Dear John —

Happy Birthday

4

D1487518

Luis and
Jeanne Tonizzo

SAILS

Jeremy Howard-Williams

Drawings by Mike Collins

FIFTH EDITION

John de Graff, Inc.

Contents

AEROFOIL. AERODYNAMIC FORCES, *Coefficients, Distribution of Forces.* CAMBER, *Position of Maximum Camber, Entry.* ANGLE OF INCIDENCE. THE SLOT. AERODYNAMIC DRAG, *Form Drag, Friction Drag, Induced Drag, Twist (Tip Vortex, Camber, Aspect Ratio, Wind Gradient, Fractional Rig), Drag Angle.* HEADSAIL. MAINSAIL. OFF THE WIND, *Close Reach, Broad Reach.* THE SPINNAKER, *Reaching, Running.* WIND, *Gradient, Pressure.*

STRETCH. FLAX. COTTON. NYLON. POLYESTER. PHYSICAL PROPERTIES *(Modulus of Elasticity, Tensile Strength, Yield Strength, Weight, Porosity, Tear Strength, Seam Strength, Resistance to Chemical Reaction, Water Absorption, Smoothness).* REQUIREMENTS *(High Aspect Ratio Mainsail, Low Aspect Main/High Aspect Genoa, Low Aspect Ratio Genoa).* CONSTRUCTION. COVER FACTOR. FINISHING, *Impregnation, Heat Setting, Calendering, Coating.* TRI-AXIAL CLOTH. FILM LAMINATES. CLOTH TESTING. SAIL OUTLINE DESIGN. CLOTH WEIGHT *(Working Sails).* CLOTH SELECTION, THE MODERN APPROACH.

ROUNDING THE LUFF AND FOOT. TAPERING THE CLOTHS. TENSION ON THE CLOTH. TENSION ON ROPE, TAPE OR WIRE, *Headsails.* LAY OF THE CLOTH, *Mainsails, Headsails.* MOULDED SAILS.

Contents

Acknowledgements

It is an awesome thought that this book was first conceived some 20 years ago. Dacron and Terylene were still proving themselves, and much of the go-fast gear which today we take for granted was unthought of: hydraulics, Barber haulers, tell-tales, big boys, self-tailing winches, electronic wind gauges and a host of others. Over the years the book has gone into four editions before this one, and has been reprinted with amendments in between, so it has been kept pretty well up to date. But there have been so many recent innovations that the Publishers agreed with me that the time has arrived for a more thorough overhaul than usual. In particular, I have completely re-written the chapters on *Theory* (where I had the generous guidance of Tony Marchaj); on *Sailcloth* (where Brian Doyle of Howe & Bainbridge was extremely helpful); on *Design and Rating* (which Roger Marshall criticised and advised upon most constructively); I have written a new chapter on what seems a strangely undocumented subject, namely *Chinese (Junk) Rig* (Robin Blain of Sunbird Yachts gave unstintingly of his time, including taking me out in his boats); finally, Peter Lucas made me free of his sail loft for photography and he checked my somewhat rusty sail-making lore.

I remain in debt to all the people who originally helped me with the first and subsequent editions, in particular Franklin Ratsey-Woodroffe (who introduced me to sailmaking), Ernie Vallender (who, as foreman of Ratsey & Lapthorn, taught me some of the mysteries of the sailmaker's palm), Richard Hayward and Sons, ICI Fibres and the RYA. To this abbreviated roll must now be added some of those who have helped with this edition (the full list would fill several pages, but I am no less grateful to those who don't get a mention): Mike Collins (who drew some 80 per cent of the drawings, often from my indifferent roughs), Col Bowden (the Delta rig), Jack Manners-Spencer (the Gallant or Aero-junk rig), John Oakeley (the Freedom rig), Dr Watson of the RAAF Academy (the first photographs in the book), and Ken Way of Windsurfing® International (sailboard sails); as I say, there were many more, some of whom receive notice in credits or captions to illustrations.

People are extraordinarily kind and generous with their time, often at some expense to themselves, and I am most grateful. The book is the better as a result of all this help, but any remaining errors are mine alone.

Many proprietory names and trade marks have passed into the language as everyday terms. Where such words have been knowingly used in this book, the first mention and the index entry have been indicated by the symbol ®; a list of those known to be or believed to be the owners of such registered trade marks is given below. Unwitting inclusion of further unidentified trade marks does not imply that they have necessarily acquired a general significance in the legal sense; I apologise for omitting them from my list, as I do for any wrong attribution which I may have made.

Brillo Manufacturing Co (UK)	Brillo
Barber Coleman Co (USA)	Tri-axial
Domestos Ltd (UK)	Domestos
duPont de Nemours & Co (USA)	Dacron, Kevlar, Mylar
Head Foil Corp (USA)	Head Foil
Hoechst AG (Germany)	Trevira
Hood Yacht Systems (USA)	Stoway
Howe & Bainbridge (USA)	Synchroweave, Temperkote, Yarn Tempered
ICI Fibres (UK)	Genklene, Lissapol, Melinex, Terylene
Montedison Fibre SpA (Italy)	Terital
Parbury Henty & Co (UK)	Spee Squeezer
Polycell Products Ltd (UK)	Polyclens
Ratsey & Lapthorn Ltd (UK)	Jibswitch, Strenlite, Vectis
Ratsey & Lapthorn Ltd (USA)	Venturi
Rhone-Poulenc Textile SA (France)	Tergal
Soviet Russia	Lavsan
Spinnaker Sally (USA)	Spinnaker Sally
Spinnaker Services (Sweden)	Spiral
Toray Industries Inc (Japan)	Tetoron

List of Photographs

List of Drawings

List of Drawings

Introduction

One of the great joys of sailing is that it is still not a scientific pastime and, try though we will to iron out the many variables with which we have to contend, there are always some problems left unsolved.

Our knowledge increases with experience – often bitter – and it is a great help when those who really know, give of the fruits of their experience in readable form. Far too many experts are incapable of communication and far too many books are written by those who are more skilful with the pen than at the helm.

Jeremy Howard-Williams is, however, one of those lucky few who both know and can communicate their knowledge. He has spent a number of years with Ratsey & Lapthorn of Cowes making good sails and listening intelligently to the ideas, some good and some not so good, of many keen yachtsmen. He has sailed in all sorts and sizes of boats from the largest in the Fastnet Race to a children's Scow, and has taken the trouble to keep up to date in his thinking.

Because of this, he knows as a helmsman what a helmsman wants; as a crew – and I know from personal experience that he is a first-class one – he has learned the techniques and the drill in handling sails, while as a Sail Maker he has applied a good brain to making the yachtsman's 'engines' as efficient as possible.

The result of his experience is this book, informative, authoritative and right up to date. Many distinguished yachtsmen do not bother to read books on yachting subjects, feeling that few of them contain anything new. I feel, however, that this book will become a yachting classic and one which every keen yachtsman should have on his bookshelves, for even the pundits will find some nuggets here and there.

There has been an absolute spate, in the last few years, of books on most of the many different aspects of sailing but there has been a lack, since the days of cotton and until now, of a good book on sails.

It is an honour for anyone to be asked to write an introduction for a friend's book, but I am especially pleased to write this one because I am sure this book will help us all to obtain a better performance from our particular boats once we realize more clearly the many problems which all Sail Makers have to face.

STEWART MORRIS

Chapter I

History

Although my subject evokes tales of handling acres of hand-sewn Egyptian cotton, the reader will look through these pages in vain for illustrations of gaff-cutters and schooners. This book is about synthetics and the present, and there is little room in it for nostalgia.

The shorter *Oxford English Dictionary* tells us that canvas is 'a coarse unbleached cloth made of hemp or flax, used for sails, tents, etc.'. The misconception that canvas means cotton to the exclusion of synthetics probably springs from this definition. In fact, if we read on further in the dictionary, we find that canvas also means sailcloth, and this is the meaning of the word as used by sailing men today. In other words, Terylene and Dacron are just as much canvas as cotton is.

The earliest sails were probably developed from palm-fronds erected in Egyptian boats for shade or ornamentation. The Romans used hide and homespun cloth, as did the Vikings, and their sails were made in a number of panels sewn together by the womenfolk. They even used to case the edges of the sails with leather for protection, in much the same way as we sometimes do today, and sealskin was particularly popular for this application.

The first record of a sailing boat built purely for pleasure in England refers to the three-masted vessel called *Disdain*. She was some 30 ft long and was built for the young Prince Henry in 1604. Yachting got its real start in this country, however, from King Charles II. Soon after the Restoration in 1660 he was presented with two yachts, *Mary* and *Little Bezan*, by the Dutch East India Company, and they brought the very name yacht with them from the Dutch language.

The King's friends soon built yachts of the same size, and races took place. With the death of the King, however, the sport lost its initial impetus and died out for about a hundred years. The Starcross Yacht Club of Devon was founded as long ago as 1773, and is the doyen of English sailing clubs. The Cumberland Fleet, which was later to become the Royal Thames Yacht Club, followed it in 1775, and the sport started up again. Rigs developed slowly, and there evolved the straight-stemmed gaff-cutters with large jack-yarders and long booms which we know so well.

The next major landmark in the history of English yachting was the arrival in our waters of the schooner *America* from the United States in 1851. Her whole concept was radically different from the bluff lines and single mast of her competitors. She was fore and aft rigged on both masts, and her sails were made of well-woven cotton, as opposed to the flax universally used in England; they were also unusual in that the mainsail and headsail were laced to booms. This is important, for it gave her the power to take advantage of her fine entry and raking bow, because the sails were much smoother and flatter than those of her rivals, and they were also a good deal less porous.

British yachts switched to cotton after this, but they did not learn their lesson properly. They reverted to flax about thirty years later and did not go back to cotton again until the turn of the century. Terylene, Dacron and nylon did not appear until after the Second World War.

Before the Second World War, international yachting was the prerogative of the rich man, and it was not until afterwards that it became more widespread, ranging from the smallest dinghy through the international day-boats to the ocean-racing fleet. This great intercourse of racing men has meant that there is a constant effort to improve performance. Ideas are tried on the smaller boats, found to be useful and then find their way to the bigger yachts. We have now reached the stage where the margin of possible improvement is so small that everything must be perfect if a boat wants to stay at the front of an international fleet.

This is a good thing as far as the Sail Maker is concerned, because it means that sails are coming in for their due measure of care and attention. And so they should, for a yacht would not get very far without them.

Chapter II
Theory

The forces acting on a yacht in motion through the water come from two sources: the apparent wind acting on the sails (aerodynamic) and the hull's speed through the water (hydrodynamic); in both cases, these can be resolved into forward and sideways forces, and into lift and drag. Figures 2.1 (a) and (b) show these diagrammatically using the familiar parallelogram of forces. If we look vertically down on a mainsail (ignoring the headsail at this stage) somewhere below its half-height, and draw an arrow to represent the magnitude and direction of the total force produced by the sail, we shall find that it acts through the centre of pressure, slightly forward of rightangles to the mean chord. This force line can be resolved by a parallelogram of forces into its components acting athwartships (heeling force) and fore and aft (thrust). F_H represents the heeling or lateral component, and the driving component is F_R acting along the fore and aft line of the yacht. Note that, for the purposes of this book, we do not need to take account of leeway[1] (and this will also hold good when we talk later of wind angle and boat's course).

The diagrams in Fig. 2.1 are not to scale, but they fairly represent a typical case. F_H is the force trying to push the boat to leeward, and is usually about 3–4 times F_R which is driving her forward. Leeway, of course, is resisted by pressure of water on the keel or centreboard (F_S), and the ensuing force couple gives a heeling moment. This in turn is opposed by another couple made up of weight (W) and buoyancy of the hull (F_B) as shown in Fig. 2.1 (b). The weight of the fixed keel (or the crew sitting out in a dinghy) is one arm of the opposing couple, and the natural buoyancy of the hull is the other. In fact, there is a similar balance of forces in the pitching plane, but we need not concern ourselves with it.

We have now balanced out the heeling force – if we have not, we shall either fill and sink, or capsize. Referring back to the diagram, we can see that we are left with F_R acting in the fore and aft line of the yacht and driving her forward. This is opposed by forces set up by the resistance of the water, and to a lesser extent by the wind. But, although they have a major

3

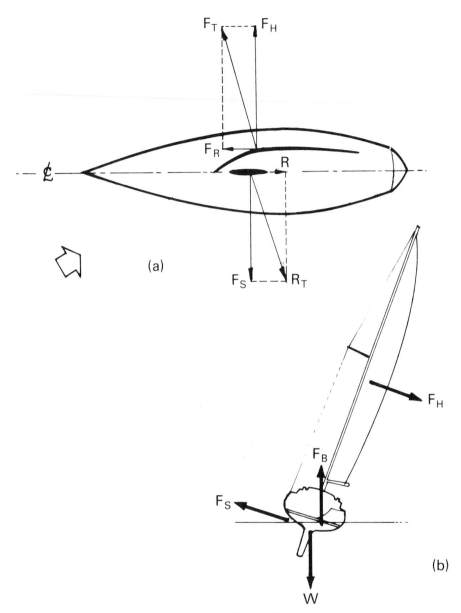

Fig. 2.1 Balance of Forces
Seen from above (a), the total aerodynamic force (F_T) acts through the Centre of
Effort (CE), usually slightly forward of right angles to the mean chord; it is
opposed by the total hydrodynamic force (R_T). In this case there is weather helm,
which would be balanced out by the headsail and/or rudder. Further opposing
force couples exist in both lateral and pitching planes. Seen from ahead as in (b),
the couple formed by the heeling force (F_H) and the lateral water force on the keel
(F_S), is balanced by one comprising the weight (W) of the boat – largely the keel –
and the buoyancy of the hull (F_B).

influence on performance, hydrodynamics are not our prime concern here. We shall, of course, be assuming certain values for hull forces, but I shall not be demonstrating how these are achieved – they are well explained in *Sailing Theory and Practice* by my friend C A Marchaj, to whom I refer those readers anxious for enlightenment (and if this does not go deep enough, his monumental *Aero-Hydrodynamics of Sailing* should be enough for anyone). The symbols used in both his books and mine are the same, even if the scholarship is different.

But sails are very much our business in this book, and it is important to know what we are striving to achieve and why. The windward condition is the one of most interest to yachtsmen (and women), because this is the most obscure and it is the hardest to improve; it is also the one where improvement is the most rewarding. So let us start with the close-hauled condition.

AEROFOIL

Airflow can be depicted by lines which show the direction and movement of the wind. When these streamlines are spaced far apart, speed is low and pressure is high; when they are close together, the reverse holds good (most yachtsmen are familiar with the isobar lines of a weather map, which show wind direction and speed in the same manner – a lot of closely set isobars means low pressure and a lot of wind). Figure 2.2 shows what happens to wind speed and pressure when airflow passes through the confines of a venturi which compresses the streamlines. As long ago as the early 18th century Daniel Bernoulli discovered that increased wind speed meant reduced pressure[3], and no self-respecting book on sails would be complete without at least one mention of the great man's name.

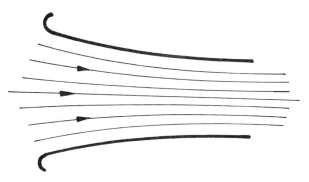

Fig. 2.2 The Venturi
Streamlines passing through a venturi indicate speed and pressure by how closely they are spaced. Flow quickens as it approaches the choke, and pressure drops in obedience to Bernoulli's law.

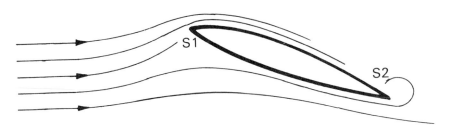

Fig. 2.3 Stagnation Streamlines
S_1 is the stagnation steamline which, in theory, impacts on the leading edge of the aerofoil, so that air on either side of it passes down the upper and lower side of the aerofoil. In accelerated flow, a second stagnation point exists at S_2, but this is soon shed downstream as steady flow is established.

As shown in Fig. 2.3, when an aerofoil is first subjected to fluid flow (and air is a fluid) at an angle, air passing each side is divided by the stagnation streamline which impacts on the leading edge at S_1. At the beginning of this century, Professor Kutta demonstrated that in accelerated flow, a starting vortex and second stagnation point S_2 originates on the upper, or leeward, surface just forward of the trailing edge. As the flow develops, provided the angle of incidence is not too large, S_2 is quickly pushed towards the leech (in the case of a sail) and steady attached flow is established. Such a steady state is not concerned with the relative positions of individual air particles as they move past the aerofoil, so we need not concern ourselves whether the familiar A_1 and B_1 at the luff are reunited with each other at A_2 and B_2 at the leech (I cannot, however, resist including the series of photographs which seems to prove that the upper particles accelerate past the lower ones when a flow system is being established; I am indebted to Dr Donald Watson of the Royal Australian Air Force Academy for these interesting prints); a fully established system is more concerned with the distribution of velocity and pressure throughout the fluid.

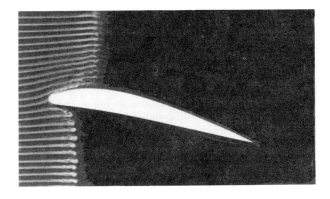

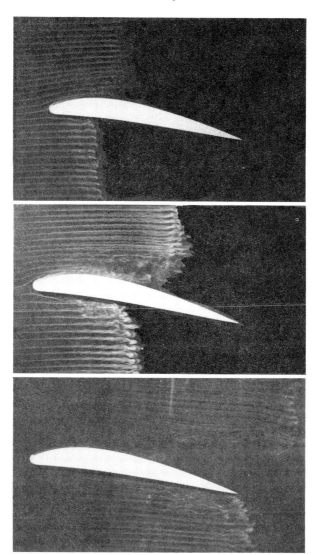

Plate 2.1 Airflow Smoke Pattern
Modern theory would have us believe that the streamlines passing over the upper surface of an aerofoil eventually rejoin those passing underneath, so that two neighbouring particles starting either side of the stagnation point at the leading edge reach the trailing edge at the same time: 'one streamline cannot be displaced laterally over another.' This series of photographs kindly taken for me recently by Dr Donald Watson at the Royal Australian Air Force Academy, Point Cook, Victoria, would seem to prove the contrary. They show smoke traces at the initiation of a flow pattern, and were a repetition of a similar pulse technique photographed in the Collins Aeronautical Research Laboratory, Cedar Rapids, Iowa, by Dr Alexander Lippisch in 1956[2]. The sequence is a vivid illustration of acceleration of air over the upper surface of an aerofoil, reducing pressure to produce lift.   *Dr Donald Watson*

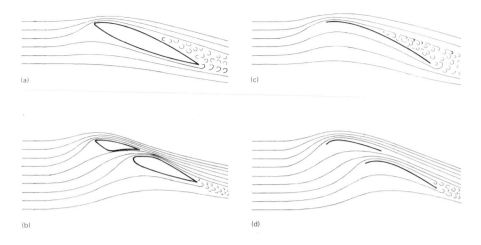

Fig. 2.4 Steady Airflow and the Slot

Established flow at an angle of incidence of 20° over a conventional aerofoil of fat section (a). Without use of slot or suction, separation occurs just aft of the point of maximum camber. Introduction of a slot (b) draws more air to the upper surface (note how streamline No 4 now passes over the aerofoil, instead of under it). Flow is speeded up to leeward, and remains attached over much more of the surface as a consequence. A single sail (c) may be compared with the first picture (a). It is the addition of the mainsail downstream in the airflow (d) which improves the performance of the headsail by diverting more air to leeward. This has the same effect on separation as the slot in (b) above.

Figures 2.4 (a) and (b) show the flow pattern over an aerofoil set in an airstream at an angle of incidence to the apparent wind of $\alpha = 20$ degrees. Of particular note is the way the streamlines are cleaned up when more airflow is diverted to the upper, or leeward, surface by introducing a slot into the system. The corresponding situations for sails are shown in Fig. 2.4 (c) and (d). In this respect, it is important always to consider the mainsail and headsail together, with the headsail acting as the leading edge of the total combined aerofoil and the mainsail providing the slot which, as we shall see below, causes more airflow to divert to the leeward surface; this speeds up the flow over the lee side of the headsail, causing lower pressure and adhesion beyond the point where it would otherwise stall into inefficient separated flow with attendant eddies – well aft along the lee side of the mainsail.

Figure 2.5 shows what happens when α is allowed to become too great. Even the slot effect cannot prevent the airflow from detaching from the lee side of the sails, and the streamlines may separate from about the position of maximum camber. This results in detached turbulence to leeward, and is usually called the stall. The reader should note that turbulence and separated flow are not synonymous, for the former occurs inside the

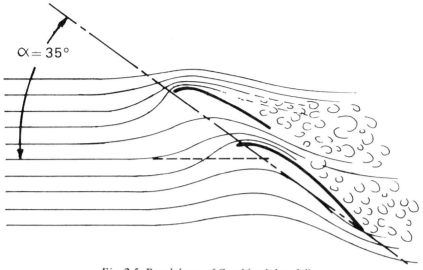

Fig. 2.5 Breakdown of Combined Aerofoil
If the angle of incidence α which the mean chord of the combined aerofoil makes with the apparent wind becomes excessive, flow separates from the lee side and thrust breaks down. The combined aerofoil has ceased to exist (see also Fig. 2.22).

boundary layer and the latter outside it (when the streamlines become detached from the surface, so that lift is badly affected). In fact, turbulent flow in the boundary layer may sometimes remain attached to a rough surface better than laminar flow, thus delaying separation[4].

AERODYNAMIC FORCES

Let us now see how those streamlines are translated into the force which drives a boat along. I shall still concentrate on the aerodynamic forces, and shall look first at the close-hauled condition.

COEFFICIENTS

In any practical study of the forces acting on sails, we need to be able to measure model sails in a wind tunnel and then relate the results to the matching full size unit. But obviously the forces developed in a sail with a luff of seven or eight feet will be different from those in one of 30 or 40 feet, even though the sails be of identical proportions and similar shape, and the winds the same. In practice, the wind speeds may also be different.

To enable the comparison to be made, an observed force is usually reduced to a common base, which is called a coefficient; this is done by dividing it by the sail area concerned and by the dynamic pressure of the wind tunnel air-flow. One coefficient can then be compared mathematically with the corresponding value for a larger or smaller sail of similar proportions. As an example, the coefficient of lift (C_L) is expressed as $\dfrac{L}{S_A \times q}$, where L is lift, S_A is the sail area in square feet, and q the dynamic pressure (which in turn is 0·00119 times the square of the wind speed in ft/sec – an expression of a term familiar to aerodynamicists as $\frac{1}{2}p V_A{}^2$).

Plate 2.2 Wind Tunnel Model
I helped to calibrate a scale model of the Ratsey wind tunnel in 1963. The full size tunnel was duly built, but eventually had to give way to demands for space, before it could produce a full volume of results.   *Beken*

For the purposes of this chapter, where we are looking at principles, we need not differentiate between observed forces and coefficients. If one is greater, so is the other; it is the manner of increase and reduction which concerns us, and how we can influence those changes.

DISTRIBUTION OF FORCES

It has been repeatedly shown in test conditions[5] that an aerofoil generates more lift on its upper, or leeward, surface through greater wind speed reducing the pressure, than on its lower, or windward, surface where the wind speed is lower so that pressure is increased (for practical purposes, air does not compress at the wind speeds we are considering, so there is very little positive pressure caused by build-up of air on the windward side of the sail). This theory of greater suction than pressure was confirmed in the USA as long ago as 1925, when manometers were introduced into the sails of the yacht *Papoose* and the results published[6]; the proportion is typically 2:1. We can illustrate the forces diagramatically, and I am indebted to C A Marchaj for Fig. 2.6, which is reproduced from *Sailing Theory and Practice*.

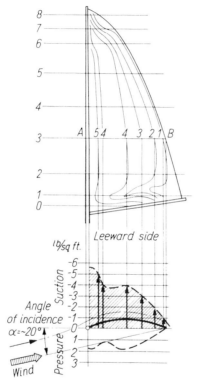

Fig. 2.6 Pressure Distribution in a Mainsail

This 'contour map' has been drawn to show the lines of equal pressure in a sail (as such there might be a temptation to call them isobars, but this would be misleading for we are talking here of dynamic pressure, not the weather man's static variety). The sketch under the mainsail shows pressure distribution on each side of the sail, from which it can be seen that leeward suction is about double windward pressure, and that most of the drive comes from the front half of the sail. Reprinted from *Sailing Theory and Practice* by kind permission of the author.

We already know that F_T can be resolved into thrust and heeling forces; these are shown in Fig. 2.7 (a), which has the dashed outline of an aerofoil superimposed as a reminder. F_T can also be resolved into lift acting normal to the wind, and drag acting in the same direction as the wind, as shown in

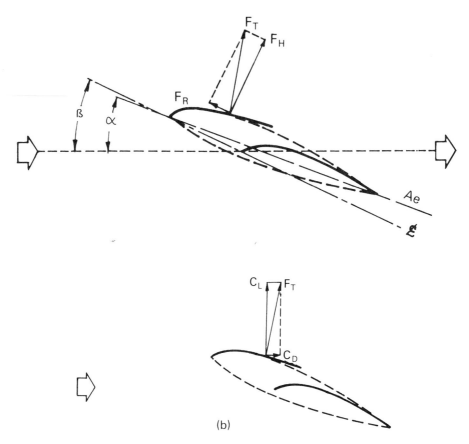

(b)

Fig. 2.7 Aerodynamic Forces in a Sail
In (a), the total aerodynamic force (F_T) resolves into forces of thrust (F_R) parallel to the boat's direction (Ç), and heel (F_H) at right angles to it. The course (apparent wind angle to Ç) is represented by β, and α is the angle of incidence (apparent wind angle to mean chord Ae of the combined aerofoil). F_T may also be resolved in relation to the apparent wind as in (b). It is made up of the coefficient of drag (C_D) acting in the same direction as the wind, and the coefficient of lift (C_L), acting at right angles to it.

Fig. 2.7 (b). In both (a) and (b) the separate forces are resolved from the total force F_T produced by the sail. So this is the common factor which is all-important: more wind means greater F_T; angling it more forward increases C_L and reduces C_D. They are both a function of trim, which will be discussed later; they also depend on several variables:

(a) Camber.
(b) Angle of incidence.
(c) The slot.

12

CAMBER

The camber of a sail affects the ability of the airflow to remain attached to the leeward surface. The amount of camber in any particular sail can be expressed as $\frac{f}{l}$, where f is the depth of camber and l is the sail's chord at that particular point; in turn this may be expressed as a percentage, so that a camber of $\frac{1}{5}$ would be 20 per cent. The theoretical optimum camber for a mainsail varies with the mean chord of the sail, as well as with the wind strength for which the sail is designed; above Force 2–3, the greater the mean chord, the flatter the sail should be. When I first wrote this book in the mid-sixties, Mr Fred Cross AFRAeS was kind enough to supply the graph reproduced as Fig. 2.8, which shows the effect of Reynolds number (Re) and wind speed on best camber; Re is the ratio of the momentum, or inertia, forces to the viscous forces. When momentum is low (i.e. Re is small) the streamlines adhere more easily to the lee side of the sail, and therefore a large camber can be used, except that research has now revealed the paradox that *very* low wind speeds require flat sails rather than extra full ones, because air which is

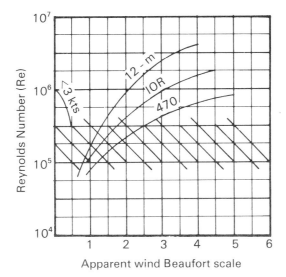

Fig. 2.8 Reynolds Number
This graph shows the effect of Re and wind force on best camber or flow. The larger the mean chord of the combined aerofoil formed by the mainsail and head-sail, the flatter should the sails be for a given wind force. Camber should be forward and moderate towards the top of the graph, and aft and large near the bottom; the changeover region is in the middle (hatched). The short curve at the extreme left relates to very light wind forces, where a flat section is required if separation is not to occur.

moving too slowly will not turn through large angles and thus cannot adhere to the lee side of a deeply cambered sail, so that separation rapidly occurs. As Re is increased beyond Force 2–3, the full camber of normal light weather sails must be decreased again and moved forward.

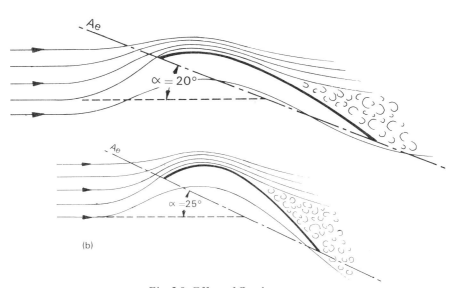

Fig. 2.9 Effect of Camber on α
The luff of the fuller sail in (b) makes a larger angle with its own mean chord (Ae) than does the luff of the sail in (a). The streamlines therefore need to approach at a larger α, in order to allow for this.

Figure 2.9 shows how a flat sail with camber = 10 per cent needs to be set at a finer angle of incidence α than a fuller one of 20 per cent, if the streamlines are to remain attached. With f:l = 20 per cent, F_T will be greater, thus producing greater drive F_R. But it also produces greater F_H, which can only be accepted in light conditions (low Re) which won't heel the boat too much (the ideal is upright; but angles up to 20 degrees make little change in sail forces[7]).

When F_H becomes too great for control to be maintained, it must be reduced to manageable proportions. Sheets can, of course, be eased so that the sails lift, but the reduction is best achieved by a flatter sail. Because of the better attached flow which this helps to maintain, the value of F_R is high; but note that the aerofoil then needs to be set at a finer angle of incidence α if separation is not to occur (see below).

It is interesting to note the actual measurements which I took of a 12-metre mainsail designed for wind speeds from 10–15 knots; the average camber in the lower two thirds was 9 per cent (it was only 6 per cent five feet

14

above the boom), and the greatest reading was 12 per cent at about half-height. Similar figures which I took for an Enterprise dinghy showed an average of 13 per cent, a maximum of 15 per cent, and 8 per cent one foot about the boom. I have known a light weather mainsail for the Dragon class which exceeded 20 per cent (and which proved inefficient as soon as the wind rose above Force 1).

POSITION OF MAXIMUM CAMBER

Not only does the amount of camber affect airflow, but so does the positioning of its maximum depth; the location of this point is usually expressed as a percentage of the distance along the relevant chord, starting at the luff.

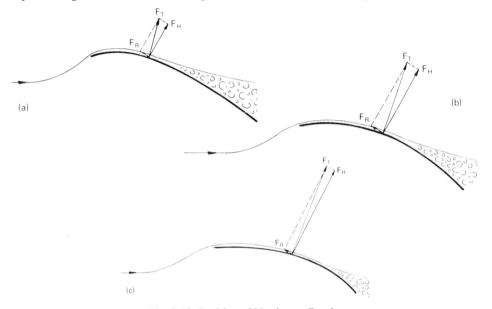

Fig. 2.10 Position of Maximum Camber

Where a mainsail operates without a headsail, turbulence sets in just aft of the position of maximum camber. In a cat-rigged boat such as a Finn or a Contender, therefore, it is logical to have this position rather further aft than usual, in order to delay airflow separation and thus get more of the sail doing useful work. Sail (a) is a conventional sloop's mainsail, with max camber at 40 per cent; if we take its F_T as being represented by 100, then its F_R is 25 and F_H is 95. Max camber in the cat rig sail at (b) has been put further aft to the midway position, with the result that F_T is increased to 175 (on the same scale) and, although the direction of this force is angled slightly more to the rear (thus reducing the proportion available as F_R), actual thrust is increased by about half over (a) to 37; but note that F_H has nearly doubled to 165.

If we decide to take the max camber further aft still, in an attempt to get even more of the sail working with attached flow, the direction of F_T is by now angled so far aft that F_R is reduced to 20. We have indeed succeeded in making F_T greater, but its principal effect is to increase F_H to over 250, or three times the value for the similar force in (a).

15

It has been shown over the years that sails with a position of maximum camber about 40 per cent aft of the luff are better all round than those where the figure is 33 per cent[8]. Provided that the sail shape at the luff allows an easy entry for the airflow, this shift of the position of maximum camber towards the leech helps to maintain attached flow over more of the aerofoil. We can see this more clearly if we look at the flow behaviour in the special case of the single mainsail of a cat-rigged boat, as depicted in Fig. 2.10, which is reproduced from my own book *Dinghy Sails*. This is borne out in practice, because boats such as the Finn or Contender have always liked fullness near the half-way point in order to go best to windward. If it were any further aft, there would be loss of F_R due to the centre of effort being too far aft, and thus angling F_T too much to the rear. Introduction of a headsail would allow attached flow to be maintained at greater angles of incidence α.

ENTRY

If a sail is to have a fairly large camber, its leading edge should offer a fine entry so that wind can flow smoothly onto the aerofoil. This means that the shape of the luff should be matched to the oncoming airflow, as can be seen in Fig. 2.11 (a). Figure 2.11 (b) shows how, if flow separation is not to occur too soon, α must be greater when the fullness is carried right forward.

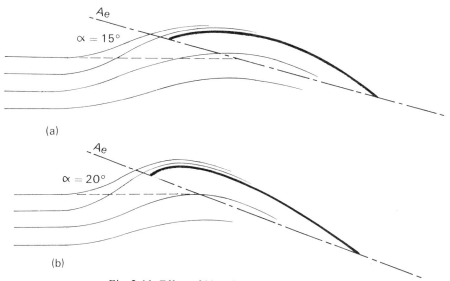

Fig. 2.11 Effect of Max Camber Position on α

The angle of incidence (α) which the apparent wind makes with the chord of the aerofoil (Ae) needs to be larger if the sail is full forward, as in (b). If the flatter entry of (a) were confronted by $\alpha = 20°$, the streamlines would have difficulty in turning through such a large angle to adhere to the leeward surface. This is a good argument for having a flat sail for use in really ghosting conditions, when the wind does not have enough energy to make sharp bends, so that it separates easily.

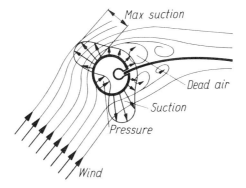

Fig. 2.12 Pressure Distribution Round a Mast
This large scale sketch shows the detailed distribution of pressure in the immediate
vicinity of a circular mast; see also Fig. 2.14. Reprinted from *Sailing Theory and
Practice* by kind permission of the author.

The leading edge is therefore important. But the mast causes a lot of
disturbance to the mainsail at this highly sensitive point, and a diagram of
mainsail lift looks like Fig. 2.12, which I have taken from *Sailing Theory
and Practice*. A headsail, on the other hand, doesn't suffer from such disturbance, so the efficiency of this sail is not impaired in the same way; it forms
the leading edge of the combined aerofoil, and is generally speaking twice as
efficient as the mainsail[9]. This superiority is by no means entirely due to the
absence of a mast at the headsail's luff, but also to the beneficial effect which
the presence of the mainsail has on the airflow round the headsail.

ANGLE OF INCIDENCE

The correct angle of incidence α on a sail ensures that upwash onto the luff
pulls extra air from windward, thus speeding up the leeward flow; this
creates low pressure to leeward and makes the soft sail take up its aerofoil
shape.

If α is too large, the streamlines cannot make the sharp turn round the
luff and adhere to the leeward surface, so that they break away in separated
flow[10]. Conversely, if α is too fine, there is little or no upwash onto the luff,
and the streamlines pass equally down each side of the sail, causing equal
speed and thus equal pressure on each side; the sail lifts and loses its aerofoil
shape.

We have already seen in Fig. 2.9 that a sail with a medium to full camber
should be trimmed with α larger than that for a flatter sail of similar proportions. Typically, a sail with a camber of f:l = 10 per cent is set at α = 15
degrees, whereas a 5 per cent sail, suitable for heavy weather, should be
reduced to 12 degrees[11] (don't forget that the combined aerofoil itself makes

17

an angle to the fore and aft line of the boat of some 10 degrees, and we are not talking about the course angle β here). To summarise:

(a) Full sail/low wind speed = wide α.
(b) Flat sail/high wind speed = narrow α.

THE SLOT

The general observations on camber should be borne in mind when considering the slot. If a headsail has too much camber, or if its position of maximum draft is too far aft, there will be a bellied leech, with airflow directed into the lee side of the mainsail; the same holds good for a headsail leech which is hooked. A flat run to the slot is essential, with airflow tangential to the mainsail at the exit[12], if separation is to be delayed.

The conventional way to discuss the slot is to imagine a mainsail alone and then add a headsail. I suggest that this method has grown up over the years largely because, in practice, we usually hoist the mainsail first, and then add the headsail. But the theory of the slot can be more easily grasped if we consider first a headsail acting on its own, and then look at the effect which a mainsail has when it is added to this system.

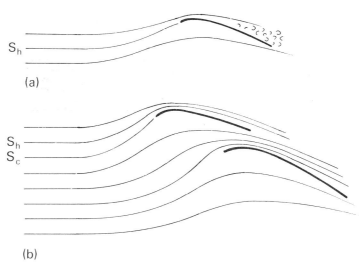

Fig. 2.13 The Slot

When a second sail is added *downstream* in the airflow (b), it will be noted that the original stagnation streamline (S_h) of the headsail alone (a) is now diverted further to leeward. This results in higher speed and lower pressure to leeward of the headsail, so that flow separation is delayed, with resulting increase in F_T.

The addition of a second sail *downstream* in the flow increases upwash, thereby increasing the effective angle of incidence. We can also compare in Figs. 2.13 (a) and (b) the path of the stagnation streamline for the headsail alone, S_h, with the line it takes when the mainsail is added, and a new stagnation streamline for the combined aerofoil, S_c, is introduced. The effect of this is to divert more air to leeward of the headsail, and thus reduce pressure in that region, so that the streamlines now adhere to the lee surface of the aerofoil past its position of maximum camber.

Because air is drawn away from the leading edge of the mainsail to pass to leeward of the headsail, the slot actually slows down the wind which passes along the immediate lee of the mainsail luff. It might thus be thought that the slot reduces efficiency, but don't forget that it is the combined aerofoil with which we are concerned, and improved efficiency of the headsail, acting as it does as the leading edge of this aerofoil, is what we are seeking. The headsail has therefore been made that much more efficient by the addition of the mainsail, rather than the other way round. We now have more total force F_T in the combined aerofoil; what we do with it is another matter, and will be examined later.

AERODYNAMIC DRAG

We have just seen how variation in camber, angle of incidence and the slot affect the behaviour of the airflow. Let us now look more closely at some results of that behaviour. Drag D from the airflow acts in the same direction as the wind, and normal to the cross-wind force, or lift L; L and D are the resultants of resolving the total aerodynamic force F_T (see Fig. 2.7). Drag may be divided into:

(a) Form drag.
(b) Friction drag.
(c) Induced drag.

FORM DRAG

Form drag results from eddies produced by what may be termed, for convenience, lack of streamlining of the mast and sail, i.e. it is caused by the form of the aerofoil. When the sail acts at a large angle of incidence to the relative wind (α), we have seen that the airflow cannot adhere to the contour of the lee side and it separates, usually just behind the position of maximum camber. Thus, at small values of α, such as occur in windward work, form drag is minimal, being caused mostly by the influence of the mast which creates eddies at the leading edge, and by any items attached to the sail such

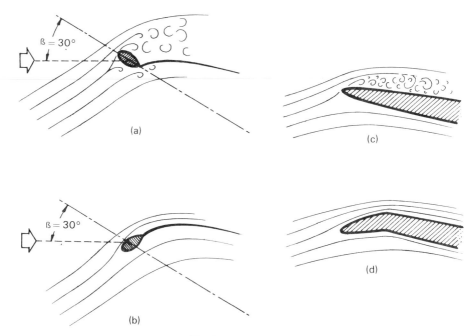

Fig. 2.14 Mast Drag

Due to upwash on the streamlines at the luff, the centre line of the boat (and mast) may make anything up to 60° with the local airflow when sailing close hauled (a). The two diagrams at (c) and (d) are taken from an instructional film made in the USA in 1972, in connection with boundary layer control[13]. They show how laminar separations, such as those which occur at the sharp leading edge of a thin profile, can be avoided by the deflection of a nose flap to alter the pressure field. Although not directly applicable to the mast/sail configuration, the principle remains a good argument for adopting a mast which swivels into line with the oncoming airflow (i.e. beyond head to apparent wind) as in (b).

as reef points or repair patches (see Fig. 2.14)[13]; attention needs to be paid to developing a seamanlike method of rotating the mast's profile.

FRICTION DRAG

Air is technically a viscous fluid, and it may be thought of as comprising millions of individual particles. The layer of particles next to the fabric of the sail is slowed down because those particles actually in contact with the sail stop; these in turn slow the next particles almost to a stop; the next ones are slowed a little less; and so on, until there is a layer of air particles being progressively slowed from full air speed some distance out, to zero next to the sail. Energy is lost in the process, and eddies form.

The layer of particles thus affected is called the boundary layer. It may be looked on as a very thin film of air, with several layers of air within it, each sliding over the other with decreasing velocity as the surface of the sail is approached. Thickness is a poor word to use for something which is so thin, but of course it does have a measurable width, being some 2 per cent of the chord at its greatest, depending on whether the surface of the sailcloth is rough or smooth. Although it may seem that friction is small, the eddies it causes affect the whole pattern of the streamlines round the aerofoil through flow separation[14]; a smooth sailcloth without too many excrescences in the form of reef points and patches is important – and this includes as few creases from careless folding or stowing as possible.

INDUCED DRAG

Induced drag may be looked on as a measure of energy lost due to vortices generated at the head and foot of the sail, as a result of a pressure difference between the windward and leeward sides of the sail. These pressure differences tend to equalise, and tip vortices are caused in the process. This effect can be partly countered in aircraft aerofoils by the use of end plates to inhibit transverse flow. In sails, a wide flat boom or a genoa which scrapes the deck can be beneficial in preventing too much flow under the foot. Twist helps reduce the vortex effect at the head, and a high aspect ratio is also useful, particularly going to windward. For a sail of any given aspect ratio, the amount of induced drag depends on the coefficient of lift C_L: the more lift, the more drag[15] (see Fig. 2.15).

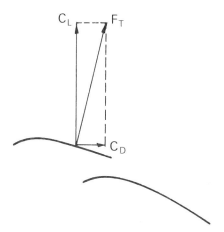

Fig. 2.15 Induced Drag
Compare the length of the force arrows in this diagram with those in Fig. 2.7. An increase in total thrust not only brings more lift, but also more drag (which has to be overcome).

21

TWIST

Before World War II few yachtsmen had heard of twist in relation to sails; fewer still did anything about it, as will be seen from almost any photograph of a boat on a reach in the twenties or thirties. In the 1950's some of the more astute keelboat helmsmen found that they could improve performance dramatically by copying the dinghies and using a kicking strap or boom vang to reduce mainsail twist. It was only a short step for the amateur theorists to tell us the reasons; the foot of the sail was being sheeted too hard, purely so that the head should not lift; it stood to reason that the whole mainsail should lie at the same angle to the wind for best efficiency. Twist was banished as kicking straps were fitted to the offshore fleet in order to pull down the boom and straighten the leech; the foot of the mainsail could then be eased without the head lifting: more F_R and less F_H (see Fig. 2.16).

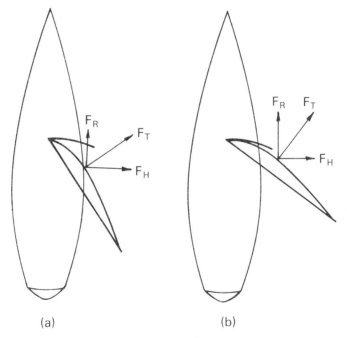

(a)   (b)

Fig. 2.16 Twist
If the main boom can be eased without allowing the head of the sail to fall off so that it starts to lift, F_R increases and F_H is reduced.

But this is not the full story. Early thoughts that the wind was constant up the luff were, of course, incorrect so, as I said in the first edition of this book in 1967, some twist is desirable. Let us look at why and how much.

Tip Vortex. Possibly the most compelling reason for allowing the head of a sail to fall away is the vortex which washes up from the head of the sail to cause induced drag. There is an increase in the local or effective angle of incidence (α_{ef}), which thus requires the sail to be twisted if the stall is not to occur at the head. This effect is most marked in light winds, when α is high (and so is C_l)[16]; some 5–10 degrees should be allowed, according to whether the wind is strong or light.

Camber. We have already discussed how a sail with a deep camber turns the apparent wind through a greater angle (upwash) than does one with a flat section. In general terms, a light weather sail should be allowed 2 or 3 degrees more twist than a flat storm sail. Happily this conforms with the increase in α_{ef} mentioned under *Induced Drag* above.

Aspect Ratio. Given a sail of high taper, i.e. triangular form, a high aspect ratio produces the best L/D ratio for windward work. It has its penalties, however, which include the need for greater camber near the head (due to low Re) and this, as we have just seen, brings the need for a couple of degrees more twist to accommodate the higher α_{ef}; this results in some increased drag, but the gain outweighs the loss.

Wind Gradient. Because of its viscosity, air is affected by friction due to the uneven surface of the Earth; this slows it progressively at altitudes under 100 feet (see Fig. 2.17). If we construct a typical triangle of forces (Fig. 2.18), it will be seen that the higher wind speeds at the mast head free the boat (regardless of tack); there is a larger α_{ef} high up than low down. So the sail must be allowed to twist if the effective angle of incidence is to be kept below the stall. The amount of wind shift will vary with wind strength (being

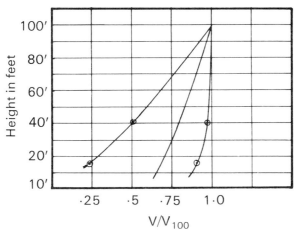

Fig. 2.17 Wind Gradient
The ratio of wind speed below 100 ft to wind speed at 100 ft.

23

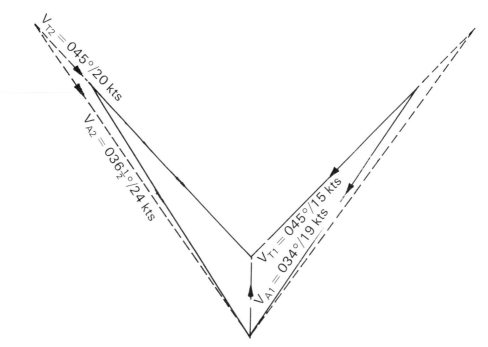

Fig. 2.18 Freeing Wind Aloft

A typical triangle of forces, using boat speed of 5 knots and true wind speed at deck level of 15 knots, 45 degrees off the bow. The apparent wind speed (continuous line) on either tack is 19 knots, 34 degrees off the bow. If the true wind speed at the mast head is increased by 5 knots from the same angle, the apparent wind (broken line) becomes 24 knots, $36\frac{1}{2}$ degrees off the bow on both tacks. There should therefore be $2\frac{1}{4}$ degrees of twist in the sails to allow for wind gradient as represented here.

If a gust (from the same direction) hits the boat and increases true wind speed at deck level from 15 to 19 knots (with attendant further increase aloft, with which we need not concern ourselves at present), the immediate effect is to free the apparent wind by $2\frac{1}{2}$ degrees until hull speed picks up and alters the hull vector further (even then, the boat would have to reach an unlikely 8 knots in this example before the apparent wind were to come further ahead).

less at high speeds), and is usually not more than 3 or 4 degrees when going to windward, or 10 or 11 degrees when reaching[17].

Fractional Rig. As has been explained above, the slot enables the leeward streamlines to remain attached to the mainsail past the point where they would separate if the headsail were not there. A fractional rig, however, leaves the upper part of the mainsail uncovered by a headsail, so that it needs to be set at a finer α_{ef} if separation is not to occur. In other words, the head of a mainsail for a boat with a three-quarter rig should be allowed to twist. This was well proved at Southampton University, when a series of tests was undertaken with a 12-metre rig at varying sail (α) and course (β) angles[18].

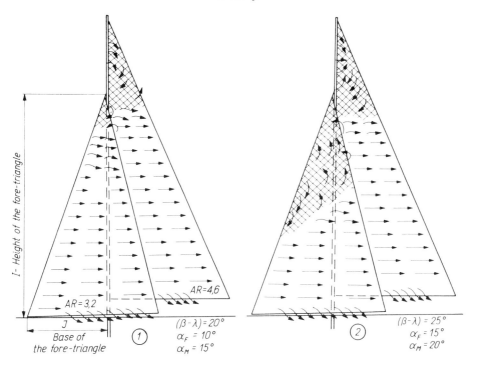

Fig. 2.19 Fractional Rig Flow

These drawings were prepared from photographs taken to leeward of a suit of model 12-metre rigid sails in Southampton University wind tunnel. Low values were used for the course angle β (20° and 25°), giving angles of incidence for the combined aerofoil of $\alpha = 17\frac{1}{2}°$ and $22\frac{1}{2}°$, and there was 3°–4° of twist. It will be seen that substantial areas of both sails suffer separated flow, particularly at $\beta = 25°$. This is because the top of the mainsail has no headsail in front of it, so that it does not form the rear half of a slot; airflow is thus not helped round that part of the leeward surface. Where there is no slot, a mainsail needs more twist aloft in order to reduce α_{ef}. Reprinted from *Sailing Theory and Practice* by kind permission of the author.

The model sails were rigid, with uniform camber disposed vertically, and predetermined twist at 3°–4°. Figure 2.19 depicts the flow with constant sail settings at course angles which, for our purposes we can say were (1) $\beta = 20°$ and (2) $\beta = 25°$. Both tests resulted in flow separation from the upper (uncovered) part of the mainsail, and the test at $\beta = 25°$ (i.e. a wider α_{ef}) could not maintain steady flow over the whole genoa; but even here, the headsail caused steady flow over the whole of that part of the mainsail covered by the slot.

The combined effect of all these requirements is for twist to be desirable in both headsail and mainsail. For any given sail, the angle will vary with aspect ratio, camber, the slot, and with wind strength, direction and gradient. It is not a question of adding together all the allowances for these, and letting the sail twist some 20 degrees, because excessive twist creates too much form drag and thus nullifies the benefit; rather is their precise interplay one for fine judgement, which can often be helped by the use of tell-tales or streamers on the leech (see Chapter IX).

DRAG ANGLE

When beating to windward, we have an interest in increasing F_R to drive the boat forward, and in reducing F_H so that she doesn't heel too much. We can see from Fig. 2.20 that the values of these two depend on the apparent wind angle β and on the coefficients of lift (C_L) and drag (C_D). A form of efficiency yardstick may be obtained from the angle which the total force F_T makes with the cross-wind component C_L (lift). This is known as the drag angle, and is represented in Fig. 2.20 by ϵ.

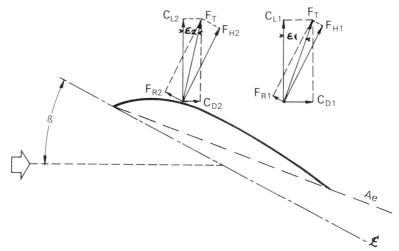

Fig. 2.20 Relationship of ϵ to C_D

The angle between thrust (F_T) and lift (C_L) is the drag angle, and is represented by ϵ in the diagram. If this is reduced from ϵ_1 (inset) to ϵ_2 in the diagram, drag angle is reduced in direct proportion (from 20° to 12° in the example, causing a reduction of C_D by 40 per cent).

Assuming that F_T remains constant (not always the case because, though wind speed may not change, the angle of incidence α and sail camber may be altered by the crew), a reduction in C_D from C_{D1} on the inset, to C_{D2} on the drawing will mean that F_T is angled more forward if the parallelogram of lift and drag forces is still to resolve; in other words, ϵ is reduced. This in turn increases F_R and decreases F_H, which is what we were requiring in the first paragraph of this section.

We thus have a direct interest in keeping drag to a minimum, so that drag angle ϵ shall be low. We shall see under the appropriate chapters later, how this requires the following:

1. *Form Drag*. Streamlining the form of the aerofoil (Ch IV, *Sail Flow Design*).
2. *Friction Drag*. Ensuring a smooth surface (Ch III, *Sailcloth*).
3. *Induced Drag*. Reducing tip vortices (Ch IV, *Sail Flow Design*).
4. *Twist and Drag Angle*. Setting the aerofoil at the optimum angle (Ch IX, *Trim*).

HEADSAIL

If we examine each sail in turn we find that, though they are mutually supporting, the headsail is roughly twice as efficient as the mainsail[9] – so it will repay our particular attention.

In its role of leading edge, the headsail forms the entry which accepts the wind, and it can thus make or mar the airflow over the whole combined aerofoil. Get it wrong, and separation occurs too soon, with resulting loss of thrust[19]. In addition, F_T for the combined aerofoil acts through the headsail (see Fig. 2.6). Fortunately there is no mast at the luff of a headsail, so that the entry is not disturbed as much as it is with a mainsail.

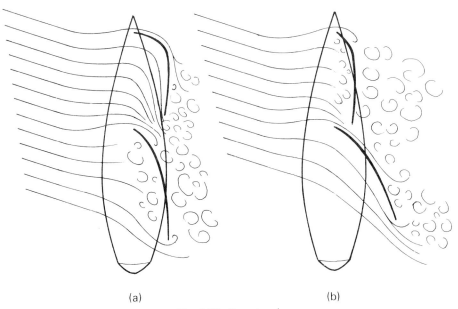

(a)   (b)

Fig. 2.21 Oversheeting
If either sail is sheeted too hard, a large area of eddies is created to leeward, as the entire airflow separates.

We must thus pay special attention to the shape and surface of the headsail. In the particular case of windward work, it should respond to the following requirements:

1. A clean entry, at an angle of incidence which will vary with the depth of camber of the sail (and thus with wind strength) somewhere between 12–27 degrees[20].

2. Maximum camber at about the 33–40 per cent position, to provide drive[21].

3. A maximum camber of 10–15 per cent. More would encourage detached flow[21] and also tend to give a bellied leech, thus increasing pressure between the sails, which might cause backwinding of the mainsail; less would reduce thrust by reducing F_T.

4. A flat run-off to the leech, so as to ensure a clean airflow through the slot, tangential to the mainsail[12].

5. An overlap which reaches the line of maximum camber of the mainsail[22]. Too little diffuses the effort; too much chokes the slot.

6. A smooth surface, free from excrescences, which holds its shape, so as to ensure low friction drag and a good streamline shape.

MAINSAIL

For its part, the mainsail must maintain the drive by means of correct shape and a good surface finish. Although it is not as efficient as its headsail, it often provides the greater area; in any event, it has a considerable influence on the final behaviour of the airflow. Assuming a sail of given aspect ratio, we may list the requirements much as we did for the headsail (for the effect of aspect ratio on α, see *Sailing Theory and Practice*, page 149).

1. Maximum camber at about the 40–50 per cent chord position (see Fig. 2.10)[7].

2. A maximum camber graded according to wind speed. In light airs, up to 10 per cent (1/10th) is best; sails of 15 per cent camber are almost always too full to windward, because there is a significant rear component at the leech, which becomes too large as soon as the wind gets above Force 1[8]. As the wind increases above Force 3–4, camber should be decreased to around 5 per cent (1/20th)[23], a profile which is also useful for ultra light winds.

3. The angle of incidence α of the sail varies with wind speed and camber. The fairly full sail of 10 per cent camber, used in light weather, should be set at some 15 degrees to the apparent wind, while the flat 5 per cent sail should be at no more than 12 degrees in brisker conditions[11].

4. Sail twist must be taken into consideration as well, particularly with

Plate 2.3 Wind Tunnel Testing

A one-third scale 14 ft International mainsail in the Ratsey wind tunnel. We measured the difference in thrust on a reach when a shelf incorporated in the foot was closed by its zipper and open; here it is closed. The result was a 5 per cent gain when the shelf was open.   *Beken*

Plate 2.4 Full Size Testing – Ashore

The mainsail shown in Plate 2.3 was also built full size and tried both ashore and afloat. Here it is with the shelf unzipped ashore.   *Author*

a fractional rig. The wind gradient (and the absence of any slot above the head of a short hoist or fractional headsail, which would otherwise deflect the airflow through an angle), gives the apparent wind a greater angle of incidence aloft than down on the deck. The mainsail should thus be allowed some 5 degrees of twist to prevent premature stall at the head[24].

5. A flat leech and smooth surface, as with the headsail.

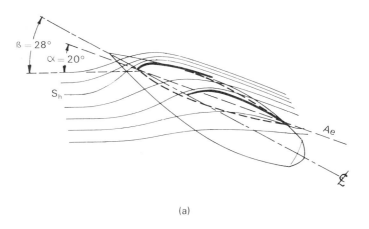

(a)

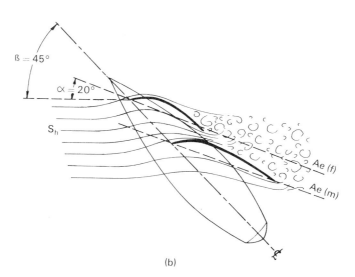

(b)

Fig. 2.22 Aerofoil Breakdown – Genoa Reach
Even though both sails in (b) are trimmed so that individually they each have an angle of incidence of about 20°, the two luffs are spread widely across the airflow, so that they cannot combine into one aerofoil, such as that shown in (a) – where β and α are more nearly aligned with the airflow. The result is that less air passes to leeward of the headsail in (b), which thus produces less suction.

OFF THE WIND

As a yacht gradually comes away from the close-hauled condition, we know from practice that it is important to ease sheets progressively. We look upon this as angling total thrust F_T further forward, so as to put more into driving the boat (F_R) and less into heeling her (F_H).

But we are doing more than this, because the angle of incidence α must not become too large, or separation will occur. Even if only one of the two sails is overtrimmed, flow will separate from the combined aerofoil, and the alert reader will surely have realised by now that this results in loss of lift; see Fig. 2.21. We shall see later (Ch IX, *Trim*) how the resulting region of turbulence to leeward can sometimes be used to temporary tactical advantage[25].

CLOSE REACH

There comes a point where the course in relation to the apparent wind (β) increases beyond that at which the mainsail is positioned close enough across the airflow to the stagnation streamline of the headsail, for the former to have a significant effect on the path of S_h. Figure 2.22 shows how the aero-

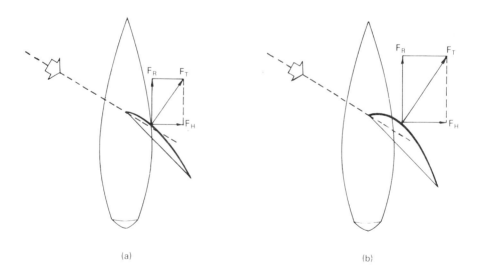

(a)   (b)

Fig. 2.23 Thrust on a Reach

A larger camber can be accepted as soon as the boat comes on anything other than a fine reach, because the larger F_T which it generates is not accompanied by a disproportionate increase in F_H. The price for the extra F_R is therefore not too high.

31

foil which we have so far postulated for the close-hauled condition has ceased to exist. Extra air is thus no longer being deflected to leeward of the headsail, even though α for each sail acting individually remains optimum, and one of the conditions for attached flow thus remains.

At this point, larger values for sail camber can be accepted, for the parallelogram of forces is now virtually a square, so that an increase in F_T does not bring an unacceptable increase in F_H; see Fig. 2.23. Attention should now be concentrated on maintaining attached flow over each sail individually (by trimming sheets according to tell-tales or streamers).

BROAD REACH

When β is increased still further, the sails can eventually be eased no more (I am assuming here that mainsail and genoa remain; we shall see below the effect of the spinnaker), and the angle of incidence α now increases beyond that at which flow remains attached to either sail, even individually. As a result, suction is sharply reduced to leeward with attendant loss of thrust[26].

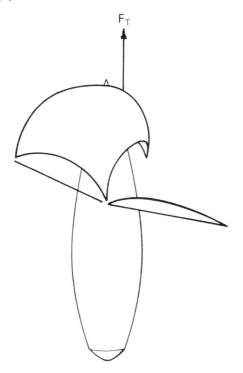

Fig. 2.24 Thrust on a Run

As the boat comes more and more square before the wind, eventually F_T is directed along the same line as F_R, so that (in theory) F_H disappears. We all know that oscillation or rhythmic rolling down wind remains, but that is a different problem and does not alter the fact that there is no steady F_H.

The sails produce a high driving force, because F_T is almost parallel to the fore and aft line of the boat, with very little F_H; see Fig. 2.24.

In the turbulent and separated flow conditions which now prevail, thrust is more a matter of area than streamline shape, and the sails revert more nearly to the concept of the early sailors in the times of the Pharaohs: they form an obstruction to the airflow so that the boat is blown down wind. The practical effect of this is that leechlines and drawstrings may be tightened and, indeed, the sails made fuller by any other controls which may be available (see Ch IX, *Trim*); this includes setting the spinnaker.

THE SPINNAKER

The spinnaker, of course, will have been set (by racing yachts at least) long before the boat comes onto a broad reach. So let us examine what happens to the airflow.

REACHING

First of all I must repeat what I have said in every earlier edition of this book: we must remember that a spinnaker is just another headsail; on a reach the airflow passes across the sail from luff to leech, just as it does with a genoa. The difference is that a spinnaker does not have the straight luff of the genoa, nor does it have the flat run-off to the leech which we have seen is desirable if the airflow is to remain attached[27]. Figure 2.25 shows how we are a long way from pretending that we have an efficient combined aerofoil, with the two sails acting in concert. But we do have two separate aerofoils, each struggling to maintain attached flow as long as possible.

The problems of flow separation have already been discussed above. The deep camber of the spinnaker (typically f:l $= \frac{1}{4}$) means that the streamlines have to turn through a large angle if they are to remain attached; in addition the position of maximum camber is near the 50 per cent position (sometimes it is even pushed by the wind to 60 per cent), so that there is always a marked return to the leech, creating a large rear component to F_R. This explains the success of flat spinnakers for reaching purposes; how to see that the stretchy cloth remains flat under stress is another matter, and is discussed in Ch XIII, *Spinnaker in the Abstract*.

We said just now that there can be no question of an efficient aerofoil when the spinnaker is up. But this doesn't mean that the slot is of no significance. The very size of the spinnaker means that the gap between the two sails is often not as much as we would like; this means that the slot will be choked in all but the lightest conditions, thus promoting eddies. When you add that the spinnaker's bellied leech directs flow into the lee side of the mainsail, it is easy to imagine the very disturbed conditions which prevail,

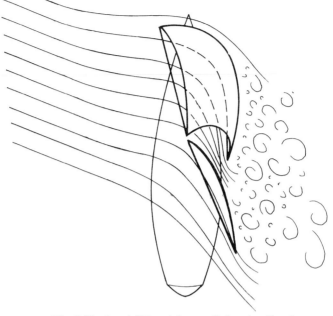

Fig. 2.25 Aerofoil Breakdown – Spinnaker Reach
As with Fig. 2.22 (b), there is no aerofoil when the apparent wind is nearer abeam than ahead.

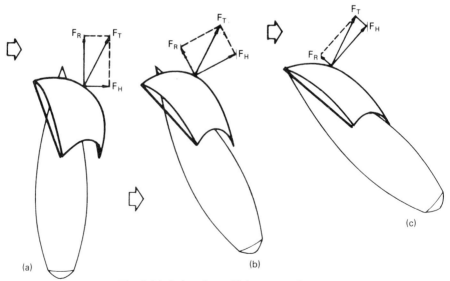

Fig. 2.26 Spinnaker Efficiency on a Reach
As a boat under spinnaker comes from a beam reach to a fine reach, it is important to visualise the dramatic increase in F_H which is taking place. Eventually, anything other than a really flat star-cut (or equivalent) will have its F_T directed more aft than forward, at which point it will pay to switch to a genoa or a double head rig.

34

often necessitating an overtrimmed main sheet if the mainsail is not to lift the entire time.

This overtrimming results in F_H for the mainsail having a higher value than we would prefer. This is aggravated by the spinnaker's relatively large area aloft, so that its CE is high, with attendant increase in the effect of total F_H.

All this seems to put the usefulness of the spinnaker into doubt. But we know that this is not true, so where does it gain? The answer lies in one word: area. The average IOR spinnaker is over double the size of its matching genoa. Provided, therefore, that F_H can be kept within bounds, F_R will increase dramatically. Because the sail normally operates with values of β in excess of 60 degrees, F_T is directed well forward, with relatively low values for F_H; a glance at Fig. 2.26 will show the principles.

RUNNING

Here again, as with mainsail and genoa, when running, all hope of attached flow over each sail breaks down as soon as the wind ceases to flow from luff to leech. But we have F_T acting parallel to the fore and aft line of the boat,

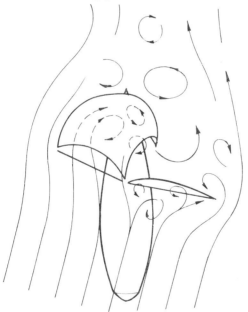

Fig. 2.27 Airflow on a Spinnaker Run

The airstream in front of a spinnaker dead before the wind is separated and full of eddies; there can be no question of an aerofoil, and reliance must now be largely placed in area. Separation occurs close to the edges of the sail, so that a smooth surface is not important under these circumstances – even irregular seams or panels do no harm (but this is no excuse for having them, because efficiency will suffer as soon as attached flow returns on a reach).

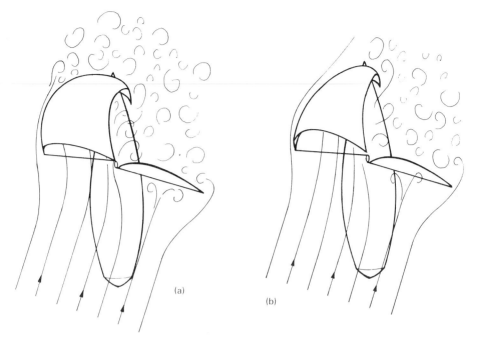

Fig. 2.28 Full and Flat Spinnakers
On a nearly dead run, the full spinnaker of (a) will create eddies at almost any α.
The flatter sail at (b) has a small chance of achieving some attached flow if the
pole is pulled far enough aft, and the wind allowed to reach the sail at a reasonable
angle rather than from square astern.

with no F_H (I am not going to get into the problems of broaching at this
point; those who can't wait, should skip to Ch IX, *Trim*). Figure 2.27 gives a
schematic illustration of the kind of flow which has been photographed in
wind tunnels and flow tanks[28], so it is easy to see that aerodynamics have
now virtually gone out of the window. This is an argument for tacking down
wind, not only to increase the apparent wind strength, but to re-establish
attached flow. Figure 2.28 (a) shows a conventional full running spinnaker
with 25 per cent camber operating with detached flow at $\beta = 160$ degrees,
whereas the flat reaching spinnaker of lesser camber in (b) might very well
re-establish attached flow at that angle, with attendant gain in speed.

WIND

Before we heave a thankful sigh and move on to more mundane matters, two
aspects of wind behaviour are relevant to this chapter: gradient and
pressure. We have already looked briefly at wind gradient when discussing
sail twist earlier in this chapter.

Plate 2.5 Full Size Testing – Afloat
The same sail as Plate 2.4, being sailed by myself on Frank May's *Sunrise* (K 545)
with the shelf closed.   *Castle Studio*

GRADIENT

We have seen that it is largely due to friction that the wind is slower at the
surface of the sea than it is higher up. The difference in speed also depends
partly on temperature, so that different meteorological conditions give rise to
different wind gradients. The graph at Fig. 2.17 shows the ratio of the wind
speed at any height up to 100 ft, to that found at 100 ft (V/V_{100}).

The graph illustrates why a tall narrow rig has a greater advantage over a
squat one on a calm day, with an overcast sky, than it has under similar
wind conditions but when fog or drizzle means a greater temperature loss. In
the former case the wind at 15 ft will be just under a quarter of the value at
100 ft, while at 40 ft it will be half; in other words the wind doubles in
strength between these two heights. In the latter case, however, the proportions are 0·90 and 0·96 respectively, so there is little increase.

PRESSURE

The pressure in a sail under given wind conditions can be roughly calculated by using Martin's formula: $W = 0.004V^2A$, where W is the total weight of wind in the sail in lbs, V is the relative wind speed in m.p.h., and A is the sail area in sq ft. This formula holds good as an approximation for most points of sailing, but remember that local areas of the sail may have a greater or lesser weight per sq ft than the average, due to aerodynamic forces; the formula gives the *total* weight in the whole sail. Remember this sum next time you have your 700 sq ft light spinnaker or ghosting genoa out in a 20 m.p.h. relative reaching wind: you will have half a ton in the sail.

Chapter III
Sailcloth

Before going into technical detail about how to make sails, it is as well to get a little background knowledge on sailcloth and how it is produced. A woven material is made by arranging a suitable number of threads (or ends) on the beam of a loom to establish the warp, or lengthwise threads, and then passing the thread back and forth through the warp, to form what is known as the weft (UK) or fill (US). The resulting weave is tightened by beating up the weft so that the fill lies more closely together. It will be seen that a given

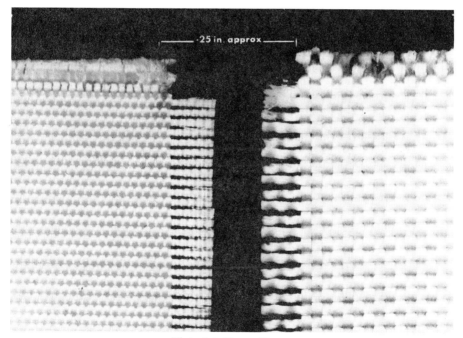

Plate 3.1 Cover Factor
Comparison of two sailcloths, magnified to show the weave. They are of similar weight per sailmaker's yard, but the one on the left has a greater cover factor and finer sett.   *Yachting World*

weight of cloth can be established by weaving at what is known as a low sett, which means having a smaller number of thicker threads, or by achieving a larger number of thinner threads through a finer sett. The thickness of an individual thread is known as its count, which used to be expressed as *denier* – the weight in grams of 9000 m of yarn. The metric system weighs 1000 m of yarn and calls this the *tex* count; this may be divided into 10 *decitex* (often written as d'tex) and 1000 *millitex*. As an example, if 9000 m of a particular yarn weighs 100 grams, its denier would be 100; 1000 m of the same yarn would weigh 11 grams, giving a tex count of 11 and a decitex of 110. It will be seen that denier and decitex are not far apart, and the precise relationship is to divided denier by 0·9 to get decitex.

The density of weave of a particular cloth, as achieved by the closeness of the ends on the beam and the degree to which the weave is tightened by beating up the fill to drive the weft closer together, is expressed as the *cover*

	1964 Dacron Hood Sailmakers Inc		1969 Terylene Vectis by Ratsey & Lapthorn		1982 Terylene	
	Warp	Weft	Warp	Weft	Warp	Weft
Fabric weight oz/yd² (gm/m²)	14 (465)		14 (465)		13 (450)	
Nominal decitex*	3/275	1/1225 1/245	2/275	3/275	400	830
	MT	HT	HT	HT	HT	HT
Ply twist t.p.i.	6 'Z'	2 'Z'	10 'S'	2½ 'Z'	5 'S'	flat
Resultant decitex*	960	1620	630	900	480	945
Decitex uptake %	15·7	10·6	13·4	8·0	17	12
Threads per inch	63·4	33	88	48	126	36
Yarn crimp %	11·6	0·9	14·0	0·5	5·5	0·02

HT = High tenacity   MT = Medium tenacity
t.p.i. = twists per inch   'Z' and 'S' = direction of twist
*To convert to denier, multiply by 0·9

Fig. 3.1 Analysis of Sailcloth Construction
Note how the 1969 Terylene had threads about one third lighter than those for the 1964 Dacron (resultant decitex of 630 and 900 as against 960 and 1620); by 1982 the warp has reduced yet again (to 480) while the weft stays roughly the same. Since cloth weights are comparable, threads per inch must increase, and we can see that this has, in fact, progressively taken place on the warp; weft has remained more static. But note also how weft crimp has reduced to an insignificant factor, showing that this is a cloth for high aspect ratio mainsails. Based on figures kindly supplied by Ratsey & Lapthorn.

factor. The highest theoretical cover factor which can be achieved for either the warp or weft threads in a fabric is 28, which represents threads placed so close together that there is no gap between them. A higher value than 28 can, in fact, be achieved by *crimping* the threads slightly on top of one another, and sailcloth with a cover factor of 32 has been recorded. A logical mind would, of course, raise this magical figure of 28 (which is based on the old cotton system of calculation; there are others giving different figures) to 100, thereby converting a measure which is almost meaningless to the layman into a percentage; but sails and sailmaking are full of illogical systems which have grown up with piecemeal development; see Fig. 3.1.

A cloth with a high decitex warp and weft, therefore, and a low cover factor, will have fewer threads, a more open weave, and consequently greater porosity than one of the same weight per yard, but containing thinner threads more closely woven; on balance, it is preferable to adopt the latter method, but there are many factors which interplay as we shall see.

STRETCH

If it is subjected to a loading on the bias, particularly if the direction of loading is at or near 45 degrees to the line of the thread, any woven fabric

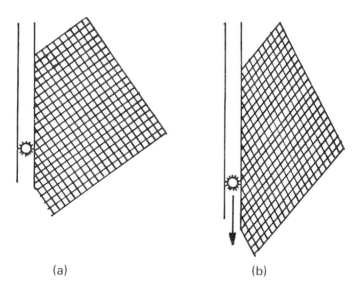

(a)   (b)

Fig. 3.2 Weave Distortion Under Load
When a loading is applied to woven material across the threadline, i.e. on the bias, the square weave (a) is distorted into a diamond pattern (b). In a sail, the luff stretches if the Cunningham hole is pulled down, but the sail does not get any bigger; the leech contracts across the line of tension to compensate.

must distort, or stretch as it is usually miscalled when referring to sails: the small squares formed by the threads crossing each other will be distorted into small diamonds as the threads move against one another; see Fig. 3.2. There will also be a very small amount of genuine linear stretch along the thread-line, depending on the nature of the fibre and the amount of twist in the make-up of individual threads, which tend to unwind slightly under load if they have a lot of twist. Finally, crimp tends to straighten under tension (see Fig. 3.3), although this also has the beneficial effect of helping the weave to lock even tighter. We shall see later how film laminate cloth virtually eliminates both distortion and stretch.

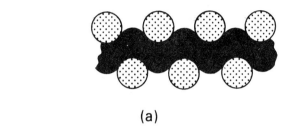

(a)

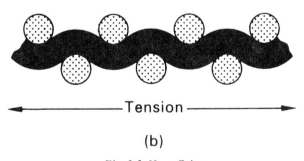

Tension

(b)

Fig. 3.3 Yarn Crimp
Where the warp yarn is heavily crimped (a), tension along it will straighten it and tend to separate the weft yarns (b). Pressure of warp against weft will increase, with beneficial effects on bias stretch.

The strength of any particular woven sailcloth comes from the basic strength of the individual threads forming that cloth, together with the way in which they are woven. Where these threads are made up of individual staples, or fibres, from a plant such as flax or cotton, the staples will in turn determine the quality of the thread. Because these staples are closely inter-locked in the thread, their length and degree of roughness control the breaking strain of the individual thread, and also how much it stretches. If,

42

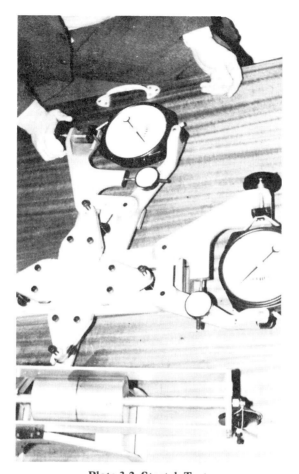

Plate 3.2 Stretch Test
This apparatus can give precise details of stretch in any direction, by interpolation
of the x and y co-ordinate strain gauges.   *Ratsey & Lapthorn*

however, the threads can be made up of filaments of one long homogeneous
substance, such as occurs in synthetics, individual thread strength will be
greater weight for weight than, say, cotton with its separate staples.

FLAX

Today, virtually all sailcloth is manufactured from synthetic yarns for the
reasons I have given, but the first fabric important to yachting was flax, a
herb with narrow pointed leaves and blue flowers, whose name comes from
the Old English word *fleax*. The staples produced when the stems are
separated in the retting process are tough, fibrous and fairly long, being as
much as 4 ins or more. These qualities make flax difficult to spin very fine,

and it is inherently a coarser thread than cotton. It is about 20 per cent stronger when wet than dry; see Fig. 3.4. The resulting cloth is therefore one which pulls out of shape a good deal, but which is particularly suited to hard use.

COTTON

After flax, chronologically speaking, came cotton. The Arabic word qutun came to Europe through Spain (where it become *coton*) and France. Egyptian and Sudanese cotton are best for sailcloth to this day, although the American variety also gives good results. The staple formed by separating the lint from the seed, in a process called ginning, is shorter and finer than flax, being seldom more than an inch long, but it is of a woolly and spiral character which causes resistance between the fibres when they are spun into thread, and naturally produces a uniform cloth.

Property	Ulstron	Terylene	Nylon	Flax	Cotton	Glass	Dacron	Kevlar
Tenacity (g/den)								
Dry	8·0–8·5	6·5–7·5	7·0–8·8	2·4	1·5–2·0	6·3–7·0	8·0	22
Wet	8·0–8·5	6·5–7·5	6·0–7·9	2·9	1·8–2·4	5·4–5·8	7·8	—
Extension at break (%)								
Dry	18–22	10–14	16–26	2–3	3–10	3–4	15	3
Wet	18–22	10–14	19–28	4	2·5–8·0	2·5–3·5	15·7	—
Elastic recovery (% from 5% extension)	88	90	98	Breaks	45	Breaks	95	Breaks
Initial modulus (g/den)	90	110–130	40–50	136	12–70	330	105	525
Moisture regain (%)	0·1	0·4	4·2	12	8	0	0·4	7·0
Specific gravity of fibre	0·91	1·38	1·14	1·54	1·54	2·5–2·6	1·38	1·44

Fig. 3.4 Comparative Filament Yarn Properties
The tensile properties quoted for flax and cotton refer to spun yarns, which have an overall tenacity lower than that of the single fibres. Based on information kindly supplied by du Pont and by ICI Fibres.

Being finer, cotton can be woven more closely than flax, and its advent meant a considerable advance in sail efficiency. Virtually its first appearance as sailcloth in Europe was with the schooner *America*, whose celebrated victory round the Isle of Wight in 1851 started something we have not yet heard the last of. Apart from any other factor, her cotton sails were much flatter than the baggy suits of flax on her rivals, thus making her closer winded.

Today cotton and flax are used only where authenticity is the prime consideration on large square sails, schooners and the like, or where an owner is a traditionalist. Both fabrics are weaker, and they stretch to a much greater degree than modern synthetic canvas; they are also badly subject to mildew. Stitching does, however, bed into the material so that it is largely protected from chafe.

NYLON

Nylon is the generic name for the polyamide fibre plastic derivative of coal, which was developed in America as a result of a long series of experiments started in 1932 by Carothers and his collaborators; it was not used for sails until after World War II (the name derives from New York and London, where the firm had its offices). Due to its inherent elasticity, nylon is particularly suitable for spinnakers, which need a certain amount of give in their cloth to help them achieve their shape – indeed, the shock loads to which they are often subjected in use practically demand elasticity. The cloth is also sometimes used for light reaching sails such as mizzen- and spinnaker-staysails, not to mention big boys. It is not damaged by mildew, but is subject to weakening through prolonged exposure to sunlight – an effect which is heightened by contacts with acids such as are found in many bleaches.

POLYESTER

In 1941 J R Whinfield and J T Dickson of the Calico Printers' Association of Lancashire, England, invented polyester. World War II prevented much immediate action, but ICI Fibres of London agreed to help with development, and they produced the first polyester yarn in January 1944, acquiring from Calico Printers the world rights in 1947, apart from the USA where these had already been sold to duPont. The licensees in various countries all produced the new material under individual trademarks: Terylene® in the UK, Dacron® in the USA, Tergal® in France, Trevira® in Germany, Tetoron® in Japan, Terital® in Italy and Lavsan® in Russia – the basic yarn is all made to the same chemical formula, and it is only in the weave that sailcloth differs. The licences started to expire in 1967, and from that date a free market began to develop.

The first sails made in England from Terylene were by Gowen and Co of Essex, in the winter of 1951–2, and the 8-metre cruiser/racer *Sonda* had the first one they made commercially – a genoa.

Polyester is made from the polymer polyethylene terephthalate, a condensation product of terephthalic acid and ethylene glycol (familiar to motorists as anti-freeze), both of which are derived by chemical synthesis from products of mineral oil cracking. The filament yarn used in sailcloth has no individual staple, each filament being one long extrusion, and the thread is made up of many filaments twisted together. When this thread leaves the manufacturer it has up to about one twist per inch according to decitex, in order to bind the individual filaments together. This thread is then processed by a specialist called a throwster, who twists it further to the weaver's specification. The more the thread is twisted, the greater resistance it has to filamentation in the weaving process, since it holds together better, but the more linear elasticity it will have as the twists tend to unwind slightly under tension.

Polyester sailcloth is usually woven with warp and weft of different decitex, as indeed was cotton and flax in some cases. The raw weave is scoured and dried, and may have various resin fillers added to improve stability and resistance to bias stretch; it is then heat-relaxed and calendered to shrink and settle the material, helping the threads to lock together. These processes are normally carried out by specialist firms of finishers on both sides of the Atlantic, and we will look at the various processes a little more closely later.

PHYSICAL PROPERTIES

It is important to understand what functions sailcloth must perform and therefore what physical properties it must possess. Then we will look at how these properties are attained.

Modulus of Elasticity. The readiness with which a material distorts is indicated by its modulus of elasticity. In sailcloth, the modulus should be high, that is to say the fabric should have a good resistance to distortion at all loads; see Figs. 3.4 and 3.5. This modulus is not the same in all directions within a sail fabric, and the ratio of the modulus in the weft (or fill) to that in the bias (or 45 degree direction) is an important consideration as we shall see later.

Tensile Strength. Tensile strength is represented by the load at which a material breaks in tension. This is its ultimate strength and is only a consideration in determining the point at which a sail will break. This applies principally to spinnakers and to some of the more exotic sails such as bloopers or big boys.

Yield Strength. Yield strength is represented by the load below which the material will return to its original shape when a given stress is removed, but beyond which the material is permanently deformed. In modern sail fabric,

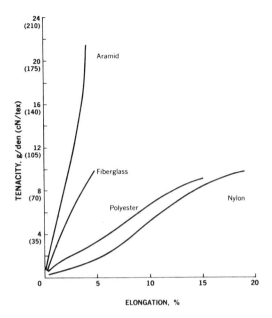

Fig. 3.5 Stress-strain Curves for Filament Yarns
It will be noted how aramid fibre yarns (Kevlar) do not stretch even as much as 5 per cent. Nylon has the greatest elongation; this, indeed, is what is required to absorb the shock loads inseparable from spinnakers. Graph by courtesy of du Pont Inc.

yield strength is generally of high importance for it determines the wind range of a given sail – if it is subjected to loads beyond the yield point of the fabric, the cloth will be permanently elongated, and the sail will lose the shape which it was designed to have. It must then be re-cut or discarded.

Weight. Sailmakers generally prefer to use the lightest weight fabric available for a particular application, because sails are then easier to handle, fold and stow. On racing boats, light sails also have an important effect on weight aloft, and thus on the sailing efficiency of the rig. The performance of a given sailcloth is often measured in terms of *specific modulus*. This is the modulus divided by the weight, thus a high modulus/low weight material has a high specific modulus.

Porosity. Porous sailcloth allows air to permeate from one side of the sail to the other, thereby tending to equalise pressure distribution to the detriment of thrust. Spinnaker cloth, being particularly thin, suffers more from porosity than cloth for other sails. 200 years ago, when a ship was trying to out-run a faster enemy vessel in light winds, hands would be set to throwing water on the flaxen sails in order to shrink them and thus close the weave,

Plate 3.3 Porosity Test
The Gurley meter used by Seahorse Sails for testing spinnaker nylon for porosity.
It measures the time in seconds for 100 c.c. of air at constant pressure to pass
through one square inch of material. 25 seconds is par, 50 is very good, and 15 or
less is poor.
Seahorse Sails Ltd

but the porosity of woven polyester used in modern fore and aft sails is so low
as to be virtually unmeasurable.

Tear Strength. All sailcloth must have a minimum resistance to tearing and
abrasion. This varies considerably depending on the application of the
fabric. Material used in racing sails may sacrifice some durability to gain
performance, while long life will be a high consideration for charter boats.
Modern synthetics are inherently very rugged, so that durability is often of
secondary importance during the development of a particular fabric. The
more exotic laminated reinforced films must also have a certain minimum
delamination quality.

Seam Strength. As stronger, lighter weight sailcloths are developed, the
ability of the material to hold a seam becomes more important. In high

modulus, lightweight materials such as reinforced Mylar® or Melinex®, the point-loading created through stitching can damage the edge of the material and seams will tear. In the highest modulus Kevlar® materials, elongation due to the small amount of shearing within the seams can exceed the elongation of the material in a very large sail.

Resistance to Chemical Reaction. Besides mildew, exposure to industrial smoke, sun, heat or cold can each affect sailcloth to a greater or lesser extent. In most commonly used sailcloth forms, polyester has exceptional chemical stability and can be inhibited against penetration by ultra violet rays; nylon is somewhat less good, but is satisfactory. Polyester film for laminates is very good in its resistance to chemicals, but Kevlar has poor UV stability.

Water Absorption. Water attracts dirt, and the combination encourages the growth of mildew — it will even grow on glass if the conditions are right. Good sailcloth should not absorb water either through a porous weave or into the yarn itself. In addition, water in sails adds weight aloft, and thus promotes inefficiency. The requirement, therefore, is for a sailcloth with a low moisture regain percentage; see Fig. 3.4.

Smoothness. We saw in the previous chapter how friction drag affects the performance of a sail. A smooth sailcloth reduces friction drag.

In addition to these basic physical requirements which all sail materials must meet, different types of sail impose different requirements on the cloth. Spinnakers and other very light drifting sails require lightweight stretchy fabrics with high yield strength, so nylon is used. Many racing boats, particularly Grand Prix IOR boats, require the highest possible performance, so more exotic materials are used, including reinforced film laminates and Kevlar. But by far the greatest number of sails, including nearly all dinghy sails, most mainsails, genoas and all other fore and aft sails, are made from woven polyester yarn. Let us, therefore, look at some of the requirements imposed by different applications, together with the methods used in weaving and resin application to meet those requirements.

REQUIREMENTS

The loads in a sail depend largely on the shape of that sail; Fig. 3.6. Sails with slightly different aspect ratios or varying end uses will have different stresses and strains, thus requiring different fabrics with appropriate physical characteristics.

Some interesting things become apparent from examining the theoretical load distributions. First, if we examine the two most extreme types of sail

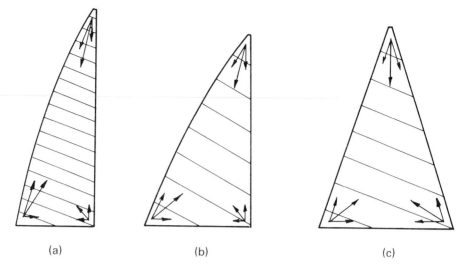

(a)   (b)   (c)

Fig. 3.6 Sail Stresses
The stresses in a horizontally cut mainsail of high aspect ratio (a) are largely up
and down the leech; resultant loading is thus on the line of the weft or fill, which
should be suitably stout. A low aspect ratio mainsail (b) also has fairly high leech
stresses, but there is high bias loading, particularly in the lower part of the sail, so
that weft and bias distortion are equally important. A low aspect genoa (c) has
loadings which are more equally distributed throughout the sail, so a square
construction is called for (with equal emphasis on both warp and weft), in order to
withstand stretch in all directions.

(high aspect ratio mainsail – (a) in the figure – and low aspect ratio genoa –
(c) in the figure – we find that the former has its primary load in the leech
direction, with only modest loading on the bias (through the mid-section of
the sail); in the low aspect ratio genoa, the sheet practically bisects the clew,
resulting in significant loads on the bias as well as the leech. The cloth
requirements for these two sails are, as a result of these varying loads,
considerably different. The high aspect ratio mainsail requires outstanding
strength across the cloth and not as high bias strength; the genoa, on the
other hand, requires great stretch resistance in both weft *and* bias directions.
A third category (low aspect ratio mainsails – (b) in the figure – and high
aspect genoas) places slightly different demands on their cloth: both require
a compromise between weft or fill strength and bias control.

Each sailcloth manufacturer approaches the problem in his own way.
Howe and Bainbridge of Boston USA are the world's largest manufacturers
of sailcloth and, having identified the three distinct needs, they produce three
basic lines of woven Dacron to meet them.

1. *High Aspect Ratio Mainsail.* To withstand the high leech loadings, the
cloth needs the best possible weft or fill strength; the relatively modest

50

Plate 3.4 High Aspect Ratio Mainsail Cloth
7.3 oz Dacron magnified 80 times. This has high decitex weft (or fill) yarns
running from left to right, which are virtually crimp-free, while the lower decitex
warp yarns crimp readily. The result is low stretch across the cloth, which is what
is needed in this type of mainsail; see also Fig. 3.3 (a).   *Howe & Bainbridge*

Plate 3.5 Low AR Main and High AR Genoa Cloth
6.7 oz Dacron magnified 80 times. Here again, the weft or fill yarns are of substantially higher decitex than the warp, but the difference is not so large as in Pl. 3.4
above. The resulting small amount of crimp in the fill yarn helps to lock the weave
and improve bias performance; see also Fig. 3.3 (b).   *Howe & Bainbridge*

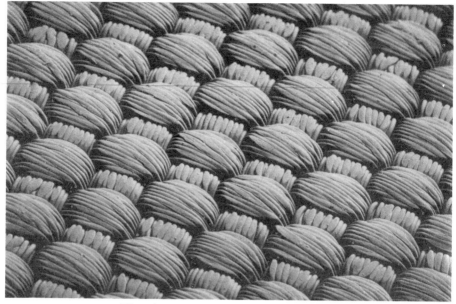

Plate 3.6 Low Aspect Ratio Genoa Cloth
3.3 oz Dacron magnified 80 times. In this cloth, warp and weft have the same yarn
(a 'square' construction), tending to equalise crimp and maximise bias strength.
This gives uniform performance right across this type of sail; see also Fig. 3.3.
Howe & Bainbridge

loading running through the middle of the sail means that resistance to bias
strength need not be so high (Pl. 3.4).

2. *Low Aspect Main/High Aspect Genoa.* Once again, high leech loadings
demand good weft or fill decitex. But the shape of these sails means that
there is no over-riding requirement, and a reasonably low bias distortion is
also needed (Pl. 3.5).

3. *Low Aspect Ratio Genoa.* This sail has loadings spread throughout the
sail, and needs maximum bias strength, even at the expense of warp and weft
stretch (Pl. 3.6).

It will be seen that the second requirement above is a compromise between
the other two. It is, however, impossible to have minimum elongation
characteristics in both the fill and the bias direction simultaneously in a
woven material (as we shall see later, this is partly the reason for the success
of homogeneous film on the racing circuit – it has uniform resistance to
distortion). As a result, the three lines of Bainbridge cloth make calculated
trade-offs between bias strength and weft strength to produce optimum
fabric for a given type of sail; they report that the cloth for requirement (2)

above has a fill almost as good as a high aspect mainsail cloth, and the bias strength is almost as good as genoa cloth bias.

In the UK, Ratsey & Lapthorn market a wide range of specialist sailcloth, including cloth/film laminate (Melinex), which they weave themselves at Cowes under the name of Vectis®. Output does not approach that of ICI Fibres or Howe & Bainbridge but, perhaps because they are relatively small, they can give a high degree of supervision to their looms.

CONSTRUCTION

The design of these woven fabrics has become a fairly sophisticated, complex pursuit, with manufacturers guarding their trade secrets closely. It will be interesting here to look at some basic principles in the design of the weave (the construction) and in the finishing or chemical treatment and resination of the fabric.

The actual choice of the yarn weights along and across the cloth length, and the counts of these yarns, is a complex problem. These four variables control the distribution of crimp in the warp and weft, the weight of the fabric, and the bias stretch or distortion of the fabric. The variables which create more subtle differences must also be considered. These are factors such as twist in the yarn, the type of loom used (tension in the weaving process), the techniques used in weaving, and the chemical treatment and finish of the loom-state cloth.

There are a few general rules which might be of interest. First, the ratio of the yarn decitex in the warp as against the weft or fill: generally, highly unbalanced fabrics (that is, fabrics with much larger yarns in the weft or fill than the warp) are appropriate for sails which have loadings concentrated in the weft direction. The best example and most common case of this is a high aspect mainsail where the loads are primarily up the leech.

The Bainbridge line of mainsail fabric constructions achieves minimum creep and highest fill strength per weight for the available yarn. On the other hand, many Sail Makers feel that balanced fabrics, which have the same yarn in both the warp and the weft, are more appropriate for sails in which the load is distributed throughout the body of the sail. As we have seen, low aspect genoas are the best example of this. Some of the warp-orientated fabrics actually have larger decitex yarns in the warp than in the weft, in an obvious attempt to carry the load along the cloth rather than across it. Much of sailcloth design involves the optimisation of a particular parameter, such as weft or fill strength at the expense of bias stretch.

COVER FACTOR

Since bias stretch is often the limiting factor in sailcloth design, it is interesting to look at several of the factors which affect it. First and foremost is cover factor. The tighter a fabric can be woven (and finished), the more inherent bias stability it will have. This effect can also be seen in the fact that lighter weight fabrics, with more yarn crossing per square area, tend to have lower bias stretch than heavy weight fabrics, made from high decitex yarns with fewer yarn crossings per area.

In balanced fabrics of square construction, which have the same decitex yarns in both warp and weft, bias stretch resistance through crimp at each yarn crossing is at its maximum. Conversely, in an unbalanced fabric (high aspect mainsail) with much larger yarns in the weft or fill than in the warp, only the warp yarns crimp as they cross each of the more rigid fill yarns; this type of crossing pivots more easily and limits bias stability.

FINISHING

Of course, resins and coatings can be used to improve bias stability, but the effectiveness of these is always limited by the inherent stability of the basic fabric. It is impossible to make a stable, durable cloth by resinating a construction which has an inherently weak base.

Sailcloth finishing is a complex, multi-step process which extensively alters the fabric; it is chemically cleaned, treated with a resin, treated with heat, and mechanically processed for flatness and to lock the bias stretch. There are many steps in the process, each with a degree of adjustment and variability, giving a nearly infinitely variable process.

Each of the basic steps in sailcloth design is additive. In other words, the finishing depends on, and is determined by, the cloth's construction, which in turn depends on, and is determined by, the choice of yarns. Every step in the chain has either a major or a subtle effect on the finished product.

IMPREGNATION

A fabric which is impregnated has been dipped through an aqueous solution of melamine resin prior to heat setting. This resin soaks into the fibres and fills the voids in the fabric; during heat setting, it chemically bonds them together. The resin is brittle and largely invisible, leaving no deposits, and adds virtually no weight to the fabric. With various concentrations of resin, coupled with heat setting temperatures and other finishing techniques, it is possible to produce a very specific modulus in a fabric – but some resins remain attached better than others, so breakdown can occur in inferior cloth which has been made to look temporarily stable.

HEAT SETTING

When polyester is heated above approximately 150°C (300°F), it shrinks, developing quite a high tension. So, although sailcloth is already among the most tightly woven fabrics in the world, density of the yarns can be further increased in this way. This is one of the properties which makes the cloth such a successful material. Thus, when the previously resinated fabric is passed through an oven, shrinkage considerably tightens the weave and decreases bias stretch.

CALENDERING

Calendering is the last step in the production of sailcloth, and its purpose is also to decrease bias stretch. A calender consists of two very large rollers, arranged in much the same way as an outsize clothes wringer, which are squeezed together with pressures measured in tens of tons. The fabric is run between them and the pressure crushes the interlacings to lock in the yarns and reduce distortion on the bias.

COATING

The lowest possible stretch in polyester sailcloth is achieved through coating. This covers the surface of the material, bonding the yarns very tightly and acting in tension as well as compression to inhibit stretch. It does, however, have the side effect of also producing a firm fabric with a harsh handle, so that coatings are generally only used for racing sails. This racing cloth is marketed under different trade marks by different firms; the Howe and Bainbridge range is called Yarn Tempered®.

TRI-AXIAL CLOTH

It will be seen that efforts are continually being made to reduce bias stretch. Logically, if we can produce a cloth with three threadlines, at 60 degrees to each other (as opposed to 90 degrees for conventional weaves), maximum bias angle will reduce from 45 degrees to 30. Tri-axial® cloth sets out to achieve this (Fig. 3.7), but it has also reduced shape control, so that it ends by being a highly specialised cloth best suited to genoas, which has been overtaken by film laminates.

FILM LAMINATES

The highest performance and best shape holding has been achieved with various reinforcements of polyester film – in other words Mylar and Melinex. An unwoven sheet of molecularly orientated polyester film has a high modulus of elasticity in all directions (it is marginally poorer than woven

Fig. 3.7 Tri-axial Cloth
The basket weave construction is formed from two vertical warp threads mounted on a circular housing. During the passage of the weft or fill pick, rotation of the warp housing results in a weave which has one weft and two warp threads, all running at 60 degrees to each other. Advantages claimed include good tear and shear resistance, a more uniform strength, and less bias weakness than conventional bi-axial weave. The resulting cloth is best suited to genoas, with their even loadings, but there is some reluctance to stretch on the luff and thus allow flow to develop.

sailcloth on the threadline, but superior in all other directions because it has no threadline itself and is thus uniform in its reaction). When used for sailcloth, this high stability means that the thickness of film is measured in thousandths of an inch (mils) with substantial savings in weight. In turn, the thin material will tear easily once a hole is started, so it needs reinforcement. This is achieved by bonding it to a specially woven light substrate to give it tear strength; Fig. 3.8.

The first attempt to build a Mylar sail was in 1964, in a spinnaker for the 12-metre *Constellation*; another was made later that year for *American Eagle*. The low tear strength of these early Mylar products made these sails ineffective, but the writing was on the wall.

Mylar was used a few years later in some one-design sails. In this case, $\frac{1}{4}$-mil film was laminated to both sides of fabric, with the aim of reducing drag. The next attempt was with the 12-metre *Enterprise* in 1977. The material was a Mylar film glued either side of lightweight Dacron, to give a cloth of about 3 oz per sailmaker's yard; it goes down in history with the unfortunate name of garbage bag material due to its dark green colour.

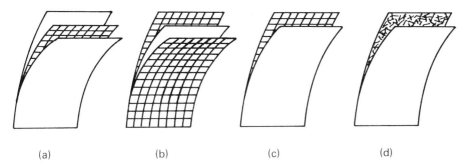

(a)   (b)   (c)   (d)

Fig. 3.8 Film Laminates

To prevent tears developing, Mylar and Melinex film is bonded to woven polyester or nylon reinforcement. Initial experiments saw two $\frac{1}{4}$-mil films of Mylar on either side of 2-oz spinnaker ripstop nylon (a). This suffered from distortion of the outside layer when the cloth was folded, so that delamination occurred. If the more rigid film is sandwiched between two layers of flexible woven substrate (b), the reduced compression effect, coupled with improved adhesives, has countered this problem. Modern Mylar sailcloth, however, is more likely to be a construction of film one side and woven cloth on the other (c), which gives a flexible end-product with no compression effect; thickness and weight can vary widely to suit the requirement. Sometimes the reinforcement is formed by a random-laid scrim cloth (d), thus producing a sail which is not woven at all.

Problems developed as a result of poor adhesion leading to delamination, but once again the way was clear to faster sails and better shape retention.

In 1978 Bainbridge introduced high strength, low weight Mylar laminate with successful adhesion: 2·85 oz Temperkote®. This was the first composite with a larger proportion of Mylar than substrate, and the 2·85 oz incorporated a sheet of 1-mil Mylar on both sides of spinnaker fabric. Through their experience with it, a good adhesive system which did not discolour was developed.

This triple sandwich developed an I-beam effect, as a result of its three layer nature (so-called from steel joists which have the I-configuration for maximum rigidity). With a layer of Mylar on either side of a solid, albeit flexible material such as the woven substrate, delamination occurred. This happened when the material was bent, causing the outer layer of Mylar to be put into tension and the woven core into compression. The solution to this was to laminate one side only, thus creating a composite construction with film on one side and woven cloth on the other. The result is a more flexible cloth with no I-beam effect. Today's sandwich cloth is also acceptable, because the rigid structure (Mylar) is sandwiched between two flexible woven substrates rather than the other way round.

Early development of one-sided Temperkote incorporated nylon substrates rather than the polyester ones which are used today, but this created problems of its own. The nylon substrate picked up water, which promoted curling and delamination. This was solved when Howe and Bainbridge designed special substrates with fill-orientated unbalanced constructions of polyester.

When it comes to spinnakers, the Mylar film may be left largely to itself, with Kevlar or Dacron mesh stuck on in the form of widely spaced ripstop material. The result is a transparent sail, whose reinforcements prevent any tear developing because the threads of Dacron or Kevlar are just pushed aside without breaking. But the cloth lacks the inherent springiness necessary to absorb the shock loads suffered by all spinnakers from time to time, so it is not an all-round replacement for nylon.

The most exotic and highest performance reinforced films employ Kevlar, which is an extremely strong, low stretch aramid fibre produced by duPont; weight for weight it is 20 times stronger than steel. Early experiments with Kevlar in sails produced poor results, primarily because it is weakened rapidly when subjected to repeated sharp flexing. For this reason, early sails made from tightly woven Kevlar failed rapidly and sometimes broke in spectacular fashion. This was enough to cause the ORC to ban Kevlar sails in offshore races. These materials often achieve a specific modulus greater than the best polyester fabrics of only a few years ago. Unfortunately, this is achieved only at great expense. The Kevlar yarn costs as much as fifteen times more than polyester, so its use is restricted to the sharp end of the racing fleet (we shall see later how the cruising owner may be very content to let it stay there, because film laminates are harsh and noisy to handle).

CLOTH TESTING

This section is meant for the owner who wishes to prove samples of cloth for himself. A simple test for conventionally woven cloth can be conducted by pulling it at 45 degrees to the threadline between the hands; see Fig. 3.9. Stretch should be low, and the resulting crease should not remain too prominently after the pull is released. Another good way to examine cloth which is suspected of being overfilled with resins, is to crumple it in the hand and observe the crazing of the surface as the chemicals break down. If you have time, it is also a good idea to nail a sample to a post in the open for 24 hours, and then look at the results at the end (the high pressure man without time to spare will tie it to his car radio aerial and drive round the block). An overfilled cloth of poor quality will quickly have the stuffing knocked out of it by this treatment (who wouldn't?), and the bias pull-test described above

58

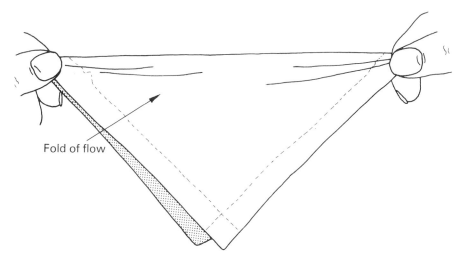

Fold of flow

Fig. 3.9 Cloth Testing
If a handkerchief is folded as shown and then pulled apart at the corners, a fold
will appear along the 'luff'. The free-hanging corners will rise, as the weave
distorts across the line of tension to draw the 'leech' upwards. This is a demonstra-
tion of weave distortion under loading, and can be repeated with a sample square
of sailcloth; the fold should not be too marked (which would betray poor resistance
to stretch), and should disappear when you stop pulling (which would show good
recovery).

will show much poorer results. This all-night test will also reveal the quality
of adhesives used in Mylar/Melinex film laminates.

When I was with Ratsey's we once had a French customer who took a
sample of 6 oz Dacron and tore it in half – something akin to meting out the
same treatment to a telephone directory, as anyone who has tried either will
know. He turned out to be a coal heaver.

Where chemicals have been used, they have been forced into the loom-
state cloth under pressure using rollers, and then cured. After the cloth has
been made up into a sail, therefore, there is no way in which an old synthetic
sail can be renovated by re-dressing the cloth as can be done with cotton.

Nylon is tested mainly for porosity and, with practice, a good deal can be
discovered by trying to blow or suck through a sample. Sailmakers use a
more exact method, which usually takes the form of some kind of hollow
cylinder made to fit vertically into a container of water. The nylon to be
tested is fastened over the upper end, thus restricting the passage of air, and
the time taken for the cylinder to descend a given distance into the water,
under gravity, is a direct indication of the porosity of the cloth under test.

Film laminate cloth can be checked for delamination as mentioned above.
About the only other test which the owner can do, is to stick a spike through

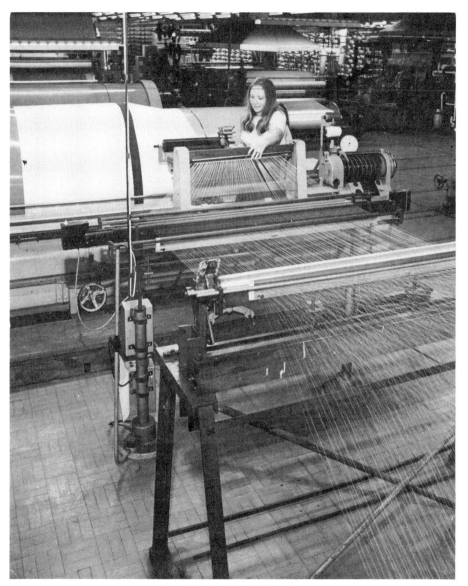

Plate 3.7 Sailcloth Weaving
Arranging the ends on a loom to form the Terylene warp threads.   *ICI Fibres*

it and check for himself that a tear won't get any worse – it won't, but it may be comforting to confirm it personally.

These simple tests are given as a guide only. Your Sail Maker is the expert, and you should normally be guided by him in preference to your own assessment. Sail Makers have a wide experience in judging cloth and, indeed,

Plate 3.8 Cloth Sampling
Removing a sample from the loom-state cloth for testing.   *ICI Fibres*

in all other matters relating to making sails. There is now such a wide range of different cloth constructions available, that it is easy for a little learning to be dangerous. The amateur may well have heard from his club 'expert' that the ratio of weft or fill yarn decitex to warp decitex should be high for a tall mainsail; so he objects to the cloth of 3:1 ratio which he is offered, and opts for one of 10:1 – but he would be wrong, because the warp would be too weak. Nothing will be more calculated to get you off to a bad start with your Sail Maker than ill-informed criticism and comment, or over-insistence on your own point of view with no more grounds than, say, a quick glance through this book.

61

SAIL OUTLINE DESIGN

Before the Sail Maker can get down to the task of selecting the right cloth for the sail under consideration, and then deciding how he is going to make it, he must know its outline shape. This is sail design proper, and should not be confused with the design of the camber, or flow, of the sail together with the round or hollow built into the edges of the sail in order to achieve the desired performance; I prefer to call this flow design, and I shall refer to it in some detail later.

In most cases the outline design of a sail will be decided for the Sail Maker. Either the yacht is a one-design boat, with strict limits and tolerances on the sizes allowed, or else there will be a sail plan, and he will be required to follow the sizes set forth by the Naval Architect or the rule. It may be, however, that the owner will ask the Sail Maker to make a sail for a specific task, and that this sail does not figure on the sail plan – or indeed that no plan exists.

Not all Sail Makers have a qualified Naval Architect on their staff, but most of them have sufficient practical experience of sailing and sailmaking to design a reasonable sail to most plans. It should be remembered, however, that they will almost certainly be working without the underwater lines of the boat, and that their answer will at best be an experienced cock-shy and not a qualified calculation. Such a course has, for the owner, the advantage that design fees are saved, but there can be no redress if the result is not all that could be desired. Redress from a Naval Architect would, however, also be hard to come by, and the Sail Maker has years of experience in interpreting sail plans from a wide variety of designers, so you need not be chary of asking his opinion.

Naturally, it will be a comparatively easy task to draw a maximum size no-penalty IOR genoa on to an existing sail plan. All that has to be done is to draw the LP one and a half times the J measurement, and then see that adequate clearance is allowed at the head, tack and clew (the last of these will require the sheer line of the deck). It is a slightly more delicate calculation to suggest a suitable intermediate genoa or working jib, and it becomes a major task when a complete redrawing of the sail plan is required, in order perhaps to alleviate weather helm or to reduce the rating. These last two aims are best met by calling on the services of a qualified Naval Architect, unless you are quite certain that you know what you want or that your Sail Maker has the necessary expertise. I shall refer in more detail to this question in Chapter XVIII *Design and Rating*.

CLOTH WEIGHT

I shall assume here that the outline shape of the sail is known to the Sail

Maker. The next task is to establish what weight of cloth will be used for the sail in question. I propose to deal at first with conventionally woven polyester cloth in single ply; I refer at the end of this chapter to the more modern approach. Those who may want to know about cotton (and it is nice to think that there are still some traditionalists left) should select their Sail Maker carefully, or try to obtain a copy of *Yacht Sails, Their Care and Handling*, published in the fifties by Ernest Ratsey and Ham de Fontaine.

Terylene and Dacron are strong enough to resist hard use, but this causes one of the most common errors to be made: too light a weight is selected. What is too often forgotten is the stretch factor. I can do no better than to quote John Illingworth on this subject, as his views coincide so closely with my own:

'In the case of headsails the answer in brief is to use the lightest weight of cloth *which will keep in shape*, in the wind strength for which the sail is designed ... care must be taken to choose a mainsail cloth *which will be fully adequate to its task* but no heavier.'[29] (The italics are mine).

A light woven cloth, while being easier to stow and handle, will stretch more readily than a heavy one, and the sail will consequently blow out of shape, usually manifested by the flow moving aft to an inefficient position. Steps must then be taken to correct the situation by pulling harder on the halyard or luff adjustment. As we shall see in the next chapter, this has the desirable effect of drawing the flow forward again to restore the proper aero-dynamic shape. Besides the size and function of the sail, the weight of cloth for a particular sail is also a function of the size and type of boat, and the winds it can expect to meet. Thus a beamy cruising boat will have heavier sails than a slim racer of the same length. Similarly for any particular boat, the larger the headsail the lighter the weight of cloth in general, for the sooner the sail will be replaced by a smaller one as the wind increases. The heaviest canvas, therefore, will be used for the storm headsail (in practice usually no heavier than the working headsail); the intermediate genoa and the genoa each becomes progressively lighter. The question of light weather headsails is slightly different, and receives attention later.

Continuing the practical approach to the problem, on a cutter we normally have the jib lighter than the staysail, because the former is usually taken off first as the wind gets up. Some owners of twin headsail yawls and ketches, however, prefer to sail in really heavy weather under mizzen and jib rather than mizzen and staysail, because the boat is better balanced; it partly depends on where the topmast stay arrives at the deck, for it may be dangerous in a blow to handle a jib on the end of a bowsprit. If the jib is the last working headsail to come off before storm canvas is set, then its weight should be sufficient to maintain shape in all winds up to this moment. Conversely, if the jib is set on a bowsprit, it will be taken off sooner and, in any case, it is not desirable to have too much weight to handle so far beyond the end of the boat.

Before we get down to actual figures, I should say something about the various methods of denoting cloth weight. The Americans measure sailcloth in ounces per yard of cloth $28\frac{1}{2}$ ins wide, whereas in Britain the square yard is used. There is thus an apparent difference of 20 per cent in our respective cloth weights, because a yard of cloth in Britain will have more material to be weighed (being 36 ins wide) than a yard in America (being only $28\frac{1}{2}$ ins wide); Fig. 3.10. Thus $3\frac{1}{2}$ oz (US) is the same cloth as $4\frac{1}{2}$ oz (UK), while $6\frac{1}{2}$ oz (US) = 8 oz (UK). Because the USA produces far more sailcloth than the UK, the American system of measurement (called oz per sailmaker's yard) is also often used by Britons who, having broken from a somewhat

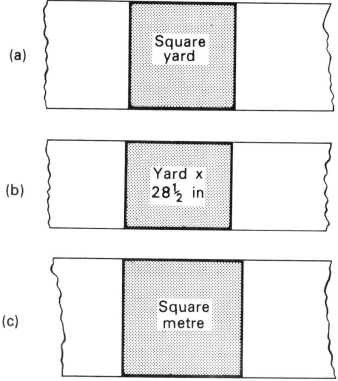

Fig. 3.10 Definition of Cloth Weight
In the UK, cloth weight is measured in ounces per yard run of cloth a yard wide (a). Americans count the number of ounces per yard run of cloth $28\frac{1}{2}$ ins wide (b). This results in an apparent discrepancy in identical cloths of some 20 per cent, and is because the USA still uses as a cloth yard the distance between King Henry VIII's nose and the tip of his outstretched hand (the king was a dumpy man, as evidenced by his suit of armour on view in the Tower of London). Thanks to the logical French, the metric system measures the number of grammes per square metre (c).

archaic yardstick (28½ ins was the standard distance between nose and out-stretched hand when King Henry VIII measured his wives for broadcloth), now find themselves back in the Dark Ages again. Roll on the metric system, which uses grammes per square metre, and the two examples above would be 155 gm/m² and 275 gm/m² respectively. I have included a comparison table at Appendix A.

Working Sails. The best way to establish the weight of woven cloth for a particular boat's sails is to decide the mainsail and working headsail first. It is not possible to be dogmatic, because different types of boat need different solutions, but it is always useful to have a yardstick. A good method is to relate cloth weight to water-line length of the boat. It is a direct indication of the size of the yacht and, unlike tonnage, there can be only one interpreta-tion of a given figure; it also has the advantage that it can be scaled straight from the sail plan. You may consider that sail area would be an equally good method, but you would be surprised at the number of owners who do not know the area of their sails. In addition some yachts carry more or less sail than the average and, in any case, headsail sizes can vary between yachts of the same size: a masthead genoa will be a good deal larger than the largest headsail which can be set on a yacht of similar proportions which has only a threequarter rig; yet they will both be used under similar wind conditions. In addition, there is always a risk of confusion between rated and actual areas.

At Fig. 3.11 is a table showing the recommended weights of convention-ally woven single-ply cloth for average boats of various water-line lengths. These should be varied either way if the boat is especially heavy or light for her size, or if she habitually sails in light winds or Atlantic gales. Besides the working sails, I have shown my thoughts on genoas. In this connection, it should be remembered that owners are tending nowadays to hold on to these sails in stronger winds than they did a while back. The tremendous pulling power of the genoa means that it is common practice to take two or three rolls in the mainsail, or pull down a jiffy reef, and leave the genoa on as the wind increases. In this case it becomes the equivalent of a working headsail, and its cloth weight should be calculated accordingly.

Use of treated or 2-ply cloth complicates the picture, as does the use of cloth with different counts in warp and weft or fill but, for those who want to carry some sort of figure in their head, a very rough guide to conventional canvas weight for working sails can be obtained from the following formula:

$$Wt = \frac{L}{5}$$

where Wt is cloth weight in oz per sailmaker's yard, and L is the boat's waterline length in feet.

Fig. 3.11 Table of Recommended Weights for Woven Sailcloth
Weights are expressed in oz/yd × 28½ ins (US system).
To convert to oz/yd² or gm/m², see Appendix A.

Yacht	Mainsail and working Headsail	Genoa	Intermediate genoa	Light genoa
Small dinghies	2¾–3½	—	—	—
Stout dinghies	4 –5	4 –5	—	—
Small keelboats	4 –5	3½–5	—	—.
Dry sailers:				
Dragon, Soling	5½–6	4 –6	—	3 –4
Large keelboats; LWL:				
20 ft	4 –5½	4 –5½	—	2½–3½
21–25 ft	5 –6	4½–6	5 –6½	2½–4
26–30 ft	5½–6½	5 –6½	6 –7	3 –4
31–35 ft	6½–7½	5½–7½	6 –8	3 –4½
36–40 ft	7½–8½	6½–8½	7 –9	3 –5
41–45 ft	8 –9	7 –9	8 –10	4 –5
46–50 ft	9–10	*	*	4 –5
51–60 ft	11 –12	*	*	*
61–70 ft	12 –14	*	*	*

* = requires individual assessment

The above can only be a guide, because cloths of so many different characteristics and qualities are available. But it will give a starting point, when conventionally woven single-ply Dacron or Terylene is being considered. The Sail Maker must be the best final arbiter.

The cloth for the mainsail of a yawl or ketch should normally be decided in accordance with the table in Fig. 3.11, tending to go slightly lighter if there is any doubt. This is because the sail will be rather smaller than a mainsail for a comparable sloop, and probably smaller than for a cutter, so it will not have as large a total pressure in it for a given wind strength. On the other hand, beware of going too light for it will not be reefed as often, due to its smaller initial size.

A mizzen should normally be not more than two weights lighter than its mainsail. It is here that calculation according to area can lead one astray, and I take issue with some on this point. A yawl of 30 ft waterline may have a mainsail of 350 sq ft and a cloth weight of 7 oz per sailmaker's yard. Its mizzen, however, may not be larger than 60 ot 70 sq ft, which some would have us give a 5-oz cloth. Yet this is the sail which may well have to stand up to the weight of a near-gale, when the mainsail has been removed. 7 oz is the minimum for such a task, even at this small area. We did, in fact, make one mizzen of about 60 sq ft at Ratsey's out of 5-oz cloth for a French owner. It was a complete failure, for the leech stretched badly out of shape and, though we recut the sail twice, it was never a success. The owner blamed poor sailmaking, of course, and I suppose he was right, because we should have refused to accept instructions to use such a light material. We were in a difficult position, because there was no doubt what had caused the leech to stretch, but we could not put the blame on the Naval Architect concerned without incurring his displeasure, to the possible jeopardy of future orders from him. On the other hand, the owner was most upset so we just had to grin and bear it. As I say, it was largely our fault for allowing ourselves to be talked into such a light material in the first place.

Reverting to the table, you will notice that light genoas do not increase their cloth weight in proportion to other sails. This is because they should never be used in winds above force 3, and the total weight of wind in the sail will thus not be great, no matter how large an area is involved. I must here make the first of several warnings about using such sails in winds too strong for them; this also applies to ghosters and drifters, with even more effect (and also to film laminates, which have an admittedly higher, but no less important, wind limit). It is a natural temptation to hold on to a sail which is pulling well, even though the wind increases a good deal. If this occurs, the sail may be ruined for all time as it is blown out of shape, and the owner must make up his mind whether the race is worth it.

CLOTH SELECTION

We have already seen that, film laminates apart, cloths of varying construction are made to meet different requirements. If a low aspect ratio mainsail is being made from a wholly woven polyester cloth, the chances are that it will be for a boat which does a lot of cruising, so there is little point in using too sophisticated a material. A look back at Fig. 3.6 shows us that the sail will be subjected to loadings which are comparable along the leech and across the wide chord of the sail, therefore the cloth should be of relatively square construction. This confers good resistance to bias stretch, and has the desirable effect that fewer fillers are required to lock the weave. We thus have a soft material, well suited to the cruising owner. By contrast, a high aspect ratio mainsail will probably be used for a racing boat, where a harder finish can be accepted. Stresses are greatest down the leech, and the weave must therefore be reinforced on the weft, so a cloth construction of heavy fill yarns is indicated. The result is increased weft strength but at the expense of slight extra bias distortion; this in turn can be partly compensated for a while by use of fillers to lock the weave. Dacron and Mylar are of the same chemical base, as we have seen, but the former actually has less elasticity; it is the yarn crimp of woven cloth which allows stretch, and the form of its construction which distorts under bias loading, hence the uniform stability of film. If

67

weight is a factor and film laminate is to be avoided, stability can be achieved by using two cloths of less than half the weight each in a ply construction, such as Howe and Bainbridge's Synchroweave®. The former involves the Sail Maker sealing two light cloths on top of each other (double-sided sticky tape helps here); the latter is a cloth which has two thicknesses joined at the selvedges, thus simplifying the sewing process. In both cases, distortion is less than that of a single-ply cloth of the same weight as the two plies added together. A similar solution is offered by the use of tri-axial weave in genoas (where loadings are more uniformly spread), but its very resistance to stretch in three directions brings its own problems, particularly with adjustable luff headsails, which may not respond to quite the extent desired. Use of highly resinated material puts a greater emphasis on built-in shape through tapering and rounding the panels, but there is still some control available to the owner through spar and headfoil bending.

THE MODERN APPROACH

Use of ply-cloth, laminates and special weaves has complicated the somewhat simplistic approach to cloth selection of the previous pages. Much depends on the role of the boat, the type of cloth and even the construction of the weave (weft/warp ratio). We have already seen how different cloths must be used for high and low aspect ratio mainsails, and different again for a genoa. The racing owner, prepared to invest in a new suit of sails for a particular series, has a separate requirement from his cruising counterpart, who wants an easily handled wardrobe which will last thousands of miles.

It is thus hard to give a general rule for cloth weight as against boat size or sail area. A laminate of Mylar or Melinex and Dacron or Terylene (or nylon) might be as low as 5–6 oz/US for a 12-metre, while more conventional polyester weave could be 7–8 oz/US; a cruising boat of comparable size would think of 9–10 oz/US. Quarter Tonners sometimes use 2-ply cloth of 4–4½ oz/US (5–5½ oz/yd²) and would certainly want different weft/warp ratios in mainsail and headsail, even if they did not go for film laminate cloth, while a cruising boat of the same size would want softer sails with less resin; this in turn would demand a heavier construction if distortion is to be kept within reasonable limits offshore. The poor tear strength of Mylar/Melinex film laminates means that they are not best suited to cruising boats which are sailing far from sophisticated repair facilities. Many different adhesives are used for bonding film to weave, and some are better than others, so that delamination can still occur, particularly where point and shock loadings are involved (hard folds, or sails flogging against the rigging); this also brings problems with some chemicals used for cleaning, as we shall see later.

The parameters are so varied and complex that, if you are going for one of the modern materials, you are best advised to discuss the problem with your Sail Maker. When it comes to storm canvas, you would be wise to consider the words of the Offshore Racing Council. They rule that trysails should be made of cloth which is 'of suitable strength for the purpose'.[30] This rather vague wording is because, due to the improvements in weaving which we examined earlier, mainsail weights have become lighter over the years. But in extreme conditions offshore, loadings are heavy and so no chances should be taken. It is worth specifying that canvas with a soft handle should be used for storm sails, because a hard finish can make sail drill difficult; any attendant slight distortion can be countered by having the sail cut flat and hoisting it hard. You should also ask about one of the coatings which can be applied to protect the seam stitching. Sail Makers don't always like using them, because they are smelly and messy, but they do seem to work. On the other hand, cloth which is inhibited against attack by ultra violet rays is not always necessary, particularly in waters where there is not sunshine twelve hours a day, every day; it is usually the stitching which is weakened first, and the cloth lasts for years anyway, so inhibition may be an unnecessary expense. By all means have a strip sewn to the leech of a roller headsail, to protect it where it would otherwise be exposed when left rolled on the fore-stay in all weathers; always have a roller headsail made of heavier cloth than standard genoa weight, because it will be used, probably half-rolled, in winds which would otherwise be far too strong for it.

Chapter IV

Sail Flow Design

After the general shape and outline form of the sail have been decided, and the cloth selected, the Sail Maker must make up his mind how he proposes to achieve the flow which has been agreed. To differentiate it from the sail design involved in drawing up a sail plan, I have called it flow design.

Not only must the controlling dimensions and weight of cloth have been decided at this stage, but also the general degree of fullness required in the finished product and the conditions under which it will be used should be known. By this I mean not only what wind speeds it will encounter, but also the characteristics of the spars or stay on which it will be set. Thus, a head-sail made for a forestay which is nearly straight (the optimum) will be cut differently from one which is to be used on a wire which sags a good deal; the luff of the latter will have to be cut to allow for a predetermined curve. The same holds goods for a mast which bends.

There are five principal ways in which a sail of single-ply woven cloth can have flow designed or controlled:

1. Rounding the luff and foot.
2. Tapering the cloths (broad seam).
3. Tension on the cloth.
4. Tension on the rope, tape or wire.
5. Lay of the cloth.

ROUNDING THE LUFF AND FOOT

If the luff and foot of a mainsail destined for a straight mast and boom are cut in a convex curve, the surplus cloth will be pushed back into the sail as flow when it is put on the spars and the edges are forced into straight lines. As soon as the mast bends, however, it bows forward and draws any surplus cloth with it, thus flattening the sail. The more the mast bends, therefore, the more round must be added to the luff to conform. We saw in Chapter II

Plate 4.1 Measuring Flow in a 12-metre Mainsail
The America's Cup has eventual spin-offs which benefit the whole of sailing. The high budgets of most challengers permit such thoroughness as shown here, where a fire-fighting ladder is being used so that flow can be measured precisely to check against calculation (one of Cowes part-time firemen worked for Ratsey's). *Author*

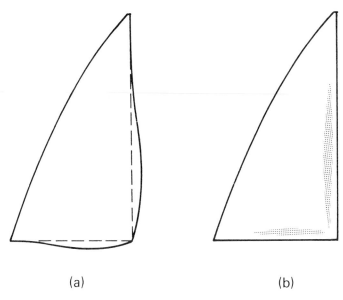

(a)   (b)

Fig. 4.1 Luff and Foot Round Imparts Flow

In (a) a mainsail is shown spread in the Sail Maker's loft before roping or taping; the surplus cloth built into the luff and foot in the form of round lies substantially flat on the floor. When the sail is hoisted on straight spars as in (b), the extra cloth is forced back into the sail as flow. This flow will lie fairly close to the mast and boom, and the Sail Maker will have no control over where it settles unless he adopts other measures as well. There are, however, many successful sails (usually small ones) which have their flow arbitrarily induced in only this way. The less round built into the sail, the flatter it will be, so there is often none built into the head, which may even be slightly hollow if it is desired to keep the sail particularly flat at this point (but remember the need for extra camber at the head, explained under *Aspect Ratio* in Chapter 2). Bendy spars must have sails with more luff round, so that the sail can accommodate the bow forward when the mast is bent, and still provide the extra cloth required for flow.

how the head of a high aspect ratio mainsail needs rather more camber than a lower aspect sail; nevertheless, we get a basic shape somewhat like Fig. 4.1 (a) when it lies flat on the floor before roping.

On the other hand, a headsail must be shaped to allow for forestay sag both aft and to leeward. This has the effect of increasing flow, as it pushes cloth back into the bunt of the sail, which must be cut accordingly. Thus, an overall hollow curve is the basis of any large headsail luff, especially where backstay adjustment is not really powerful enough to keep the forestay straight (so, if your Sail Maker asks whether you have hydraulics on your boat, don't think that he's just being inquisitive). Having said that, there needs to be a certain amount of flow in the lower half and, whatever method is used to achieve it, some luff round is needed low down (one Sail Maker spreads the joined-up sail for its final shaping, and then draws the clew aft under tension. This pulls the lower luff inside the straight line, thus taking out much of the effect of bunching caused by broad seam, so that subsequent hollowing of the luff does, in fact, allow some round to reappear when tension is taken off the clew again).

Plate 4.2 Luff Round on the Spreading Floor
Enterprise sails in W G Lucas' loft, spread on top of those for a 14 ft Bermuda dinghy. Apart from the disparity in sail size for the same length boat, readily evident is the amount of round built into the luff of the smaller mainsail (to its right). Flow in the sail is revealed by the folds of cloth which do not lie flat.

W G Lucas & Son

The Sail Maker is usually very much in the hands of the owner in this respect, and is sometimes given misleading information. Word has got round that a straight forestay is a good thing aerodynamically, and owners do not like to be thought unaware of this requirement. The tendency is therefore to assure the Sail Maker that the forestay is 'as stiff as I can get it. We have the permanent backstay ground right down, you known, and there's very little sag.' A photograph would surprise that owner, if it were taken from dead ahead, or at right angles from down to leeward.

It is interesting to note that this basic shape, which has been used by Sail Makers for centuries, was confirmed after extensive wind tunnel research at Southampton University.[31]

TAPERING THE CLOTHS (BROAD SEAM)

If some of the cloths are tapered, the sail will alter shape accordingly. If, in addition, the sail has a certain amount of extra cloth built in, in the form of

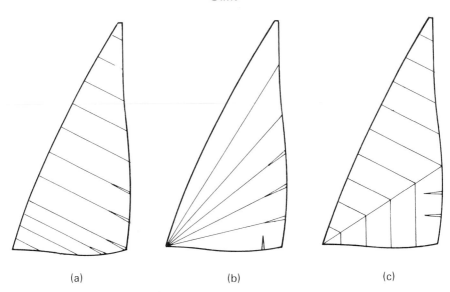

(a) (b) (c)

Fig. 4.2 Mainsail Cuts

The horizontal cut (a) is efficient as regards broad seam, because its cloths arrive at the luff at a convenient angle for that purpose. It is for this reason that sails cut in this manner usually have a seam exactly striking the tack, for that is where maximum shaping is required. A radial or a mitre cut mainsail, such as (b) and (c), must inevitably rely more on darts specially put in for the purpose, with the attendant danger of small knuckles appearing where they end.

The leech can also be shaped by means of these tapered seams. In this area, however, it is not curvature which is required, but complete flatness to allow the wind to run off cleanly. Thus, leech seams which have been tightened right out to the tabling should be suspect, because they will tend to hold the leech to windward. Rather should we expect to find these seams eased slightly, particularly near the head and clew, to help free the leech where it has to come up to windward a little to rejoin the top of the mast and the outer end of the boom. Care must be taken not to overdo it, or the whole leech area will go slack and sag to leeward.

luff and foot round, the position of the resulting flow can be controlled by means of tapering the appropriate cloths to a predetermined point; see Figs. 4.2 and 4.3.

This tapering of cloths is called 'broad seam', and is subdivided into luff seam, tack seam and foot seam. The overall flow given to the sail in the form of luff and foot round will have its point of maximum draft along the line where the inner end of taper ceases. The first time a particular sail is made, this basic line is established on the cloths as they lie side by side after being cut out on the full-size pattern, and before they are sewn together. We shall see more of this in the next chapter.

Similar broad seam can be put into headsails, although they need less flow or camber, and can usually be relied upon to take up more nearly their correct shape with only the mitre being adjusted and without the necessity

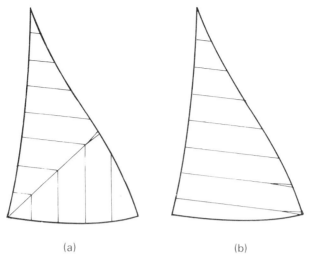

(a)   (b)

Fig. 4.3 Headsail Cuts

The mitre cut (a) was the most popular way to fashion a headsail for nearly a century, because it ensures that cloths run at right angles from both the unsupported edges of the sail; the resulting lack of bias reduces distortion at the leech and foot. But the cut sometimes gives trouble at the mitre itself, where development of flow is inhibited by the extra thickness of material; broad seam may be incorporated into the mitre to counter this.

Development of stable cloth (not only film laminates and tri-axial weave, but better standard conventional weaves) allows the more efficient horizontal cut (b) to be exploited with its consistent characteristics. Broad seam can be conveniently introduced – in the case of all-woven cloth, roughly every third seam up to three-quarter height for cruising sails and every other seam for racing genoas; film laminates usually have every seam shaped.

Some large genoas are cut vertically, with the object of putting the leech stresses along the run of the cloth on the warp.

for darts. A horizontally cut headsail will, of course, present plenty of scope for adjustment in this manner.

TENSION ON THE CLOTH

As woven cloth stretches on the bias, so it causes a fold to appear near the line of tension. To check this, take a clean handkerchief and fold it corner to corner diagonally in half, so that it forms a triangle. Let the two ends hang down while you pull on the other two corners. A fold will appear in the 'luff' of the handkerchief as tension is applied on the bias of the cloth by pulling outwards, and this will deepen as you pull harder; see Fig. 3.9.

When the weave in a sail is treated in the same way, a similar fold will appear along the line of tension. If it is correctly controlled, this tension can be used to induce further flow in a sail. A mainsail is deliberately made shorter on the luff and foot than its full size, so that tension applied by means of the halyard and outhaul will induce flow near the rope or tape. If this tension is applied only lightly, there will be little induced flow, as I call it, and the sail will take up the shape given it by the round and broad seam also built into it. As the wind blows harder, this flow will move aft and up into the sail under the influence of pressure and friction drag. It can be brought back nearer to its starting point again by further tension on the luff and foot. This is one of the principal ways in which an owner can control the shape of his sail in use. If the halyard and outhaul are stretched to their maximum, the flow will appear as a tight fold near the bolt rope, and only the strongest wind will move it further into the sail to the correct place. The flow in a headsail can be controlled in a similar manner if the luff is adjustable in some way – either by being sewn to a rope or tape like a mainsail, or by being free to slide over the luff wire. We shall deal with this more fully in the chapter on trim, but it is as well to know exactly what is happening and why.

Plate 4.3 Sailboard
This shot down the luff of a Sea Panther shows clearly the smooth flow in the sail, and the slight bend at the mast head. *David Eberlin*

TENSION ON THE ROPE, TAPE OR WIRE

To be effective, induced flow must be properly controlled. It is no good allowing a sail to be stretched as far as the cloth will go, for this will almost always result in too great a fold appearing in the adjacent area. First and foremost, allowance must be made by the Sail Maker so that the sail does not stretch beyond its marks.

MAINSAILS

If we are to deal first with large one-off mainsails, the cloth would pull out a great deal too much if left to its own devices, especially under the influence of powerful halyard winches. However, there is usually a rope or tape on the luff and foot of a mainsail, and this will restrict the distance to which the sail can go. The Sail Maker uses a material with known elasticity, which he first of all pulls to a certain tension before sewing on to the sail. This ensures that there is less rope or tape than sail, thus restricting the amount which the sail can stretch. The exact calculation of the right amount of pre-stretching for the rope is another of the Sail Maker's secrets, and each one has his own ideas, which extend to varying the preset tension along the rope, in order to vary the induced flow up the luff.

The majority of sails these days are fully moulded to shape, and the bolt rope is pre-stretched on both luff and foot. This has no elasticity at all, and the sail can be cut to its exact shape without having to take account of induced flow through bias stretch. It will still be necessary to pull the sail out to its marks with a certain amount of tension, because the action of sewing the sail to the rope causes a degree of puckering. Alternatively the rope can be sewn on slack, so that the cloth is pulled a little as the rope straightens out under tension.

The use of luff tape was pioneered by Ike Manchester of the United States of America; its adoption gives the headsail an adjustable luff free from corrosion. It is important to use the right weight and type of tape for each particular weight of cloth, so that the tape will allow the correct amount of stretch to take place in the cloth. In both cases the luff of the sail will stretch just about the right amount to reach the designed length, while at the same time inducing the right amount of flow by stretching the cloth on the bias. We shall see later about how to pull less on halyard and outhaul in light winds, and how to pull more when it is blowing hard.

HEADSAILS

When a traditional headsail is made with a conventional luff wire, the Sail Maker ensures that the length of the luff is slightly shorter than the wire on which it has to be fitted. The allowance varies with the type of sail and with the Sail Maker concerned (secrets again), but it is in the order of two or three per cent. The tack eye is worked into the sail and the luff is pulled until the cloth stretches the full distance along the wire. The head is then seized at its stretched position and the sail made fast to the head eye. The induced flow is left to lie along the luff as a fold.

The exact amount which the sail is pulled depends on a number of factors, including the weight and quality of the cloth, the type and role of the sail, the size of winch which will be used for the sheet and whether the sail should be full or flat. No two traditional sails pull exactly alike, even if they are supposed to be identical; the cloth or stitching will vary sufficiently to cause a slight variation, so each headsail had to be finished off individually by someone who knew what he was looking for and how to achieve it. The sail may then either be seized at intervals along the luff wire, which is sewn close up all along its length so that it lies at the edge of the luff tabling at all times, or else the wire is left to lie freely inside the luff tabling. In either case, when the headsail is spread on the floor without pulling the wire taut, the wire will

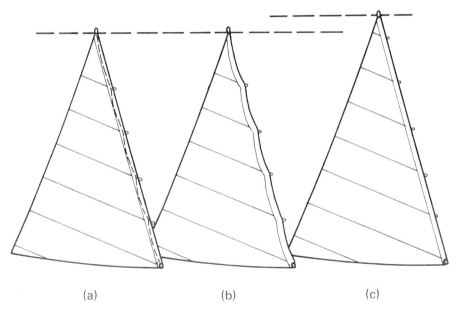

(a) (b) (c)

Fig. 4.4 Headsail Luff Measurement (Woven Sails)
In (a) a wire is fitted loose inside the tabling, but the luff has not been pulled tight enough to stretch the cloth and straighten the wire, which can be felt lying along the dotted line; the sail appears short. When the wire is seized at intervals all along the luff as in (b), its sinuous course will be readily apparent and the reason for any shortage in length is obvious. In both (a) and (b) there will be no fold of flow in the sail. When the luff is pulled correctly to straighten the wire (or pull the kinks out of a tape), the sail achieves its designed length and flow is induced up the luff. Film laminate sails, of course, do not stretch but are pre-shaped panel by panel.

lie in a series of S-bends, either taking the luff with it, or else lying loose inside the tabling. This is because the cloth will only spread to a certain size and the wire, being longer, must zigzag to stay confined within the length of the unstretched luff. Not until the wire is pulled taut will the luff of the sail stretch to its designed length, producing induced flow as it stretches.

There seem to be popular misconceptions about two facets of stretch. First, nearly every mainsail and many foresails will appear to be under size if they are laid flat on the floor and measured. We have seen that a mainsail is often deliberately made under size so that it shall stretch to its designed length under the influence of its halyard and outhaul, thus achieving induced flow. In addition the rope or tape is sewn on tight, to prevent the sail being stretched too far; this will cause the sail to pucker slightly when little or no tension is applied. A traditional headsail is also made under size, but it is often easier to see the intended length of the luff if it is seized at intervals to the wire along its length.

The second point is that stretching a sail on the luff and foot does not make it any bigger. All you are doing is to cause the threads to move against each other, thus transforming the little squares formed by the warp and weft into little diamonds. To enable the luff to increase in length beyond the size it was cut, some cloth must come from elsewhere, and it usually comes from the leech. The more you pull on the halyard the less roach you will have. You cannot get something for nothing, so there is no point in pulling the sail as hard as you can in light airs in the mistaken belief that you are getting maximum area by so doing. The reverse is desired from a flow point of view, as you will not want the induced flow hard against the bolt rope. I shall revert to this in the section on setting sails.

LAY OF THE CLOTH

Since woven Terylene and Dacron distort as soon as tension is even slightly on the bias, the Sail Maker has to pay great attention to the way in which he lays the cloths of a sail. Cloth stretch is the greatest single factor to be considered in making sails of woven cloth – or else why all the excitement about Mylar? By manipulating his cloths so that the strain is either on or off the threadline, the Sail Maker can control how much a sail distorts in a particular place. Similarly, the faulty lay of a cloth by as little as one or two degrees can upset the shape of a sail to a point where it is useless. This explains why most leeches have cloths running away from them approximately at rightangles, since stretch on this part of the sail is undesirable, and the threadline must be followed. The cloths are therefore often tripped round the roach of a mainsail and the hollow of a headsail so that the weft follows approximately the line of the leech. This has the additional desirable effect of

Fig. 4.5 Mainsail Leech Stresses

There are two important stress lines in the leech of a mainsail, where woven cloth is concerned. One goes straight from the clew to the head, and the other runs along the perimeter of the leech itself. It is obvious that we cannot have the weft running along both of these, particularly in the upper and lower thirds of the sail, where these directions are anything up to 20 degrees different from each other. However, we are particularly interested in having the leech very slightly slack in the upper and lower regions, otherwise the sail will tend to hold up to windward as it comes up to meet the appropriate spar; this will occur if the cloths are set at right angles to the straight line joining clew to head. On the other hand, if we have the thread-line aligned with the leech itself, then the cloth must be on the bias along the straight line clew to head, particularly in the upper and lower thirds. This means that the sail would go slack just inside the leech, principally near the clew and head.

keeping outward pressure on the battens, thus reducing any tendency to batten pocket 'poke'; see Chapter XVII.

MAINSAILS

This is not the full picture, however, and we can look at a typical horizontally cut mainsail leech to see why. If we set the threadline parallel to the straight stress line (head to clew), you will note from Fig. 4.5 that the cloth is slightly on the bias at the leech in the upper and lower thirds. This gives us the slight stretching we require near the head and clew, so that the sail will not hook to windward at these two places. It also reduces the stretch in the middle third, where the sail will naturally tend to sag more to leeward, because the leech edge and threadline more nearly coincide.

Once again this is not the final picture, because a very small variation from the threadline makes a big difference in the degree of stretch. Each sail

Plate 4.4 Measuring Flow in the Loft
General shape and flow (as well as particular faults) can be examined at close
quarters on mainsails up to 800 sq ft on Bruce Banks indoor test rig. The mast has
a groove large enough to take most luff slides.   *Yachting World*

has to be studied, therefore, according to how much roach it has (and hence
the divergence of the upper and lower leech from the straight line head to
clew), and each Sail Maker has his own closely guarded secrets about how
much bias he allows in different places. The thickness and type of tabling
will alter the amount of leech stretch, and some Sail Makers prefer no bias at
all, with a very light tabling so as not to hold the sail too tightly; some prefer
rather more bias (around 5°) with a stout tabling to help cut down stretch,
which can also be controlled by tightening one or two seams the appropriate
amount; there is one who determines a catenary line, running from the clew
to a point forward of the headboard by a percentage of the foot length –
cloths are then laid at right angles to this line, thus ensuring more leech bias
at the head than the foot.

You will see from Fig. 4.6 (a) that the conventional horizontally cut
mainsail allows the cloths to strike the luff and foot with plenty of bias, so
that induced flow can be made to play its part to the full. If the cloths were
on the threadline at the luff or foot, there would be little or no fold as a
result of applied tension. This is one of the drawbacks of the mitre cut mainsail in Fig. 4.6 (b), which has to have the foot cloths deliberately offset from
the line of the weft if induced flow is to be encouraged.

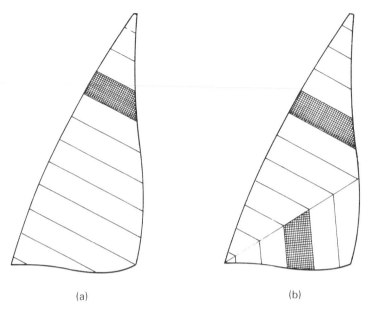

Fig. 4.6 Mainsail Cloth Bias (Woven Sails)
The horizontal cut (a) has plenty of bias evenly distributed up the luff. The mitre
cut mainsail (b), on the other hand, has two different bias angles at the luff, and
must have the foot cloths deliberately offset if there is to be any give in the foot.

When the cloths depart from these conventional patterns, strange things
happen to the leech. This is not always detrimental to the sail, but often is. A
radially cut mainsail presents a leech which has a varying bias angle, and
thus a varying stretch, for which there are no ready-made seams for corrective measures. In addition the cloths will arrive at the luff at varying angles,
again with different stretch results. Attempts to resolve the leech problem,
therefore, by means of a series of short horizontal cloths at the after-edge,
only represent half measures, for the luff will still stretch differentially. The
sail's chances of success after several hours' sailing are small unless made by
a loft which specializes in this cut.

On the racing circuit there has recently been a rash of vertical cut mainsails, which started in the USA, as such cults often do. The loads which are
imparted to a mainsail are principally down the leech, so that any non-
resilient cloth such as film laminate will benefit from not taking these stresses
across the joins of horizontally laid cloths, but will be better by accepting
them along the length of the warp of the substrate. Let it be quite clear that
conventionally woven polyester cloth absorbs shock loads better than film
laminate, so that the vertical cut is best suited to the latter. Mylar/Melinex
mainsails cut in this way work well, but they are for the racing owner so, if
you are a cruiser, don't be tempted to follow suit.

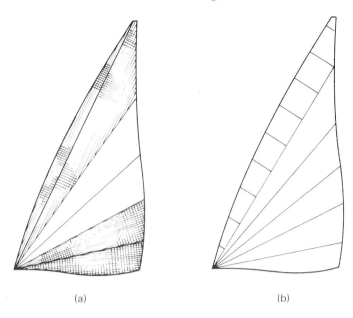

(a)   (b)

Fig. 4.7 Sunray or Radial Mainsail Bias (Woven Sails)
The leech panel has varying bias along the curve of the leech, and none at its forward edge. In order that uneven stretching shall not occur, panel number 2 should meet this with no bias at their juncture. This means that there will be bias at its meeting with panel number 3, which must also have the same bias if counter stresses are not to be set up. And so on through the sail. If the cloths are to be cut so that they have bias at both edges (which would avoid alternate seams which don't stretch at all), as shown at the foot of the sail, there is a lot of cloth cut to waste, so it is expensive. To hold the leech distortion in check, sometimes individual panels are laid in this area as in (b). In both cases there will be differential stretch up the luff, due to varying bias.

HEADSAILS

The same basic principles apply to a headsail, which requires careful attention to its leech, so that the clean run off we have postulated is achieved, and so that it never hooks to windward. A racing sail with a light tabling (and a designed life of a dozen races) may therefore have no bias all the way round the leech. A more robust sail for a long-distance cruiser, with its strong tabling and perhaps even a leechrope, should have one or two degrees of bias to counteract the tightening effect of the tabling. The ocean racer who wants his headsails to last properly for a couple of seasons as racing sails, and then to go on for cruising, should have a tabling graduated somewhere in between, with rather less than one degree of bias on the leech. The foot will also need some stretch – indeed, rather more than the leech, because the bunt of the sail will pull aft under the action of powerful

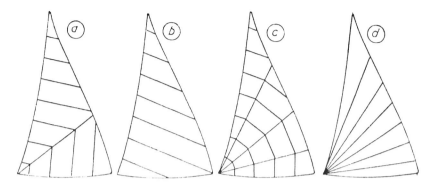

Fig. 4.8 Headsail Cloth Bias (Woven Sails)

(a) *Mitre Cut*. In the days of cloth which distorted badly off the threadline, the conventional mitre cut headsail gave the simplest solution to containing bias stretch along unsupported edges. However, not only do its cloths strike the luff at two different bias angles up the luff, but the doubled thickness of cloth at the mitre exerts a restricting influence on development of draft in the sail. This tends to produce a hard line along the mitre itself and the danger of a flat lower half to the sail.

(b) *Horizontal Cut*. Murphy & Nye of America virtually pioneered large-scale cutting of horizontal headsails. With development of more stable cloth, bias problems at the foot have disappeared, so that this highly efficient cut can take advantage of consistent bias angle at the luff and convenient seams for shaping. In the case of Mylar or Melinex film, there is no bias to worry about, but this cut is the simplest and most efficient for shaping.

(c) *Spider Web*. The spider web or multi-mitre cut has two or more mitres and still retains its weft threadline parallel to the leech and foot. The panels are remarkably small, so that stretch is reduced to a minimum – often too low, and this is a style which is only suitable where the sail is large and the stresses are large, such as in a 12-metre (which will probably avoid the issue by using Mylar).

(d) *Radial Cut*. The radial or sunray cut headsail suffers from exactly the same drawbacks as a mainsail cut in the same way. From time to time a cult arises, but I am convinced that it stems from a couple of leading helmsmen doing well with it, and the rest of the fleet slavishly following suit in the belief that it is the sail which is winning the race. As in many other fashions afloat, the truth is often that the helmsman would win with any reasonable sail, and I can find no overriding advantage for this cut, despite the fact that one or two individual Sail Makers make a habit of producing excellent radial sails.

winches. The foot cloths may, therefore, have anything up to 7° or 8° of bias so that the whole sail can move aft, thus flattening the leech area.

MOULDED SAILS

Where we are considering sails for dinghies and one-design day racers which, because they are relatively small, are not subjected to loadings high enough to destroy their shape in a couple of races, a hard, highly resinated woven cloth may be used. Shape is then built in by means of taper and round, so

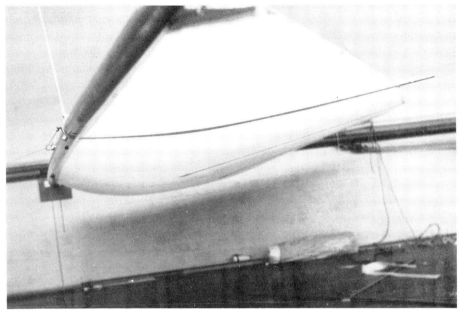

Plate 4.5 Bendy Mast
Where a sail is made for a bendy mast, it is sometimes useful to check that it sets
according to the offsets which have been specified by the customer. Here a 5–0–5
mainsail is set on the flexible spar in Bruce Bank's Sarisbury sail loft.

Yachting World

that the sail sets to its designed flow with little or no adjustment from the
owner. This also applies to those larger sails made from Mylar/Melinex film.
The vast store of cutting information (length of each panel, amount and
length of taper, luff and foot round, and bias angle if appropriate) can be
stored on computer and called up for any particular sail; the computer can
up-date or vary its information in discussion with other computers in allied
lofts across Europe and in America, so the precise shape of every panel will
be known before the first length of cloth is cut from the bolt, together with
details of how each one is to be sewn.

The result may be imagined as being made from fabric which does not
stretch, almost as though it were from pliable sheet metal. Particularly in the
case of film laminates, this gives a flow which is moulded-in and does not
respond to varying tensions on luff and foot; the sail stays the same shape
over the whole wind range for which it was designed. There is therefore little
or no need for adjustment in use, apart from varying mast bend or headsail
sag. But owners brought up to control sail shape by means of halyard,
Cunningham hole, kicking strap and the rest may take a little time to revert
to the leave-well-alone attitude of their forebears before World War II, and
we shall examine this in Chapter IX.

Chapter V

Cutting and Sewing a Sail

The physical task of making a sail once it has been designed and planned, can be divided into five stages:

1. Cutting out.
2. Putting together.
3. Rubbing down.
4. Tablings, patches and pockets.
5. Finishing; this will be treated in the next chapter.

CUTTING OUT

Where the precise shape of every panel is not stored by a computer (or calculated from that data), or available from a pattern or book, a one-off sail is drawn full-size on the floor, with an allowance of several inches all round so that the doubled edges, or tablings, can be put on the luff, leech and foot. Traditionally, the cutter first draws in chalk the three (or four) corners of the sail, marks these with prickers stuck into the floor, and stretches a twine round the basic triangle. He then makes further crosses to mark the amount of round or hollow at predetermined points along the luff, leech and foot. He next bends a spline along the curve he requires or alternatively he 'throws' his tape, or roll of webbing, along the edge to be drawn, by anchoring it at one end with a pricker stuck in the floor and adjusting it to a fair curve by hand and eye from the other end, so that it exactly cuts the several crosses determining the amount of round or hollow. The line of the luff, leech or foot is then chalked on the floor, using the spline or tape as a marker. Where the sail is a recurring one-design, the pattern may be permanently painted on the floor, or the size and shape of all the necessary cloths may be stored in a computer, drawn on to a pattern or written in a book, so that they can be cut out on a table. The selected bolt of cloth is then passed back and forth across this pattern according to the flow plan, and the cloth is cut exactly to size; due

Plate 5.1 The Lucas Auto-Plotter
The pen is controlled by a micro-processor, and draws the panel shapes direct onto
the bolt of cloth (a), as instructed by the basic computer (b).   *Author*

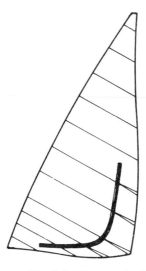

Fig. 5.1 'Throwing' a Tape

Where broad seam has to be calculated by eye, the Sail Maker marks two or three points on the laid out cloths where he wants the maximum draft to lie. He then 'throws' a webbing tape along this line and marks each cloth individually. This represents the end of broad seam taper and will mark the position of maximum camber in the sail.

Plate 5.2 Cutting a One-off Mainsail

A large mainsail being cut out by Peter Lucas; the cutter is trimming off waste cloth at the foot while Peter is discussing the sail with his designer. There is extra panel overlap in the tack area (lower right) to allow for tack seam.

W G Lucas & Son

allowance has to be made, of course, for the overlap of one cloth on another, and for the amount of broad seam to be given to each cloth. It is at this stage that the webbing tape is thrown on the cut-out sail to establish the seam pattern, if the sail has been cut full size on the floor.

BROAD SEAM

Where panel taper is not pre-determined by recorded data, the cutter marks one or two places on the sail where the maximum draft is to be, say one-third aft of the luff at points 6 and 9 ft above the foot. He then throws his webbing tape along the line where he wants the maximum camber to lie. The broad seam will then end at this line, and he marks the sail accordingly.

Each panel is then numbered, and the amount of broad seam it is to have

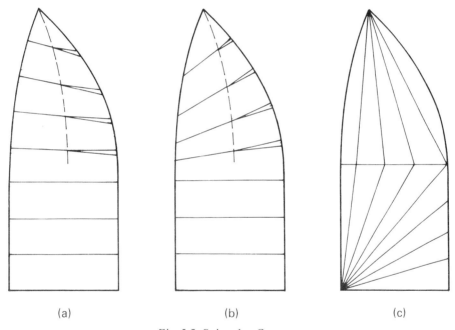

(a)   (b)   (c)

Fig. 5.2 Spinnaker Cuts
A spinnaker will normally lie fairly flat on the floor when it is folded in half about its vertical centreline. The long-established horizontal cut (a) is normally made in two halves and joined together down the middle; cloths run at right angles away from the luff/leech (so there is little bias stretch), and broad seam is incorporated into the panels at the middle of the sail (on the right side in the drawing). If the cloths are kept at right angles across the line of the centrefold as in (b), they can be doubled back on themselves, to make a sail without any centre seam. There will be rather a lot of bias angle where the cloths strike the luff/leech at the head, but this can be allowed for by tightening the seams; broad seam is once again fitted into the cloths across the middle of the sail. The star-cut spinnaker (c) has panels radiating from the three focuses of stress lines — head and both clews; there are plenty of cloths for incorporation of broad seam.

is written on the end of it. This may be as little as $\frac{3}{8}$ in for a distance of 2 ft 6 in, or as much as 10 in for a distance of 6 or 7 ft, according to the size and function of the sail and the position of the particular cloth. The surplus cloth can either be trimmed off so the overlap of one panel on another is maintained constant, or it can merely be lapped on the next cloth by the extra amount of the total broad seam of the two cloths. The former is time consuming and, apart from looking nicer, merely serves to make it more difficult for another Sail Maker to find out the broad seam pattern.

A spinnaker will not lie flat on the floor when fully spread, but most modern cuts can be laid out if the sail is folded in half down the centre. Often there is a seam running down the middle, but even if there is not, the cloth will usually double back on itself about the centrefold. The broad seam, or taper, which is put into the sail will lie, as with a mainsail, in a multiplicity of small pleats and folds when the sail has been sewn together.

The tape is 'thrown' on the cut-out sail, as it is on a mainsail, in order to mark where this broad seam shall end.

Progressive Sail Makers use computers to determine the degree and location of broad seam, but there are still those who rely on traditional methods of hand and eye, particularly where one-off sails are concerned. Use of low-stretch material in any of its many forms puts a greater responsibility on the loft to produce the correct flow in a sail, and considerable care should be exercised in selecting a Sail Maker for one of the more modern sailcloths — all the more so as the money involved may be considerable.

W G Lucas & Son of Portsmouth have developed their own auto-plotter for marking the cutting lines on sailcloth. The basis is formed by two computers. The first is a normal ITT 2020 data bank, for which they have written programmes containing all the details for determining the precise shape of every panel needed to make up sails of all shapes, sizes and flow. These include the number of panels, the amount of broad seam and its location, the position and length of batten pockets, and the ability to turn the bolt on alternate panels to minimise waste where the cloth is cut on the bias at one end. The operator can select the depth of flow, its position in the sail, and the leech gore he wants at the outset. The ITT computer then puts the information for the particular sail onto a disk in a form which can be read by the second computer, which is based on a Motorola 6800 and which controls a large x/y plotter mounted on a 40-foot table.

This micro-processor translates the disk instructions into pulses, which are picked up by two stepper motors whose job it is to guide the pen. A length of cloth is unrolled onto the table, and one motor moves the pen along the warp (in the x co-ordinate), while a second moves it along the weft or fill (in the y co-ordinate); a third stepper motor is controlled by an edge-follower which continually senses the selvedge of the cloth, thereby ensuring a constant reference datum. When Peter Lucas kindly demonstrated his brain child to me, I was interested to see that 20th century technology still can't do without elastic bands – one was being used to tension the pen so that it drew its lines properly.

Lucas are to be congratulated on their business acumen in producing what is certainly the first of its kind in Europe (only one plotter anything like it is known to exist in the USA). It is an expensive but valuable piece of equipment, which confers ability to convert the Sail Maker's data bank into cutting instructions without further ado, giving accuracy, speed and efficiency, allowing any variable to be altered at will, yet retaining an infinitely repetitive capability. It is, of course, well protected by patent.

Panel Width. Cotton used to be made in various widths, from 12 to 54 inches, and sails were made in as many different panel widths. Polyester and nylon today come predominantly in 32 and 36 ins widths (though the metre is also coming in); there are narrower cloths for special application, especially where racing is concerned. The introduction of non-stretch film laminates brings the possibility of much larger widths, with the only limitation being the need to introduce shaping of some sort; advanced technology cannot be far from the successful one-piece sail, truly moulded to its finished shape. Sailing may turn out to be a little duller when that time comes, and I can only hope that whatever it is will have a softer handle than present film laminates.

The use of narrow cloths with synthetics is sometimes desirable for two reasons. First, there may not be enough seams in the luff of a sail to allow the Sail Maker to get all the shape he wants through tapering the cloths. This only applies to the smallest sails as a rule, and then more often to those cloths striking the foot of a mainsail, in which case the bottom one or two panels only can be split. An alternative is to put darts into the sail, as we have seen in the previous chapter. Secondly, it may be required to use a particularly light cloth for a certain sail, which would stretch out of shape if full-width panels were used. Splitting the cloth once, or even twice, will keep the stretch down to a minimum. We once made a 35-ft luff mainsail for *Micronette*, a 30-ft sloop owned by John Britten and Desmond Norman. We used a 6 oz all-woven Terylene cloth with 11 in panels, which held its shape very well.

PUTTING TOGETHER

I am glad to have had the chance of seeing 28 oz No. 2 heavy cotton being sewn by hand into a 90-ft luff mainsail (in 1964 for Herr Burmester's schooner *Aschanti IV*). But this is a dying requirement, not only because of

Plate 5.3 The Machine Shop
Light and airy conditions for Ratsey's machinists. Each has his or her own table, some of which may be let into the floor for ease of handling big sails (which may also be carried on travelling tables for the same reason). Les Day, the foreman on his knees, did his full apprenticeship, and can wield a needle and palm with the best of them. *Ratsey & Lapthorn*

the advent of synthetics, but because yachts of the right size are few and far between. While they rightly pride themselves on their craftmanship in this hand-seaming, Sail Makers realise that they must not rest on their past laurels but look to the future. Side by side with these highly skilled craftsmen are young men and women who sew synthetics together with double needle machines equipped with pull-feed and travelling tables.

The standard claw-feed on a sewing machine only operates on the lower of the two cloths being sewn together, and the slippery nature of the material means that this lower cloth goes through the machine faster than the one on top, unless the machinist holds it back with one hand and pushes the top cloth through with the other. This makes it hard to stick to the match marks put across the two cloths as they are 'struck up' when lying side by side on the full-size pattern in the cutting-out stage. A pull-feed does away with this problem, as it squeezes the two cloths tightly together in the sewing machine, and ensures that the top cloth is fed through at the same speed as the bottom one, thus eliminating the need to strike up the cloths in many cases.

Use of double-sided sticky tape permits the cloths to be laid one on the other and held firmly in place, without the attendant danger of one sliding over the other as they are being sewn. This enables inexperienced machinists to sew accurately, but it is time-consuming and not conducive to series production by skilled operators.

Where a cloth is too heavy for a double-needle machine, it must be passed through a single needle twice, or even three times where triple stitching is required – for instance, at the corners and in places of likely chafe. It is useful to use a thread which contrasts sharply with the colour of the cloth, so that any broken or chafed stitching will stand out and receive quick repair. Tan thread is usual for white sails, and white for coloured ones.

Discussion of chafe leads me to the question of hand-sewing. In the days of cotton there was a great advantage to be obtained through hand-sewing, because the stitching (which could be pulled much tighter) was able to bed right into the relatively soft material. Polyester is so hard that this bedding-in process does not occur, with the result that the stitching stays proud and exposed to the effects of chafe. Nevertheless a much heavier thread, waxed for protection (which causes it to lie closer to the surface), is used with hand-sewing, and anti-chafe patches for heavy-duty synthetic sails for the largest vessels should certainly have this refinement. It costs a good deal more initially, due to the time taken and the skill required, but it will save its cost in the long run through longevity and greater security. I would expect to see at least the lowers of any large trading or training vessel hand-sewn, unless the owners want to spend their time repairing the ravages of chafe.

The lap of the cloths should be carefully controlled so that either it is constant or any change, such as is required by tapering the cloths to build in the flow, takes place gradually. If one cloth is allowed to overlap its neighbour unevenly for a short distance, the finished sail will show a hard spot in its surface. Spot welding the seams at close intervals offers advantages by doing away with the need to sew, but the technology is not so simple (continuous welding makes the cloth unyielding). Glueing is not strong enough offshore at present, but a lot of research has been going into adhesives in connection with laminated cloth, so the efficient glued seam cannot be far off.

RUBBING DOWN

When the sail has been joined together, it returns to the pattern on which it was cut, so that the raw edges can be turned over and creased along the line of the final size of the sail. This is called rubbing down, and the crease is formed with a tool called a rubbing iron. The exact shape of this tool is not fixed, indeed a flat piece of steel can be used; the rubbing iron is as old as

Plate 5.4 Rubbing Down
Half of a 4000 sq ft spinnaker spread out for final shaping at Ratsey's loft; note the prickers holding the sail to the wooden floor and the tape 'thrown' down the centre seam (left) to get a fair curve. At the right, the cloths meet the luff at 90 degrees to avoid bias stretch; they arrive at the centre seam at right angles in the lower part of the sail, becoming progressively more off the weft threadline as the head is approached. *Ratsey & Lapthorn*

sailmaking, however, and drawings of them can be found in many old prints and books on the subject.

It is, of course, important to be accurate at this stage, particularly with those sails which have closely controlled dimensions. The turned over raw edge will then become the tabling, to reinforce the outside of the sail.

TABLINGS, PATCHES AND POCKETS

The next process in sailmaking involves putting on all the strengthening pieces, fitting the rope, tape or wire, and working all the eyes, eyelets, rings, cringles or holes by any other name; slides, hanks and other refinements also come under this heading, but I shall deal with them separately as they merit rather closer attention from the owner than the more routine work of finishing.

TABLINGS

Tablings are often achieved in dressmaking, where they are called hems, by simply folding, or rolling, the cloth over and tucking the raw edge inside itself (Fig. 5.3). This can give rise to creases, however, particularly where the edge is a curve, or where the cloths strike the edge on the bias (Fig. 5.4). It is better in both cases (curved leech and angled luff) to trim off the tabling and lift it back on to the edge of the sail without turning it. The curve at the leech and the threadlines at the luff will then marry up with the minimum risk of distortion (Fig. 5.5). An alternative for any luff, or for the foot of a mainsail, is to use flexible polyester webbing or tape in the place of the tabling, often with the bolt rope incorporated.

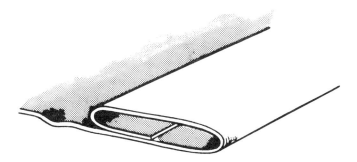

Fig. 5.3 A Rolled Tabling
This is the quickest and cheapest form of tabling. It is really only suited where the threadline runs parallel to the edge in question, when it causes little disturbance to the set of the sail.

If, on the other hand, the edge is straight, or a series of straight lines (perhaps from one batten pocket to the next), and the cloths strike it on or near the threadline (either warp or weft), then there is no danger in simply folding the edge over to form the tabling.

A tabling which has been trimmed off and resewn will either be turned under at either side, or heat-sealed so as not to fray; similarly with the edge of the sail itself. This means that there may be as many as four thicknesses of cloth at the very edge of the sail, or else two thicknesses plus a double line of heat-sealing. This is sure to have less stretch than the single layer of cloth immediately inside the tabling, with the attendant danger of a 'cup' appearing just inside the leech, unless the Sail Maker has taken appropriate measures to forestall it by means of laying the cloths slightly on the bias, or sewing the tabling on with a little slack.

Great care is needed to see that a separate tabling is not sewn on too slack, thus causing the leech to 'motor-boat', or be too tight, which will cause it to curl and to aggravate the 'cup' effect. Naturally, the width of the tabling will also affect the amount of stretch it allows the very leech of the sail.

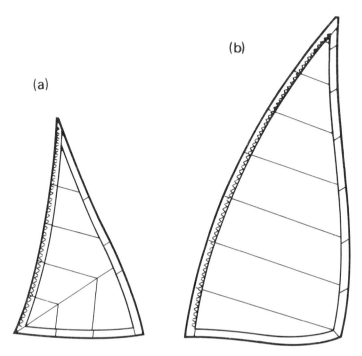

Fig. 5.4 Effect of Rolled Tablings

The inside circumference of any two concentric curves will be shorter, and thus a rolled tabling will have to crimp up in tiny pleats as it disposes of unneeded cloth around a curved leech. Where the tabling is more on a straight line, but is on the bias such as at the luff of a mainsail, the action of folding the cloth back on itself will mean that the threadlines of the tabling will cross those of the sail itself at double the angle at which they arrive at the luff; the result is that as the sail is stretched on the luff, the cloth may move according to the angle of the threadline, and there will be a significant difference between the action of the tabling and that of the main part of the sail. This is often the reason for small wrinkles at the luff, which are hard to remove.

A rolled tabling will, of course, avoid most of these pitfalls, but its very nature may allow too much stretch to the leech, particularly with large sails which are going to have a good deal of wind in them.

There is thus some reason for doing away with the tabling altogether, at least on the leech, if the sail is not going to be subjected to too much weight of wind, and if the job will be permanent and strong enough. I would like to discount the idea for mainsails straight away, even for the smallest sails. A mainsail's leech has a great deal of stress transmitted through it when beating to windward: there is the steady pull of the mainsheet when the sail is full, and the flogging effect during tacking. I do not believe that heat-sealing the raw edge alone is enough to withstand these stresses and to prevent it stretching too much even if it does not fray out; it is definitely not recommended for mainsails.

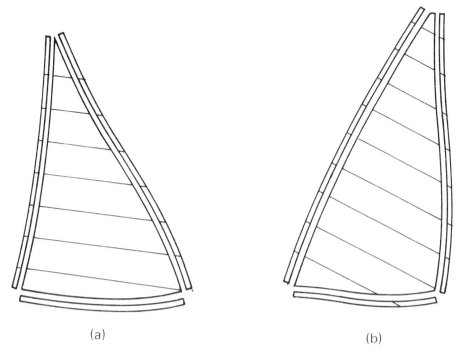

(a)   (b)

Fig. 5.5 Separate Tablings (1)
When the outer two inches or so at the edge of the sail are cut off, note how the seams (and thus the threadlines) and the curves all match perfectly if the narrow strip is then picked up and placed back on the edge of the sail as the tabling. There will be no bias conflict, nor will there be crimping of the cloth due to unequal distances round an arc.

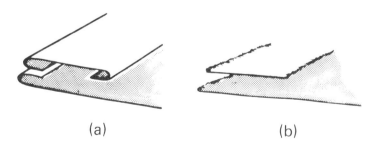

(a)   (b)

Fig. 5.6 Separate Tablings (2)
If the cloth is folded over at the raw edge, there will be four thicknesses at the very leech (or luff or foot) as shown in (a); this extra cloth can cause differential stretch between sail and tabling. If all the raw edges are heat-sealed as in (b), this danger from extra thickness is avoided, but care must be taken not to cause too hard a rim where the melted thread hardens on cooling.

Similarly, any boat larger than a small dayboat will have too much weight of wind in its headsails for a heat-sealed leech to hold up for long; on any boat which goes offshore it would be a most unseamanlike practice to say the least. This leaves dinghies and small keelboats like the Dragon and Soling. There is no doubt that a leech without a tabling gives an easy run off to the wind, and will probably never curl to windward. It may, however, easily go slack, which is hard to cure once it has stretched at the edge. Racing dinghies can often get a good jib this way, although it will not last so long as a conventional sail because chafe will soon fray out the most careful heat-sealing (which can always be resealed, however), and the sail will suffer more from mishandling. The small one-designs, whose owners are prepared to have a jib for only a dozen races, can also try the idea with a good chance of success. For an individually cut sail, however, get your Sail Maker to cut the normal tabling when he makes the sail, and put it on one side for later addition; but be prepared to find that later on is too late to cure your problems.

PATCHES

The loads on a sail are naturally concentrated at the corners, and it is important to see that these parts of the sail are adequately reinforced. Several thicknesses of stout cloth should extend well into the sail, so that the strain on the single layer of cloth in the sail proper is well spread. This also gives a strong base into which the cringles or eyes at head, tack and clew can be worked. But the Sail Maker has to remember the IYRU rules on sail reinforcement which might be classed as stiffening[32]. It is an interesting fact that the extreme toughness of modern sailcloth adds to the problem in its own way: the cloth itself can saw away at the stitching to cut it through. When you add to this the degradation caused by sunlight, you can get trouble. This manifests itself in areas of high loading, so that seams come apart, and nowadays we see Mylar and Melinex sails which have their leeches and heads quite heavily reinforced, sometimes with dark material to inhibit ultra violet rays.

The extremely heavy loads imparted by modern sheet winches call for even stronger reinforcement patches. It is good practice to put several lengths of webbing tape looped round a heavy stainless steel clew ring in large headsails, or in those which will be used with powerful winches; also at head and tack eyes. This webbing should extend a foot or so into the sail, to share out the load more evenly.

Sails are carried in much stronger winds than they were even ten years ago. This is the result of keener competition for the top honours. It also means that sails must stand up to increased strains. I am thinking here particularly of spinnakers, and I am sure that the natural desire of an owner

Plate 5.5 Mylar Reinforcement

The Mylar sails of *Spartan* show reinforcement patches, not only at points likely
to chafe, such as on the genoa in way of the spreader ends, but also at the mainsail
head and leech where stresses are high. Note the creases in the hard material,
which don't smooth out in light winds (stand up, the boy who said 'Oh for a suit of
cotton sails').   *Author*

to have as light a spinnaker as possible cannot be married to this keenness to
hold on to the sail as the wind increases. The Sail Maker can help by increasing the size of his head and clew patches and even, perhaps, by putting a
long tongue 3 or 4 ft into the sail, but I believe that there is still insufficient
awareness of the limitations of spinnakers. Whereas most owners know to
within 10 per cent the weight of cloth used in their headsails, they are
remarkably ignorant when it comes to spinnakers. Yet there is an increase of
33 per cent between a $1\frac{1}{2}$ and a 2 oz cloth, let alone the 170 per cent increase

from 1·1 to 3 oz. To many owners, however, the sail is merely a spinnaker to be used at all times until really strong winds require a heavy weather spinnaker which, as far as some owners are concerned, is distinguishable by its smaller size and the fact that it is flatter in the head, not by its heavier cloth weight.

BATTEN POCKETS

There is still the odd deep sea sailor who prefers to have tie-in battens, on the grounds that the slip-in type may work their way out. This is a sensible precaution but, apart from chafe, battens are the single cause of more sail trouble in blue water cruising than any other factor and, if he were to take the matter to its logical conclusion, he would have his mainsail cut straight on the leech and thus banish battens altogether; it is really only looks which suffer from abolishing the leech roach, because the loss of sail area is minimal. I would also replace the headboard with a stout ring for similar reasons, if I were going round the world.

With slip-in pockets, it is quite important that the batten ends should be rounded to facilitate easy entry, and ideally the pocket should be slightly overlong with a piece of elastic sewn in its inner end so as to force the batten gently towards the outer end of the pocket, thus keeping it right at the leech. Pockets without elastic must, of necessity, present a tight fit for the batten, which will be hard to fit, and which will tend to chafe the inner end.

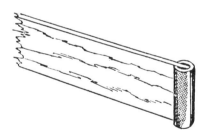

Fig. 5.7 Full Length Batten Ends
A strip of split PVC tubing can be fitted to the ends of full length battens, only where there is no external protector requiring a thin end to fit inside it.

The inner ends of full length pockets should have a pair of nylon protectors sewn one each side, to take the chafe which will always occur. The ends of the battens themselves should be carefully shaped to take up the line of the luff, and they may have a short length of PVC tubing which has been split down its length, fastened to the end. This tubing, however should not be used if external protectors are available, because the batten will not fit snugly into them due to its bulk.

LEECH ROACHES

Mention of battens leads naturally to leech roach. In most classes this represents 'free area' since it is not measured; it is thus subject to much attention from area hungry owners, who often demand from the Sail Maker more roach than he can safely provide without endangering the set of the sail (Fig. 5.8).

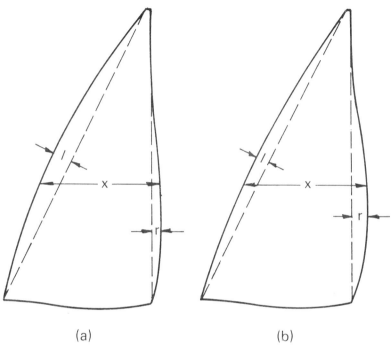

(a)   (b)

Fig. 5.8 14 ft International Mainsail Roach

x = Half-height cross-measurement. l = Leech roach. r = Round to luff.
Assuming a half-height maximum cross-measurement of 6 ft, sail (a) is made for a fairly stiff mast and only has 4 ins of luff round; this gives it a leech round which reaches 19 ins at its greatest — too much to be supported by battens which are 40 ins long. Sail (b), however, is made for a bendy mast, and has 8 ins of luff round to cater for this; if the cross-measurement is to remain within the maximum, the roach must be reduced by 4 ins, so that the battens will just about support the resulting 15 ins.

Battens will support approximately one third of their length in roach extended beyond the straight line from clew to headboard. Beyond this the whole leech will tend to fall away in an inefficient manner. This manifests itself in one of two ways, shown in Fig. 17.6.

These symptoms are similar to those of a sail which has a slack leech due to incorrect lay of cloth, or poor material. I will not attempt to go into the cures available at this stage, but refer the reader to Chapter XVII *Faults and Creases*.

A large roach which falls off to leeward is inefficient when beating to windward or close reaching. Only when the sail has the wind blowing into it rather than along it does the extra area pay off. Yet the area lost by 4 in off the leech of a Fourteen is under 5 sq ft, which can so easily be put efficiently into a spinnaker or genoa for work off the wind. The result would be a faster suit of sails to windward, where seconds so often count.

There are many racing boats which have no limiting cross measurements on mainsails, yet they do not go in for exaggerated roaches at the expense of efficiency. The dinghies should take note, and either be grateful for a sensible restriction if they have one, or else follow this good example.

An instance of the reverse happening, where offshore racers have followed the small boat trend, is the way the mainsail is shaped at the leech. It was found that a fair curve often caused the leech tabling to flutter between the battens, as there was no support for this small area which projected beyond the ends of the battens. Accordingly it is now usual to cut leeches straight, or even very slightly hollow, between the battens, not only on dinghies but on bigger sails as well. The loss of area is negligible, improvement in efficiency is small, but morale goes up out of all proportion!

HEADSAILS

Most headsails are not allowed battens on the leech. The offshore fleet allows them as a rule, if the forward end of the batten comes forward of the mast. They are unseamanlike appendages if they have to come into contact with the mast or shrouds when tacking, and I do not advise them except in certain instances. There are some headsails which are tall and narrow (anything with a head angle of less than 20°), and where the leech comes forward of the mast, which can be made to set better by the inclusion of three or four short battens. There is no point in trying to build up a roach on the leech of such a sail, because this would defeat its own object. The extra cloth would probably cause the leech to foul the mast, which in turn would break the battens. If a greater area is desired in a headsail which is tall and narrow, it is better to draw the clew further aft, so that it overlaps the mast and the sail achieves a lower aspect ratio.

Tufnol is good for headsail battens, because its greater flexibility for a given weight and thickness does no harm in such short lengths. It is more resistant to the rough usage it will get in a headsail, perhaps because of the very flexibility it possesses. Pockets should be securely fastened, and it is perhaps preferable to have the battens permanently sewn or tied in.

As a rule, of course, a headsail has the opposite of a roach on its leech. A hollow leech will stand better than a straight one, and this will help in the slot effect if the sail is an overlapping one. If a correctly graduated leech hollow can be made to follow the curve of the leeward side of the mainsail just aft of its point of maximum flow, the resulting streamlines will be at their most efficient.[12]

Roach to the foot of a headsail is also free area, and is sought after. Certain classes like the 5–0–5 allow a batten in the foot, but most do not. A foot roach of approximately 3 per cent will stand unassisted; beyond this amount (which is about 1 in of roach for every three feet of foot length), either the Sail Maker has to tighten the foot seams (which means a danger of the foot curling), or else the foot will not stand at all while beating to windward, and the owner reaps his reward of extra area only when sailing off the wind.

Chapter VI

Finishing a Sail

ROPING

Modern methods have all but done away with hand roped mainsails. Either
the luff and foot are taped and fitted with slides, or else a rope is put on to a
tape or tabling by machine; sometimes it is only attached at the head, tack
and clew, and then left to float freely inside the tape – a method which
ensures that tension on the bolt rope is even throughout its length. Hand
roping, however, is immensely strong and is to be preferred for sails on larger
yachts which will have to withstand specially heavy loadings, such as those

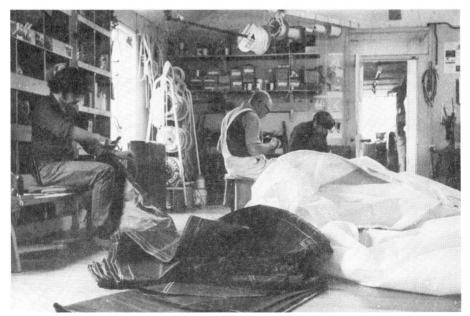

Plate 6.1 Handwork (1)
A study of light and shade emphasises the more traditional side of sailmaking,
where handwork is being used to finish a sail in Gowen's West Mersey loft.

Gowen Sails

for around the world voyages or storm conditions. Sometimes also, the rope to be used is so large (trading or training schooners) that it cannot be put on by machine. The search is then on for that rare commodity, an expert hand roper – for it takes years of practice to become adept at it. The drawback is the difficulty of ensuring even sewing of the rope, particularly if two workers are put on the job (possibly starting from different ends). Let us therefore first of all deal with the old fashioned method.

Even pre-stretched polyester rope may elongate slightly over a distance of 40 or 50 feet when it is subjected to tension. So the rope must be pulled somewhat before it is sewn to the sail. This is done by first ensuring that there are no twists in it so that it lies quietly, a line is then drawn along its length to guide the Sail Maker as he sews. The sail is then spread with the luff fair, the rope is laid alongside and the correct amount is deducted from its length; this amount is a function of the length of luff, the size and characteristic of the rope, and the flow required. On one occasion at Ratsey's there was a little trouble with Italian hemp rope in the days of cotton. The manufacturer changed the treatment of the hemp in such a minor way that he did not feel it necessary to inform his customers. Sail Makers made a number of cotton sails which did not set too well, and this was enough to cause a major disturbance. Everything was checked and rechecked, until there was nothing left save the rope which could be the cause of the bother. The manufacturer

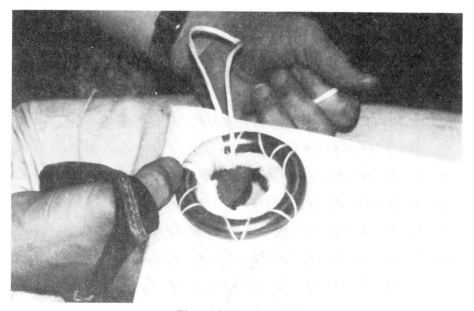

Plate 6.2 Handwork (2)
The hole is deliberately cut too small, so that cloth is caught by the thread and bound firmly to the ring.
Author

was asked, and the mystery solved. The minor change had altered the stretch characteristics of the rope enough to alter the set of the finished sail.

The rope is next pulled to the stretched length finally required from the sail, to see if it goes correctly (Sail Makers are not going to be caught again); a strain gauge may be used by the progressive at this stage. It is next struck up at intervals, which may be graduated along its length to give a different tension near the head from that lower in the sail, thus varying the flow. The luff tabling is also struck up with similar, but not identical, intervals. The sailmaker then sews to these marks. He must take care that he keeps the rope straight by watching the longitudinal pencil line, and that the marks match correctly, or there will be a tendency for the luff to twist or to gather too much cloth at one point. One of the tendencies in poor hand-roping is for the rope to go on too slack; the rope runs out before the end of the sail is reached.

The advantage of machine-roping is that the stitching will be evenly tensioned throughout the rope, and with little danger of gathering. There will, however, be less flexibility in the relative tension on the rope and sail, and the finished job will not be as strong as a hand-sewn rope. Machining is, of course, quicker and does not have to be done by a highly qualified sail-maker, paid the appropriate wages. Machine work is to be preferred where it is important that all sails should be as nearly alike as possible, such as in classes of rigid one-design like the Firefly or 420 dinghies. There is a third possibility, much used in smaller sails. This is for the luff rope to be allowed to run loose inside the tabling, being merely seized at the head and tack; the same applies to the foot rope. This is all very well on small sails, but anything larger than a five tonner will often have enough weight of wind in its mainsail to cause the seizings to pull away. This will have disastrous results, which are not surprising when you pause to think how the strain is concentrated on three points. It has the advantage, however, that the luff and foot ropes are sure to be absolutely evenly stretched along their entire length.

LUFF TAPES

Ike Manchester, of America, has been taping luffs of sails since 1955. Because wire and synthetic rope do not have anything like the same characteristics as synthetic fabric, he felt that they should not be used in conjunction with Dacron. He knew that similar materials will react in a similar way under similar conditions, so he used Dacron cloth throughout the sail.

The adoption of adjustable luff headsails has done as much as anything to accelerate the acceptance of taped luffs. The alternative to this type of sail involves a luff rope, but Manchester's early opinion about dissimilar materials being unsympathetic still holds good. An additional gain is that a headsail without a luff wire will not suffer from oxidization.

ROPE IN TAPE

The modern quick method is to use a combination of rope and tape. Either a special machine sews through the rope on to the tape (Fig. 6.1), or else the tape is wrapped around the rope and the two halves sewn together so that the rope is free to float inside the doubled tape (Fig. 6.2). In both cases the rope is sure to be put on evenly and, if it is not of the pre-stretched variety, it can be pulled first to a given tension and then used with the latter system.

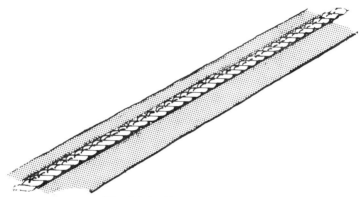

Fig. 6.1 Luff Rope in Tape (1)
A special sewing machine sews through the bolt rope onto the length of tape or webbing, which is then folded round the edge of the sail to form the tabling.

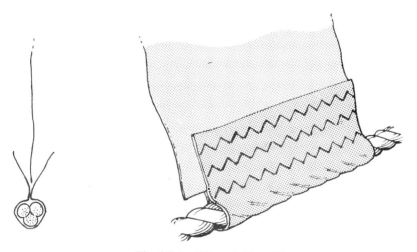

Fig. 6.2 Luff Rope in Tape (2)
Take a length of 2–3 in wide webbing or tape, fold it round the bolt rope and then sew along the two parts of the tape as close to the rope as you can get, either by machine or by hand. If the machine will not get close enough, take out the rope and sew in a length of thin cord so that you can pull the rope through later. Rope and tape should be used as tabling for the luff or foot, being struck up to the raw edge; one part of the doubled tape is sewn to each side of the sail so that the tape forms the reinforcement.

WIRE

The commonest wire for headsail luffs is PVC covered galvanized, and this is probably the best for temperate climates. Care must be taken to seal the break in the PVC coating where the tack eye is formed, and it is here that most trouble occurs. The head eye is not so subject to frequent salt-water duckings, and is thus less susceptible to corrosion. Galvanized wire is not suitable for tropical climates unless it has a completely sealed covering; it corrodes quickly at exposed places and seldom lasts more than a year. Stainless steel wire is also used a great deal, particularly in the United States of America. It reacts with synthetics, however, and causes discolouring of the cloth which eventually leads to weakness. If stainless steel wire is covered with a protective coating, it will be starved of oxygen which will lead to shielding corrosion. Cranfield and Carter make a number of luff wires for the tropics in monel, which I believe is good, but which has a lower breaking load than stainless steel.

In short, PVC coated galvanized wire is good for temperate climates, but watch the tack eye for corrosion. Stainless steel uncovered is best for the tropics, if a hermetically sealed, covered galvanized wire is not available, but one must accept the stains which will appear on the cloth.

Plate 6.3 Stainless Steel Eye
The four parts of Sea Sure's stainless steel eye, which is used for pressing into a sail by means of an hydraulic machine. At the top are the top and bottom flanges; to the left is the liner; to the right is the spur ring which grips the sail under pressure.   *Author*

EYES

For a long time eyes which were pressed or punched in were much weaker than those sewn by hand, and were therefore only suitable for smaller sails. Modern sailcloth, however, is often so closely woven that improved pressing equipment and materials often produce a result which is less damaging to the cloth, while being quite strong enough for the task. Stainless-steel punched eyes are thus usually to be found on most sails. Hand-worked eyes remain the stronger in coarser cloth, however, and should continue to be used where loadings are expected to be really heavy; webbing can be used to help spread the load (Fig. 6.3).

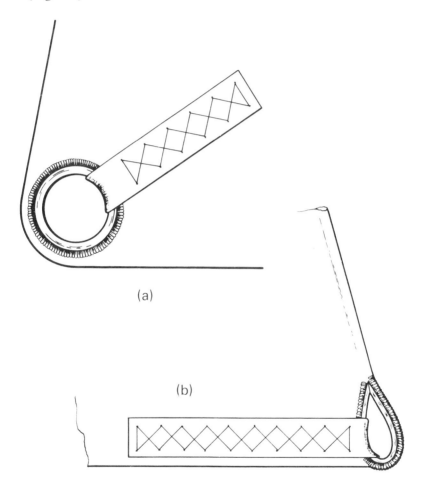

(a)

(b)

Fig. 6.3 Webbing Reinforcement at Eyes
A short length of webbing either side of the sail and running along the principal stress-line will help take the load from an eye, even if it is retro-fitted.

109

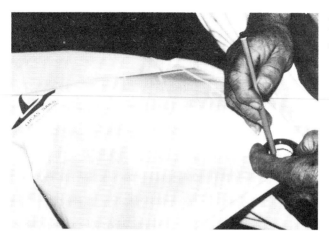

(a) The ring is placed on the sail, which is marked accordingly.

(b) The circle is cut slightly smaller than the inner diameter.

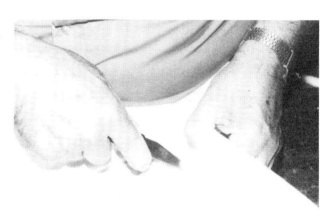

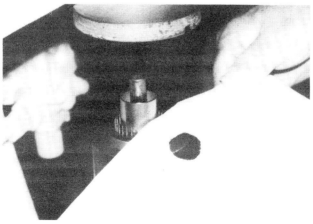

(c) The base ring, spur ring and liner are fitted to the press.

(d) The cut-out is placed over the liner and the upper ring added.

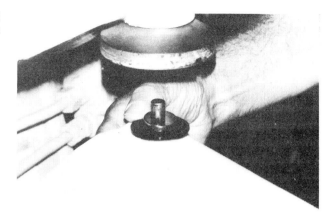

(e) The press is activated and the two sides come together.

(f) The job is finished.

Plate 6.4 Fitting an Hydraulic Ring *(Author)*

Because of this risk of damage to the cloth from close hand sewing (or of one stitch being pulled too tight and thus starting a crease), where an eye is being hand sewn modern practice is to sew with four parts of thread, and even six on the bigger sails, instead of the more traditional two parts, thereby making half the number of passes with the needle in order to reduce the possibility of wrinkles appearing.

Reef eyelets should have individual patches for extra strength, and the eyes at luff and leech correspondingly larger patches running into the sail, as these will become tack and clew when the reef is taken in. Most other eyes find ready made extra thickness for strength, because they will usually come at the tabling or at the clew or tack patch.

Hand-sewn eyes have a metal ring sewn into the sail to form the basis of strength, with a turnover of the same metal pressed in afterwards to protect the thread from chafe by whatever is to go into the eye: shackle, wire, hank or slide seizing.

BATTENS

The most common material for battens used to be wood, but this has now been largely overtaken by plastics. There are still plenty of wooden ones about, however, and they should be well rounded and tapered towards the inner end both as to width and thickness, in order to make them bend more at the tip. They should, of course, be well varnished to make them resist water soakage. A good idea, particularly if the end is thin, is to strap the tip with adhesive tape. This both prevents it breaking too easily, and protects the sail if a break does occur. A strip of adhesive tape the full length of the batten serves as a protection from sharp corners in a break, and also enables you to pull the broken end out if the worst should occur.

Tufnol Battens. There is an increasing use of Tufnol for battens these days, and it is a satisfactory material. It does have a tendency to bend rather too much, so care must be used. This flexibility makes it a suitable material for the top batten, which is often the better for having more of a curve than the lower ones, but it means that lower Tufnol battens have to be rather thick if they are to do their job properly. $\frac{1}{16}$ in is enough for the top batten of a small mainsail, but thickness can range up to $\frac{1}{4}$ in for the larger yachts. A very rough guide is $\frac{1}{16}$ in for every 10 ft of waterline length. Width can be the same as wooden battens, and the rough guide here is one inch for every 10 ft of waterline. Thus a boat with a waterline of 25 ft will have Tufnol mainsail battens which are $\frac{5}{32}$ in thick, and $2\frac{1}{2}$ in wide; the pockets should be one-third as wide again, if the batten is to slip easily in and out.

GRP or FRP Battens. There are many other synthetic materials which are used for battens with success; plastics in general and fibreglass in particular spring to mind. One of the advantages which fibreglass enjoys is that of a high strength/weight ratio; it is also less bulky than wood. This means that a batten can be made which is strong, flexible, light and slim although it tends to stiffen with age. In fact, one of the pitfalls to watch for is a tendency to bend in several directions, which can be countered by ribbing the material. These slim battens usually have spade-shaped ends in order to give a large bearing surface when pushed into batten pockets.

Full Length Battens. Full length battens take some of the inefficiency out of a mainsail when going to windward. The sail becomes much more allied to a solid aerofoil, because its luff does not lift so much under the influence of backwinding by the headsail or, in the case of a mizzen, by the dirty wind off the mainsail. This means that laminar flow is maintained over a greater area with resulting improved efficiency. The point of maximum camber should be about one-third aft at the head, becoming almost half-way near the foot. To achieve a full camber in light winds, push the battens in hard when you tie them in; use less pressure in strong winds so the sail is flatter. Test for stiffness by standing each batten vertically on a set of bathroom scales and pushing on its upper end until it takes up roughly the right shape. The scales should read between 3–7 lbs; any batten needing more than about 15 lbs is far too stiff. Curvature can also be changed by use of the leech line, although this seems to have most effect in the top third of the sail only. Be careful not to overdo this, because a hooked leech will have a marked breaking effect at the high speeds enjoyed by some fully battened multihulls. The forward ends of the pockets are subject to a lot of chafe, so they must be well reinforced.

HEADBOARDS

Headboards for the larger mainsails may be hand made of wood or, more economically, machined from light alloy; others can be plastic, stainless steel, aluminium or fibreglass. They are hand sewn into a large sail, but smaller sails tend to show creases unless great care and skill are taken; these can often be avoided if the board is slipped into a pocket at the head, and left to float freely inside (but this nullifies some of its strengthening effect). Rivetting is a good solution if the board is slim enough. Any deep water cruising boat is better off without a headboard at all, for they are troublesome if they break; fit a stout ring instead.

Plate 6.5 Headboards

Headboards on the bench of Leonard Hackett, who has been sailmaking for
W G Lucas for over 50 years. At the top are two wooden boards, which are sewn
in by hand; next come an alloy and a white plastic board, which may be rivetted;
finally, a stainless steel board can just be made out, which may be rivetted or
slipped into a pocket. *Author*

SLIDES

The traditional method of attaching slides is with waxed twine, and this has
served well for many years. Its chief drawback is chafe, for only one part of
the seizing has to break for the whole thing to be in danger of coming
undone. Various methods of overcoming this have been tried, the best being
to use a thimble to take the chafe at the slide; sometimes a shackle is
preferred (Fig. 6.3).

But this means that the slide is that little bit slacker on the sail, and thus
more prone to twist and jam on the track. Shackles chafe the luff rope
heavily, which has to be well protected in way of every slide by means of hide
of cloth casing. Alternative systems involve stainless steel screws, plastic
snaps, leather thongs and even wire. There are internal and external slides
(see Appendix F), slug slides, slides for mast grooves and, of course, the
simple bolt rope; there are special tracks with shields to stop airflow seeping
between mast and sail. Each has its own advantages and disadvantages:
price, simplicity, durability, efficiency, gimmick value, and ease of handling.
The two advantages of the shackle are strength, and the fact that it can be
quickly and easily fitted by the owner. The disadvantages, however, make a
formidable list which more than outweighs the points in favour.

1. The shackle itself can corrode, so that the pin will not undo. Electrolysis between shackle and slide often accelerates this.

2. The shackle will chafe the bolt rope, which has to be cased with leather or cloth as some measure of protection.

3. The softer of the two metals will chafe, either on the slide or on the shackle.

4. There is an extra weight aloft.

5. If an odd sized shackle has to be used for one or two slides, the bolt rope will not run in a straight line.

Which brings me to the question of what the solution is. To my mind the answer lies in the system adopted by *Stormvogel* in 1963. This is to attach the slides by means of synthetic tape. The tape is strong enough to resist chafe by the slide, and is soft enough not to chafe the slide or the sail in return (Fig. 6.4).

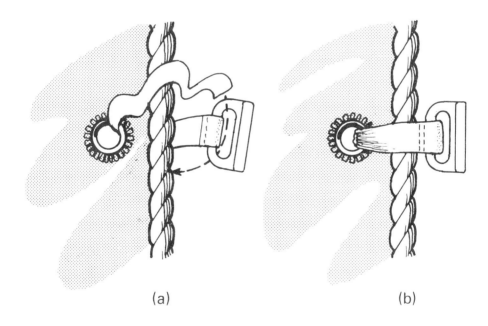

(a)   (b)

Fig. 6.4 Taped Slides
One end of about one foot of $\frac{1}{2}$ in tape is first sewn to the slide. The other end is passed through the eyelet at the luff or foot of the sail, and then back through the slide. This is repeated as many times as it will conveniently go, usually about three or four times to give 6 or 8 parts. Care should be taken to see that a slight amount of lateral play is allowed the slide, so that the sail can swing from side to side on the mast. The loose end should then be sewn through the 6 or 8 parts several times with a stout waxed thread. The result is a neat and workmanlike fitting which will last a good deal longer than most other systems, and which will not damage the slide or sail.

Types of Slide. Slides themselves are better from the Sail Maker's point of view if they are made of plastic, because they do not then need greasing. Grease picks up other dirt particles and spreads across the canvas in an unsightly smear; it is most difficult to remove. A certain minimum thickness is necessary if a plastic slide is to be strong enough. This virtually means that external slides cannot safely be made from this material, save for the smallest sails, for the slide would be too thick to pass behind the track. Some of the smaller sizes of internal slide are also suspect when made in nylon or similar material, because they either break at the handle, or elongate at the shoulders.

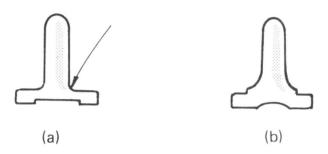

(a)   (b)

Fig. 6.5 Nylon Slides
The face of the slide needs to be hollowed to allow it to pass easily over screw heads in the track. If this is done on the square as in (a), there may be a weak point (arrowed); it is stronger if the face is sunk in a curve as shown in (b).

I tested a number of such slides in 1964 and found that the average breaking strain of the $\frac{5}{8}$ in (16 mm) variety was 550–700 lb. This is enough for a five-tonner, but is low for anything larger, particularly when you remember that it is often shock load which has to be sustained. I have not seen many of the larger type, from $\frac{7}{8}$ in (22 mm) upwards, which have given trouble.

A standard alloy slide can be coated with a film of nylon which will last a season or so. This does away with the need for grease, and is stronger than an all-nylon slide of similar dimensions. The nylon coating tends to peel off after a year's use.

I do not like external slides, which are so popular in America, for several reasons. Not only can they not be made in nylon thin enough and yet strong enough, but I have yet to see an external slide smaller than $1\frac{1}{4}$ in which has a really suitable handle for the synthetic tape attachment which *Stormvogel* developed. The gap left by the usual small handle is not large enough to allow many thicknesses of tape, which normally has to be very narrow to get

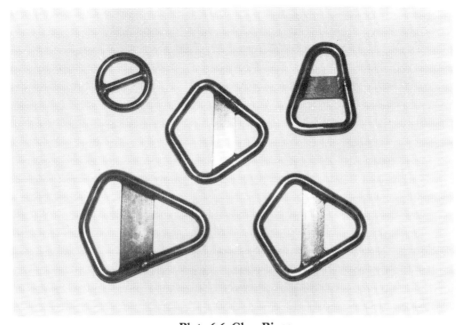

Plate 6.6 Clew Rings
Various types of stainless steel clew ring produced by Sea Sure. They are for
different sizes and shapes of genoa and spinnaker.   *Author*

through in the first place. In addition, the thinness of the metal which is
often used, makes them ideal machines for cutting anything which is used to
fasten them to a sail, even synthetic tape. It is for this reason that many of
them come already equipped with a brass thimble for a grommet or seizing;
this makes them very slack on the sail.

In certain very large yachts it is sometimes an advantage to be able to
remove the mainsail without taking the slides off the boom. To effect this
there are heavy-gauge gunmetal external slides, made by Merriman, which
are attached by means of their own screw pins. When taking the sail off the
boom, the screw pins are undone, and the sail lifted bodily off sideways.
Yachts which are in the region of 100 ft overall adopt this system, because
their mainsails are too heavy to pull forward off the boom. In addition,
yachts of such a size usually have an internal track with an external slide.
This is because really heavy-gauge track only comes in this form; the slides
which go with it are also heavily constructed and able to stand up to the
severe loads involved.

Several firms produce a slide which will not only run in a track of the
appropriate size, but will also go into a groove. This can be useful, should
the owner decide to change his boom from one to the other. They also have
the advantage that they are often made of nylon, and thus do not need

greasing. The body of the slide is stoutly constructed, and I can thoroughly recommend them.

Finally, some neat little slides originated in France and America (where they are known as slugs) which are cylindrical in shape, also designed to run in a groove. They are about the same diameter as the appropriate rope would be, and they fasten to the sail just like any other slide. It seems to me, however, that it is a waste of opportunity to have a grooved boom and not to run the bolt rope inside it. There are a number of disadvantages associated with slides, and I would not want to go out of my way to fit them, expect perhaps on the luff.

HANKS OR SNAP HOOKS

Dinghies have a wide variety of hanks or snaps from which to choose. Besides the end- and side-pull piston type, of either bronze or stainless steel, there are wire clips like overgrown safety pins, nylon and metal twist type attachments, and tab hanks; zip-fasteners also come under this heading.

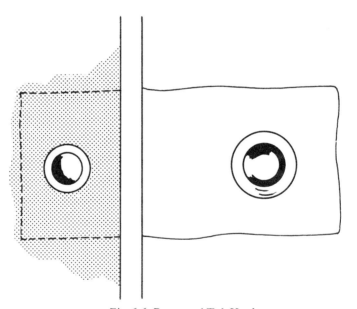

Fig. 6.6 Press-stud Tab Hank

A short piece of synthetic webbing, about $1\frac{1}{4}$ in wide, is sewn to the luff of the headsail so that it protrudes some $1\frac{1}{2}$ in beyond the luff, as in this full-size drawing. This is passed round the forestay and fastened to itself by means of a press-stud. Its advantages are lightness, minimal disturbance of the airflow, and unlikelihood of its catching on the spinnaker. Disadvantages are chafe of the tab by the forestay, and the undue reliance which has to be placed on the fastener, which may give corrosion trouble at its spring. I don't see why velcro shouldn't work, certainly for light weather sails.

Selection of a particular type is very much a matter of individual choice, and I would be the last to make a single recommendation in this rather specialist field. Whatever I say is bound to displease some people, because there are plenty of dinghy men who spurn hanks altogether in a laudable pursuit of aerodynamic efficiency from a clean luff. Wire clips will not stand up to the heaviest weather without tending to bend, nylon twist hanks chafe on the forestay, metal twist ones are sometimes hard to get off with cold fingers, and gunmetal or stainless piston hanks or snap hooks are not always perfection – although there is not much wrong with them to my mind. Tab hanks are light, aerodynamically clean, and can be easily fitted by most dinghy owners (always provided that he or she can find someone to punch in the press-studs to order).

Ocean-racers mostly use piston hanks or snaps of one kind or another, the choice being merely one of materials, and whether the piston should be operated by a side- or an end-pull. A side-pull hank can be worked with one hand, which is a decided advantage when working on a heaving deck; an end-pull hank is possibly more reliable. If you fit a short thong or strop on the end of the plunger to make it more easily operated, don't form it into a loop which will catch on snags, but leave the two ends free. The traditional material for hanks is gunmetal, and it has stood the test of time well. In the early sixties, however, Goiot of France and Ratsey & Lapthorn of England each came out with an improved material. The latter have their hanks made by an aircraft company, of a metal which is both lighter and stronger than gunmetal. The Strenlite® hank, as it is called, is an easily operated, tough hank which takes advantage of modern materials. It has an end-pull operation and is virtually corrosion free (the prototype was hung on a sea wall at half tide for three months, and was as smooth to operate at the end as it was when first put there). A destruction test, which had broken other types of hank at 300 kg tension, was halted at 1,500 kg for fear of breaking the test equipment. They are, however, rather expensive and thus rare these days.

Many piston hanks are still attached to the sail with a seizing. This is an old fashioned system, with drawbacks similar to those attendant upon seized slides. The tendency up to medium-sized sails nowadays is to squeeze a metal arm round the eyelet, possibly using a plastic chafe protector; larger craft can use leather thongs.

Zippers. There is no doubt that a zip-fastener provides a smooth and efficient system of attaching a headsail to a stay. There are no projections for the spinnaker to catch, and the sail is given a clean leading edge aerodynamically. A certain conservatism exists regarding the zipper, not only among owners but also among those responsible for drawing up rules. Far too many classes ban the zippered luff, and I suspect that they would be hard put to it to set down why they ban it. What is certain is that governing bodies have seized upon the pretence that a sail which zips on to its stay is a double luffed sail, and is thus conveniently banned under the rule which deals with such devices[33]. The ban on double luffed sails, however, was brought in to prevent owners from inflating their sails by allowing air to enter at the front of a double sail. To pretend that a zippered luff is attempting the same advantage is nonsense, and I am glad to see that the IOR permits them subject to a minor measurement addition.

The zipper and its slider must be corrosion resistant, and this virtually means that the former should be all plastic and the latter heavily enamelled metal (for the slider has to be thin in places in order to work, and this would weaken plastic too much). The method of attaching the sail to the stay is for the zipper to be open-ended and to close towards the tack. One side of the zipper is passed round the stay, and the two ends are joined at the top, just like the bottom of a zip-fronted jacket. A hand then holds the slider as the sail is hoisted until it is two blocks, and the slider reaches the bottom.

To change sails, the slider on the sail to come off is unzipped for about 6 ft at the tack, while the replacement sail has its head started on the now exposed lower end of the stay. The new sail is then hoisted on a second halyard, while a hand holds the slider as before. The act of hoisting the new sail unzips the old one, so there is never a period when the boat is without a headsail.

GROOVED FORESTAY

A grooved forestay has the advantage of a clean aerodynamic entry for the leading edge of the driving aerofoil, and of fast sail changes. Being smooth, as opposed to the serrations of a wire, a spinnaker slides off it more easily and so resists the tendency to wrap round it if the sail falls in (a quality it shares with a rod forestay). A grooved rod forestay is expensive, but has the advantage of simplicity over the cheaper alternatives, which usually involve mating two lengths of metal or plastic extrusion round an existing wire forestay, to produce a pear-shaped entry (which is better aerodynamically) for the headsail luff rope on its trailing edge. Improvement in aerodynamic efficiency is marked, but the IOR takes account of the fore and aft dimension of these stays or attachments when calculating the yacht's J measurement, so the grooved rod will affect your rating less than the cheaper and bulkier alternatives. Twin grooves enable a replacement sail to be set before the old one is lowered (Fig. 6.7).

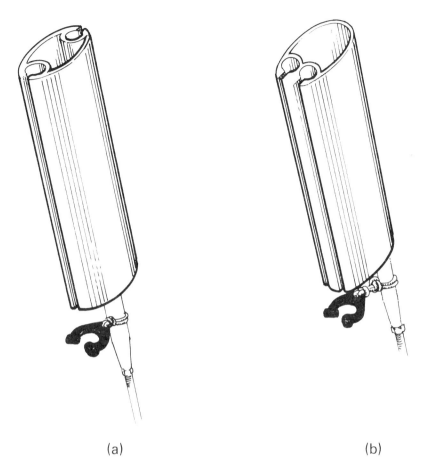

(a)   (b)

Fig. 6.7 Grooved Forestays
If twin grooves are on opposite sides of the rod (a), fitting a second headsail is
rather more difficult than if they lie side by side (b). In both cases a feeder helps
the luff rope to run easily.

WINDOWS

Many classes allow windows in sails. They give improved visibility and thus
contribute to safety in crowded waters. The material used is resistant to
creasing, although particular care should be taken not to maltreat this part
of the sail. A window is normally fitted to a finished sail by forming an
envelope of the correct size with a second piece of cloth sewn to the sail. The
window material is then slipped into one end of the envelope and sewn all
round to keep it in place; this ensures that it lies flat in the sail and does not

pull at the corners. The middle portion of each side of the envelope is then cut away and the edges tucked under and sewn neatly round. Alternatively, the window material may be sewn straight to one side of the sail, and the sail then cut away on the other side. This leaves a slighty rough surface where the window is not covered at the edge on one side, but it has the advantage of economy.

Chapter VII
Rigging

We have seen in Chapter II some of the theoretical factors which affect a yacht's performance to windward. I now want to discuss how the static nature of the boat plays its part *vis-à-vis* the sails, and how you can improve performance by careful attention to it. This covers all those parts of the boat which directly or indirectly affect the set of the sails, such as spars and their rigging, kicking-straps, boom vangs, winches, halyards, etc.

We all have our pet rigging likes and dislikes, some of them for no more valid reason than because we have never used anything else. I cannot hope to set forth the optimum rig for all boats, because each class differs from the next, thank goodness. I say thank goodness, for it would be a dull sport without variety. All that can be done is to point out some of the effects, and to suggest a profitable approach to each problem.

SPARS

The earliest masts were tree trunks, on to which the sails were tied at convenient points. The only real refinements over the centuries were for the branches to be trimmed off neatly and for a particular type of tree to be preferred. We thus came to solid spruce masts which were straight and tapered towards the top; girth was decided by trial and error. The same generalization holds good for all other spars.

The rise of the aircraft industry in the twentieth century saw the need for accurate calculation of strength/weight ratios in this kind of structure and, in particular, for cutting down weight while maintaining strength. This led to a more widespread understanding of lamination, hollow construction and, later, to the use of metals and light alloys.

A metal mast of given section will normally be stronger than an equivalent wooden one; equally it will be stiffer and lighter. This means that a good saving in weight aloft can sometimes be made, because the section can be smaller than a wooden one for the same boat, thus also reducing the size of the fittings required. Modern methods of anodizing offer a permanent protection against corrosion, such as is not available against rot in a wooden spar.

You might assume from the foregoing that metal spars are a necessity for all yachts. An expensive, custom-made, wooden mast can sometimes actually be lighter than a metal one, however, and will certainly have a lower centre of gravity. We shall see shortly the advantages of a bending mast, and it should be remembered when reading this section that, while a wooden mast can be made to bend more than a metal one, the latter will be more consistent. It is too broad a generalization to say that no two wooden masts bend alike, but they are more often different than otherwise. On the other hand, the dinghy owner can alter the bend of a wooden mast by carefully planing it down in the appropriate place.

Strength/weight ratios and fittings are largely outside the scope of this book, where I am chiefly concerned with sails and the flow of air over them. This is directly affected by such obvious factors as mast rake and bend, but we must also briefly consider spar shape, how the sail is attached to it, and how it is reefed; neat fittings are desirable in the interests of reduction in parasite drag.

MAST SHAPE

A clean entry for the wind on to the leading edge of a sail is what we want. The mast and its fittings, therefore, disturb the air just where we least want them to do so. A round, or even a flattened oval, section causes eddies in the airflow which bring a drop in efficiency. When you add to this the fact that the mast section is never at the optimum streamline angle to the wind unless the mast rotates, you can see how important it is to study the shape we present to the wind. The undoubted efficiency of a headsail can be partly explained by the absence of the disturbing influence of a mast at the luff.

BOOM SHAPE

The boom presents a different problem. The shape of its section does not have to be streamlined for efficiency, because the wind flows along it; consistent with adequate strength, therefore, we can allow our desires regarding bend characteristics partly to control the section. However, the boom does perform a useful function in acting as an endplate to the mainsail. The tendency of the wind is to curl downwards under the boom from windward to leeward. If the top of the boom presents a moderately flat surface, this tendency will be resisted, thus cutting down induced drag and improving the efficiency of the airflow. In dinghies, a second factor is the free sail area which the boom affords. As deep a spar as the rules allow can give an appreciable increase in area downwind, but it will reduce vertical bend.

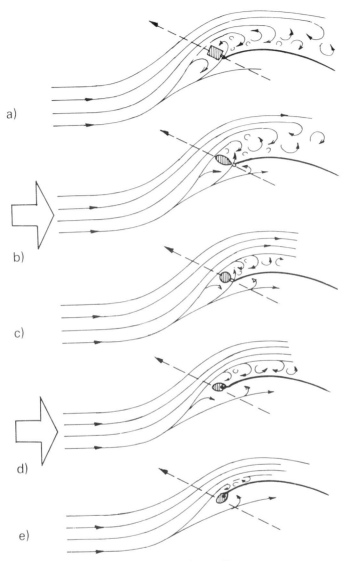

Fig. 7.1 Mast Streamline

The square shape of early built-up hollow box wooden masts (a) was an aero-dynamic disaster, not much improved by so-called streamlining to an oval (b); this is because both sections never point into the wind. Reversion to first principles of a round section (c) did little to improve matters, and it is only when a rotating oval (d) points towards the apparent wind that turbulence at the mast is reduced. But this is not the end of the matter, for the actual airflow at the mainsail luff is at a greater angle of incidence as the streamlines bend in anticipation of the aerofoil; the mast should rotate to point into the actual airflow (e) if disturbance is to be reduced to the minimum. Abolition of slides through incorporation of a grooved luff reduces loss of lift by stopping air bleeding from windward to leeward between mast and luff.

SLIDES OR GROOVES

Where a sail is attached to its mast by slides, there is a loss of efficiency caused by air leaking to leeward through the gap between the spar and the sail. This reduces the pressure differential between the two sides of the sail. Various methods of stopping this leak have been tried, and the only really successful one is to use a groove for the luff rope. This is all very well for boats which take off their sails every time they stop sailing, but a large mainsail cannot be stowed on the boom without taking it right out of the luff groove and thus detaching it from the mast altogether. This is an unseaman-like operation, as well as being irksome, so we have to accept luff slides as soon as the mainsail gets around 250 sq ft in area. Whatever the size, however, there is no doubt that a groove is more efficient aerodynamically. Not only does it stop the air-leak, but it shares the load on the luff rope evenly throughout its length. Modern masts are made so that chafe at the luff groove is reduced to a minimum, and I do not think this need affect our choice. This is particularly important since you can now get masts with a groove which has a track running inside it; the groove starts far enough above the tack fitting to allow the sail to emerge and furl on the boom, still retained on the mast by the exposed track beneath the groove entry.

A groove is nearly always best for a boom for several reasons. First, the boom acts as a more efficient barrier to the wind which is trying to curl under it and form flow-disturbing eddies, for there is no leak between sail and spar. Secondly the strain is shared more equally along the foot rope. Thirdly, if a roller reefing system is used, the sail will take up a more even shape when rolled down if there are no slides to cause lumps (and chafe) along the foot. Finally, people will use metal slides which need grease, and this makes a mess on the sail which it is almost impossible to remove. If your spars have already got a track which takes an internal slide, fit one of the modern all nylon variety which does not need greasing to make it run; if you are in doubt about the strength of this type, you can get metal slides which have been coated in a thin film of nylon, but this tends to peel off with use. See that the track is carefully cleaned before bending the sail with its new slides. If, however, you decide to have a grooved boom, be sure to have one or two strongpoints where you can attach a boom vang, because you will not be able to pass one round the boom, as you can with a sail fitted with slides along the foot.

In this connection, a very efficient and usual system is to have one or more rings running on a short length of heavy track recessed into the underside of the boom at its forward end – they might be called ringslides as opposed to ringbolts (which are, of course, bolted into the deck). The vang is then attached to one of these ringslides, which can be adjusted so that it is in the correct position over the strongpoint on deck.

REEFING

I have long been an advocate of roller reefing, but the advent of jiffy reefing has made me think again. The whole operation is easy and free from wheels and gears (with their attendant risk of mechanical failure), so that it is a Best Buy (Fig. 7.2). The result is a reef, aerodynamically sound, which can be taken in even if only needed for the last quarter of a mile of a windward leg. The bunt of the sail which is left flapping along the boom may then be tidied up at leisure by means of a lacing line but, while helping to spread the load, this is by no means essential if the reef is not expected to be in for long or the situation requires the crew elsewhere.

There are four main drawbacks to roller reefing, which can all be overcome. First, the gear may fail: in this case the wise owner will have had an emergency lacing reef fitted in the two- or three-reef position. Secondly, the sail may not take up quite the desired curve at the foot when reefed, due to the shape of the boom: but a boom which is slightly thicker at its outer end will allow for this, and will raise the clew slightly as the sail is rolled on to it;

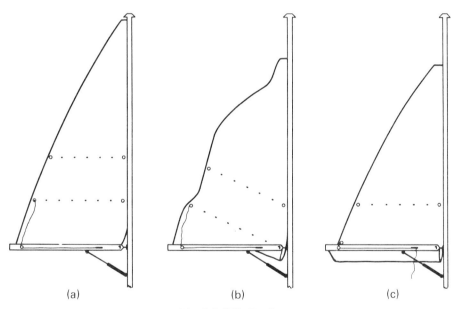

(a)   (b)   (c)

Fig. 7.2 Jiffy Reefing
This may also be used with a leech Cunningham, either alone (to top up the clew and flatten the leech), or in conjunction with a luff Cunningham (to flatten the whole foot area). First see that the hydraulic boom jack or the topping lift is holding the boom level (a). Ease away the main halyard until the luff reef earring can be slipped over the hook at the gooseneck (b); take up the slack on the halyard. Finally pull on the (permanently rove) leech reefing line, to bring the leech reef earring down to the bee block or fairlead – it should also pull aft to put tension along the foot. The intermediate reef points or eyelets may then be secured if time permits.

if you have a straight sided boom, you can either have slats fitted each side at the outer end to increase the diameter, or you can roll some tea towels or old canvas into the leech as you reef down. Thirdly, the leech is not pulled aft on a roller, as it is with a tie reef which has a cringle and positive outhaul: however, John Illingworth always recommended that the lower leech of the mainsail should have hauling-aft loops attached from the clew to about the deep reef position, so that a hand can exert a steady pull with a boathook as the boom is being rolled; this will keep the wrinkles out of the foot. Finally, the luff rope tends to bunch on the roller gear as the sail is wound round the boom: a sail made correctly for roller reefing, however, will have reinforcing webbing or tape, instead of rope, on the lower luff so that this does not occur.

A boom vang can be fitted to a rolled down mainsail if a length of synthetic webbing or reinforced cloth is rolled into the sail as the reef is taken in. The free end should have an eye worked into it for the attachment of a purchase (Fig. 7.3).

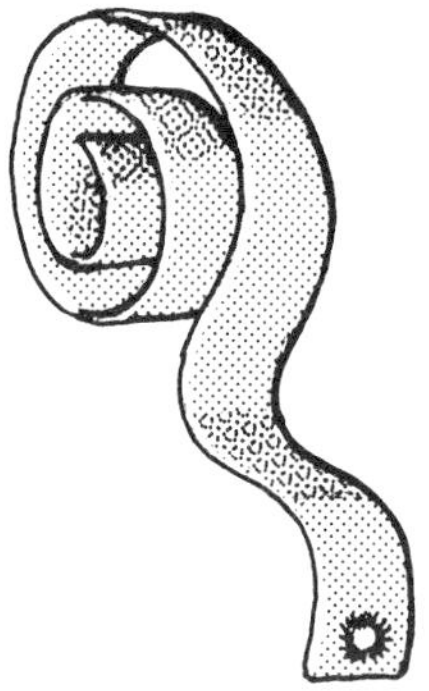

Fig. 7.3 Roller Reefing Boom Vang Strop
A 3 ft length of 3 in webbing, with an eye hand-worked into one end. The plain end is rolled in with the last two feet of sail, leaving the eye hanging free for attaching a boom vang or kicking strap.

Through-mast roller reefing entails a fixed gooseneck and a reefing gear which works from the forward side of the mast level with the boom. This method is extremely quick in operation; so quick, in fact, that it is often used for furling the mainsail in harbour.

You should ensure that the boom rises a little with each reef; this will keep it progressively clearer of heads in the cockpit and of the water on a reach, as the wind strength increases and successive reefs are taken in. With points or lacing reefs, you should have at least two reef positions, and sometimes three. Each reef should reduce area by about 20 per cent; alternatively you can estimate the luff end of the reef as being approximately one-eighth of the total luff. The leech distance will be about 10 per cent longer than the luff distance.

A jib or staysail can also be reefed. In this case individual points are the best system: they will more easily be tied under the loose foot of the sail. If the distance along the luff is the same as that along the leech, the angle of the luff will ensure that the clew rises a little as the reef is tied in. Aim to reduce area by about 30 per cent with one reef; you should not normally need more than this. A modified form of jiffy reefing can also be used for reducing headsail area. In either case, the excess cloth (tied down or free) offers plenty of windage in a gale, and can easily flog free or be torn on the rigging while tacking, so this should not be looked upon as a cheap way of providing a storm jib (the ORC condemns it), but rather to prevent the boat being overpowered as the wind rises from, say, Force 4 to 6.

STRAIGHT SPARS

I cannot, of course, tell you whether you need straight or bendy spars: this is a matter for you to decide. All I can do is to set forth some of the advantages and disadvantages of each rig and leave you to make your own choice. We will deal with straight spars first, as they are uncomplicated.

A straight mast and boom give the Sail Maker the best chance of cutting a sail which responds accurately to your requirements; he knows what the luff and foot of the sail will look like when set on your spars. However, you have to pay for this stiffness in weight and windage. The mast itself has to be of a fairly robust section in order to give it a certain amount of inherent ability to stay straight; it then has to be propped and stayed to hold it dead upright when the wind blows. All these jumpers, diamonds, cross-trees, spreaders, uppers, lowers, intermediates, backstays, forestays and runners create air turbulence and add to weight aloft. Nevertheless, they produce a straight mast. The boom is an easier task, because it does not have the same stresses, and it can be made with a deep section, since this does not affect the airflow over the sail to any great extent. In addition its weight is low in the sail plan, and is therefore not so critical except in light airs.

BENDY SPARS

The dinghies have taught us that bending spars increase the range of wind in which we can use a given mainsail. They have also given Sail Makers a headache, because bend characteristics vary from mast to mast, and even on the same mast if the rigging is altered.

A three quarter rigged mast which bends aft at the head normally bows forward in the middle, unless it is restrained. This means that the sail must also bow forward in the middle as the mast bends, thus surrendering some of the round built into the luff. This flattens the sail. A similar change takes place along the foot when the boom bends downwards in the middle, under the influence of a centre mainsheet arrangement. If the mainsheet leads to

Plate 7.1 Bent Mast

The permanent bend in this Thames A Rater's mast gives her an aerodynamically efficient sailplan. There are topmast forestay, threequarter forestay, lower shrouds, uppers, diamonds and running backstays; somewhat surprisingly, there is no permanent backstay (because of the large leech roach). Her sails are setting beautifully, and the panel seams reveal the flow. She would probably go better with a full width mainsheet traveller.   *Eileen Ramsay*

the boom end, the boom will tend to bend upwards in the middle, and this will increase the fullness along the foot.

It is important for the Sail Maker to know the bending characteristics of the spars on which the sail he is making will be used. If the mast bends more than he thought, the sail will flatten too much and almost certainly will produce a hard spot somewhere up the luff, if not a positive crease running down towards the clew. If the mast bends less than anticipated, the sail, which was cut with extra round in the luff to accept a greater bow forward, will stay too full in stronger winds. Even if the mast bends the correct total amount, but the position of maximum bend is higher or lower than expected, the sail will pull out of shape as soon as bending reaches a certain point, because the correct amount of cloth is not in the right place.

For many years bending masts were the prerogative of the dinghy boys, largely because it was not easy to see how big spars could be constructed strong enough to withstand the flexing loads, without at the same time being so heavy as to make impractical the forces necessary to bend them. In addition, shroud angles which are all right for a straight spar often become doubtful when it bends, and can easily fall to a point where the load becomes unacceptable. The whole thing was considered unsafe for keelboats (other than such notable day-sailer exceptions as the Star and Soling classes), and best left to the seemingly bottomless pockets of the America's Cup 12-metre fleet.

The introduction into mast-making of sophisticated materials, at one time so ruinously expensive that only millionaires could afford them, has allowed the mast maker to become more adventurous. The IOR outlaws permanently bent spars, but a straight mast which can be bent by adjusting the rigging is allowed. It helps sail control, and at first this meant a return to the $\frac{7}{8}$th rig, so that the mast was bent about the forestay attachment point, and running backstays were re-introduced to control the degree of forward movement. So successful was the result that ways were soon being sought of bending the masthead rig; the adjustable babystay or inner forestay made its appearance to bow the mast forward, and also to add one more item for the harassed foredeck chief to remember during the gybe ('Have you unclipped the baby-stay?'); see Fig. 7.4. The idea reached a peak when C A Marchaj used his earlier research[34] to suggest an exaggerated bend at the masthead of the British 12-metre *Lionheart*, during her crack at the America's Cup in 1980; it certainly gave her a lot of boat speed in the lighter wind ranges, largely through improved aerodynamic shape, but also partly due to some increase in area. At all events, the Australians quickly copied the idea for their own challenger.

The introduction of film laminate sails, with their lack of response to different halyard tensions, has made bending masts even more important, as

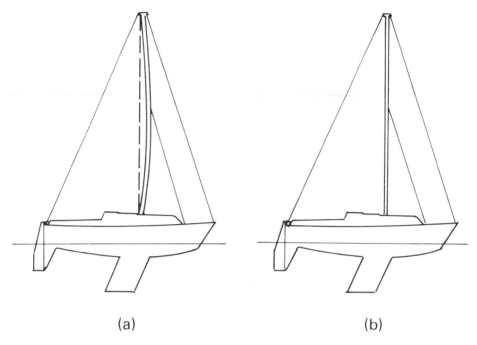

Fig. 7.4 The Baby Stay

In order to bend a spar which is masthead rigged, it must be pulled forward at the lower half. This means having a special stay, which must be tensioned hard to pull the middle of the mast forward (a), or held in control to prevent it bowing aft (b).

they offer one of the few ways of flattening a modern racing mainsail. If, therefore, you have a bendy mast, see to it that your spreaders or crosstrees have the ability to accept the change in direction of load which will result. It should be remembered, however, that a bending boom will remove draft from precisely that part of the sail where it contributes most thrust and least heeling moment: low down near the foot. Thrust is still needed, so don't go and throw it all away in an attempt to get the mainsail as flat as a board.

It is a fortunate coincidence that the stronger the wind, the more tension is needed on the mainsheet, and so the more the mast and boom will bend if they are made that way. The more they bend the flatter becomes the sail — which is what is needed in a strong wind.

We have been talking about fore and aft bend so far. Lateral bend is not so good, because it distorts the leading edge of the sail as it is presented to the wind, and will disturb the regularity of the airflow. Nevertheless a slight bend to leeward (and aft) at the head of a dinghy mast helps to feather the head of the mainsail in heavy weather, thus making it easier to hold the boat upright. A light helmsman will therefore probably have a more flexible mast than his heavier rival, who will be able to use his weight to keep upright with more of his sail drawing. This bend to leeward at the head brings with it a corresponding bend to windward below the hounds, which also carries a certain advantage. It has the effect of opening the slot a little between the mainsail and the headsail. When we remember that all this flexibility only occurs in strong winds, it will be appreciated that a slightly larger slot will be beneficial, because it will allow a less disturbed airflow over the lee side of the mainsail.

Mainsails can be cut with the correct flow in them when set on a straight boom, so it does not need to bend sideways to impart this flow, at least until nearly at the after-end. It can pay, however, to allow the final 20 per cent of the boom to sag off to leeward; Fig. 7.5. This frees the lower leech of the mainsail from hooking to windward where it returns to the boom at the clew, and also helps the whole mainsail to present less frontal area to the airflow – thus cutting down form drag. Be careful not to overdo it, however, or you will encourage a slack leech.

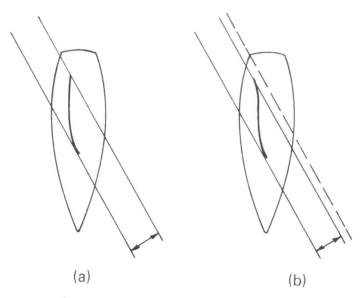

(a)   (b)

Fig. 7.5 Boom Bend (Lateral)
If the outer end of a boom is flexible enough sideways to bend to leeward in a blow (b), it means that the mainsail presents less area to the airflow and thus creates less drag.

It is difficult to generalize about the advisability of flexible masts, but if your dinghy has a lot of sail area for its size, such as a 14 ft International or a Flying Dutchman, or if you are particularly light, without a trapeze, then have bendy spars to help take some of the hard work out of keeping your boat upright. If you own an under-canvassed boat like a Snipe, or if you are heavy, you may prefer to avoid the complications of too much flexibility, because you will usually be able to use full power. Secondly, if you are in doubt as to degree, have a stiffer rather than a more bendy mast; you can always bend it by brute force in a blow, yet you will have a straighter fore-stay for light airs, because the stiffer mast will hold it up better.

If you are considering having an ocean-racer built, or are wondering whether to have your present boat remasted, my advice is graded according to your temperament. If you are out to win at all costs, and don't mind the extra complication in your crew drills, then you must seriously consider the benefits which a bending mast will bring. This is particularly true if you are using a fully moulded mainsail of film laminate cloth, because you won't get much control over its shape without bending the mast. The fractional rig is more easily adapted to the system, but there is no bar to using it (by incorporation of a babystay) if you are a dedicated believer in the advantages of the masthead genoa.

If, however, you do not treat your racing as a religion and are mainly interested in cruising, then leave the complication to others and stick to the straight spar as we have known it for so long. You should also be staying with conventionally woven cloth, so that a Cunningham and a slab (jiffy) reef will go a long way towards flattening the mainsail (which, for cruisers, should err on the flat rather than the full side anyway) sufficiently to offset the sail control disadvantages of a stiff mast.

KICKING-STRAPS

I do not propose to argue whether the words 'kicking-strap' correctly describe what is also known as a boom vang and a boom jack; they are understood by all, and form a popular term. The kicking-strap's prime function is to keep the boom down and reduce mainsail twist at the head. In a dinghy it has two secondary roles to perform; those of preventing a Chinese gybe and of helping to impart mast bend. We have already discussed mast bend, and I do not propose to get involved in how best to control the bend you decide that you want. We all know that a Chinese gybe is spectacular and embarrassing; it is not my job to tell you not to do it. But sail twist is very much within the scope of this book, and a few words are indicated.

If a mainsail on a reach is allowed to develop too much twist due to the absence of a boom vang or kicking-strap, the boom must be sheeted in so that the upper part of the sail is not lifting. This means that the lower two-thirds is generating its thrust too much athwartships, and is contributing too much of its effort to heeling the boat and not enough to driving it forward; Fig. 7.6. If we can reduce the twist, we can ease the boom, thereby achieving a greater forward thrust component and reducing the amount of weather helm

Plate 7.2 Kicking Strap – Manual
Multiple purchases shift this kicking strap rod back and forth along a traveller.
Author

Plate 7.3 Kicking Strap – Hydraulic
The hydraulic ram is the ultimate in kicking strap control.   *Author*

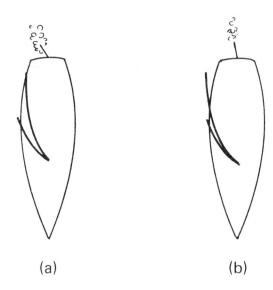

(a)   (b)

Fig. 7.6 Effect of Twist
In (a) the boom is well in towards the centreline, in order to prevent the upper half
of the mainsail from sagging off too much, and thus lifting. Pulling down on the
boom also pulls the head of the sail down and in; this means that the head will still
be full of wind when the boom is eased more (b). Apart from increased thrust from
the lower half of the sail, there is less weather helm and thus less turbulence in the
water astern from the correcting rudder.

required to keep the boat going straight ahead. The latter advantage is not
always fully appreciated, but it is every bit as important as the former, if not
more so. Don't forget, however, that we saw (in Chapter II) how some twist
is useful, particularly in tall sails, to allow for wind gradient, which effectively frees a boat as height is increased.

A full width mainsheet traveller, coupled with a centre boom lead, is
aiming at the same result, and these refinements have spread from widespread use in dinghies and the smaller keelboat one-designs into the ocean-
racing fleet. Indeed, a centre mainsheet is not easy to accommodate in a
two-man dinghy under about 14 ft long, because it gets in the way, whereas
the ocean-racers have no such problems. At all events, make sure that your
kicking-strap is powerful and easy to use. The hydraulic ram offers the best
(and most expensive) solution. It cannot be used with roller reefing, but
governs boom angle up and down, and thus gives excellent control over sail
shape if used with a slab reef and adjustable clew outhaul. A roller boom, of
course, means that a claw has to be used for a centre boom sheet lead, and
this often gives trouble from jamming and from chafe; it is for each owner to
make his own decision as to whether it is worth it.

It is not enough for a dinghy to have a good kicking-strap; it must also have an effective means of controlling the amount of mast bend which it imparts. This may take the form of chocks or an adjustable piston or strut.

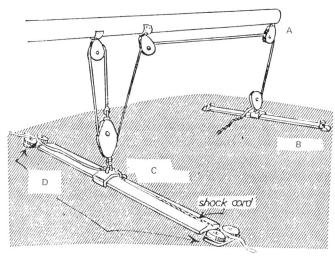

Fig. 7.7 Novex Block Mainsheet

A = Novex block.   B = Transom.
C = Traveller.   D = Cam cleats.

Use of a Novex self-locking block enables the helmsman to jerk the mainsail with a centre-boom sheeting arrangement, when he wants to strike the sail and get on the plane. On a reach, a quick snatch at the sheet brings in the boom end as if on a single part, while the central purchase still acts as a boom bender and kicking strap when required. Both centre and transom parts have travellers, so that easing the sheet when close-hauled lets the boom move sideways on the centre traveller without rising.

Dinghies have probably paid more attention to the problem of sail twist than other boats, because the effects are so apparent. It is particularly important to keep a dinghy upright in planing conditions, and the boat with an effective kicking-strap and a full width mainsheet traveller will soon demonstrate its superiority. One of the drawbacks of a centre sheet arrangement on a planing dinghy is that the helmsman cannot easily strike his sheet to give the boat those sharp kicks needed to get on to a plane, and make the most of the apparent wind suddenly coming farther ahead. Guthrie Penman developed an arrangement on his 14 ft International, whereby a Novex block at the boom end gave him this ability; Fig. 7.7.

MAST RAKE

Varying the rake of the mast moves the centre of effort in relation to the centre of lateral resistance or plane, and this has a considerable effect on weather or lee helm (see next chapter). But to achieve this variation, the forestay has to be adjusted as well as the backstay; the mast must also be able to pivot on its heel – easy enough if it is deck-stepped, but a through-deck spar needs a slot at the deck (or else a pivot at that point, with a heel which will slide back and forth on the keelson). All this movement is considered by the Offshore Racing Council to be unseamanlike, and they have banned the idea by the simple introduction of a rule which prohibits adjustment of both forestay and backstay (one or the other is all right, but not both)[35]. But it must come because, with proper safeguards, its use increases the sea-worthiness of a boat (we can most of us think of yachts where we would have been glad to be able to remove excessive weather helm at the touch of a couple of controls).

WINCHES

The job of a headsail sheet winch is to provide enough power to pull the clew of the headsail concerned far enough aft to flatten the leech of the sail when beating to windward. With many genoas it is the only way of ensuring a flat

Plate 7.4 Cockpit Layout
Thought needs to be given to cockpit layout if inefficiency is to be avoided. All controls here are nicely to hand, winches and cleats are well arranged, and handle stowages are handy. There are a lot of jammers, which will regularly eat up all those lines.   *Author*

leech in a blow. Equally, with many winches (and crews) it is the quickest way to overstrain a sail. If you possess powerful winches, therefore, you should tell your Sail Maker when ordering headsails. He can then see that the canvas is the correct weight to avoid distortion, and he can cut the sails appropriately. Many crews feel that 'just one more notch' on the genoa winch is the hallmark of a hard racing man; it is often the ruin of a perfectly good sail.

If you do not possess powerful winches, then your Sail Maker can cut your genoa with a flat leech which does not have to be hauled in bar taut when on the wind. In addition, it is no good making a jib heavily for use on a coffee-grinder, if the boat is not equipped with winches powerful enough to make the sail set properly.

Winches are frequently too powerful. It has become fashionable to own the latest equipment, and to have a higher power ratio than your rival. When you consider that some quite small standard winches have a mechanical advantage of over 70:1 (and I am not talking of coffee-grinders, which are much more powerful), you can imagine the stress you are putting on your sails every time you harden right in. If the sail is cut correctly to start with, there should be no need for more than half this ratio in boats with a water-line length of under 25 ft or so.

Let me here explain that *gear ratio* is represented by the number of turns of the handle, to one of the winch drum. *Power ratio*, or *mechanical advantage*, also takes account of the radius of the winch handle (and thus the leverage which can be exerted on it), and the diameter of the drum (and thus the amount of rope which is pulled in at each turn of the drum); it can be expressed as

$$\frac{\text{Gear Ratio} \times \text{Handle Radius}}{\text{Drum Radius}}$$

HALYARDS AND OUTHAULS

Mainsail halyards must be powerful enough to stretch the luff of the sail properly. In dinghies this presents little problem, but the bigger boats need the help of winches. A downhaul is an excellent way of getting that little bit extra when it is needed, and it has the added advantage of providing a first-class system of regulating the flow in a conventionally woven sail according to the weather. A fixed gooseneck means that the main halyard has to be adjusted in order to alter the tension on the luff, and this is sometimes a tiresome process which becomes too much trouble as a result. Remember that rope halyards will stretch with use and spoil the set of the sail if they are not trimmed after you have been out for a while.

139

An ocean-racer's main clew outhaul should be a positive fitting, preferably a jaw with a through-pin, running on a short heavy track; adjustment can be made either by means of an outhaul line on a purchase, or through a worm drive. The cruising man can stick to the old-fashioned lashing, which gives less trouble from the maintenance angle. Whichever system you adopt, see that the footrope of the sail continues in a straight line throughout its length, and does not rise sharply at the clew.

Dinghies and the smaller keelboats are keenly aware of the importance of adjusting tension on the foot of a woven mainsail, as much as on the luff, when the wind varies or the boat changes between beat and reach. A lashing cannot be altered easily in a dinghy, and many helmsmen adopt a long outhaul line leading under the boom to a jam cleat; alternatively a worm gear is used, but this means allowing your attention to be distracted for too long at a time and can only be adjusted when the boom end is within reach. John Ogle adopted a good system in his 14 ft International as long ago as 1964. He had a footrope entirely made of shock cord, tensioned so that it was about 4 in short of the black band when lying slack. The clew outhaul was coupled to a Highfield lever which allowed 3 in of play. The clew was pulled right aft to the black band for beating to windward and was allowed to go forward 3 in as soon as the boat came off the wind. Admittedly this only provides two alternative positions for the clew, but it has the great advantage that it is simple. Its simplicity means that it is used more often than a more complicated system, even though the latter may give infinite adjustment.

Chapter VIII
Tuning

In this chapter I shall look at those aspects of tuning which have an effect on the sails. Such things as a clean bottom, centreboard position, rudder shape and so on are as important as sails and rigging, but they do not directly concern my subject, even though some of them might do so indirectly through affecting the degree of weather helm a boat may have. Before we leave this area, however, I would just like to illustrate that sails are not the only part of a boat where experts can agree to differ.

In 1965 Stu Walker and Mike Peacock both bought new 14 ft International dinghies to the same design and with the same J measurement from Souters of Cowes. Peacock asked for his centreboard to be 4in *aft* of the design position, and Walker asked for an adjustable pin. Peacock found that his boat went best when he sat right forward, whereas Walker decided that the best combination was to have the centreboard 4 in *forward* of the datum, which meant that he finished up sitting right aft in the boat. Both men had tuned with two major factors almost as far apart as they could go.

If I use a good many examples from the Fourteens it is not only because they are such a suitable class due to the latitude allowed in their rig, but also because of the nature of the members themselves. I have visited many different classes to advise on sails and help repair them during important meetings, and the owners who stand head and shoulders above the rest for courtesy and consideration are the Fourteen Footers. The attending sailmakers work hard at these meetings to repair and alter sails, often until eleven o'clock at night. At the end of the race, when the plaudits have died down, it is invariably the Fourteen owner who will push his way through the crowd at the club, or walk half a mile to the temporary sail loft, purely to say thank you. They have their foibles like anyone else, and are just as particular about the odd half inch as the next man, besides which their mainsails are not easy to make and are even more difficult to correct once they are not made right, but it is small wonder that I have a soft spot for the class as a whole.

CENTRE OF LATERAL RESISTANCE

The centre of lateral resistance (CLR) is the geometrical centre of the under-water profile of the boat, and is normally determined by the Naval Architect; see Fig. 8.1. It will vary slightly when under way, due to lateral and longitudinal trim (in practical terms, due to angle of heel, and to weight distribution fore and aft); it will also vary slightly with hull speed, and much more with rudder angle.

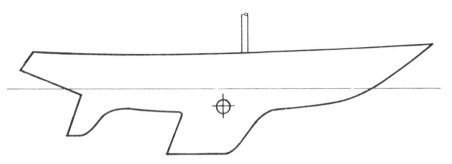

Fig. 8.1 Centre of Lateral Resistance
The static CLR is the geometrical mid-point of the boat's underwater profile; the amateur may determine this approximately, by cutting out the shape in cardboard and then balancing it on a pin. The centre will shift when under way, depending on speed, angle of heel, and fore-and-aft trim, and it will generally move forward as the bows dig in, or aft if the boat squats by the stern.

CENTRE OF EFFORT

The static centre of effort (CE) of a sail, or sails, may be found as shown in Fig. 8.2; this is the geometrical centre point of the area involved. The dynamic CE will differ as a result of several factors: the camber on the sail (different parts of the area generate different thrust in different wind strengths – some of the thrust will be angled well forward and some of it more sideways; a flat sail has its CE forward, a full one has it aft); the angle of heel; drag in its various forms; and, of course, the sheeting angle. In general terms, the dynamic CE is forward of its static counterpart, but it will be aft if the sails are too full.

The position of the CE in relation to the CLR is of prime importance. If we imagine thrust as acting through the former, and the resistance of the hull to sideways displacement as pivoting about the latter, we can see from Fig. 8.3 how their relative positions affect control of the boat and, by extension, its speed. The object is an even balance, where CE and CLR are correctly aligned. Where this is not achieved, rudder must be used to keep the boat straight; the result then is the drag of a turbulent wake from the angled rudder blade, which reveals wasted energy – and energy is speed. If

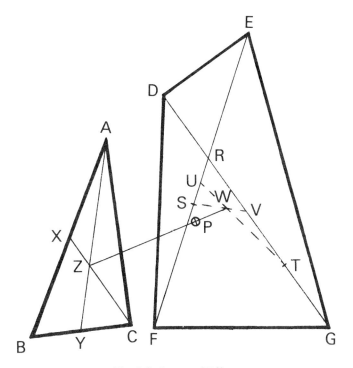

Fig. 8.2 Centre of Effort

The static CE of any sail is its geometrical mid-point. For a triangle, this is found by joining each corner to the mid-point of the opposite side. I have also drawn a four-sided sail, as this is slightly more complicated: GT = DR and FS = ER, then mark the mid-point of RS as U and of RT as V; the CE is W.

The CE of both sails together is P, which lies along ZW in inverse proportion to the two areas. Either divide jib area by total area times WZ = WP, or draw a line to represent jib area to any convenient scale, vertically upwards from W (mainsail CE), and another to represent mainsail area to the same scale, vertically down from Z (jib CE); the line joining the two ends will cut ZW at the combined CE.

there has to be an imbalance, it is better to have a slight amount of weather helm (CE aft of CLR), particularly when close hauled; this means that there is a slight feel to the tiller or wheel, and the boat is trying to work up to windward rather than lose ground to leeward.

The position of the CLR can only be varied to any great extent in boats with a pivoting centreboard: raising it slightly moves the CLR aft as can be seen in Fig. 8.4. Some influence can be effected through shifting crew weight fore and aft, but the result is minimal. The best way to change the CE/CLR relationship is to shift the CE, either through varying sail camber (pulling down on a Cunningham hole will draw the flow of a woven sail forward, thereby doing same for the CE; flattening the mainsail by bending the mast will also move the CE forward), or through raking the mast (see Fig. 8.5).

143

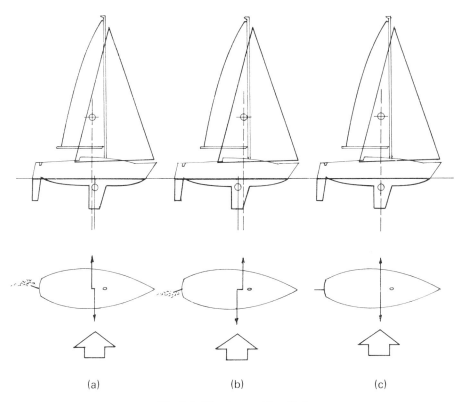

(a) (b) (c)

Fig. 8.3 Weather and Lee Helm

If the total dynamic CE is aft of the CLR, there will be a force couple tending to pivot the boat into wind (a); this must be countered by use of rudder. If, on the other hand, the CE is forward of the CLR (where the text books tell the budding designers to ensure that it is established – the so-called 'lead'), the boat will tend to bear away (b); since few boats in fact carry lee helm, one or both of the centres must move inwards to balance in the dynamic situation, if the CE leads the CLR on paper. The ideal, of course, is a balanced rig where no helm is needed to steer a straight course (c).

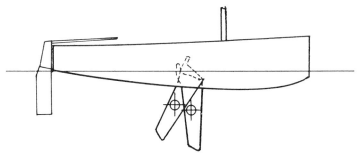

Fig. 8.4 Effect of Centreboard Position on CLR

Because the centreboard pivots aft when it is raised, the CLR will move accordingly. Weather and lee helm can thus be taken out or increased at will.

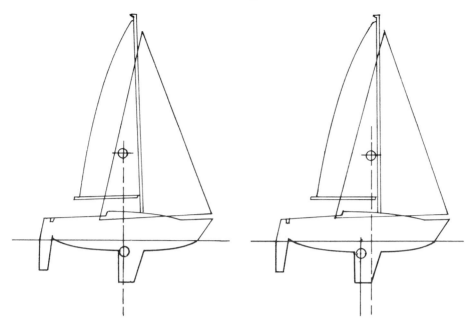

Fig. 8.5 Mast Rake
Raking the mast aft moves the CE aft; raking it forward has the opposite effect.
This is because the moment with the CLR changes accordingly, and thus weather
and lee helm can be varied at will.

RIGGING

The object of tuning is to balance a boat in such a way that she will sail to
best advantage under certain conditions of wind and water. This usually
involves ensuring that the airflow over the combined aerofoil formed by at
least two mutually interfering sails is efficient, and that the driving force
which they generate is optimum in strength and direction. A great many
variable factors play their part in this search, as we have already inferred in
previous chapters. Not only does the initial shape of the sail make a big
difference, but also the size and shape of the slot, the angle of the luff, the
run-off at the leech and the way the sail is set and sheeted. Let us, therefore,
go through those tuning factors which can affect the set and drive of the
sails.

ASHORE

If your boat is small enough to be hauled out easily for setting up ashore, so
much the better. There is little more helpful to an owner than to walk
round his boat with a critical eye when all working sail is set. If she is too
large for this treatment, a similar result can be obtained at the moorings if
you row round her in a dinghy.

STARTING POINT

First of all you must decide from which basis you are going to start. Don't forget that we are assuming here that all points not connected with sails have been covered, so the position of the mast is probably the most elementary factor. If you do not know how you want the mast placed, have a look at two or three successful boats in the same class as yourself and average their ideas. Decide where you want to put your own mast as a result of this.

The first task is to see that the boat is dead upright. If she is ashore, take care that the chocks are firmly positioned; if she is at her moorings, transfer weight until she is floating exactly to her marks. Next, see that the shrouds on either side are the same length, and that they and the forestay have the right amount of travel on their adjustments.

Classes vary as to whether rigging should be slack or tight[36]. In general, a boat will normally go better to windward with the mast raked slightly aft, and better downwind with it raked forward. In order to achieve this double requirement, many two- and three-man boats use slack rigging. This allows the mast to lean towards the bows when the wind is astern, so that the main shrouds take the weight. When the boat is close hauled, the mast is raked aft by the pull of the mainsheet; the slack of the forestay and headsail luff is thus taken up, so that the latter in particular is nice and straight. Slack rigging should be somewhat tighter in heavy weather, or the mast will go too far forward on a run and tend to bury the bows to the detriment of speed. Remember also that it is no use spending time finding the exact length for your forestay so that the mast behaves as you want it, only to sweat up on your headsail halyard and thus pull the mast too far forward on a beat. The headsail should be hoisted to the same tension for all races where the rigging is unaltered; the surest way to do this quickly is to have an eye on the halyard and a hook on the mast, so that the headsail luff just takes the weight off the forestay.

Many of the larger boats are putting their masts nearly upright nowadays, for an ocean-racer cannot afford to have a mast which moves backwards and forwards when facing force seven winds offshore.

The competition generated by such series as the Admiral's Cup, the One Ton Cup and the RORC points trophies means that an ocean-racer has to remain in tip-top condition over a long period. The amount of stretch, even in modern wire, is sufficient to interfere seriously with tuning, particularly as regards the forestay. I said something about straight headsail luffs on page 73, and I cannot over-emphasize this point. If the forestay of an ocean-racer stretches, the headsail luff will sag to leeward and the boat will not point properly. For this reason many owners are specifying rod rigging, particularly for the forestay.

When Camper & Nicholson's were building one of the *Yeomans* for Owen

Aisher, an empty lorry drove into their yard in the south of England, having come all the way from Scotland. Peter Nicholson looked mildly surprised at this phenomenon, until he saw tucked along one side of the lorry the rod forestay for the new boat. In those days it was never rolled, as it is now, and road transport was about the only way of delivering it. The rigging itself is expensive enough, and this only added to the final bill.

Once you have decided the basic mast position and whether you are going to have slack or tight rigging, comes the question of the relative tension of the various wires. There is no problem with a simple rig comprising main shrouds and forestay; it is when we come to many shrouded types like the Dragon that complications set in.

Jumpers. Jumper stays should normally be fairly tight, to the point where the head of the mast is arched slightly forward (Fig. 8.6); this will straighten as soon as the mainsail is full and on the wind.

Shrouds. It is important that main shrouds should be evenly tensioned, and a strain gauge is useful when setting up. Cap shrouds are normally fairly tight and the forward lowers nearly the same; aft lowers may be somewhat slacker

(a)   (b)

Fig. 8.6 Jumper Stays

If the jumper stays are slack, a fractional rig mast will be pulled aft under any tension (a) – either from the topmast backstay or else from the mainsheet when close hauled. If the jumpers are tight, the situation in (b) occurs until the mainsail fills on the wind, when the mast will probably straighten under tension from the mainsheet through the mainsail leech.

147

to allow for some mast movement (Fig. 8.7 shows the effect of various adjustments).

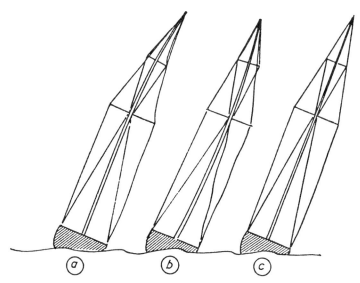

Fig. 8.7 Cap Shrouds

If the cap shrouds are slack, the masthead will fall off to leeward, with an exaggerated effect if the lowers are tight (a). The opposite situation will cause the middle of the mast to fall away under the slack lowers, while the tight cap shrouds hold the masthead amidships (b). Hard cap shrouds, with lowers not quite so firm, allow the mast just a little athwartships play, and often seem best (c).

Forestay. Either the forestay or the backstay may be adjustable while racing under the IOR, but not both[35]. It is better to be able to adjust the backstay, so the forestay is usually set up to length, and its tension then varied by means of the backstay. The general rule is to have the forestay as tight (and therefore straight) as possible when going to windward with the mast correctly raked. Figs. 8.8 and 8.9 show masthead and fractional rig backstays, together with the effect of various adjustments on the forestay.

Backstay. An adjustable masthead backstay should be capable of pulling the masthead back so that the forestay is correctly tensioned when the mast is vertical. On racing boats of any size, adjustment is usually by means of hydraulics, otherwise it may be a wheel tensioner, a turnbuckle or a simple lashing; sometimes twin backstays are drawn together by means of a system of pullies. Be prepared for the backstay to go slacker when the boat comes hard on the wind in a breeze, for the action of the mainsheet will tend to pull the mast slightly aft. Downwind, the backstay should be eased to allow the mast to rake slightly forward.

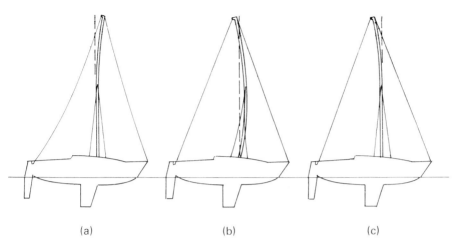

(a)   (b)   (c)

Fig. 8.8 Backstay and Forestay – Masthead Rig

If the backstay on a masthead rig is allowed to go slack when beating to windward with little mainsheet tension in light winds, the forestay will sag badly and the boat will not point (a). If the forestay is too long, so that the backstay has to be pulled down excessively to keep the genoa luff straight, the mast will bend and pull the mainsail out of shape, because it will not have been cut with this in mind; the bend will be in the middle if the lowers are slack (b), or at the head if they are tight (c).

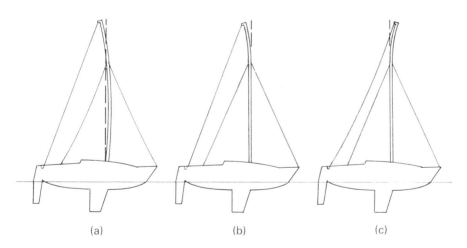

(a)   (b)   (c)

Fig. 8.9 Backstay and Runners – Fractional Rig

To bend the topmast of a fractional rig, the backstay is hardened. The degree to which the resulting bend extends down the mast may be controlled by slackening the running backstays *very slightly*, which increases the extent (a); alternatively, they may be held tight to confine the bend to the topmast only (b). If the permanent backstay is allowed to go slack on the wind, the masthead will bend forward, increase flow in the mainsail and cause a lot of creases (c).

Plate 8.1 Forestay

The genoa luff is all-important. Place a straightedge along the genoa luff of *Second Luv*, and you will find little sag (see also *Sanction* in Pl. 9.5). Try the same on a photograph of your own boat, and you may be persuaded to get a better backstay adjuster. *Second Luv* has a lot of pullies and purchases at the stern, but she also seems to have had some trouble – it looks as though the two middle battens have started to come out of their pockets, and I can't believe that all that tangle at the stern relates to the lee runner. *Author*

Plate 8.2 Backstay Adjuster – Manual

Backstay adjustment may be by pulley and purchase as in (a), or by wheel tensioner as in (b).   *Author*

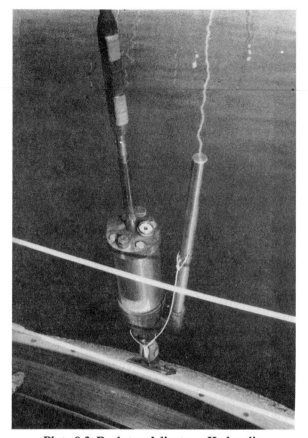

Plate 8.3 Backstay Adjuster – Hydraulic
This hydraulic adjuster has its own pressure gauge incorporated into the barrel of
the piston.   *Author*

Running Backstays. With a fractional rig, there will be runners which join
the mast at the same level as the forestay; these do the same job as a single
masthead backstay. When combined with a topmast backstay, mast bend can
be controlled (Fig. 8.9).

Inner or Babystay. A babystay is normally only fitted with a masthead rig,
its job being to force the lower part of the mast forward to flatten the mainsail (Fig. 8.10). Above Quarter Tonner size, hydraulics are virtually essential
due to the forces involved and the poor mechanical advantage.

While setting up the basic tune, keep checking up the mast to see that it is
straight athwartships with possibly a slight bow forward at the head. Now go
sailing in a force 3 wind.

A steady bend to leeward as in Fig. 8.7 (a) means that the upper shrouds,

Fig. 8.10 Babystay
If the babystay of a masthead rig is pulled tight, with the forestay and topmast backstay firm, the middle of the mast will bend forward and flatten the mainsail. This and jiffy reefing are the two quickest acting and most effective methods of flattening a film laminate mainsail.

and probably the jumpers, need tightening to control the sag at the head. Tighten both sides at once and make a note of how much you adjust. The bend shown in Fig. 8.7 (b) is the result of loose lower shrouds coupled with tight uppers. If you are seeking a slack rig, then tighten very slightly the lowers (but do not overdo it), and ease off on the uppers; this should result in slightly more movement than the picture at 8.7 (c), bearing in mind that the running backstay should be helping to keep a fractional rig mast from sagging too far to leeward in the middle.

Do not forget to watch the fore and aft situation. Figure 8.6 (a) is the result of jumpers which are too loose while 8.9 (c) shows either tight lower shrouds, if these are led forward of the mast, or tight forestay and slack backstay.

Where there is only one set of shrouds, as on the average dinghy, you will find the effect I described in Chapter VII, where the head of the mast will tend to fall slightly off to leeward above the hounds. This in turn means that the middle of the mast will bow to windward to compensate. Correctly adjusted upper and lower shrouds on multi-shroud masts will have the same effect. This is what opens the slot between the leeward side of the mainsail luff and the windward side of the genoa leech. Ideally, you should be able to adjust dinghy rigging to suit the weather. Here again Highfield levers can help by giving a two-way adjustment, which at least gives you an advantage over the boat with no adjustment at all. Some dinghies have this system on their main shrouds.

HEADSAIL LEADS

We have already seen that the slot between the headsail and the mainsail is critical. This means that the angle which the foot of the headsail makes along the deck when viewed from above is critical[36].

DECK ANGLE

This deck angle will be affected not only by the wind strength and the main boom sheeting angle, but by the fullness and shape of the mainsail (including where that fullness lies in the sail), as well as the draft of the headsail itself and its amount of overlap. In addition, if a boat has a large wetted area for her size or has bluff sections, hull drag will be high, so she will need more power to get to windward; this in turn means a wider sheeting base at the expense of pointing ability. The variables are many (see Fig. 8.11), so look critically at the slot as you determine the inboard or outboard position of the headsail sheet fairlead. The angle will vary from 7 or 8 degrees for Stars,

Plate 8.4 Sheet Leads
The deck of *Pen Duick IV* looks like the dream of some model railway enthusiast. Tracks can be seen for the headsail sheets, kicking strap, running backstays, and mainsheet; it looks as if the two figures in the middle are as puzzled as I am over the reason for the track which runs straight across the deck between them (Barber Hauler?).   *Author*

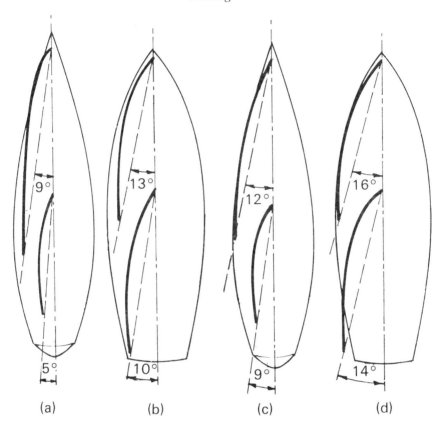

Fig. 8.11 Jibsheet Fairlead Position – Deck Angle

In general terms, sails may be hauled inboard (Barber-hauled) and sheeted close as shown in drawings (a) and (b), for higher pointing in light winds and smooth water. If the headsail is sheeted via an inner fairlead, the main boom should also be trimmed fairly well inboard. Under these conditions, the average offshore racer (a) should have a genoa with flow forward and a fine entry; the mainsail flow should be central, also with a fine entry. A heavy cruiser (b) won't get away with this sophistication unless the overlap is small, because the slot will be choked and thrust will be low.

Headsails should be sheeted outboard (drawings (c) and (d)) in stronger winds and rougher water; the main boom should also be eased down to leeward, and the boat will power her way through the seas, not pointing quite so high and with less weather helm. The average offshore racer (c) should have a genoa with its flow central, and a mainsail with flow slightly forward and a fine entry. This is the normal state for a heavy bluff cruising boat with a lot of wetted area, which needs the power to keep her going through the waves (d).

Solings and the metre boats in light weather and smooth water, to 20 degrees for a bluff cruiser in rough weather when power is needed to push the boat along[37]. As the boat luffs into wind, the headsail should lift at the same time as the mainsail; if it is sooner, the headsail needs sheeting harder or more inboard, and vice versa.

FORE AND AFT POSITION

When deciding the fore and aft position of headsail fairleads, adjust so that, as the boat points too high into wind, the whole luff starts to lift at the same time. If it lifts aloft first, move the fairlead forward; move it aft if it shakes first near the tack (see Fig. 8.12). But also look at the leech. If the mainsail is full or has a lot of twist, the headsail lead should come aft to ease its own

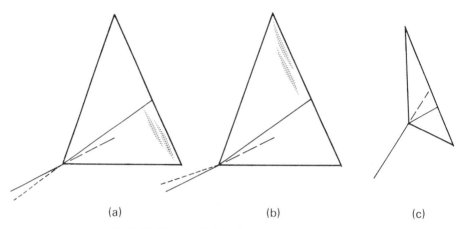

(a)   (b)   (c)

Fig. 8.12 Jibsheet Fairlead Position – Fore and Aft

The main factors governing fore and aft position of the headsail sheet fairlead are the outline shape of the headsail and the slot. Pull on the sail must be such that, as the boat turns into wind, the luff of the sail lifts simultaneously along its entire length, and that neither the leech nor the foot is overtensioned, which would cause curling of the edge concerned. When all headsails had a mitre which bisected the angle at the clew, there was a useful reference datum for the sheet lead. A low clewed sail like a genoa should sheet so that a projection of the sheet – the dashed line in (a) and (b) – runs below the bisector; a yankee with a high clew should project above the bisector (c).

If any headsail lifts first at the tack as the boat points progressively into wind (a), the sheet is too far forward (dotted line) and needs to be brought aft; if it lifts first at the head (b), the sheet is too far aft (dotted line) and needs to be taken forward. There are also other influences, which can best be shown in tabulated form:

Factors	Lead Forward	Lead Aft
Headsail shape	High clew	Low clew
Slot	Closes it	Opens it
Mast rake	If raked aft	If raked forward
Headsail halyard	If eased	If hardened
Tack Cunningham	If hardened	If eased
Headsail twist	Straightens it	Twists it
Mainsail twist	No main twist	Twisted main
Mainsail draft	With flat main	With full main
Main traveller	If amidships	If eased
Winds	Light	Strong
Reaching	Untwisted main	Twisted main
Luff lifts at tack first	Makes it worse	Improves it
Luff lifts at head first	Improves it	Makes it worse

leech so that it falls off in sympathy and opens the slot; this can also be true if the mainsail twists when freeing off onto a reach. An efficient kicking-strap, however, will keep the mainsail leech fairly straight, so the headsail lead may then go *forward* when reaching, to ease the foot, stop headsail twist and allow more draft. If the main traveller is down to leeward when beating, perhaps to ease weather helm, the genoa fairlead may come aft slightly to ease its leech and re-open the slot. If the headsail luff is adjustable, the clew must follow suit: harden the halyard and the clew rises, so the lead should go aft (if the tack is pulled down by a Cunningham, then the clew will come down rather than up), and vice versa. Equally, strong winds can mean some aft movement of the lead to ease the leech and allow it to fall off slightly to open the slot.

CHECKING

The slot is all-important, and the headsail leech should follow the line of the mainsail at the slot exit; if the mainsail twists, so should the headsail. Sail in about force 3 and gradually luff – if the headsail lifts before the main, the fairlead should be moved inboard a little; if it is some time after the mainsail, then you can afford to take it outboard. Take care not to kill speed in a desire to point high, and see *Tell-Tales* (Ch. IX). Dinghies seem to prefer 10 to 12 degrees for their headsails, but slim round bilge racers sailed on calm waters and with sails which are not too full, can go down to about 8 degrees; the same boat would need to increase this angle by 2 to 4 degrees if sailed on more open waters. A bluff beamy boat might need to go to as much as 20 degrees in similar conditions. Degree lines can be marked on the deck for those boats which allow alteration of the fairlead. If class rules permit, yet your fairlead has no lateral adjustment, an extra hook or snatch block should be placed right on the rail for use when reaching; this should normally be slightly forward of the standard close hauled position. As with all tuning, only try one alteration at a time, write down what you have done, and restore it before trying something else if it doesn't work. If you alter one factor, you will almost certainly have to alter at least one more, and the best summary of advice which I can offer is contained in two lines:

Keep an eye on the slot,
and *When in doubt, let it out.*

Barber Haulers. These are named after Californian twins, who developed the system on their *Lightning* in 1963 (although I have a movie I took aboard *Evenlode* at Cowes in 1947, when Tom Thornycroft hung a weight on the light genoa clew to give the sail more camber on a reach). In light airs and smooth water, some boats can foot as fast yet point higher, if the genoa clew is pulled in towards the coachroof by a tackle or an athwartships traveller. The main boom must also be trimmed amidships, even up to windward, in order to keep the two sails far enough apart to maintain an efficient slot. Another use of the device is to alter the fore and aft headsail sheet lead, thus varying sail shape to suit the wind or point of sailing.

MAINSHEET LEADS

We can now turn our attention to the mainsail. We have already discussed the question of bending spars, thus touching on centreboom sheet leads. Whether your sheet leads from the middle or the end of the boom, its travel on the deck is important.

If the sheet is permanently attached to the centreline of the counter, its pull will always be down towards the middle of the boat. This means that every time you want to have the sheet hard in, you will have to have your main boom too far in. A wide track for the traveller means that the boom can be well over the counter, yet still pulled hard down to flatten the mainsail (and tighten the forestay where slack rigging is used). The same length of track for a centre mainsheet arrangement means a greater range of control than would be the case with a boom end attachment.

This is a field where the offshore fleet profit to the same extent as the dinghies, and a reinforced coachroof is a ready made base for a centreboom sheet arrangement. The 12-metres developed the recirculating ball-race traveller, which runs smoothly even when full tension is applied to the sheet. Those who scoff at the money spent on the America's Cup are sometimes liable to forget the many spin-offs which are the direct result, to the subsequent benefit of the sailing fraternity as a whole.

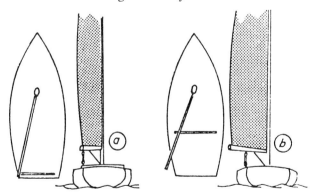

Fig. 8.13 Mainsail Sheet Leads
Where the traveller runs along the transom (a), the mainsheet must be eased as soon as the boom end goes outboard. Use of a centre boom attachment and traveller (b) means that the boom can be eased substantially outside the transom while the mainsheet is still two blocks.

ACTIVE TUNING

When you have got your mast and rigging set up as you want, go out for a sail in company with another boat of the same class and performance as your own. Set the sails and rigging of both boats to the same adjustment, trim them the same, and sail alongside one another so that you both have the wind free. Now comes a slow process of improvement, during which you must not expect spectacular results.

When you have decided that you know the relative speeds of the two boats, change one item only of the tuning in one of them. Write it down in a book as you change it, and see what effect it has. If it improves performance, make the same change on the other boat and then try altering something else. If it has a bad effect, put it back where it was and try again.

Most helmsmen like a small amount of weather helm when beating to windward. If the boat does not have enough, it can be induced by raking the mast aft, thus moving the centre of effort towards the stern. Equally, if you have decided to rake the mast more in an effort to improve windward performance, be prepared to feel more weather helm. On the other hand, if the boat has too much weather helm, raking the mast forward will help to cure it. Raking the mast, however, will only effect minor alterations in trim and, if the tendency to weather helm is pronounced, a change in mainsail thrust will cure it best. This can often be done by bending the mast or taking in a slab reef along the foot to flatten the mainsail, or simply by pulling hard down on a Cunningham hole (if the mainsail is not film laminate). If these don't work, try getting the Sail Maker to trim some cloth from the leech of the mainsail, to remove area from aft of the centre of lateral resistance.

The International One Design class at Cowes decided in 1962 that they were afflicted in this way, so they had 14 in cut off the foot length of their mainsails at the clew, and faired the reduction up to the head. This cured the excessive weather helm and actually made them faster to windward. Had they been a handicap class their rating would also have been reduced, due to the smaller E measurement.

It is sometimes possible to have your cake and eat it.

BROACHING

Modern fin and skeg offshore designs, while benefiting from increased hydrodynamic efficiency and usually from a reduction in wetted area, sometimes suffer from a tendency to broach, particularly when close reaching in a stiff breeze under spinnaker; this is a case of extreme weather helm in a particular situation. Such craft frequently have fairly firm quarters and a fine bow so that, when the boat heels, the stern tends to lift and the bow digs in; this is accentuated by the downard pull of the spinnaker from the mast-

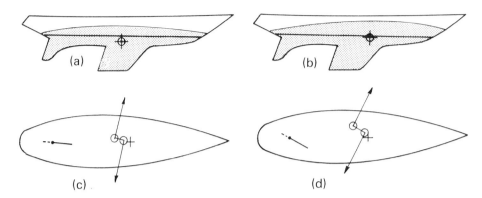

Fig. 8.14 Broaching
The shaded portions of (a) and (b) show the difference in wetted area when a boat
is heeled on an even keel fore and aft under genoa as in (a), and when the bow is
buried on a close spinnaker reach as in (b); the latter moves the CLR forward,
increasing the force couple trying to turn the boat into wind. If we now look down
on the CE/CLR relationship, we can see that in (c) there is a small couple easily
countered by the rudder; this is increased when the boat heels under spinnaker in
(d) as the CLR moves ahead as shown in (b) above, and the CE moves to leeward
as the boat heels. When this becomes too great for the rudder to control, the boat
gyrates wildly into wind; this is precipitated if the effect of the rudder is reduced
because it is half out of the water (as can happen when a transom mounted rudder
is heeled excessively).

head and a shift of the CE to leeward. The centre of lateral resistance thus
moves forward with increasing heel, so that there is a mounting tendency for
the bows to push up into the wind.

At rest, therefore, the centre of effort of the mainsail and foretriangle area
should normally be some way in front of the CLR, so that the two are
correctly balanced when the boat is under way. Movement of the CE to
leeward of the keel as the boat heels increases the broaching couple. I will
digress into the next chapter at this point and suggest that, if your boat has
this habit of broaching badly in a breeze, it is no good raking the mast, or
even cutting down the area of the mainsail as an attempt at a *sole* solution.

You should consult a Naval Architect, who may suggest moving the mast,
trimming area from the mainsail leech, fitting a dagger plate aft and/or
increasing the depth and area of the rudder. But you can't do any of these in
the middle of a race, so you should bring the crew right aft to help lift the
bow, and you should do all you can to reduce the angle of heel. Thrust must
be dumped from the mainsail before the situation gets out of hand. Release
the kicker and allow the boom to sky clear of the water, so that wind escapes
from the top of the sail and eases pressure. This demands instant action, so
one man should be on the kicker and a second on the main sheet – the

traveller has little effect under these conditions. Hydraulic vangs can be rather slow to react to a sudden release, so some form of block and lever system is better. In addition, keep weight aft and to windward to hold the bows up and the mast as upright as possible.

Releasing pressure from the spinnaker will reduce the tendency to bury the bow and also bring the boat more upright. As the wind is now entering at the foot, letting the sheet run out will collapse the sail and quickly restore control, but of course it loses speed.

Light displacement craft with short keels or dagger plates are so critical that they can broach going to windward, or at least on a very close reach. There is usually nothing which can be done to reduce heel by shifting more weight to windward – the crew should already be hanging on to the weather rail by their toenails. In the same way, the Cunningham should already be hard down to keep the mainsail draft forward. But bending the mast will flatten the sail and help considerably, as will raking the whole rig forward if the rules allow.

Read my words in Chapter XIV about the pros and cons of reaching under spinnaker or headsail, and have second thoughts about hoisting the big one when you are less than 75° to the apparent wind above force 3, unless you have a really flat-cut reaching spinnaker, genniker, star-cut spinnaker or what-have-you.

Chapter IX

Trim

CHOICE OF SAILS

Trimming sails starts in the clubhouse with the correct selection of which sails to use. Those ocean-racing men with only one mainsail can smile at the indecision of the dinghy or Dragon owner as he worries over the weather forecast. I recall Stewart Morris at the Prince of Wales' Cup race at Weymouth some time ago. He used to work up for this race for about six months, and the POW week was the final tuning of a precision instrument, which reached its peak on the day of the Prince of Wales' Cup race itself. He went to bed at nine the previous evening and was awake in time to hear every weather forecast from the farmers' bulletin at 06·45 onwards.

The Thursday of the week dawned with somewhat unsettled weather for the big race. Stewart selected a new medium weather mainsail and started to rig his boat well in advance. All the time his eyes kept wandering to the clouds, and he paced the dinghy park restlessly. Finally he changed mainsails for an old flat faithful which had served him well in the past. But it was obvious that he was not happy, from the way he kept asking his crew, other competitors, and even myself, what we thought the wind would do. After another glance at the sky, he changed back again to his first choice, and we started out on the long push over the sand towards the sea. We had lifted the boat off the trolley, which I was preparing to take back to his berth, when he took yet another look at the sky.

'If any wind comes out of that cloud I'm sunk,' he muttered and hurried up the beach once more. He reappeared with a sail bag and threw it into the boat.

'I can always put it aboard the committee vessel just before the start,' he grinned as he shoved off.

He must have used up enough nervous energy in those thirty minutes to ruin the chances of a lesser man. But the POW was almost a religion to Stewart, and he is the exception who proves the rule, for he won it again that day; but he was a tired man in the evening. I have always thought that part

162

of the reason for his indecision was that his medium weather sail was relatively unknown to him, for he had not had it very long, whereas his heavy weather sail was tried and proved, and thus was a known factor. None of the top helmsmen likes using gear on an important occasion which has not been proved under actual racing conditions, and this holds especially good for sails.

Stewart Morris usually had two mainsails currently in favour, but there are those who have three. This is too many in my opinion, for you will be haunted by the fear of a wrong decision long after the choice has been irrevocably made. I was a far happier man when I got rid of my very light weather mainsail for the Dragon, and contented myself with two sails. One was for winds up to force 4, and the second was for force 4 upwards. During any season in England, the number of races which are completed in ghosting conditions can be counted on the fingers of one hand. You are more likely to be caught out by winds of force 1–2 increasing to force 3, then by them dying away to nothing. If you have an ultra-light weather sail, all the zippers and Cunningham holes in the world won't stop the boat being knocked down and generally overpowered as the wind increases, unless you have a really flexible mast.

Offshore racing and cruising men will only have one mainsail, but a selection of headsails will be at their disposal; the number and use of sails is controlled by the IOR, and reference should be made to the current rule book. If they are caught out by strengthening winds they can switch headsails accordingly, but this does not always happen, and I make no excuse for repeating the following warning. Many is the offshore racing man who has set his drifter of 2 oz Terylene or Dacron in force 1, only to find that the wind has slowly increased. The boat is going well, however, and it seems a shame to take off the sail; so he hangs on to it into force 2. What he does not realize is that the light canvas is being punished out of all proportion to its strength. Any woven cloth will stretch as the threads are pulled on the bias, and a light cloth will soon stretch past the point where it will resume its original shape as soon as the pressure is relaxed. With the wind forward of the beam a 2 oz sail should be taken off as soon as the wind goes above force 1, and a 3 or 4 oz sail should not be expected to deal with anything stronger than force 2.

This does not apply so much to ply-cloth sails or those made from film laminate. The latter in particular hold their shape very well over a wide wind range and for a long time; nevertheless, if you overstress one beyond its yield point once, you've blown it. What is more, it will never recover. Consult your Sail Maker when taking delivery, for he should give you the maximum apparent wind speed which a particular sail should never exceed.

I have digressed enough. We must assume that the correct choice of sails has been made (if, indeed, a choice exists; happy the man in many ways for whom it does not). Now comes the time to hoist them.

HOISTING SAIL

Before going further we must recall what happens to woven cloth when it is hoisted. The Sail Maker has built flow into the sail by means of making the luff rounded, and by tapering the appropriate panels. He also makes it slightly shorter than the stretched size, so that further induced flow can be put into it when it is pulled to its designed length. You will find that no successful fore and aft sail is made with the cloths running either parallel or at right angles to the luff; this is because of the bias stretch to which the cloth is subject when tension is off the threadline, and stretching helps it to achieve shape, as we discussed in Chapter IV.

Do not, therefore, be a slave to your black bands. Just because a sail is made to set between certain marks, there is no need always to pull it right out to those marks. You will not make a sail any bigger by stretching it, so you are not gaining area. There is only a certain amount of cloth in any sail, and no amount of pulling can put any more into it. If you increase the length of the luff by stretching it, the round to the leech of the sail must come in to compensate.

Here are half a dozen reasons why a particular mainsail may set better if it is short of its marks, by one or two inches on a dinghy and anything up to 8 or 9 in on a larger boat; they are in order of likelihood:

1. The sail was cut for wind strengths greater than those prevailing.
2. The luff is roped too tightly.
3. The sail has been altered at some time, changing its characteristics.
4. The gooseneck fitting is not as given to the Sail Maker.
5. The black bands are wrong.
6. The sail has not got enough cloth up the luff.

On the other hand, the sail may come easily to its marks, and still be undertensioned. This is where the Cunningham hole comes into its own, by enabling extra power to be exerted on the luff without overstepping the black bands. I shall go more fully into this device in Chapter XI.

Light Weather. Thus, in light weather, do not set up the mainsail halyard too tight, even to the point where a multitude of small wrinkles appears along the luff. When you have the flow as you want, take in what Uffa Fox called a 'nattigram' to allow for halyard stretch or a slight increase in wind, and make fast. Similar careful attention should be paid to the clew outhaul. It is important not to put too much tension on the foot tape in light weather or a fold will appear along the foot. The clew should be eased forward from its medium weather position, between 1 and 3 per cent of the foot length according to the inherent flatness of the sail. In these circumstances Jack Knights went so far as to suggest that dinghy owners should have a specially light boom in order not to drag the mainsail down too much and thus flatten it; I would not disagree with this slightly fastidious recommendation.

Heavy Weather. On the other hand, heavy weather demands a firm pull on halyard and outhaul to force the flow of Terylene or Dacron forward. It is safer to err on the ham-fisted side under these conditions, because once you have started it is simpler to ease the halyard if it is too tight, than to pull it harder. The sail may look a poor shape in the initial stages, but the wind will immediately blow the flow aft into its correct position, perhaps even too far if the halyard is not tight enough.

Fully moulded sails of ply-cloth or film laminate need to be looked at particularly carefully for shape when hoisted. Mainsails should go right to the black bands, genoas to the same point near the masthead sheave, when pulled firmly but not excessively on the luff. There is a danger of delamination when a Mylar or Melinex sail which is fitted with slide or hanks is underhoisted; this is because the attachments are subjected to local over-stressing. Halyards should be painted or whipped at a point to indicate the fully-up mark.

Before leaving the question of hoisting sail, do not forget to take the weight off the boom until the sail is up. If you let the boom hang on to a half-hoisted sail which is flogging about, you will run the risk of delaminating a Mylar/Melinex sail or overstretching the leech of Dacron/Terylene. This may sound obvious, but you would be surprised at the number of mainsails which are returned to the Sail Maker by their owners, complaining of a juddering leech for this reason. While we are on the subject, it may sound even more obvious not to pull a sail down by the leech, but it is amazing how an otherwise top class skipper will do this if he is in a hurry.

UNDER WAY

When checking a sail for correct trim under way there are three cardinal rules: first, always sight up the mast to see that it has no abnormalities on either tack; secondly, see that all leech lines are completely slack, for they can give a false impression if tight; finally, have a look at the sail in question from leeward and in front if possible, it will look totally different from this angle and will reveal its faults more easily.

MAINSAILS

Apart from the curve of the mainsail, there are two points to watch when beating to windward. The first is the amount of twist you allow the leech of the sail, and from this comes the position athwartships of the mainsheet traveller and the tension on the boom vang or kicking-strap. The second is the interrelation of the headsail and the mainsail, and from this comes the shape of the headsail leech.

Twist. When a mainsail suffers from twist, the head sags off to leeward and lifts earlier than the rest of the sail. To stop this, the boom has to be trimmed closer, which means that the lower half of the sail is too tightly sheeted for its own efficient working, and there will be more sideways thrust than necessary. If the boom is pulled down by a vang, twist will be reduced and the sail can thus be eased to give more forward thrust. It also makes the sail

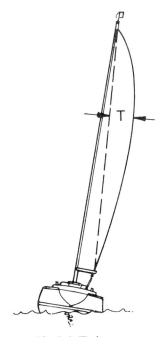

Fig. 9.1 Twist

Twist is the degree to which the upper part of a sail falls off to leeward (T), and thus presents a lower angle of incidence to the wind. We saw in Chapter 2 how wind gradient (Figure 2.17) frees a boat as wind speed increases with altitude, so some twist is desirable in all sails, depending on conditions. In calm weather with an overcast sky this is particularly true, because from 15 to 40 feet above sea level the local wind speed doubles, thus freeing the boat considerably. Under these conditions, Lowell North, sailmaker and World Star champion many times, has recommended one foot of twist (T) for every 15 feet of mainsail luff[37]; this makes a good starting point when considering trim.

more efficient, because wind flows off the top of a twisted sail. A limited amount of twist is, however, beneficial for tall sails, particularly in light conditions.

Mainsheet Traveller. For smooth water and light winds the traveller should be fairly well in towards the centreline of the boat. This will enable you to point better, and the slight hook to windward which it gives the lower leech will be more than offset by the greater speed made good to windward. Do not, therefore, try to eliminate all twist by pulling hard down on the mainsheet; the sail should not be flattened too much, and a certain amount of twist can be accepted to this end. As the wind increases towards force 4, however, it becomes vital to remove any tendency to hook to windward, so the traveller should be eased until the boom makes an angle of about 8° or 9° with the centreline of the boat. If you do not have a traveller, ease the sheet, having seen that the kicking-strap or boom vang is tight to reduce twist.

As the sea and wind both increase further, so should the traveller be eased to its fullest extent. If there is a lumpy sea, the boat will move more slowly than if the same wind were blowing over smooth water, so the apparent wind will be farther aft. The boom should therefore be out more to accept this. In addition, most boats go better into a chop if they are freed slightly and driven into it. The mainsail can therefore afford to be a little fuller, so the tack can be eased up if the wind is not so strong that a flat sail is necessary to avoid too much weather helm; see that the mast is not bent too much.

If the mainsail lifts near the head before the main body of the luff falls in, there is almost certainly too much twist. This can be corrected by easing the traveller and hardening the sheet to pull the boom down over the counter.

A boom which is trimmed too close will soon make itself felt through excess weather helm. As the wind increases, the flow in a woven mainsail will be forced aft and the boom will tend to rise. These will cause the lower leech to curve to windward, which will drive the bow round towards the wind. If the traveller is already eased fully, the luff of the sail should be tightened to draw the flow forward again (either by tacking down harder or by use of a Cunningham hole), and the clew pulled out more to flatten the lower leech. A bendy mast will probably be under maximum curvature already, due to the influence of the tension of the mainsheet; if it can safely be bent more (on dinghies by harsh use of the kicking-strap for instance), then you should do so. If your mainsail is film laminate, take in a slab reef as well as bending the mast. This will flatten the whole foot area, raise the boom and reduce weather helm; the boat heels less and is easier to control. The last resort should be to ease the mainsheet so that full power is not delivered, but this should also be done if the boat is obviously fighting the rudder and heeling too much. The loss of power from the mainsail must be weighed against the reduction in weather helm; it pays in many classes to ease the mainsail until it is lifting along its entire length in a stiff blow, because the easier rudder lets the headsail pull her along more quickly.

HEAVY WEATHER MAINSAIL

Most of us know that a heavy weather sail needs to be flatter than one cut for light or medium winds. We should beware, however, of cutting a mainsail so flat that it loses nearly all its drive. The ocean-racing man will have to

Plate 9.1 Twist
This Panther sailboard is using a fathead sail, which is designed to have extra area aloft so that the board shall maintain thrust when down in the troughs between large waves. Note how Gordon Way is holding the wishbone down in (a), thus eliminating twist to windward. Opposite, he has allowed the clew to rise, thus causing the sail to fall away at the head while reaching.   *David Eberlin*

forgive me for a while, because discussion on the requirements of a heavy weather mainsail does not directly concern him, as he is all too often prevented by the rules from having such a specialized sail. The upper third of a mainsail designed for strong winds for a dinghy or one of the two- or three-man keelboats should be quite flat, so that it presents little or no resistance to the wind and so that it 'feathers' easily on a beat; this will reduce the heeling moment. The middle third of the sail should start to take some shape, so that the lower third can be comparatively well rounded, particularly over the boom. It is from here that the boat will get its drive. The heeling effect is minimized because the centre of effort on such a sail will be fairly low down.

Most authorities agree that it does not often pay to have small mainsails for heavy weather racing in dinghies. Boats with full area may lose a little on the windward leg, but they will more than make up for it off the wind. It is far better to have flexible spars which can be controlled by the helmsman; this will take the excess fullness out of the mainsail, and make the boat easier to keep from too much heel. As mentioned in Chapter VII, there must be some means of controlling mast bend and, if the complication of setting up individual stops or chocks is to be avoided, an adjustable compression strut is often easiest for most small boats. The man who can set full sail and maintain control of his boat will normally have the legs of the man who either has a small mainsail or who rolls down a reef. There are, of course, exceptions to this rule but not many, and much depends on what is meant by 'maintain control' of the boat.

It is in heavy weather than the beneficial effects of a boom which bends slightly to leeward at the outer end will be felt. The reduction in drag and the easing of the lower leech will both have a marked effect on performance. Be careful, however, that the boom does not bend so much that it causes the whole leech to go slack, for this may give rise to a crease along the inner ends of the battens, especially in those classes like the 12 ft National which often have too much roach for the battens to support properly; it may also weaken the boom beyond the safety point for heavy weather.

The foregoing remarks are meant primarily for dinghies, but many of them can be applied to the offshore racing fleet as well, where the rules permit the use of specialized heavy weather mainsails, such as in racing round the buoys. The bigger boats, of course, often meet stronger winds than the dinghy fleet, and I do not pretend that they should seldom reef; we shall see more of this later in this chapter.

HEADSAILS

If you have a large overlapping headsail, either on a dinghy such as the 14 ft International or on an offshore racer, then you will not be able to ease your mainsail quite as much in heavy weather and still keep an efficient airflow, particularly if the genoa is a mastheader. You will have to be careful not to close the slot between the sails too much, and there will come a time when the boat will go faster with a smaller headsail, because she would otherwise by overpowered. A dinghy cannot switch headsails without too much loss of ground on a relatively short beat, but the keelboat will need at this stage either to change to an intermediate genoa, or to take a reef in the mainsail. An intermediate genoa can be sheeted hard in and the mainsail eased slightly because there will be a wider slot between the smaller genoa's leech and the lee side of the mainsail; a reefed mainsail will cause the boat to heel less, thus enabling the full-sized genoa to be kept at the main job of driving the boat along. The tendency nowadays is towards the latter solution.

It becomes progressively more important to examine your headsail leech critically as the wind freshens. The flow in the sail will tend to move aft under the action of the wind, and any tendency to curl at the leech will be accentuated. This can be helped somewhat by pulling harder on the headsail

Plate 9.2 Trim – the Slot
You must be careful not to close the slot too much. A crew member standing in the slot will cause turbulence and loss of thrust. Note the curl in the genoa leech; the lady is completing the task of lousing up the airstream.   *Eileen Ramsay*

sheet, but be sure that the pull is at the correct angle and beware of over-stretching the canvas. A light sail will curl more than a heavy one, and should be changed as soon as this starts to happen. At all events you should avoid the extremely unfavourable airflow created by a tight genoa leech. Make sure that you have not got the leech line tight, and also see that the sheet lead is not too far forward. It is better to have a genoa leech which vibrates, than to have a quiet leech which curls to windward. The former will allow the wind to run off freely, but the latter will direct it into the lee side of the mainsail.

HEAVY WEATHER HEADSAILS

When it comes to heavy weather headsails, dinghies and the smaller keel-boats most probably have the one-sized sail, which should be cut flat with rather more hollow to the leech than a medium weather headsail, in order to open the slot. If a small headsail is allowed, one may be used in really strong winds before the mainsail is reefed. This is an efficient way of reducing sail area, while keeping the full sized mainsail for reaching and running. Here again, however, the winning boats are often those who hold on to full sail, while the lesser men change down. An effective way to overcome this conflicting requirement is to have a full size genoa cut with a good deal of hollow to the leech, thus opening the slot and also reducing sail area less drastically. The bigger boats will have a range of headsails from which to choose, descending in size as the wind increases. With this in mind, it is easy to see why the largest headsails in a boat's wardrobe have the lightest cloth, and vice versa.

ADJUSTABLE LUFF HEADSAILS

What I said just now about tension on the luff of the mainsail also applies to headsails of woven cloth which have means of adjusting their luff tension. If the sail is adjustable over the luff wire, you will have some form of downhaul at the tack. You will also have a useful datum from which to judge the amount of pull you are applying: when the tack of the sail reaches the bottom of the wire, you have set up the sail for the strongest winds it should encounter. The wire itself is often painted or served by the Sail Maker, so that you can tell how much tension you have applied by noting how much wire is showing at the tack. If the headsail has a tape luff, you may either adjust it on the halyard, in which case you should mark the halyard, or by means of a tack downhaul which should be similarly marked. The former is the more efficient system, because the tack is then always as low as possible, thus keeping the driving force low, but the latter is simpler to operate and therefore preferable. Remember that adjustable luff headsails will alter their clew positions as they adjust, and the sheet lead must be varied accordingly.

While on the subject of headsails, see that the luff is as straight as possible when beating to windward. The forestay must not be allowed to sag too far off to leeward in the pursuit of mast rake and slack rigging as discussed earlier in this book, or the boat will not point properly. No boat can have an absolutely straight luff to her headsail, for this would bring unacceptable stresses to the mast, and this factor must be borne in mind when setting up the forestay. If there is too much sag to the headsail when on the wind, however, equal adjustment to *both* the forestay and its opposite numbers towards the rear must be made if you are not to rake the mast out of its desired position. 'Opposite numbers' can include the pull of the mainsheet, runners, permanent backstays, and shrouds, depending on where the forestay attaches to the mast. You may also have to readjust the jumper stays.

The whole question of a straight forestay can lead to excessive loading on the mast of a large boat, and it is one where the Sail Maker's requirement of no sag to the headsail luff can conflict with the designer's ideas on what the boat will stand. I remember sailing in the 12-metre *Norsaga* when she had her first outing, after re-rigging as the Red Duster group's test bed for a new

Plate 9.3 Trim – Headsail Luff (1)
To judge by the fact that she is wearing a burgee, this boat is not racing – yet she
presumably does not want to take longer than necessary to get to windward, so she
should sweat up on her genoa halyard. *Author*

challenger for the America's Cup. Besides the owner Lord Craigmyle, there
were on board Arthur Robb who had undertaken the re-design, and Franklin
Ratsey-Woodroffe who had been responsible for the sails. Franklin took one
look at the genoa luff and ordered more tension on the weather-runner, and
on the backstay and forestay turnbuckles. He returned to the bow of the
boat, had another look and ordered more turns on the rigging. Arthur Robb
watched this for a few moments and then went to have a look up the mast.
Finally he called a halt to the proceedings, and the two opposing requirements were forced into a compromise. At all events a straight luff is

173

Plate 9.4   Trim – Headsail Luff (2)
This is what the genoa in Pl. 9.3 on the previous page looks like when sighted up
the luff. It will cost the boat at least five degrees in pointing ability, or five miles on
a 60-mile leg – enough to put her the wrong side of a tide rip.   *Author*

important for good performance on the wind, and I make no apology for
repeating it. This means a tight forestay (preferably a rod) on a boat which
has straight spars and tight rigging; and sufficient movement on the mast,
coupled with a forestay slightly slacker than the jib luff wire, on a boat
which has slack rigging.

A headsail should usually be cut on the flat side rather than the opposite.
Naturally a full headsail can be useful in light airs, but a flat sail can
normally be given a little extra draft by easing the sheet, whereas over-
hardening the sheet will only pull a full headsail out of shape and will not
make it much flatter.

If a woven headsail is too full, the flow will be forced aft as the wind
increases in the same way as happens in a mainsail, and it will tend to backwind the mainsail. There will also be a rearward component of the driving
force at the leech.

The moral of this is that headsails should err on the flat side and their
sheets should not always be pulled hard in unless it is blowing fairly hard; it

174

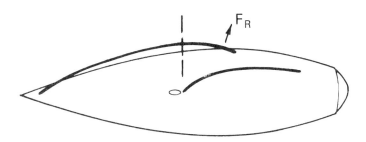

Fig. 9.2 Genoa Bellied Leech
If there is a belly to the leech area of a genoa, besides choking the slot, there will be an appreciable aft component to thrust, all of which contributes to drag and heeling moment.

is the owner's task to check the enthusiasm of his sheet hands. As the wind grows lighter, so should the sheet be eased further and the fairlead brought inboard if there is adjustment. It is good practice when racing neck and neck with another boat to try easing the headsail an inch or two; you will be surprised how often this will make just the difference to your speed. Also check your sheet lead for fore and aft position; a small variation may give you enough extra speed to establish an overlap at the buoy. Don't forget the findings of the Southampton University research team, which reveal that headsail sheeting is more critical than mainsail sheeting[12]. Corny Shields said that he usually had his headsail sheet leads further forward than most people, as he considered that this gives a better shape to the lower half of the sail[38]. It will certainly free off the foot and allow it to take up a better aerofoil shape, but watch out for a curling leech. I do not imagine that the American master advocated more than half a degree or so, and I would be the last person to contradict him.

On the other hand, let me here say that another American, Jack Sutphen of Ratsey & Lapthorn Inc., said 'as a rule of thumb, it generally is better to have the leads too far aft than too far forward'. This shows that the whole question is open to experiment, and that they were dealing in very small differences. It is more than likely that both were ending at the same point, having started from a slightly different datum. Each helmsman has his own preference and I feel that Sutphen is the more orthodox in his approach; Shields confessed that he was in a minority in his point of view.

Reaching. The question of adjustment holds doubly true when reaching. The headsail hand should play the sheet constantly to take advantage of wind shifts. It may well be that too tight a headsail is backwinding the mainsail and thus giving the helmsman a false impression. Easing the headsail sheet

Plate 9.5 Tell-Tales
Here *Sanction* has the tell-tales of genoa and mainsail streaming nicely; note the shape lines (and the straight genoa luff). Both her Mylar sails have been reinforced at the leech, and a lot of attention has been paid to the head of the mainsail.
Chris Howard-Williams

will let the mainsail go off that little bit extra, and both sails will give more drive. Watch the luff of the sail about a third of the way up, ease until it just starts to quiver and then harden in very slightly; keep feeling for the quiver so that you have always given the sail as much sheet as it will take. Just because the boat is now off the wind, the constant shifts in wind direction which you were at such pains to chase when close hauled have not disappeared. The same applies to the headsail, and the dedicated racing owner will not have the genoa sheet cleated, but there will be a trimmer constantly easing and hardening to take advantage of the puffs. If the rules permit, switch the sheet to a hook or snatch block further out and further forward than the normal fairlead (if you don't have an adjustable track), as

176

suggested in Chapter VIII. If the sail is not too big and the wind too strong, the sheet should be held in the hand, either on or off the winch, and the crew encouraged to play it as he or she sees fit.

TELL-TALES

Tell-tales are one of the most effective trim indicators, because they give instant indication of airflow over the sail (breakdown of laminar flow into separated flow is bad news, as we saw in Chapter II); they are also certainly the cheapest. They should be wool or nylon of contrasting colour to the sail, and are best fitted as shown in Fig. 9.3. The object is to maintain all streamers flowing evenly. If a windward tally lifts, sheet the sail harder or bear away; if it is the leeward streamer which reveals loss of attached flow, ease the sheet or luff. The mnemonic for the forgetful is TASTES: Turn Away or Sheet Towards Erratic Streamers.

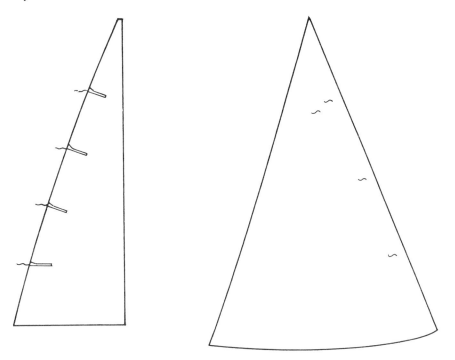

Fig. 9.3 Tell-Tales

Tell-tales should be about 6 inches long and of wool or nylon. Dark colours often show through white sails but, if there is any problem, small windows can be fitted to the genoa if rules permit. Make sure that tell-tales on a headsail are fitted so that they cannot quite reach the luff, or they will catch on it in light winds; they can even snag on the stitching of a seam, so keep them well clear. The second tell-tale at the genoa head should be at about the mid-chord position, and clear of the one at the luff.

Mainsail. If tell-tales at the mainsail leech flick round the back of the sail, clearly there is unwanted turbulence and normally the leech should be eased by slackening the sheet or kicker slightly, or possibly by bending the mast.

Genoa. If the genoa tell-tales break first either at the top or the bottom, halyard tension of an adjustable luff sail may be wrong, but it is more likely to be the sheet lead. If the bottom windward one goes first, the lead must go aft to bring the sail closer to the wind at the tack; and *vice versa* for the top one. The opposite holds good if it is a leeward tell-tale which breaks first high or low. Adjustment must be accompanied by altered sheet tension. The extra tell-tale at the head of the genoa in Fig. 9.3 gives an indication of how much twist is required in the sail, and it usually responds to sheet tension. The interplay of all these factors is a matter of trial and error for each boat in different conditions of wind and sea.

Tactics. We saw in Chapter II how oversheeting on a reach causes excessive turbulence. If we look back at Figs. 2.21 and 2.25, it does not need much imagination to picture the effect which this will have on the airflow over the sails of a boat which is dead to leeward or very slightly astern. Even when the leading boat's sails are trimmed to best advantage, the leeward boat suffers from the wind shadow in which she is sailing. Extra turbulence will cause extra suffering, so for short periods it can be exploited by the leader for temporary advantage. The sort of situation I have in mind is just before the leeward boat is about to claim an inside overlap at a mark. If the overlap exists five or six lengths from the mark, try trimming your sails too far inboard, in an attempt to break it before the critical two lengths point is reached. You have nothing to lose, for you must give way if your opponent maintains his overlap; if you break it, you go round the mark clear ahead. But be careful, because oversheeting will lose you speed as well as him – it's a question of who loses more than the other.

REEFING

A badly reefed sail will materially affect the speed of the boat, not so much because it does not produce the maximum driving component, but because this component will be heavily reduced by increased drag and knockdown effect, caused through too much fullness aft. If you allow the sail to be sloppy over the boom, you will form a bag near the leech and this will hold the boat back and heel her over without producing any drive. It is here that Illingworth hauling-aft loops and a carefully shaped roller boom pay for their keep. The fixed reef man will be able more easily to adjust a continuous lacing reef than one tied with individual points. Those two great authorities, one on each side of the Atlantic, Wallace E. Tobin and John Illingworth have both written their opinion on reefing. They are united in their verdict that most people roll in and shake out their reefs too late. You will make a neater job of reefing if you do it before the wind gets too strong; when the wind starts to go down, you will outdistance your rivals if you overcome your natural desire to let the next watch increase sail when they come on in an hour's time. There should be no excuse for this laziness now that jiffy reefing has made it so quick and easy.

When dinghies or small keelboats have to reef mainsails, it is often only really necessary on the windward leg. This is where a simple system like the Banks reefing gear can pay dividends, in that it will enable you to set full sail again for the reaching leg; but remember that you may have to roll down again for the next beat, and you should be confident of making a good job of it.

HEAVY WEATHER TECHNIQUE

I do not intend to get too involved in technique, but it is difficult to explain the requirements relating to sails in heavy weather without going slightly into the way it should be done. You may not agree with the methods I advocate, but the principles are sound enough; providing you arrive at the same result, and know why you are doing what you are doing, we shall not argue.

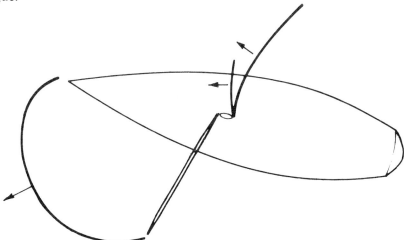

Fig. 9.4 Rhythmic Rolling

Divergent thrust forces contribute to rhythmic rolling. Note how a section through the top quarter of the mainsail pushes to windward. In addition, the spinnaker sheet has been eased too much, giving further windward push. Quartering seas and gusting winds both contribute to the unpleasant rolling condition, which in turn can lead to a broach when all the factors mount up.

Twist is one of the faults which must be corrected as much as possible in heavy weather. Not only does excessive twist mean that, when beating to windward, the boom has to be further in than need be the case but, when sailing downwind, it also promotes what John Illingworth christened rhythmic rolling. Because the head of the sail sags far enough forward to contribute pressure to windward, there comes a time when the action of the waves on the hull and the forces acting on the sails combine to cause the phenomenon we all know. This is aggravated when the spinnaker sheet is allowed to slack off too far, thus adding to the windward tendency.

Beating to windward in a dinghy is often a matter of keeping the boat upright and staying as close to the wind as possible. A heavy crew combination can free sheets slightly to drive the boat through the water, keep their sails full and sit right out to hold the boat upright. By playing the sails enough to allow them to quiver, but not to flog, they can hold the boat upright by a combination of weight and minor playing of the sails. A light crew cannot hope to adopt the same tactics without a trapeze, and must rely on a bendy mast. With kicking-strap and mainsheet bowsed hard down, the top of the mainsail will feather so as to give least drag and heeling moment. The headsail is kept hard in for as long as possible and the boat is balanced between being too close to the wind and becoming overpowered through being too free. This is a solution which has to be practised assiduously to achieve competence. In both cases remember that it is necessary to have some power in the sail, and that this is best placed in the foot where it has least heeling effect, and will help you climb over the big waves.

The mainsheet traveller should be right out, and the kicker or vang adjusted to bend the mast according to the amount of power you can control, which in turn depends largely on your weight (assuming skill as a constant). As soon as you come off the wind, the kicking-strap should be hard enough to stop the boom from rising too much, but it should not be quite as tight as usual, so that some of the strain is taken off the rig. In addition, a boom end which is constantly dipping in the water stops you spilling wind and slows the boat. A centre mainsheet fitting will help flatten the sail, but may take a little getting used to at the start. It is not my job to tell you how to do this, merely to say that I think that it is a device which amply repays its incorporation and will lead to a more flexible sail. A boom end fitting, in fact, allows the boom to bend upwards in the middle, which is exactly the opposite of what we want as the wind increases, for this will only make the sail fuller over the boom.

SPINNAKERS

The spinnaker is so important that it has a chapter to itself. Correct trimming of this sail can win a race as easily as its mishandling can lose one.

SAIL HANDLING

It goes without saying that sail handling should at all times be smooth and efficient. A good crew member will spend the first half-hour on board a strange boat finding out where all the various sheets and halyards lead, how the boom vang is rigged, the purpose of all the winches, and the location of all sails not in use, together with ancillary gear such as reefing handle, tack pendants, handy billy, spinnaker net, etc. Some of the best crew drill I have seen was displayed on board the little Dutch sloop *Hestia*. One year the late Mr Van Beuningen had ordered a quadrilateral with such a high upper clew that we had to put three sheets on it, instead of two. The lowest sheet led through the normal genoa fairlead, and the two upper sheets went via a couple of 'monkeys' running on the permanent backstay, the upper one of which needed to be some 20 ft above deck. Besides their sheets, both these 'monkeys' had halyards and downhauls of their own so that they could be trimmed to the correct height. This meant six lines at the backstay alone.

We set the sail in a light breeze of about force 2 and put her on the wind while we sought the correct ·angle for the upper sheets. After a certain amount of experiment we felt that we had the sail setting well, and the owner announced that we would try it on the other tack. This meant lowering both 'monkeys' by means of their downhauls, unreeving the two upper sheets, reeving the sheets from the other side, and hauling the 'monkeys' back up the backstay. Meanwhile, the boat was being tacked in the normal way and the lowest sheet had to be tended as well. The whole operation proceeded with the utmost calm and efficiency, just as if it were the most normal operation afloat – but remember that this was the first time that the sail had ever been aboard. I know, for I took it straight from the loft to the boat before we sailed. It was obvious that Mr Van Beuningen had worked out the drill beforehand and had practised his crew in it.

Headfoil. The biggest step forward in headsail handling in the second half of this century has been the headfoil® or grooved forestay. It not only speeds up handling generally, but gives a better airflow at this important part of the aerofoil, avoids bald headed changes and does not snag a spinnaker in the way that the serrations of a conventional laid wire will do.

Headsail Cartridge. Headsail changes can also be speeded up by the cartridge system, such as Ratsey's Jibswitch®. If a foil or grooved forestay is used, special slides are fitted to the sail and a short length of foil is removed from the bottom of the forestay, with the lowered sail bunched on it; the replacement sail, also stowed on its own cartridge, is clipped in place and lined up with the groove in the foil. The sail is thus ready for immediate

Plate 9.6 Ketch Rig
The somewhat cluttered look of these sails reveals how important it is to trim
properly. If one is wrong it will interfere with most of the others, but they seem to
have got it right. The boat is conveniently rigged, for her working canvas is
divided into main, mizzen and (not hoisted) boom staysail; she also has a roller jib
on the topmast stay for use in light weather.   *Author*

hoisting, and times for headsail changes have been cut dramatically. Similar systems have been evolved for use with standard piston hanks or snap hooks, but they are not quite so convenient.

TRIM TIPS

Nobody can learn all about trim from a book, because each boat differs in different conditions – and these include wind, water, tune of the rig and, indeed, mood of the helmsman. But it obviously pays to read what others have found, and some broad generalisations can be helpful. Jim Allsopp, of sailmaking and International Star fame, suggested ten points at a 'Smart Course' run by North Sails in London[39].

1. Always sail on a lift.
2. Stay between the opposition and the next mark.
3. Trim the main so the upper tell-tale flows behind the leech (i.e. he likes less twist than normal).
4. Stream the mid-girth main tell-tale evenly.
5. Stream all genoa tell-tales evenly.
6. Never stall the leeward tell-tales (i.e. don't fall away too much).
7. Keep the spinnaker clews level.
8. Keep the spinnaker luff just on the break.
9. Don't forget your sea-sick pills.
10. Never race with your wife.

He went on to suggest lightheartedly that 12-metres are no fun: 'just a lead mine – but the night life is fun.'

Trim Lines. Sailmaker and America's Cup sail trimmer Robbie Doyle has advocated stencilling a short line on the headsail clew to give the optimum lead of the sheet when this has been established[40]; Fig. 9.5. This enables the correct lead to be regained when sheets are eased (move the lead forward until the sheet lines up again) and is particularly helpful with a reaching headsail, where wind angle is seldom identical each time the sail is set.

Shape Stripes. Addition of shape stripes across both mainsail and genoa will help the sail trimmer recognise whether he has got a smooth entry with maximum flow at the correct distance along the chord. These are also shown in Fig. 9.5.

Forestay Sag. The most effective way to adjust a headsail's flow is through the backstay – indeed, it is the only way to alter the camber of a film laminate genoa. If the forestay sags even a couple of inches, the headsail will

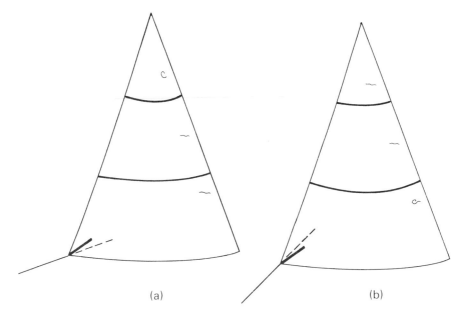

Fig. 9.5 Trim and Shape Lines

In (a) the top windward tell-tale has broken, so that part of the sail needs to be sheeted closer to the wind; move the fairlead forward. This will bring the projection of the sheet into line with the trim line marked at the clew. The reverse is the case with (b). Note how the shape lines at one third and two thirds height reveal the amount of camber in the sail.

Fig. 9.6 Genoa Stowing

Flake the genoa as you would a mainsail (see Figure 15.2), and place a temporary tie round the finished package to hold it together while it is stowed into a long bag. Head, tack and clew are then readily identifiable for the sail to be hoisted neatly from the bag – which should have hold-down ties strategically placed for the mooring cleat and/or toe-rail.

184

fall away from the centre line of the boat and become fuller, so the sail trimmer can increase or decrease camber by easing or tightening the backstay. As with all trim, use this with caution. If the backstay is eased too much in the pursuit of more power, the boat won't point and the whole rig can slam in a seaway, with attendant disruption to the airflow.

Genoa Hoisting. My final tip on trim paradoxically starts when the genoa is taken down. All too often the sail's next appearance entails it being 'poured' out of its bag on to the foredeck. Besides being unwieldly in a breeze, this merely adds to the time taken to locate the three corners before hoisting it. If the genoa is always folded and stowed as shown in Fig. 9.6, much time and frustration will be saved – and the sail will be less likely to attract leech creases.

Chapter X

Working Sails

One of the pleasures of owning a boat, no matter what her size, is to indulge in planning extensions to her wardrobe. This exercise usually takes place during the winter, and has the advantage that it does not cost anything, at least while it stays in the planning stage. The following three chapters are designed to help these daydreams, and I have listed some of the more popular sails to be found in an inventory. I have deliberately stuck to the more conventional sails which may be found on the average yawl, ketch, sloop or cutter, or else the list would have been never ending. The schooner owner will therefore find nothing here to help him design a fisherman staysail or a golly-wobbler; but there are regrettably not many schooners about these days. Similarly, I do not mention the flying jib, the square sail or the mizzen spinnaker, as these are all too rare.

I had thought of writing this section alphabetically, that is to say that balloon headsails would come first and yankee jibs last. This, however, presents problems of natural succession, besides the fact that many sails are known by two or more names. I have accordingly written about them in groups, and the reader will have to turn to the index first if he wants to find one particular sail quickly.

The percentage in brackets immediately following the name of the sail, represents a guide to its cloth weight. All sails are related to a yardstick of the standard weight of fully woven cloth for the working sails for that particular boat, which is 100 per cent. Thus a yacht with a mainsail and working headsail of 8 oz cloth will have an intermediate genoa (85 to 100 per cent) between $6\frac{1}{2}$ and 8 oz; a similar sail for a standard working canvas of 6 oz would be between 5 and 6 oz. If you want a specialist cloth such as 2-ply Dacron or Terylene, or a film laminate such as Mylar or Melinex, you should seek the advice of a specialist Sail Maker as explained in Chapter III.

MAINSAIL (100 per cent of cloth weight of working sails)

The mainsail and the working genoa are the two most important sails on the boat: the latter because it produces most of the drive when it is set, and the former because it is up most of the time. On a dinghy or one of the smaller inshore two- and three-man keelboats, of course, they will be the only sails apart from the spinnaker. It is important that they should work well together, and they should preferably be made by the same Sail Maker. If you are going to be unwise enough to provide your ship with second rate sails, at least ensure that the mainsail and genoa come from a good firm.

Do not be misled into ordering an all-purpose mainsail of a cloth which is much lighter than the recommended weight, as derived from the table I have given in Chapter III. This is especially true if a light weight is dictated by reasons of economy and not of aerodynamic efficiency. At the risk of boring you, let me repeat that a light weave may not tear, but it will stretch out of shape as soon as it is subjected to any weight of wind. I shall have something more to say about this under the section on light weather sails in the next chapter.

An all-purpose mainsail should have its flow just forward of the sail's mid-point, and it should have a reasonable degree of fullness over the boom. A narrow boat will normally need a flatter mainsail than a beamy one, because the headsails of the former will have a narrower sheeting base than the latter, and will thus tend to backwind more. The amount of headsail overlap also has its effect in this respect: the greater the overlap, the flatter the mainsail. In addition a large penalty overlap may produce a case for having the maximum flow of the mainsail a little farther aft, so that the slot is formed according to the principles we saw in Chapter II; improved sail-making, with a fine luff entry, has increased this trend in recent years. A dinghy will normally be able to carry a rather fuller mainsail than an ocean-racer because its spars will be able to take out some of the fullness by bending, be it ever so little, and also because a dinghy will not have to stand up to the strong winds which can buffet a yacht offshore; see also the graph at Fig. 2.8.

We have already seen that a depth of flow, or camber, of 10 per cent of the chord is a reasonable amount of fullness for medium weather, and that 5 per cent is the figure we can expect to be efficient for a heavy weather sail. In any case, flow should be carried right down a mainsail so that there is plenty of drive low down near the boom, and it can always be flattened with a slab reef.

We have also seen that a high aspect ratio is efficient in reducing the effect of induced drag at the foot. I go more fully into this question later, in Chapter XVIII *Design and Rating*. Suffice it to say here that a mainsail luff length should not be more than just over three times the length of the foot, unless the yacht is undercanvassed for her size or there are special considerations which apply, e.g. with catamarans or to achieve a desired rating.

Plate 10.1 Mylar Sails
Sometimes a Mylar mainsail is doubled for the full length of each side of the leech, as with *Ultimatum* (K 734) here; sometimes it has a series of reinforcing patches, as with *Whirlwind VI* (K 1990, ex-*Imp*).   *Chris Howard-Williams*

188

Battens are almost always limited in length by the rules under which a particular boat is sailing. The length of battens will, in turn, determine the amount of roach which the Sail Maker can safely put on the leech of a mainsail, and still expect to stand. A batten will normally support one third of its own length outside the straight line from the headboard to the clew. You go beyond this limit at your peril, as we have discussed earlier.

The best aerodynamic efficiency is obtained from a mainsail which runs in grooves in both the mast and boom, because wind will then not be able to escape from windward to leeward between the spar and the sail, as is the case when slides are used. However, a mast groove is not seamanlike where the mainsail would normally be left bent to the spars when sailing is over, because the sail has to come right off the mast when it is lowered; slides are normal in this case, and we can generalize that it occurs where the mainsail area reaches around 250 sq ft.

Virtually the only disadvantage of a boom groove is that a vang cannot be passed round the boom at any point along its length to make a kicking-strap: either an adjustable ring, or specially reinforced attachment points have to be provided at two or more places, and these have to be recessed if the boom is a roller.

I shall not repeat here all the arguments put forward in Chapter VII regarding roller reefing *vis-à-vis* points or lacing reefing. Suffice it to say that, in the absence of jiffy reefing, I feel that the average offshore yacht of up to 35 ft water-line length would need to consider carefully before adopting anything other than a roller boom, with a row of emergency lacing in the deep reef position.

This does not, of course, preclude a slab reef being incorporated in any mainsail from a dinghy upwards, and I shall have more to say on this subject (and that of Cunningham holes) in the next chapter, when we come to examine light weather sails. It should be remembered here that these devices can be incorporated to add to the flexibility of an otherwise medium weather mainsail.

MIZZEN (75 per cent of cloth weight of working sails)

The main advantages of a mizzen are twofold. First, it offers a useful quick reef to the cruising man: a yawl or ketch under mizzen and headsail alone gives a most comfortable ride, even in the strongest winds. Secondly, it can help add some bite to the helm if it is strapped in hard on the wind. For these reasons it should be made of cloth which will stand up to a blow. It does not need to be as heavy as the mainsail, because its area is usually substantially less, and thus the total weight of wind in the sail is less. Nevertheless it presents a good argument against deciding cloth weight on area alone and it should not be more than two weights lighter than its mainsail, and only one

Plate 10.2 Static Test Rig
A 14 ft International mainsail, a Dragon mainsail and spider-web genoa, and a suit for a cruiser being examined on the static test rig.   *Ratsey & Lapthorn*

if its area is more than one-third that of the mainsail. For the racing man, the mizzen is not heavily rated under the IOR, and the second mast confers the relatively lightly taxed area of the mizzen staysail when off the wind.

When beating to windward, the mizzen is operating permanently in the dirty wind of the mainsail, so its apparent wind is at a finer angle (if such turbulence can be said to have an angle at all). It should thus be cut flat and sheeted hard. It also helps if the leech is not too long, so that a firm downward pull can be exerted on the boom, which is still out of the way of the sunbathers on the afterdeck (a serious consideration not to be lightly ignored, let me add). A row of reefing eyelets can be incorporated by the pessimistic, even on the smallest mizzen, in case the foot of the sail should tear.

WORKING HEADSAILS (100 per cent of cloth weight of working sails)

A working headsail should usually be the same weight as its mainsail, with only rare exceptions, such as when the latter is unduly large and therefore is, in fact, one weight heavier than the standard for the size of boat.

Unless considerations of rig or area dictate otherwise, the working staysail of a cutter, or working headsail of a sloop should be cut with the clew approximately level with the main boom, and so that it does not foul the mast or shrouds. This is so that it will not pick up water in a fresh breeze, the helmsman can see under it, and it will not chafe too much. Battens should only be used if the sail is tall and narrow, say with an angle at the head of less than 20°, because the simpler the sail the better. It should, of course, be cut flat since it will normally be used in fairly strong winds. A mitre cut working headsail will usually lead to a fairlead so that the sheet is below an imaginary prolongation of the mitre aft.

One-design dinghies and two- and three-man keelboats with small headsails (that is to say, without overlapping genoa jibs), such as the Enterprise, Fireball, Star, 420, International One Design and Soling, will need rather different consideration from the simplification set forth above. They will certainly need a flat cut headsail for heavy weather, and one with a little more draft in it for light to medium going. Not disposing of a large jib for light weather, they could well have the latter sail made of a canvas one weight lighter than the standard, if the rules allow. In addition, a leech roach will make a significant increase in area on such a small sail. Thus, if battens are allowed by the rules they should be used to this end on a light weather sail, which will also have as much foot round as the Sail Maker can include within the rule.

BOOM HEADSAIL (100 per cent of cloth weight of working sails)
A working headsail is sometimes set on a club boom. Be it a boom staysail, boom jib, or boom foresail, it will obey all the requirements of a normal working headsail as regards clew height and weight of canvas. The point to watch here is that the sheet has enough travel athwartships, or the sail will backwind the mainsail badly. This requires a fairly wide horse if the clew is not to rise too high, and it can thus become an obstacle on the foredeck; for some reason recessed sheet travellers are not common for boom headsails.

A headsail boom which is mounted on a pedestal gives added flow to the sail as it is freed off, and is thus aerodynamically more efficient than a full length boom.

In order that the sail can be fully lowered down the stay, while remaining attached at the clew, some device is needed to allow the clew to come forward, or the luff to come aft, as the sail comes down the stay.

Let us assume there is a hank or snap hook at the luff opposite the clew, so that the line joining the clew and the hank is perpendicular to the luff. This will be shorter than the distance from the clew to any point on the stay below the hank in question, so that the hank will not then be able to slide down the wire since the clew is restrained by the boom.

191

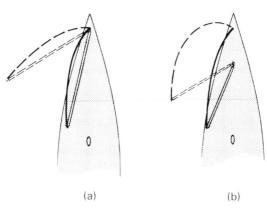

Fig. 10.1 Headsail Booms

In (a) the staysail boom is attached to the forestay, so that the camber of the sail remains unchanged as the boom is eased onto a reach. If the boom is hinged on a pedestal just aft of the forestay (b), the sail's camber increases as the sheet is eased, giving a better shape for the reach.

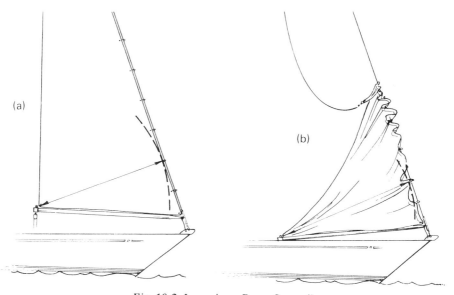

Fig. 10.2 Lowering a Boom Staysail.

As a boom staysail is lowered, any sail hank or snap at or near the point of the luff which is opposite the clew will not slide down the forestay while the clew is still attached to a fixed boom end, because it must get further away from the clew as it nears the deck; this it cannot do because the sail is not made of elastic. Methods of overcoming this include a complicated system whereby the appropriate hanks are fitted to a jackstay, which allows them to pull away from the luff on their own wire when tension is relaxed; use of a club boom which is only attached to the sail (and not the deck or forestay), and so can freely ease forward complete with clew; and incorporation of a pedestal mounted on a slide, so that both pedestal and boom can be moved forward when necessary, thus shortening the distance from clew to forestay.

If a jackstay is fitted to the headsail, the hank or snap hook (and any others at a distance from the clew which is less than the length of the foot) can allow the luff to fall aft as the weight is taken off the halyard. Another system is to have the club boom sufficiently short at the tack to allow the sail to move forward as it is lowered; in this case the boom is attached only to the sail and not to the stay or the deck of the boat. A third method is to allow the pedestal to move in a short track, so that it goes forward as the sail is lowered. Finally, of course, some system of releasing the clew of the sail can be used, but this means another operation to remember when lowering sail.

JIB OR YANKEE (66 to 85 per cent of cloth weight of working sails)
A cutter's jib will be used in conjunction with a staysail, and the pair of them can not only confer more area than a genoa for the same fore triangle, but the jib also forms a slot with the staysail. The latter is thus working to better aerodynamic advantage and developing greater thrust. In addition, reduction in sail area is more efficient than handing the genoa and setting an intermediate, because there will always be a sail set and drawing in the fore triangle. Finally, two sails forward of the mast seem to make a boat steadier offshore than a single one.

A working jib, also called a yankee in Great Britain if it is cut with a high clew (a name which is not used in America, by the way), should normally be one or two weights lighter than the standard, if it comes off before the staysail, and particularly if it has to be handled on the end of a bowsprit. There are, however, owners of twin headsail yawls and ketches who prefer to sail in heavy weather under mizzen and jib rather than mizzen and staysail. In this case, of course, the jib should be 100 per cent of the standard, or one weight lighter at most.

Care must be taken that the jib does not interfere with the airflow over the staysail. To this end there should be a reasonable gap between their respective stays, which are best if they are nearly parallel, and the jib should be cut high in the clew to allow room for plenty of wind to pass to leeward of the staysail. The sheet lead will run slightly forward of the average for a headsail: the higher the sail is cut, the further forward will come the sheet lead. In practice, the height of clew is usually controlled by this requirement. It will be as high as possible and still sheet inside the boat – on or near the counter, providing the base is wide enough at that point to keep the leech free.

GENOAS

The genoa in its various forms is such an efficient sail that it is now looked upon more or less as a working headsail. As the wind increases to a point where reduction in sail area is necessary to keep the boat sailing at an efficient angle, modern technique is to hold on to the genoa and reef the mainsail. I have therefore shown as cloth weight percentage guides the lowest figure normal to a particular genoa, where it would be changed for a smaller sail before the first or second reef is taken in the mainsail, and also the full 100 per cent for hard driving.

WORKING GENOA (70 to 100 per cent of cloth weight of working sails)
The working, or medium, genoa is the sail which wins races for the sloop, and its shape is all-important. Not only does it provide immense thrust on its own account, but it controls the flow of air over the mainsail. It is crucial, therefore, that this sail should hold its shape, so its cloth selection is important; in a racing boat, it is the first candidate for film laminate or tri-axial cloth.

In the vertical plane a genoa should cover as much of the mainsail as possible, and so should be taken as near the top of its stay as it will go and still clear the shrouds; the width of the sail at the head is small enough to outweigh considerations of disturbing the airflow so near the mainsail. It should be cut with its flow well forward, and with a flat run aft to the leech. It is most important that the leech itself should not curl to windward, because the streamlines will then be directed straight into the lee of the mainsail, and the slot will be choked. A well-hollowed leech will open the slot and pass more air, thus backwinding the mainsail less. Modern materials and techniques enable lighter cloth to be used than was common a few years ago, particularly if the sail has a control luff to regulate flow position.

A good idea is to have a kind of jiffy reef. Extra cringles fitted at luff and leech, usually in a horizontally cut sail, can be pulled down in far less time than it takes to change sails; the slack can either be left lying on deck or tied off. This saves a sloop without a twin groove forestay from being bare-headed during a change; it saves another sail (useful where the wardrobe is limited by special rules); and it can be used where conditions are marginal or will be of short duration. Disadvantages are weight of the cringle and its reinforcement at the leech, finding a weight of cloth to suit both conditions, and the gap in the wardrobe if you rely on the reefed sail and it tears; thus effectively depriving you of two sails, not one.

Before the advent of the IOR, the RORC limited headsail size by controlling the horizontal distance between the tack and a perpendicular dropped from the clew. To get maximum area within this rule the clew had to be kept as low as possible. The IOR controls the distance from the clew perpendicular to the luff. Not only is this something which can be physically measured on the sail, but it allows the clew to be raised as high as you like without loss of area (the clew is brought aft as it is raised, along a line parallel with the luff, thus maintaining constant area; this line is technically known as the LP, or longest perpendicular, line). It is therefore tempting to recommend that a full size IOR genoa should have a clew high enough to enable the sail to clear the lifeline comfortably. Alas, although there would be no loss of area, efficiency would be impaired, so the clew still has to be low.

This is because it will take advantage of the quicker airflow over the hull and of the end plate effect which the deck has in restraining air escaping under the foot of the sail. Where regulations prevent a break in the lifeline to allow the genoa foot to be led outside the rail near the tack (the RORC, except as shown below, demands an unbroken lifeline at least 2 ft high all round the yacht), a low clewed genoa must be sheeted inside the rail when

Plate 10.3 Vertical Cut Genoa

Countdown's vertical cut genoa has a series of short panels laid along the leech, to give better bias control at this critical point. *Chris Howard-Williams*

195

beating to windward. This means that it must be led between the main shrouds and the rail, which is often difficult. Nevertheless, maximum efficiency requires this, and it should be done by any dedicated owner. It is a good idea to angle the stanchions slightly outward in way of the shrouds (the RORC allows a maximum of 10°) to make room for the sail, which should be adequately protected from chafe by suitable patches each side of the foot where abrasion will occur. The RORC permits overlapping pulpits so that a gap may exist between the lifeline and the pulpit. This allows a low-cut headsail to set without the difficulties described above.

The owner for whom a slight loss of efficiency is more than offset by greater convenience, will have his genoa cut high enough in the clew to avoid this problem. The sail will then pass over the rail well forward, and will set round the shrouds without any bother. He will also be able to close reach with his genoa, without having to re-reeve the sheet outside the rail. But he will lose out to his more painstaking rival, who puts efficiency before convenience. Incidentally, there should be a second chafing patch on the foot of the sail near the tack, where it rubs on the top rail when reaching.

HEAVY GENOA (85 to 100 per cent of cloth weight of working sails)
This is a sail which will not normally be in the locker of a boat with a working or medium genoa. It requires a light genoa to complement it, and has a limited wind range from, say, force 4 to $5\frac{1}{2}$, and then not on a boat which is tender. It is a full size sail and the only difference from a working genoa, besides the weight of canvas, is that the clew is cut a little higher, so that the foot is kept out of the water, and also so that the sail can clear the lifeline. This avoids having someone up to his knees in water every time a tack is made, and the sail has to be tucked between the rail and the shrouds.

INTERMEDIATE GENOA (85 to 100 per cent of cloth weight of working sails)
The intermediate genoa is the first change down when the boat begins to be overpowered by the full size working genoa. It represents a reduction in area of about 25 to 33 per cent of the larger sail, and it is tending to replace the working headsail more and more these days; its cloth weight is therefore more inclined to be 100 per cent of the standard than 85 per cent.

It should be shorter in the luff than the standard genoa, in order to keep the centre of effort low, and also shorter in the foot in order to reduce area. It should have an area about half-way between the genoa and the working headsail so that it makes a logical reduction to the total area carried as the wind reaches the point where it replaces the larger sail. As with a dinghy's heavy weather jib, the intermediate genoa should be cut very flat, with a fair amount of hollow in the leech to open the slot; the clew should also be higher than that of the genoa, with little or no round to the foot. These last two points are so that the sail will pick up less water as the boat heels under the influence of the strong wind and so you can see under it. When considering the length of foot for this sail, it should be remembered that it has to set properly. If it is to go adequately round the main shrouds, setting outside them so that it may be freed off on a reach, the foot must be long enough so that the clew does not bear hard against the shrouds and cause a kink in the lower leech; about $1.25 \times J$ is the minimum which will do this. You may decide that you want to lead the sail inside the main shrouds, between them and the lowers. This means that the upper leech will have to clear the lower spreaders, and that the sheet will have to be re-rove outside the main shrouds when you free off to a reach, or it will bear against them and chafe, besides giving a wrong lead.

LIGHT GENOA ($2\frac{1}{2}$ to 5 oz)

A light genoa is essential for a boat which has a heavy, but not a medium genoa. There must be a full area headsail which can cater for wind strengths up to force 3, and the heavy genoa will not do this properly. The light genoa will be cut along the lines of the medium equivalent, with particular emphasis on plenty of round to the foot, in order to achieve maximum area. Draft will be full and with a fine entry, so that the leech does not have a belly, while the line of the leech itself can be nearly straight (i.e. without hollow), because the slot may be narrower in these weights of wind with little danger of choking.

Most boats up to 45 ft LWL will use a cloth of fixed weight, as indicated above, rather than one related to the standard weight, and the temptation to use it in winds stronger than those for which it was designed must be firmly resisted. If there is only a mile to go to the windward mark and the wind is increasing, it is sometimes impossible tactically to change sails. The owner in this position – perhaps with a rival just under his lee – must be prepared to see the sail ruined, possibly for all time. He should confess his sins to his Sail Maker as soon as possible, and be prepared to buy a new sail. Such is the price of racing. If, on the other hand, an owner can foresee that he will often need to hold on to the light genoa in winds of force $3\frac{1}{2}$ and more, he should have it made of heavier canvas, and it then becomes a light-medium genoa. At all events, do not use it in strong winds and then blame the sail for being out of shape. Although the upper wind limit of a Mylar/Melinex light genoa may be higher, there is nevertheless still a limit which must be observed – and it is easier for the Sail Maker to detect if it has been exceeded, so he will known where to place the blame for a blown out sail . . .

BOARD SAILS

It is tempting to think that sailboards have such simple looking sails that there is little which can be written about them. This may have been true when the sport first started but, like anything new, technology and techniques have advanced as boardsailing has expanded — and we all know the tremendous growth in the number of people who 'do it standing up'.

REQUIREMENTS

Boardsailors look for varying outline shape in their sails according to the following broad principles.

All-round Sail. There is obviously a need for a general purpose sail, which can be used in average wind strengths, by the average practitioner, for average club purposes. It will be round about 5 m² in area, with a relatively high clew for ease of handling, and have a straight or even hollow leech so that there is no need for battens; Fig. 10.3 (a).

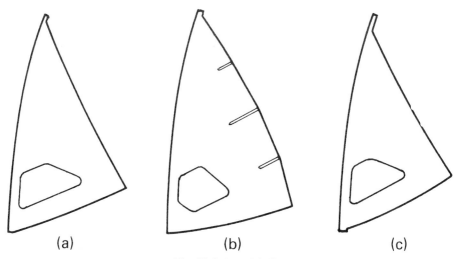

(a)   (b)   (c)

Fig. 10.3 Board Sails

Board sails have a somewhat harder life than those of the average dinghy. They are repeatedly dunked in the water, left lying flat on the beach, rolled casually on the mast, and sometimes taken home on the car roof rack without benefit of a mast or sail bag.

(a) *All-round Sail.* A 5 m² sail with a high clew, designed for ease of handling in most normal wind conditions.

(b) *Racing Sail.* A full area sail (6·3 m²) to maximum International Boardsailing Association sizes. It has three battens to support the leech roach.

(c) *Storm Sail.* A 4·3 m² sail with a slightly shorter luff and a reduced diagonal; the leech is hollow. The area is low and forward for better control in strong winds (not storms . . .); a short wishbone is beneficial with this configuration.

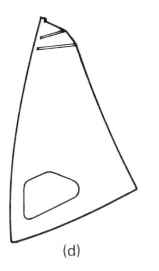 

(d) *Fathead*. Designed for speed sailing and wave jumping, this sail may, and often does, exceed the ISBA racing measurements, particularly as regards its batten arrangement. It has extra area aloft, supported by two full length battens, so that thrust is maintained when the board is in the sheltered trough between waves.

(e) *High Aspect*. A reduced area sail, principally for racing in strong winds. Size may be graded according to the board sailer's weight by deciding on a longer or shorter diagonal, but the full luff length is needed to catch the wind high up. A short wishbone may often be more convenient if the diagonal will accept it.

Racing Sail. Rules limit the size of racing sails, whatever boat is used, and sailboards are no exception. Equally, owners never like to have under-size sails for competition work, so this one is right up to international measurement, and has battens at the leech to give a roach; Fig. 10.3 (b).

Storm Sail. Somewhat optimistically described as far as the average sailor is concerned, the storm sail has a lower area through a shorter luff and a reduced diagonal. A high clew helps control, and a hollow leech not only keeps area down, but does away with the need for battens; Fig. 10.3 (c).

Fathead. In the troughs of deep waves, there is a danger that most of the bottom half of the sail will be masked from the wind. This requires extra area aloft if drive is to be maintained, for instance for wave jumping. A high clew ensures that the board sailor can control the leech by bearing down on the wishbone; Fig. 10.3 (d). Some Hawaian surfers overcome this problem by using a taller mast (over 5 m instead of 4·5 m).

High Aspect Sail. When racing in strong winds, a reduced area sail is necessary – but once again area is needed high up, for the moments when the board is low in the wave troughs. So the full luff length is maintained, and area graded according to requirement (weight and skill of the owner) by varying the length of this diagonal; Fig. 10.3 (e).

MAST

As with all sailing craft, the mast plays an important part in the final set of the sail. Because there is no rigging to tweak, the board sailor is very much at the mercy of the manufacturer – rather like a Finn sailor, he is stuck with what he gets, so some care in selection is important. The options lie in material and shape – in broad terms between fibreglass and aluminium, and between parallel sided and tapered.

Fibreglass. Polyester resin reinforcement is too weak to stand up to the flexing loads and general rough treatment inherent in board sailing. In order to get the strength, most manufacturers use epoxy reinforcement; even so, such masts bend rather too much in strong winds, so that a large section is required – with attendant weight problems. However, the material stands up well to the rough and tumble of club sailing where, because heavy weather often finds the boards left ashore, flexibility is not the problem it might be for the expert.

Aluminium. Light alloy gives the rigidity required, if the mast is not to bend too much and open the leech excessively. The material does, however, have a tendency to accept a permanent bend after use in a strong wind. This may take some of the fullness out of the luff, but it makes the leech difficult to control in heavy weather, when it is not easy to keep a downward pressure on the clew because the sailor is leaning so far to windward.

Parallel Sided. A constant section mast is naturally very stiff, and thus good for strong winds in that the leech is kept under better control. But the extra weight becomes tiring after it has been lifted from the water a number of times, and it doesn't have enough curve for light winds.

Tapered. So we come to an aluminium spar with a tapered topmast. This offers the extra rigidity of alloy, with some bend aloft when required. Here again, however, there is the danger of a permanent bend being induced. Most champions use aluminium masts, tapered at one or both ends.

Kicking-strap. To overcome problems caused by incorrect mast bend, some board sailors have turned to the kicking-strap to help keep downward

Plate 10.4 Sailboards
No two windows are alike in this Sea Panther fleet racing at Nottingham. Note
how the booms are all shoulder high – if yours is at your waist, you will never hang
out in a breeze. *David Eberlin*

pressure on the leech while lying parallel with the water in strong winds.
This is a line from the base of the mast to the boom end at the clew, and back
to a handy pulley-block and cleat which can be adjusted while sailing.

FLOW

Flow can be controlled partly by hoisting harder and partly by downward
pressure on the clew to alter twist. But different camber is required for
different conditions much as with other types of boat.

Light Winds. A very flat sail ensures that airflow remains attached in winds
of less than Force 1, as we saw in Chapter II. If the draft is allowed to
become too full, separation occurs and turbulence sets in.

Medium Winds. Between Force 1–3 a fuller sail can be accepted, so that the
mast should not bend too much to take this out; raising the clew can help to
give twist and impart thrust.

Strong Winds. Over Force 3, a small flat sail is wanted. The fact that the mast will bend doesn't help as much as it may sound, because the leech then falls off with attendant control problems. The sail should be basically flat, with a high clew to help leech control.

Tips to remember when considering a board sail include seeing that the head of the mast sleeve is adequately reinforced, because constant pressure downwards promotes a certain amount of chafe. Secondly, the height of the luff cut-out, where the wishbone ties to the mast, is important: if it is down by the knees, it will be virtually impossible to hold the boom when leaning to windward in a blow – it needs to be about shoulder height. Finally, many Sail Makers fit a small zip pocket for personal belongings – it's about the only stowage you have on a sailboard, so is worth specifying.

GENERAL

You may well ask what the ideal working wardrobe should comprise. This depends on your pocket and your dedication. The aim is to have a sail which will respond to most conditions of wind and sea, and the minimum would appear to be a light genoa to cover all winds up to force 3, a working genoa from 100 per cent standard to take over above this, with an intermediate as next buy. On the other hand, you may prefer to have a light-medium genoa of 75 per cent standard to cover force $2\frac{1}{2}$ to 4, with a ghoster below and an intermediate above; next buy is a heavy genoa to fill force 4 to 5. Take the advice of your Sail Maker and try not to use your sails in winds which are too strong for them. Conventional weaves and plycloth can be helped back to a reasonable shape after abuse; film laminate cannot (though it holds a good shape for much longer than normal cloth). The variations are many and offer pleasant fireside speculation.

Chapter XI

Light and Heavy Weather Sails

LIGHT WEATHER SAILS

CLOTH

There are those who believe that a light weather suit of sails, particularly for a dinghy, should be made of a light cloth, and there are those who say that it should be heavy. The former maintain that the merest zephyr will fill out a light cloth immediately, while the latter say that the heavier material is sufficiently stiff not to lose its aerofoil shape even when the wind has gone completely, and thus is ready to receive the first whisper of wind and turn it into power. There is merit in both schools of thought, and I would be loath to dissuade an owner from either proposal. On balance, I would advise that dinghies should use a light cloth if they really want a light weather suit of sails.

You will note that I specify dinghies. Offshore racers are often prevented by their rules from having a special light weather mainsail (the IOR, for instance, has just such a prohibition) and, in any case, such a large sail could not be made of the 2 or 3 oz material which I have in mind as the sort of sail which will respond quickly to the first puff of wind as it fills in. These larger boats will, of course, have their ghosting headsails designed to catch this nascent breeze, and I shall deal with these separately later.

Light weather sails should never be used in winds stronger than those for which they have been designed. It is no good asking your Sail Maker to make you a suit of sails for force 0 to $2\frac{1}{2}$, and then trying to use them in force 3. Not only will they be too full but, if they have indeed been made of a lighter cloth than normal for the type of boat, they will stretch out of shape never properly to recover. This latter effect can be minimized by making the sails with narrower panels than usual, thus cutting down the amount of bias available to pull out of shape, or by using ply-cloth or film laminate.

Finally, bear in mind my earlier remarks about ultra-light weather sails losing more races than they win. It may well happen one day, in a near calm, that a boat with very full sails will trounce you. Her owner will doubtless extol the virtues of this suit, but remember that he has to take every advantage of such a rare occurrence, and that he does not tell you how many races it has lost for him.

When considering sails for light weather it is not enough to say that they should be fuller than usual. There are qualifications, particularly regarding the headsail, which can always be given extra fullness by easing the sheet, and the spinnaker which, as it increases in size at the head, increases its total weight aloft and thus its tendency to collapse in ghosting conditions. There is

Plate 11.1 Ruination of a Light Genoa
I have included this photograph in every edition of this book since it was first published in 1967. The alert reader will spot that the sail is, in fact, a quadrilateral; this dates it, because these sails have been outlawed by the rule for many years (a quad was a lightweight sail, so the argument is not affected). The fact that a light cloth will be blown out of shape if it is used in winds too strong for it is even more true for Mylar/Melinex than it is for polyester, and I make no apology for retaining the photograph. *Beken*

also a special art in setting and sheeting all sails in light airs, and I must repeat some of the factors about sails which make a boat go fast under these conditions. The same holds good for heavy weather as we shall see later.

LIGHT WEATHER MAINSAIL

It is the very full mainsail which loses the race for you as the wind gets up beyond the strength for which it was designed. Many are the dinghy owners who choose a mainsail admirably suited to the force 1 wind prevailing at the start of a race, only to find themselves knocked down on the second beat to windward because the wind has increased. Unless you have a method of taking some of this fullness out of the sail, such as a bendy mast or an efficient slab reefing coupled with a Cunningham hole, it does not pay to own such a sail. I naturally except waters where ghosting conditions are the rule rather than otherwise, or where light airs are predictably constant, such as parts of the Mediterranean.

By its very fullness, an ultra-light weather mainsail must have a leech which returns sharply to windward so that it can rejoin the boom at the clew. This return means that the leech of the sail will be actively trying to thrust the boat astern as soon as the wind can get a grip on it. In very light airs the luff is not lifting and thus is contributing all its power, the bunt is not heeling the boat because the wind is not strong enough, and there is not enough force in the wind to cause the leech to do much harm. As soon as the wind increases to a certain critical point (which will vary according to the fullness of the sail), the luff may lose drive through lifting, the flow will move aft slightly under the action of the wind, thus aggravating the leech return, and the bunt of the sail will heel the boat; the leech itself will be trying to drive the boat astern (see Fig. 11.1). See my remarks in Chapter II under *Camber* regarding the need for a flat sail in really light weather.

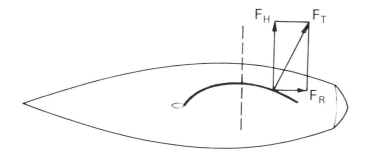

Fig. 11.1 Over-full Mainsail
If a line is drawn down the middle of a very full mainsail, more often that not the rear half of the sail is actively working to drive the boat astern. It can be seen above how F_T for the after section of this mainsail resolves with F_R facing aft.

Slab Reef. The boat which does not have a bendy mast can, as I indicated just now, employ a slab reef and a Cunningham hole to do the job of flattening the mainsail when required. A slab reef, also called a roach reef or a flattening reef, is one which runs along the foot of a mainsail, starting at the tack, curving up into the sail as it proceeds aft, and coming back to the boom at the clew. When it is pulled in it removes some of the cloth at the foot, thus flattening the sail as though it had less foot round cut into it in the first place. The reef can be effected by means of a continuous lacing line, but a simpler system employs the zip fastener. Providing a non-corroding zipper is used, such as nylon or one of the more modern plastics, it is a way of taking in a slab reef quickly; this in turn means that it will be used more often than the old-fashioned lacing system. It is important to use a zipper which has been tested and found serviceable, for the slider can also corrode or the whole thing may be found to be too weak. There are problems involved in enamelling or plating sliders, because their tolerances are often measured in thousandths of an inch. Incidentally, it is usually better to leave such a zipper open when you stow the sail in its bag, for closed teeth can disengage when the zipper is bent or twisted. It is also a good idea to follow Bruce Banks Sails practice of fitting a second slider at the outset to act as a spare should the first one break while sailing. Easier still is to pull down Cunningham holes above both tack and clew in a kind of jiffy reef, leaving the spare cloth to flap idly over the boom.

A zipper can also be used up the luff of a mainsail, where the class rules permit (the IOR prohibits it), in a similar manner. While it will take out fullness from a better place for effective flattening of a mainsail, it should be remembered that zippers are by no means infallible, and it is easier to get at a jammed slider along the foot of a sail than half-way up the mast. I do not like luff zips.

Cunningham Hole. The Cunningham hole is a simpler device, which is possibly even more effective than a slab reef; it may be used in conjunction with the latter and can be most useful on its own. Invented by Briggs Cunningham in the 6 metre days, it is a method of putting more tension on the luff of a woven mainsail which is already out to its black bands, also on the leech and clew outhaul.

It is no good having a Cunningham hole if it is never used. Many a mainsail has one fitted, yet the owner does not have the tackle to enable him to adjust it quickly. If a lacing has to be rove between the Cunningham hole and the tack eye, and tension applied by drawing the two together and tying a knot, then it will seldom be done. A line should be led from the tack, through the Cunningham hole, and down to a sheave on deck, from where it can go to a convenient cleat. Similarly a permanent line should be rove

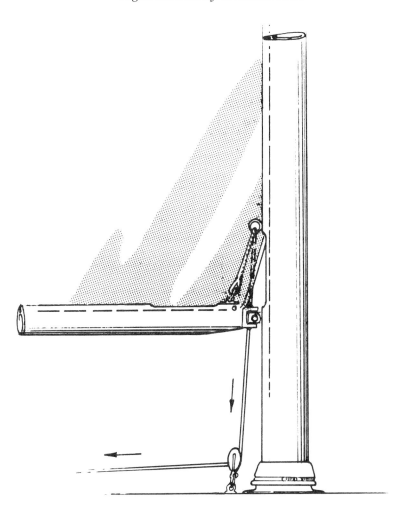

Fig. 11.2 Cunningham Hole

Most woven mainsails are made to hoist right to their marks all the time. When the wind freshens and forces the draft back towards the leech, so that thrust is lost and weather helm becomes noticeable, some means of restoring the *status quo* is needed. The owner would like to stretch the luff a little more by means of the halyard, to draw the flow back towards the luff again, as we saw in Figure 3.2, but the sail is already hard up against the black band. Cunningham's idea was to have an eye worked into the luff tabling, just up from the tack – about 6 ins on a dinghy and up to one foot on a medium sized offshore racer. A line is passed through this hole and tension applied downwards on the luff, stretching it more. The flow in the sail is thus drawn forward, although small creases appear in the tack area as the sail bunches. This, however, is by far the lesser of two evils, and is easily outweighed by greater overall aerodynamic efficiency in the sail. If similar treatment is given to the leech, you are effectively reefing out the fullness in the bottom 6–12 inches of the foot, thus flattening the whole sail. The leech Cunningham must pull aft as well as down, or there will be no tension along the foot, which will then not set properly.

through the leech Cunningham and taken via a ringslide to a cleat on the boom.

Some dinghy classes have developed the slab reef beyond the stage where it flattens a sail for heavier weather. A large shelf is built into the foot of the sail, and a zipper incorporated in order to close if off when required. The shelf is unzipped off the wind, to provide a really full sail for reaching and running, and closed for the windward leg, where a more conventional shape is needed. I once did some wind tunnel tests on this idea, and releasing the shelf on a reach gave a 5 per cent increase in driving force over the sail with closed zipper, with little change in heeling force.

LIGHT WEATHER HEADSAILS

QUADRILATERALS

The IOR requires headsails to be sheeted from only one point on the sail, and specifically excludes quadrilaterals or similar sails[41].

GHOSTER (2 to 3 oz)

The ghoster is a headsail suitable up to and including force 2. It will take the boat to windward in these conditions, and should be made of a cloth slightly above the minimum available. It is cut in the same way as a light genoa for greatest area: low clew, maximum foot round and no hollow to the leech. It should have lightweight sheets tied to the clew (to avoid the weight of a shackle), and hanks or snap hooks should be double spaced. Strength of mind is needed to take the sail off as the wind gets above force 2.

DRIFTER (1 to 2 oz)

The drifter is virtually synonymous with a ghoster, but I have chosen to differentiate between the two for the purposes of this book. Let us say, then, that the drifter is the sail which indicates when the first puff of wind arrives, and then has to be changed immediately; it is suitable up to and including force 1. Anything above this will blow the very light cloth out of shape, so it is a sail of limited application to say the least.

As a good deal of its time will be spent hanging lifeless from its halyard, the drifter can be made with or without hanks or snaps according to preference. There is a strong case to be made for doing away with them, so that the light genoa can be hanked on to the stay, ready to go up at the first sign of a steady wind. This practice helps to encourage early removal of the drifter, thus prolonging its life.

The clew will usually be rather higher than that of a ghoster, so that the greatest area is kept fairly high, where the first whisper of breeze occurs.

This, of course, means that the sheet fairlead must be further aft for correct trim. Sheets must be as light as possible, and may be single.

I generally try and discourage owners from ordering drifters, on the grounds that the sail would almost certainly be used in winds stronger than those for which it was designed; the truth of this assumption has been demonstrated to me many times both ashore and afloat. Perhaps a good solution is to have a drifter cut from heavier cloth – whereupon it becomes a ghoster – but it is necessary to remember that it will still have an upper limit of force 2. For windward work it should be cut flat; see Chapter II *Camber*.

LIGHT WEATHER DINGHY HEADSAILS (2–3½ oz)

The light weather dinghy headsail can afford to be cut rather flatter than one might believe suitable, since flow can always be achieved by easing the sheet; there should be little or no induced flow to leave a fold up the luff. It will, however, be used in winds above its designed range, particularly if it is a good looking sail, so it should be cut accordingly. You will note that I state categorically that it *will* be misused, not that it *might* be; this is as sure as tomorrow's sunrise, and the better the sail, the greater the likelihood of dawn coming up as usual. The sail should have maximum foot round, with little or no hollow to the leech. A window is not recommended, as it will almost certainly be stiffer than the rest of the sail and this, coupled with the danger of tight stitching around its edges, can give rise to creases. Very light wire luff clips, such as those marketed by Lewmar, are better than normal snaps or hanks because they are lighter and they allow a better airflow; they will be quite strong enough for the light winds the sail ought to encounter (and if they bend or break it will serve the owner right for using the sail in too strong a wind). Many dinghies, of course, use no hanks on their jibs at all, preferring to hoist them flying in the laudable pursuit of aerodynamic efficiency.

STORM SAILS

Many rules, including both the RORC and the CCA, require a yacht to have storm canvas capable of taking her to windward. This means that a sloop or cutter should have a sail of reduced size to set on the mast (a yawl or ketch can sail to windward without the mainsail), and that all yachts should have a headsail which can safely be set in a storm.

TRYSAIL (85 to 120 per cent of cloth of working sails)

A trysail is a most seamanlike storm sail, as it does away with the need for a boom, which can be a danger in a heavily rolling boat under storm conditions. In addition, the boom may be broken, yet the trysail can still be set.

Plate 11.2 Heavy Weather
The neatest roll will not prevent heavy seas from tearing a spare headsail from its
stowage on the lifeline if it is left there as the wind gets up.　　　　*Granada*

It is difficult to suggest weights of canvas, due to the advent of modern light
cloths, but the ORC requires a heavier trysail weight than the mainsail[42].
Big cruising boats with woven Dacron or Terylene sails may, in fact, go one
weight lighter than the ideal mainsail range suggested in Chapter III
because, at these weights, there is more than enough strength in polyester.
This may sound odd for a storm sail, but polyester is so strong that there is
plenty of margin in the standard weight. The only reason that the mainsail is
not made lighter is that it would stretch out of shape, but a certain amount
of stretch is acceptable in a trysail, which is not expected to enable the boat
to tack in 90°; a lighter and softer cloth will be easier to handle (it is worth
specifying softness to your Sail Maker for this reason), and will take up less
space in the locker.

The sail should be cut so that the clew is lower than the tack, and the sail
is then hoisted so that the clew comes above the level of the boom. It is a

good idea to have a permanent strop on the tack, so that the correct height is automatically found, and so that it can be shackled straight on to the normal tack fitting without having to search round for a suitable length of strong lashing.

When the trysail is set, I prefer to see the boom lashed to its gallows and twin sheets led either side of it, so that they pull down and aft like a head-sail's. Indeed, the sail is usually cut with a mitre, so that the cloths run at rightangles to the loose leech and foot for the same reasons as they do on a headsail. Some owners, however, prefer to leave the boom free, and to sheet the trysail to its end with a view to avoiding the need to tend sheets when tacking, but the ORC requires that it shall sheet independently of the boom.

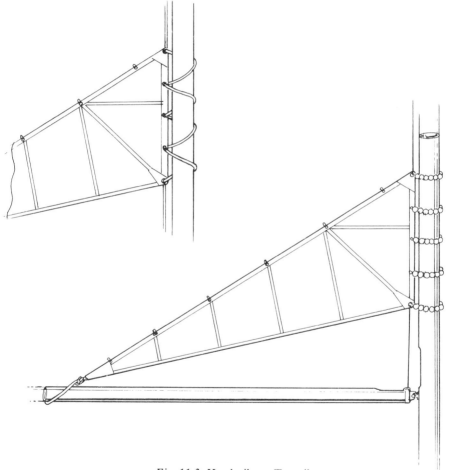

Fig. 11.3 Headsail as a Trysail
The foot, reinforced with tape, becomes the luff and is fastened to the mast with parrel beads. See insert for a method of lacing which will run up and down the mast without jamming.

In area, the sail should be substantially smaller than the close-reefed mainsail; the ORC specifies a maximum size of 0·175 P × E, which is about one third of the mainsail area. To avoid the use of battens, it should have a hollow to the leech and a straight foot. Luff slides may be used in the normal way, particularly if a second emergency track is available on the mast, as these are so much easier than the old-fashioned parrel beads. The eyelets for the slides should be large enough to allow a lacing to be passed through, should the track be unserviceable. A small headsail can always be made to serve as an emergency trysail, if eyelets are provided in the foot (which should be adequately strengthened with tape). The sail is bent to the mast with a lacing, and the sheet is made fast to the head, which has now become the clew.

I was always surprised to see that more owners did not have their racing number put on the trysail. Most rules require an alternative means of displaying this information when the mainsail is not hoisted, and it used to strike me that it is a simple way to do so on the trysail. I see that the ORC now makes this a requirement.

SWEDISH MAINSAIL (100 per cent of cloth weight of working sails)

Some people prefer to use a storm mainsail set on both mast and boom, as this is felt to give better control of the sail and does not involve separate sheets; in addition it will make the boat as close-winded as an ordinary mainsail. The Swedish mainsail answers this requirement, though its use of the boom puts it out for the ORC.

It is sail about three-quarters of the length of the ordinary mainsail on the luff and foot, and it loses more area by pronounced hollowing of the leech. The result is a sail about half as large as the full-sized mainsail, and which will sail as close to windward as the boat will lie under storm conditions. Needless to say, the hollow leech does away with the need for battens, which is all to the good, and there will be a ring at the top instead of a headboard. The sail should, of course, be cut flat for the strong winds it will encounter, and there is no reason why it should not have a reef if desired. Its main disadvantage lies in the fact that it has to be set on the boom, which may slam across the cockpit under certain conditions, or may even be broken by the very weather which necessitates the setting of the sail. A slamming boom may be thought more acceptable than flogging trysail sheets of wire, particularly if the leech of the Swedish mainsail is made short enough to lift the boom well clear of heads in the cockpit.

STORM JIB OR STORM STAYSAIL
(100 per cent of cloth weight of working sails)

The storm jib or staysail should be standard weight, as it should not be

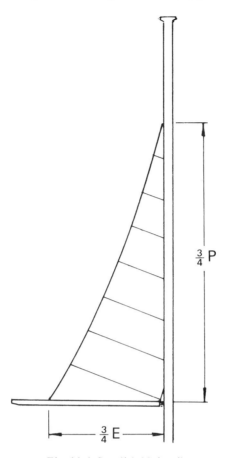

Fig. 11.4 Swedish Mainsail
The sail is roughly three quarters of the length of the regular mainsail on both luff
and foot. The leech is cut hollow, and there are no battens; the headboard is
replaced by a stout ring. The sail allows the boat to be closer winded than a trysail,
but it does mean that the main boom has to be used.

allowed to stretch unduly, or the boat may develop poor handling qualities.
It should be about half the area of the working jib or staysail, or even less,
and should have a high clew in order to keep the sail out of the water; this
also helps to bring the sheet lead to the working headsail's fairlead. Some
boats carry their storm jib on a small tack pendant to keep it well above the
water, but this should not be overdone or the centre of effort will be too high.

Here again, Terylene and Dacron are so strong that a leech rope is not
necessary unless the boat is large – say over 50 ft LWL. A roped leech will
tend to curl and flog, to which storm jibs are prone anyway. I do not favour
battens, such as are recommended by some Naval Architects, because they
represent something else to break or work loose; it should be possible to cut

Plate 11.3 Reefed Genoa
A number one genoa may be adapted to the intermediate role by using second tack and clew eyes, and tying off the surplus cloth by means of reef points rather like a jiffy reef. This should not be extended to gale conditions, because the bunched part of the sail would quickly flog to death in the wind and sea. When racing round the cans, the bunt is often not tied off if the reef is only needed for half an hour or so. *Author*

the leech with sufficient hollow and skill so that it lies fairly quiet in the strongest winds. If it does not, then take it back to its maker for attention.

It is quite feasible to use a working jib as a heavy weather headsail, if a reef is employed. Points reefing is as good as anything for this purpose, as they tie firmly under the loose foot. Care should be taken that the result is a sail which responds to the requirements of high clew and sheet lead position. Gale conditions, however, will cause the reefed part of the sail to flog and tear, so its use should be limited to force 6–7. Indeed, the ORC rightly requires that any heavy weather jib shall not incorporate a reef; any storm jib proper must be 'of suitable strength for the purpose'[42]. It goes on to specify that, if either sail is designed for a seastay or luff-groove device, it shall have an alternative method of attachment to the stay or a wire luff. There are also rules regarding maximum size.

Chapter XII

Reaching and Running Sails

The introduction of synthetic cloth after World War II gave rise to a revolution in sailmaking. In no area was this more true than in down wind sails – and it hasn't stopped yet. The aerodynamics of the close hauled condition received most attention to start with, and this was fair enough because this is where many races are lost and won. In racing, a premium is placed on windward work for, despite the fact that a boat has to sail close hauled only if she wants to proceed towards less than a quarter of the 360 degree compass, the average yacht race comprises over 50 per cent beating to windward. This is partly because boats have to sail further when tacking to cover a given distance when turning to windward, but also partly because it forms a good test of skill; committees are also mindful that boats all too often sail at nearly the same speed as each other when off the wind, so there is little change on the reaching legs.

The better skippers, however, soon started to find that they could also make significant gains when off the wind by careful selection of sails and attention to trim. They started thinking about airflow, sail shape and the interaction of sails. This gave rise to new drills, different sails and better trim even when they were not on the wind. There came big spinnakers with large skirts, two headsails set with the spinnaker, the tallboy, the reaching spinnaker, the genniker or spanker, the big boy or blooper, and various flat cuts for the spinnaker itself: star-cut, tri-radial, and radial head; eventually the cruising chute appeared for the non-racing owner. Many factors determine which sail from this wide choice is best suited for prevailing conditions, among them type of boat, balance of the existing sail plan, wind strength and, indeed, crew ability. A general guide for medium conditions is given at Fig. 12.1.

REACHING

REACHING GENOA (66 per cent of cloth weight of working sails)
A reaching genoa should normally be one or two weights lighter than the

windward going genoa it replaces, assuming that the latter is not to the full standard weight. That is to say that a light genoa of 4 ounces will be replaced by a 3 ounce reacher; a medium genoa of 6 ounces will be replaced by a 4 or 5 ounce reacher, and a ghoster of 3 ounces will be replaced by a 2 ounce reacher. This, of course, is because a given wind has less apparent force on a reach than to windward. In addition, the sail is better if it is fairly full in the middle, which a light cloth will ensure. To this end it can be set

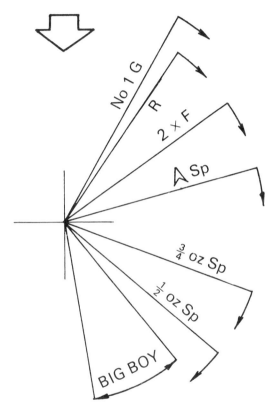

Fig. 12.1 Guide to Apparent Wind Angles

No. 1 G = No. 1 Genoa
R = Reacher
2 × F = Double head rig
Ⴠ Sp = Star-cut spinnaker

$\frac{3}{4}$ oz Sp = $\frac{3}{4}$ oz (30 gm/m²) spinnaker
$\frac{1}{2}$ oz Sp = $\frac{1}{2}$ oz (20 gm/m²) spinnaker

Big boy = Arc of big boy or blooper

No one chart can hope to show which sail should be used for which wind angle under all conditions of boat, wind speed and crew ability. This one gives a guide to use as a base for force 3 winds. Bear in mind that lighter conditions will allow spinnakers to be used with the wind more ahead; stronger weather will favour, for instance, the double head rig increasingly, because the extra area of the spinnaker is no longer so important. The star-cut spinnaker in particular can be kept full closer to the wind than 75 degrees, but above force 3 its advantage over the double head rig is progressively diminished.

flying, that is to say without snaps or hanks, as the sag in the luff will not be detrimental to performance.

The clew may be cut low (unless the sail is principally for light weather reaching when it should be higher clewed to catch the wind), because it will rise as the sheet is eased, and the fairlead should be further aft than the standard genoa position, or it may be sheeted to the end of the main boom with great advantage. This is a rich man's sail of limited application, for the average genoa will work nearly as well on a reach, whereas the reacher will be no good to windward, except in light weather, when it should not be sheeted too hard.

SPINNAKER-STAYSAIL ($1\frac{1}{2}$ to 2 oz)

The spinnaker-staysail (also known as a saveall and even as a demi-bra at times) sets under the spinnaker on a reach, in order to fill a gap forward. It is usually made of Dacron or Terylene, but may be made of nylon if preferred. The former makes a slightly better sail as it stretches less than nylon, but the difference is marginal and not so important that it should prevent those owners' wives who wish for a coloured sail from having what they want (most Sail Makers stock coloured nylon but only white Terylene or Dacron); boats with a waterline above 45 ft may increase the weight of cloth by not more than double the above recommendation. The sail can tack to the stemhead, in which case its size will be limited by the same rules which govern a genoa, and it may hank to the forestay and carry about two thirds up it, thereby acting as a spinnaker net at the same time. Alternatively a second tack eye several feet up the luff can be tied to the weather pulpit rail by means of a short rope pendant; this will give it a rather less disturbed wind, and will see that it disturbs the spinnaker as little as possible in turn.

A spinnaker-staysail set in this manner ranks as a headsail, and the rules may have something to say about it. For instance, the IOR requires that no headsail shall have a mid-girth (measured between the mid-points of luff and leech) more than 50 per cent of the foot length. In addition, the J measurement shall be taken to the luff of any headsail set flying if this is forward of the forestay. The IOR, however, allows headsails to be tacked athwartships, and the IYRU makes specific exception to the spinnaker-staysail when it requires jib tacks to be fixed 'approximately in the centre-line of the yacht'. The meaning of all this is that the spinnaker-staysail may be tacked to the weather pulpit rail provided it is not forward of the forestay. There is an overall requirement in the IOR that no staysail or jib may be tacked so that its clew, if trimmed flat along the centre-line of the yacht, would fall abaft the LP line (normally a line parallel to the forestay, and $1 \cdot 5 \times J$ aft of it). The effect of this is that no staysail or jib clew should come aft of the largest genoa clew close hauled, no matter where the former sail is tacked in the foretriangle.

A better airflow is obtained if the luff is not allowed to get too near the spinnaker, so the halyard is best led to a point just over half-way up the mast, and the sail allowed to set flying without hanks. If no special halyard is available, it can certainly be hoisted flying on one of the normal headsail halyards; in any case, the head of the sail should preferably not go much higher than half-way up the mast, or it will interfere with the set of the spinnaker. The clew is usually drawn below the deckline on the sail plan, because it will rise as the sail fills on a reach.

THE TALLBOY (3 to 5 oz)

The tallboy was a tall narrow sail, designed to form a slot in front of the mainsail when off the wind, thereby cleaning up the airflow. It took a long time to set up and trim properly and is now rarely used.

MIZZEN-STAYSAIL (2 to 3 oz)

Much of what I have just said about spinnaker-staysails holds good for mizzen-staysails. Recommended cloth weight is rather heavier for the latter because its larger area means a greater total weight of wind in the sail at any one time, and this would tend to stretch it more; this in turn would belly the sail into a bag, with consequent danger of its approaching the mainsail and interfering with the air flow. Once more, yachts with a waterline over 45 ft should consider increasing cloth weight above my recommendation, but not more than twice the figure above.

The clew is drawn below and just short of the mizzen clew, so that it can sheet comfortably to the mizzen boom end or to the counter. It is set flying, with the tack to windward, and the luff wire should be cased with leather in way of the permanent main backstay, to guard against chafe.

The IOR formula requires mizzen-staysails to be three-cornered, tacked abaft the mainmast and secured to the railcap, deck or cabin top; it may be sheeted to the hull or to the mizzen boom but not to any other spar. Several mizzen-staysails may be carried depending on the size of boat, but not more than one may be set at the same time. It follows that mizzen spinnakers are permitted (they set, of course, without a pole). Only half the rated area of either the mizzen or the mizzen-staysail goes into the rating, but the formula requires that the larger of the two *rated* areas shall be used. Thus an enormous mizzen-staysail setting as a spinnaker from the mizzen masthead will be paid for in the rating.

Some heavy cruising yawls and ketches use the mizzen-staysail more as a working sail. In this case it will possibly be hanked to a removable stay, and made of a cloth between 75 per cent and 100 per cent of the standard for the

Plate 12.1 Mizzen-Staysail (1)

A large mizzen-staysail can help a yawl when off the wind. But the mizzen itself is a doubtful asset other than as a balancing force – it is small, operates in the dirty wind of the mainsail when close-hauled, disturbs the mizzen staysail on a reach, and upsets the mainsail on a run. *Gitana IV*, on her way to the Fastnet in 1965 (yes, we had an easterly at the time) seems to have her sails setting well in this aerial shot (and so she should, or my presence on board as sail trimmer would have been anomalous). *Associated Newspapers*

Plate 12.2 Mizzen-Staysail (2)
This photograph was taken at about the same time as the one opposite, and shows
the mizzen staysail tack carried right across the deck, on a short strop.   *Author*

working sails. In passing, it is interesting to note that one Italian name for
this sail is *carbonera*, and this stems from the days of trading boats which
were half coal-fired and half sailing vessels. The mizzen-staysail used to set
over the smoke stack and quickly became dirty.

THE MULE (66 per cent of cloth weight of working sails)
The mule, or main backstay sail, sets on the permanent main backstay of a
yawl or ketch, and sheets to the head of the mizzen mast. It is a complicated
sail, and adds to mainsail area RSAM[43]; cruising yawls and ketches are
better off with a mizzen-staysail.

DOUBLE HEAD RIG
A genoa and a short hoist staysail, or even a high cut yankee and a staysail,
make a good combination under special circumstances. If the wind is force
$3\frac{1}{2}$–4 and is within the arc 55–70 degrees off the bow, boats with a tendency
to broach under a close reaching spinnaker will be more docile under a
double head rig; see Fig. 12.1. There is not the large area aloft to heel the
boat and thus offset the CE too far; in addition there is little or no aft
component of thrust, as there often is with a spinnaker strapped alongside
(see Chapter VIII). Both sails should have straight luffs, and this is some-

221

times not easy for the staysail if there is no inner forestay, so it is important to make sure that it is hoisted really hard.

TWIN HEADSAILS WITH A SPINNAKER

For a short time there was a vogue for hoisting a full masthead light genoa plus a short hoist spinnaker staysail under the spinnaker. This fills the foretriangle to overflowing, and the trim of all these sails calls for delicate judgement if they are not to upset each other's airflow. Those who may groan at the thought of having to struggle with this in order to compete, will be glad to learn that its efficiency is doubtful, and those exponents who achieve

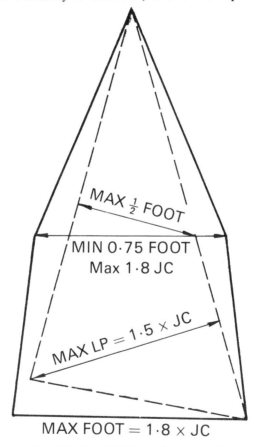

Fig. 12.2 The IOR Genoa/Spinnaker Rule

The IOR limits a genoa to a maximum LP of 1·5J without penalty; a further mandatory limit keeps the half-height cross-measurement to no more than half the foot length. This prevents unseamanlike roaches being added to simulate a spinnaker as much as possible. The spinnaker rule limits the foot to 1·8J without penalty, and requires the half-height to be at least 75 per cent of the foot, again mandatorily[44]. This prevents a host of reaching spinnakers shaped like oversize genoas.

success with it probably rely on an ability to cause as little harm as possible, while rivals are making a bigger mess of it and dropping astern. You will be better off using just a light genoa under the chute.

GENNIKER OR SPANKER (2 to 3 oz)

This was the result of early attempts to get more area into a reaching headsail. Shaped to meet the then RORC rule on spinnakers (now the IOR rule[44]: max foot and width anywhere 1·8 J, min half height width 75 per cent of the foot, and symmetrical about its centrefold; see Fig. 12.2), it had to be set with the spinnaker pole bowsed down on the foredeck, and was not very efficient because its half height measurement requirement meant that it could never have the straight luff needed by the reaching genoa.

DOWNWIND SAILS

Downwind sails are mainly spinnakers, as far as we are concerned, but I have also added a few words on twin running sails as advice is sometimes required on their design.

WORKING SPINNAKER ($\frac{3}{4}$ to 2 oz)

Dinghies and cruisers up to 25 ft waterline can use the lower end of the above range for their working spinnakers, boats over this size should be higher proportionately; standard cloths are usually produced in $\frac{3}{4}$ and $1\frac{1}{2}$ oz, and these will do for all but the heaviest yachts. As its name implies, this is a reaching and running sail for most weather conditions up to force 4. It should not, therefore, be extreme as regards fullness in the head (i.e. not too full, nor yet too flat) but should, of course, be to the maximum area allowed by the rules.

LIGHT SPINNAKER ($\frac{1}{2}$ to $1\frac{1}{2}$ oz)

Normally, the light spinnaker for boats of all sizes should be made of the lightest nylon available on the market – providing the owner remembers this fact. Much so-called $\frac{1}{2}$ oz spinnaker material is, in fact, rather heavier and often comes out at about $\frac{3}{4}$ oz.

The light spinnaker will, of course, be used in light airs, so it should not be unduly small. On the other hand, a sail which has every inch of area crammed into the head will not set well, except with a force 2 wind dead aft: the sail will be too broad and full aloft to set on a reach, and there will be so much cloth in the head that even a lightweight nylon will produce a total weight aloft which is more than very light airs can blow out. The 12 metres found that their really large orbital spinnakers were of limited application, and some of their best sails were no more than moderately sized. Extra area can more efficiently be got into a light weather spinnaker by adding a skirt along the foot.

HEAVY SPINNAKER

Heavy spinnaker is usually a misnomer for a working spinnaker or, sometimes, a heavy weather spinnaker. Owing to its ambiguity, the name is best not used at all, particularly as no spinnaker should be heavy.

HEAVY WEATHER OR STORM SPINNAKER (2 to 4 oz)

The demands of modern ocean-racing are such that a spinnaker must be used downwind whenever it is safe to do so. The heavy weather spinnaker is a common sail in the locker of the top offshore boats and, indeed, the top boats of any class where such a sail is permitted. It should normally be of 2 to $2\frac{1}{2}$ oz for all cruisers of any size, the lighter material of 2 oz/yd² only being used by dinghies and those cruisers with a LWL of less than 20 ft; owners of yachts over 45 ft on the waterline should consider carefully whether or not to go heavier than $2\frac{1}{2}$ oz, and may well have the heaviest cloth recommended above, namely 4 oz. This is a marginal decision, however, and I once designed a storm spinnaker for Herr Burmester's KR yacht *Dorothee*. The sail measured 65' 5" on the luff and leech, and 36' 0" on the foot and widest part, yet we only used 3 oz nylon, admittedly of the reinforced ripstop variety.

A heavy weather spinnaker for a dinghy will be the same on the stays and

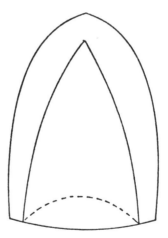

Fig. 12.3 Heavy Weather Spinnaker
Those who say that only fools hoist a spinnaker in heavy weather, have never been leading in an important offshore race when the wind pipes up. This drawing shows such a sail from the front, compared with a standard spinnaker, and it can be seen how much area is lost aloft; the dotted line represents a possible further reduction if desired (which has the additional advantage of improving the view forward).

foot as the working spinnaker. It will merely be of a heavier material and cut flat in the head to help control. This also suits the sail admirably as a reacher, and it can easily double the two jobs. The International keelboat day-racers, such as the Dragon and Soling, usually have such varying rules that it is not possible to generalize. All I can say is that, where little tolerance is allowed, cut as flat as possible and go up one in cloth weight; where the tolerance is great, reduce the size of a large sail (such as the Soling) and cut it flat.

So that the heavy weather spinnaker of an ocean-racer shall reach from the halyard sheave to the spinnaker pole, and so that it shall pass round the forestay, the luff/leech and foot should be within 10 per cent of the full-sized sail. The sail is cut narrow and flat in the head, so that area is lost aloft, where it is least wanted in a blow. If it is desired to reduce size even more, a segment can be cut out of the foot, which has the added advantage of improving forward visibility.

STAR-CUT SPINNAKER ($\frac{3}{4}$ to 2 oz)

After the demise of the genniker, experiments to produce an efficient reaching spinnaker continued. Sail Makers tried as many different cuts as there are days in the year, so that panels ran back and forth like a barnyard hen, in spinnakers which were more or less efficient depending on the quality of the cloth and the skill of the sail trimmer, rather than the lie of the panels. What was needed was a cut which was scientifically thought out and could easily be set by the average owner; it was Bruce Banks who eventually devised it in the 1960's[45].

He worked on the principle that the main loadings in a spinnaker which is full of wind radiate from the three corners. It is thus logical to lay the cloths so that the threadlines also radiate from the three corners; see Fig. 13.1 (d). The star-cut was born. It reduces distortion in the middle of the sail, so that a flatter section can be achieved; the fact that the weft is at right angles to both leeches or luffs also helps cut down stretch at these edges when reaching. The flatter run-off for the airflow is far more efficient than the old fashioned bellied shape, which tended to heel the boat excessively and hold her back.

TRI-RADIAL ($\frac{1}{2}$ to $1\frac{1}{2}$ oz)

The star-cut was so successful that people used it as a general purpose sail, rather than only as the reacher it was originally designed to be. The answer was to give slightly more draft to the middle of the sail, and this was achieved by incorporating horizontal panels right across the central part; see Fig. 13.1 (e). These cloths make the sail easier to make and can be shaped by

Plate 12.3 Star-cut Spinnaker

A beautiful example of the star-cut on *Impulse* (it should be good – it was made by Bruce Banks), showing the principle of cloths radiating from the corners. A large skirt is tending to emphasise the rather tall narrow form of the sail; see Chapter XVIII for the I:J ratio which gives a well-proportioned spinnaker.

Bruce Banks Sails

the Sail Maker to give the degree of flow which he requires. Because the sail is not normally hoisted with relative angles of less than 90 degrees, wind strengths are not quite so strong as for the true star-cut reacher, so the cloth weight can be somewhat lighter.

Plate 12.4 Trimaran Tri-radial

Though difficult to detect here, the original print shows that this is a tri-radial spinnaker. The masthead vane reveals that the apparent wind is nearly abeam, but the wide sheeting base enables the sail to be set perfectly. This trimaran was sailed by Dame Naomi and Rob James to win the 1982 two-handed Round Britain and Ireland Race. Note the roller headsail for ease of handling and, more difficult to spot, the Spee-Squeezer bell mouth at the head of the spinnaker, again for simplicity. The latter was used with much success in the race by several boats.

Chris West

RADIAL HEAD ($\frac{1}{2}$ to $1\frac{1}{4}$ oz)

The logical development was to make a full sail specially for down wind use where the wardrobe already includes a star-cut. This only incorporates the radial concept at the head, and cloth weight is usually light; see Fig. 13.1 (f). This cut had, in fact, appeared from several lofts some time earlier, but it did not catch on until the theory had been proved more convincingly by the star-cut.

BLOOPER OR BIG BOY ($\frac{3}{4}$ to $1\frac{1}{2}$ oz)

The blooper improves stability, and thus speed, when running before the wind. Its use does not warrant the extra expense and complication for a cruising boat, so it is primarily a racing sail and must be made within IOR restrictions for a genoa (max LP = 1·5 × J, max half height = 50 per cent of the foot). The object is to increase thrust on the lee side of the boat to counter the imbalance in area between the mainsail and spinnaker, and it is set flying so that it sags off to leeward to catch wind round the leech of the mainsail. Airflow is thus from the leech forward, which helps keep the sail pulling ahead; see Fig. 12.4.

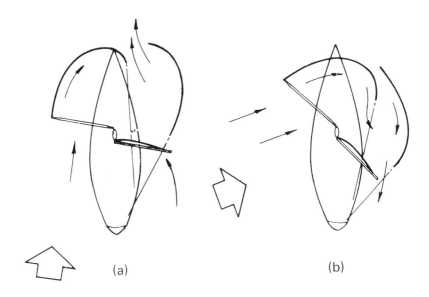

(a)   (b)

Fig. 12.4 Blooper Trim

Air should enter a blooper from aft (a). The halyard is slack, so that the sail can blow out to leeward, beyond the leech of the mainsail. As soon as the wind blows from luff to leech (b), the baggy nature of the sail means that it is only serving to hold the boat back. Because it does not set well with the wind dead aft, there is thus a cone of some 30 degrees either side of 10 degrees off the stern, through which the blooper or big boy operates; it also only pays in winds of more than some 7 or 8 knots over the deck.

The sail is cut with a lot of hollow to the luff, and the corresponding extra inches are added as round to the leech (some bloopers are made with a notched luff and hooked leech). The tack is held to the stem head by a strop which enables it to clear the pulpit and sag well to leeward; the halyard is from the masthead (a blooper is not so beneficial to a fractional rig, because

Plate 12.5 The Big Boy

The job of the big boy, or blooper, is to balance the sail forces down wind, to delay the onset of rhythmic rolling. This photograph shows how the sail catches the wind from round the leech of the mainsail – if it tries to enter the big boy from the luff, the airflow pattern will collapse. The helmsman is blinded through a large arc.

Hood Sailmakers

the difference in area between spinnaker and mainsail is not so great that it needs balancing), and it is never hoisted hard up. The sail thus flies well out beyond the mainsail leech, often with its foot intermittently just brushing the water. It only pays when the wind is within 10–40 degrees of dead aft and force 3 apparent or over.

The sail is popular with crews, because it is easy to set and lower, but care must be taken that its correct trim is not at the expense of the spinnaker; 'The blooper will set better if you square the pole/free off a bit.' Its other drawback is that it makes the helmsman practically blind forward on the lee side, but it does help to steady a boat down wind, thereby improving speed. In this connection, the sail sometimes works better if the mainsail is hauled amidships or lowered altogether to give it unrestricted airflow (but once again take care that solicitude for the blooper isn't at the expense of boat speed). I have long been surprised that 12-metres with their big spinnakers haven't tried them.

CRUISING CHUTE (1 to $1\frac{1}{2}$ oz)

The blooper is so easy to use that it has obvious advantages for the cruising owner if it can replace the spinnaker altogether. Because there is no racing rule restricting its measurements to bother about, any development may be made somewhere between a genoa and a spinnaker in size, and may be hoisted without the complication of a pole and its attendant gear; it can be used in a wide range of relative winds.

It has a straight luff (or nearly so), so that it can be used as a reaching headsail when the wind is forward of the beam, a roach to its leech to add area down wind, and a clew which is slightly higher than the tack to give visibility. Its narrow head means that it loses a lot of area aloft, so the spinnaker's heeling effect is not so apparent, but it has a good deal more pulling power than a genoa because it is bigger; see Fig. 12.5. Size and fullness may be varied within wide parameters, from a near-genoa to a near-spinnaker.

When used on a close reach, the tack is pulled down to the deck and the halyard hoisted hard up to give a straight luff. As the boat comes off the wind, so tack and halyard are eased, until the sail is sagging off to leeward like a blooper, but it sets better with a pole. Being symmetrical, it must be taken down to gybe and then re-set on the other side, but this is so easy that it takes a matter of seconds. It is not allowed in IOR racing because its half-height cross-measurement is more than 50 per cent of the foot (so it is not a genoa), yet it is often not over 75 per cent of the foot (so it is not a spinnaker); in any event, it is not symmetrical and is set without a pole. But it is a simple sail, with few problems, and gives near-spinnaker performance and fun to a cruising boat, without the extra gear, expense and hassle.

Plate 12.6 The Cruising Chute
The cross between genoa and spinnaker can be clearly seen from (a), where the cruising chute is being used as an oversize reaching genoa. Note the tight luff revealed by (b); down wind this will need to be eased a lot, and a simple bearing out spar would make things easier.   *Author*

TWIN-RUNNING SAILS (66 per cent of cloth weight of working sails)
Twin-running sails are an excellent method of making good time on passage sailing before a trade wind. They avoid the constant trim required of a spinnaker (and can be kept up in stronger winds) as the boat is being pulled rather than driven, and they can be quickly reefed by easing forward both clews at once.

A typical running sail has its clew rather higher than the average working jib or staysail, but careful drawing can often make the one double as the other, thus effecting a saving in the wardrobe. As they are down wind sails, they will usually be lighter than the standard weight for the boat but, here again, an effective compromise can often be reached and a heavier weight accepted for the running sails, so that they shall also serve as working jibs or staysails.

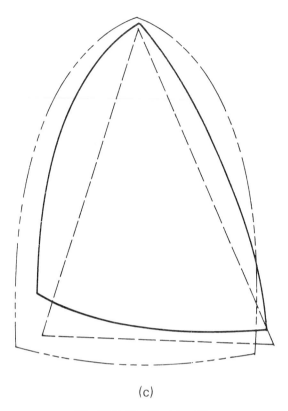

(c)

Fig. 12.5 The Cruising Chute
The cruising chute owes its origin to the big boy or blooper. Designed to have an area half way between the genoa and an IOR spinnaker, it is hoisted on a long tack strop with a relatively slack halyard when down wind; this allows it to fly out to leeward and act like a spinnaker (but they often set better poled out to windward). As the boat comes progressively onto a reach, so the luff must be straightened by shortening the tack strop and hardening the halyard. Some cruising chutes err more towards the spinnaker in area and shape, while others are nearer to a genoa; much depends on what the owner wants – an unruly sail but plenty of area to give extra speed, or a quiet life but not too much improvement over the genoa. This drawing shows a cruising chute (solid line) half way between the spinnaker and No. 1 genoa (pecked lines).

The tacks of the two sails should be between two and four feet abreast, at points about 20 per cent along the base of the foretriangle from the mast, although there is nothing to stop these figures being altered considerably; successful twins have been hanked together to the forestay, and at varying distances apart at most positions in the foretriangle; Fig. 12.6. The tacks should ideally be raised from the deck by about three feet, because there will be virtually no wind lower down, and this will help them disengage the deck somewhat; it will also help the foot of any low-clewed foresail clear the life-lines. The sails may be hoisted from the normal headsail halyards and will, of

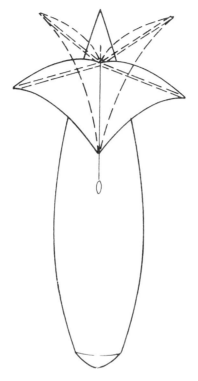

Fig. 12.6 Twin Running Sails
If the mainsail is lowered when twins are hoisted during a long ocean passage, apart from cutting out any chafe on the mainsail, there is no danger of gybing. The wind can swing through an arc of some 90 degrees astern, without the sails needing any trim; even greater changes only require slight alteration of sheets.

An additional advantage is simple reefing. Both sheets are eased forward to the dotted position, so that wind flows straight past the sails.

course, be set flying if tacked back from the stay, so the luff should be suitably stout, preferably of 1 × 19 construction. The poles should be rather shorter than the perpendicular distance from the clew to the luff, so that some shape is given to the sails when they are braced aft.

SPINNAKER NETS

A rod or foil forestay allows the spinnaker to slide easily off it, whereas the serrations of a wire tend to catch light nylon; something to stop spinnaker wraps is thus useful. The standard method is a net of webbing, hoisted on the jib halyard and hanked to the outermost stay. The three sides of the net form an outline not unlike that of a working headsail with a horizontal foot. Since the important part of the forestay to cover is the upper two-thirds, the head should be only two or three feet down from the halyard sheave, and the net should continue downwards to cover the danger area; there should be enough room underneath so that a man can walk upright on the foredeck. A single light 'sheet' may be led straight to a convenient point aft, or may double round its own halyard and back towards the bow. Hanks should be smooth so that they do not, themselves, offer possible snags to the spinnaker. A good type are the Swedish snaps or hanks, which operate pincer jaws by means of a central press button catch. The net should be fitted with a

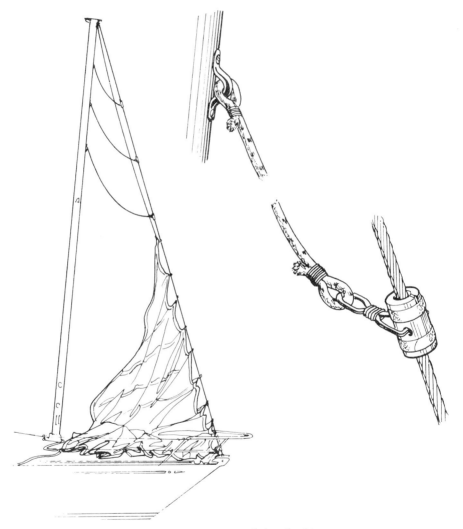

Fig. 12.7 Permanent Spinnaker Net
As the headsail is hoisted, the sliders on the forestay are pushed towards the masthead, carrying the net-lines with them. When there is no headsail set, the net falls into place under the force of gravity. Shock cord may be used instead of the lower lines, if too much slack is to be avoided.

permanent tack pendant to ensure that it is hoisted to the correct height every time.

Permanent Net. The permanent net tries to solve the problem from a fresh angle. It consists of a series of lazy lines attached to the mast, which are free to slide up and down the forestay at their other ends (Fig. 12.7).

When a headsail is hoisted, the rings are pushed up the stay by the head of the sail (a better job is made of it if the halyard has its own hank). If it is desired to keep the lazy lines from sliding too far down the stay when they are free to do so, they can be shortened if shock cord is used ($\frac{3}{16}$ or $\frac{1}{4}$ in diam.), but care should be taken to see that it does not have to stretch more than about 30 per cent of its length when the highest headsail is hoisted.

Spinnaker Area. There has long been disagreement among the pundits about deciding spinnaker area, largely because it is difficult to calculate the curved upper part. All sorts of proposals have been made, reaching the height of complication and impracticality where computer scientists have sought to achieve perfection. But, apart from reasonable accuracy, what is needed is a formula which is simple enough to retain in the mind in the sail loft, the dinghy park and club bar, and which can be worked by all those interested, so that everyone is using the same yardstick, whether it be for purposes of quoting prices, comparison of sails or general interest. It we accept that the fullness in the head just about makes up for the taper of the sail's outline towards the top, a simple rectangle gives a working base. Thus, area may be expressed as the luff (or I – the difference is marginal to all except IOR measurers) times the foot (or $1 \cdot 8 \times J$); where a sail is cut narrow in the head and/or flat for reaching or heavy weather, a deduction of 10 per cent should be made; a 10 per cent *increase* should be made for any side of the sail which is specially rounded (thus +10% for a skirt, and +10% for each of the shoulders of an orbital/spherical spinnaker).

A cruising chute offers a slightly different problem, in that it always has a narrow head and is not usually as wide as a normal spinnaker. The rectangle remains the basis of calculation, and is formed in this case by the luff (or I) times the foot (say, $1 \cdot 7 \times J$); this should then be reduced by a quarter to cater for the tapered head (and often the shorter leech), so that we get $0 \cdot 75$ ($I \times 1 \cdot 7J$). Here again, a variation of 10 per cent either way would cater for a sail which was reckoned to be larger or smaller than average.

The principle of the rectangle is easy to remember. Reduce it for the cruising chute. The 10 per cent factor allows for individuality.

Chapter XIII

Spinnakers in the Abstract

ORIGIN

There has long been much discussion regarding the origin of the spinnaker, and many conflicting theories are suggested. To a certain extent, it depends on the exact interpretation you care to put upon the word. If by spinnaker you mean any sail thrust out to the side of a sailing-boat by means of a long pole, to help down wind speed, then it is virtually impossible to decide who started it all, and when it first occurred. Fishermen boomed out their masthead jibs when running before the wind for centuries. Before them, the square riggers used studding sails, set on spars thrust out as extensions to the yards.

There are grounds for believing that the word is a corruption of 'spin-maker' and there are those who maintain that it originally referred, in this context, to a triangular sail set between the end of the bowsprit and the dolphin striker in sailing men-of-war. This sail was also known as a 'Jimmy Green', and its purpose was to counteract weather helm by making the ship 'spin' to leeward.

If, however, you mean a sail specially made of light canvas, to be boomed out opposite the mainsail down wind by racing yachts, we can pinpoint the origin more accurately. On 5th June, 1865, two yachts were match racing off the Isle of Wight. On reaching the weather mark, Mr William Gordon's *Niobe* hoisted a huge jibheaded sail to her topmast head, boomed it out and drew rapidly away.

The racing spinnaker had been born.

Mr Gordon, need I add, owned a small sailmaking business in Southampton, just across from the Isle of Wight. History does not relate whether he prospered as a result of his invention, but he sold one to Mr Herbert Maudslay, owner of the *Sphinx*, for use in the following year, and there are those who trace the origin of the word spinnaker to this fact. Before we examine this supposition, however, let me return to the earlier use of the sail on board *Niobe*. The famous old British racing skipper Tom Diaper tells us in

Plate 13.1 Spinnaker Testing (1)

Testing the 4000 sq ft spinnaker shown in Pl. 5.3, with half of it spread on the loft floor. We had to get the help of British Road Services and wait for a light wind. Even so, the crane operator was surprised at the power of the sail, which shifted his jib, if I may put it like that.   *Ratsey & Lapthorn*

his memoirs[46] that his grandfather was skipper of *Niobe* when she first used the new sail. His father, who took over as skipper on the old man's death, told him that when the sail was set, one of the hands said:

'Now that's the sail to make her spin.'

A 'gentleman' on board, Diaper continues, took the phrase and reversed it to *spin-maker*. This was shortened, in the same way that *pendant* becomes *pennant*, to *spin-aker* or *spinnaker*. The new sail was also known as a *niobe* for a short while.

In the following year Mr Herbert Maudslay, owner of the *Sphinx*, had his similar sail made, and it was first used in a match race of the Royal Victoria Yacht Club at Ryde off the Isle of Wight. The boat was known to the hands as the *Spinks*, and the locals called the sail a *spinker*, in the same way they had called it a *niobe* the year before. This became *spiniker* or *spinniker* and appears to have joined forces with the corrupt version of *spinmaker* to settle down as *spinaker* or *spinnaker*, both of which are correct usage.

The first recorded use of the word in print is in the British sporting weekly the *Field* of 18th August, 1866. Mr Dixon Kemp, compiler of the monumental *Manual of Yachting & Boat Sailing and Naval Architecture*, mentioned the *spinniker* in a description of a race on 15th August, 1866, in which he took part aboard the *Sphinx*. The form *spinnaker* appeared first in the *Yachting Magazine* for September 1866.

Authority is lent to this timing of the origin by Admiral Smyth's 744 page *Sailor's Word Book*. First published in London in 1867, it makes no mention of either *niobe* or *spinniker*, yet we have two instances of the latter appearing in print in 1866. This leads one to suppose that the word had not found common usage by the publication of the dictionary in the following year. It must therefore have only just started its life at this time.

In the years before the introduction of the spinnaker, a square sail and a square topsail, or raffee, were used. Sometimes a large jib was hoisted on a block half-way up the topmast, and was boomed out by the tack if the rules allowed it. These large jibs were not generally allowed, however, until 1865. In that year the Royal Thames Yacht Club rescinded the rule which read:

> . . . but no jib to exceed 2 ft in the head, nor to be hoisted above the mainmast head (*i.e. from the topmast*), neither shall it be boomed out.

DEVELOPMENT

Since then, of course, great strides have been made. Early spinnakers were asymmetrical and straight sided, mainly due to the influence of using large jibs for the task. These were cut of light cotton with the cloths running parallel to the leech; they were set inside the forestay. The fashion persisted until the late 1920s, when thought was given to making spinnakers symmetrical. The first such sails were made at Ratsey & Lapthorn's New York branch in 1927, and the first one in England was made by the same firm's Gosport branch, to the order of Mr Sven Salen, for his 6 metre *Maybe*.

Development of this kind usually starts in the smaller classes, because it is cheaper to experiment. 6 metres were small boats in those days, but before long most of the International classes were using spinnakers which had the same luff and leech, and which were wide enough to set round the forestay. The newly started International One Design class, however, thought the idea novel enough to include in their rules in 1936:

> . . . spinnakers may be carried around the jibstay and sheets may be trimmed outside the shrouds.

The newer sails were made in two halves, joined vertically down the middle, with nearly straight stays and most of the shape built into the centre

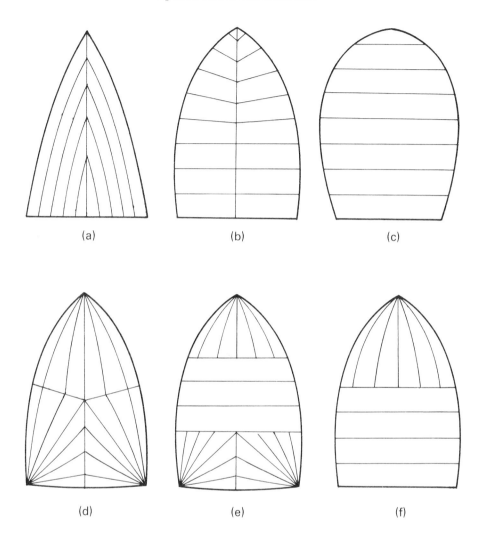

Fig. 13.1 Different Spinnaker Cuts
(a) Early Ratsey double sided spinnaker (1927)
(b) Hood horizontal cut (1951)
(c) Hard spherical spinnaker (1955)
(d) Banks star-cut (1969)
(e) Tri-radial spinnaker (1972)
(f) Radial head spinnaker (1973)

The Hood horizontal cut (b) enabled the shoulders of the spinnaker to be built out in a roach, exactly as the same cut does for a mainsail. When Hard Sails pioneered the spherical spinnaker (c), the centre seam was obviated because all cloths crossed the centrefold at right angles. Banks' star-cut (d) absorbed the stress lines from all three corners along the warp; note that the sail is very slightly narrower (and flatter) in the head than (b), (e) and (f) which are all made for running more down wind.

seam. Sail Makers laid the cloths parallel to the leeches, which gave an acute angled inverted V shape when seen from ahead or astern. The angle in the middle varied slightly, but it was not until M. Herbulot of France widened it so that the cloths struck the leeches at quite an appreciable angle, that any great change was achieved. By this time, however, development had advanced apace and the new cut only enjoyed a short vogue before it was superseded by further improvements (Fig. 13.1).

Originally it was enough to control the lengths of the three sides of the spinnaker, but the new rounded sails had a good deal more area. The rule had to change if it was to remain a fair one. There are three basic types of spinnaker rule today.

ONE-DESIGN RULE

The first requires that the sail be symmetrical and made with straight seams, i.e. no broad seam is allowed. It so closely limits the maximum and minimum dimensions at several predetermined points (usually seven at least), and the tolerances are so small, that all spinnakers to a particular rule are the same shape if folded in half about their centre, when they are required to lie substantially flat on the floor. The only way a Sail Maker can influence the shape of such a sail is by laying the cloths at varying angles, which in turn affects the degree of localized stretch. The Dragon is an example of this rule.

RESTRICTED RULE

The second classification is one where the length of the stays (luff and leech), the length of the foot and the maximum width of the sail at any point are all limited. This gives a maximum size for the sail, within which the shape may be varied at will. There is often also a minimum width at half height to prevent a spinnaker being cut so flat that it virtually becomes an oversize genoa which sneaks in under the spinnaker rule.

The RORC is a good example of this. There was no mention in their rules prior to 1937 of any limit on the spinnaker boom, although there were penalties if the luff or leech was more than 95 per cent of the leading edge of the foretriangle (this is the same as saying $0.95\sqrt{(I^2+J^2)}$, which is still the present IOR limit), the foot more than $1.33 \times J$ and the width at half height more than two-thirds of the permissible width of foot (or $0.88 \times J$).

In 1937 the maximum foot was increased to $1.5 \times J$ and the width at half height to $1.25 \times J$. This still produced a sail too narrow to set properly round the forestay. In 1948 a maximum foot and half height of $1.8 \times J$ was introduced in order to conform with the CCA rule, with a minimum half height width of 75 per cent of the foot; this is now the IOR requirement. This sets comfortably round the forestay and gives a seamanlike sail which can be handled on the open water.

In 1951 Ted Hood of America, in consultation with Ray Hunt, found that laying the cloths of a 210 Class spinnaker horizontally instead of in an inverted V, helped to broaden the shoulders, because the cloths could be more efficiently tapered at the stay ends in order to hold the shape of the upper half better. This was particularly useful with CCA and RORC spinnakers, the Carleton Mitchell used the first such sail to Bermuda in the following year.

FREE RULE

This rule allows whatever sail the owner is courageous enough to set. It may sometimes (but not always) restrict the length of stays and foot, but allows the sail to be as wide as you like above the foot. The rule usually applies to the International classes, and results in sails of all shapes and sizes. In particular, the usual sail is one with a large width at half-height.

The seams were laid in the conventional inverted V for many years, but Hard Sails of America turned their attention to the problem a few years after Ted Hood had introduced the horizontal cut. They came up with the spherical spinnaker (also called the orbital in Great Britain). This does away with the central seam, but flattens the middle portion of the sail by trimming off part of the cloths along their length near the middle. The sail can then be made a good deal wider at half-height than at the foot, and virtually becomes the greater part of a sphere.

OTHER RULES

A few classes, particularly in America, permit the half-height to be wider than the foot, without allowing complete freedom. If the limits are carefully set, the half-height being about 130 to 140 per cent of the foot, a good sail with more natural shaping results.

A second type of rule for the more progressive is one which limits the total perimeter of the sail, measured along the luff, leech and foot, but allows complete freedom within this restriction. This results in all sorts of shapes and sizes, but encourages experiment and is easy to measure.

CLOTH

Not until nylon was developed during the Second World War did spinnakers enjoy a change of material from the light cotton out of which they had been made since they started, with the possible exception of one or two silk sails which had been made in the 1930s. *Ranger* used a quadrilateral made of rayon in her 1937 defence of the America's Cup, but this material does not seem to have been used for spinnakers. The advent of Terylene in the 1950s got everybody excited, and for a short while it was thought to be superior to

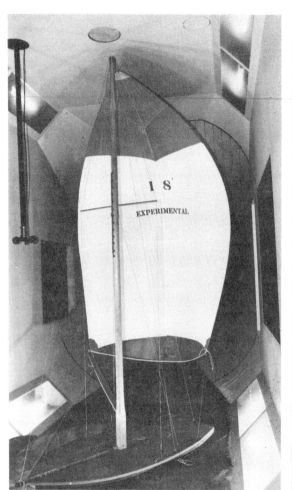

Plate 13.2 Points of View

Your spinnaker (a), the narrow-gutted affair with the spindly top, becomes *their* spinnaker (b), a big breasted bursting beauty, when viewed from ahead. These two photographs were taken from the same distance in the wind tunnel.

Ratsey & Lapthorn

nylon. Spinnakers need to stretch a certain amount, however, and polyester does not have as much elasticity as nylon, which is still the best cloth for this type of sail. It has been shown repeatedly that a low degree of porosity is desirable in spinnaker material. If the cloth passes a lot of air, then it is obviously allowing the pressure to equalize on either side of the sail. Rather than drag the boat through the water and expend its energy in this way, air will choose the line of least resistance and leak pressure through a porous material. A cloth which has a lot of fillers in it will be non-porous to start

242

with, but the chemicals will soon break up to leave the original loose weave; what we require is a tightly woven fine cloth with the minimum of finishing to render it air-tight.

The eighties brought the successful use of Mylar/Melinex film; we have already seen in Chapter III something of its properties. In working sails it is usually stuck to a substrate of woven cloth, but for spinnakers it is often used with only a quarter inch mesh of Kevlar threads bonded to it as reinforcement. The cloth is light and non-porous, and tear-strength from the Kevlar is good (the mesh moves apart slightly, but does not rupture), but it has no give and there is weakening from sunlight.

FLOW DESIGN

The design of a spinnaker, like any other sail, can be divided into outline design and flow design. Outline design is the sphere of the Naval Architect, who is nearly always bound by rules, so that his influence on the shape of a particular spinnaker is only achieved through alteration of measurements of the yacht which govern the outline of the sail: usually the foretriangle measurements I and J.

In considering flow design we have to understand what happens to the wind in the sail. On a reach it behaves very much as in a headsail, in that it flows across the sail from luff to leech. On a dead run it flows from the centre towards both sides, with a bleed downwards off the foot.

It follows that old-fashioned ideas about very full cut spinnakers have to be re-examined and more flatness achieved, particularly in the head where the stays are most tender to a reaching wind. This calls for skill on the part of the Sail Maker, as he tries to keep the springy nylon from stretching into too much of a Roman nose. He achieves his aim by subtle manipulation of the cloth, and by tapering each seam with a mathematically calculated precision (the information is stored on a computer). We have already seen how a careful analysis of the problem by Bruce Banks resulted in the star-cut sail, leading in turn to the tri-radial, but some fancy cuts still turn up from time to time. The low stretch characteristics of Mylar allows scope for ingenuity as Sail Makers grapple with the task of getting the best results. But nylon has proved durable, and I shall deal here largely with conventional cloth, as this provides a better explanation of the complex problem. Equally, I have used the horizontal cut to explain broad seam in Fig. 13.4, but the principles apply to all spinnakers.

The drawings at Fig. 13.1 are the conventional way of showing a spinnaker graphically, that it to say seen from head-on. This method, however, cannot give any indication of the fullness of a particular sail, which must be presumed to bulge out of the paper towards the reader to an

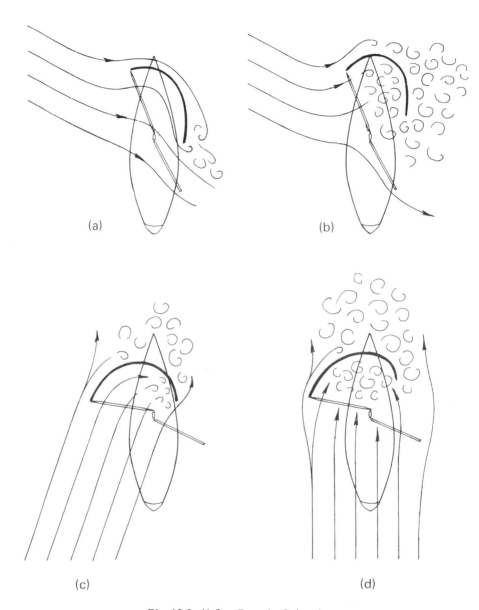

Fig. 13.2 Airflow Round a Spinnaker

Except when the apparent wind is within 10–15 degrees of dead aft, airflow over a spinnaker is (or should be) from luff to leech, as with a genoa. In (a) the streamlines pass as smoothly as can be expected over a nicely flat reaching sail. If the spinnaker is too full for reaching, as in (b), a lot of separated flow results. When the apparent wind is some 20 degrees on the weather quarter (c), there is still some attempt at airflow from luff to leech; but when the wind is dead aft (d), it enters both sides of the spinnaker, and causes a pocket of dead air in the middle.

244

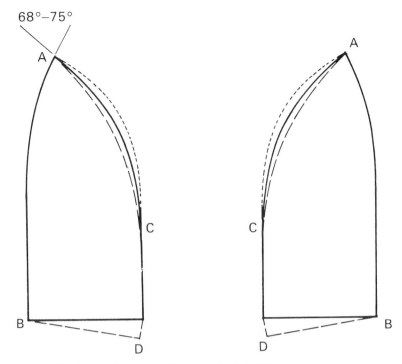

Fig. 13.3 Spinnaker Fullness on the Loft Floor

A = head   C = centrefold or seam
B = clew   D = extra area in form of skirt

When the two halves of a spinnaker are laid out on the loft floor just before being joined together, they appear as above. The central seam is then sewn together, from the middle of the foot all the way up to the head, to give a three-dimensional shape. The dotted line represents a sail which is full in the head, and the broken line is a flat one; a medium spinnaker lies somewhere between these two extremes (solid line), and will usually have an angle at the head of the half sail somewhere between 68°–75°.

unknown degree. Short of a three-dimensional illustration, therefore, we have to turn elsewhere if we want to have a proper idea of the shape we are trying to imagine.

Since a spinnaker is usually symmetrical about its vertical line, a Sail Maker lays out the sail in two halves when cutting it. He therefore has to draw the left or right half of the sail full-size on the floor, and this is how we must envisage the sail on paper. It means a fresh mental approach to the problem, but the result is easier to envisage when this has been mastered.

RESTRICTED RULE SPINNAKERS

Let us therefore examine a spinnaker to the maximum size under the IOR; Fig. 13.1 (b) shows such a sail in the conventional manner. In that drawing the leeches appear to be a good deal longer than the middle seam which bisects the sail vertically. In fact, however, they are shorter, as a glance at the correct drawing at Fig. 13.3 will show. For the IOR, a typical spinnaker will be rectangular from the foot up to a point about 55 to 60 per cent of the hoist (or stay, as it is known). This achieves full size in the lower half of the sail, and any attempt to take it higher up must usually be at the expense of reaching properties. Spinnakers have been made where the curve in to the head does not start until nearly three-quarters of the way up the stays, but they will only set on a dead run, and then usually only in force 2 (which is enough to fill the sail, but not too much to cause it to oscillate).

The curve at the head is not the only way in which draft can be given to a spinnaker; as with fore and aft sails, the cloths can be tapered to increase or decrease the basic flow imparted by the outline shape. There are some classes which prohibit this tapering or broad seam in the interests of uniformity (the Dragon is an example), but they are getting sails which are not as efficient as they might be. The correct draft is further complicated by the fact that an efficient sail does not only depend on draft, but also on the area it offers to the wind when it is set. Thus a very full spinnaker, with a lot of area and draft in the head, will probably blow forward in the middle at the top and become narrow. This will certainly happen in light airs because there will not be enough wind to spread the sail properly; in heavy winds the top will most likely fill with too much air and this will become stagnant, destroying the smooth flow of air across the surface of the sail, thus promoting oscillation.

Nylon obeys the same laws as Terylene or Dacron in that it will distort its maximum if tension is applied on the 45° bias to the threadline. This becomes progressively less as the angle is reduced, although the light nature of the cloth means that there will always be a certain amount of give, even on the threadline itself. This inherent elasticity, which is more than that of the equivalent weight of polyester, means that the cloth should be woven with little or no twist in the thread if threadline stretch is to be kept as low as possible. This in turn will mean slower weaving, and greater likelihood of thread breakage in the process, but it is the price which has to be paid for the best material.

Consequently, the Sail Maker has to make up his mind how he is going to lay out his panels for a particular spinnaker, what broad seam he is going to give them to achieve the shape he has in mind, and how he will control any cloth stretch at the luffs. The spinnaker has all three sides unsupported by a spar or stay, and stresses run throughout the sail (though they tend to radiate from the corners). This means that, no matter how the cloths are laid, bias stretch will result somewhere; it is as well to keep it away from the luffs. The problem is greatest, of course, with a large sail where the loads are considerable; the dinghy spinnaker gets away with it much better.

Broadly speaking, we want to keep distortion at the edges to the minimum so that the luffs and foot will not be slack and inefficient, whereas we can accept a certain amount of stretch towards the middle of the sail. Figure 13.1 (a) shows the early double sided spinnaker with virtually straight luffs; this sail could, and did, have its cotton cloths parallel to the luffs in an inverted vee. When roach was built onto the shoulders of the sail, the thread-line could no longer follow the curve of the luffs if the vertical cut were maintained. So the horizontal cut was developed (Fig. 13.1 (b)), and it was the weft and not the warp which followed the lines of tension along the luffs. This is a highly successful cut, which allows ample opportunity for shaping by broad seam near the centrefold, but the Sail Maker must remember that the more seam he incorporates, the more the head of the sail will be pulled over as the cut away darts are drawn together (Fig. 13.4). The horizontal cut's principal disadvantage is that the middle of the sail distorts too much under load, so that it is difficult to make a good reacher which will retain its shape.

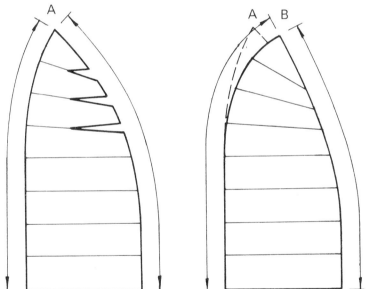

Fig. 13.4 Broad Seam in a Spinnaker
A = head of sail starts at this point
B = head is pulled over, when seams are sewn up.
Horizontal panels, which run away from the luffs at right angles, ensure that the weft or fill threadlines are parallel to the unsupported edge; the clew often makes an angle of 90 degrees, so the warp threads are parallel to the foot. This cut presents plenty of suitable cloths for incorporation of broad seam. When three or four darts are sewn together, the contraction of the centrefold pulls the head over from its starting point; this makes for broader shoulders, and the possible danger of not setting on a reach.

STAR-CUT ($\frac{3}{4}$ to 2 oz)

Distortion of the horizontal cut was the reason for the emergence of the star-cut spinnaker (Figs. 13.1 (d) and 13.5 (a)). We saw in the previous chapter how this evolved, and I can only repeat here that the cloths running out from the corners tend, if anything, to flatten the middle of the sail as they come under tension.

Because any boat on a reach will be subjected to greater apparent wind strengths than when she is running, the star-cut proper is usually made of slightly heavier cloth than a down wind sail; this is all the more valid because the star-cut's flat shape tends to make it also used as a heavy weather running spinnaker. I say 'star-cut proper' because the very success of the sail meant that it gave birth to others: the tri-radial, the radial head, and the super star-cut.

TRI-RADIAL ($\frac{1}{2}$ to $1\frac{1}{2}$ oz)

The star-cut is an expensive sail which is specially cut for reaching purposes, and we have seen that it gave birth to the tri-radial; Fig. 13.1 (e) and 13.5 (b). This was partly as a result of the living proof offered by the star-cut principle of radiating panels from the clews. But it was also because a general purpose sail does not need such overall flatness nor the slightly heavier cloth of the reacher, and so the more economic incorporation of horizontal panels at the mid-height of the sail came about, to allow development of rather more flow in the central portion. The benefits of both the star-cut and the horizontal cut were thus combined to produce a spinnaker which is highly efficient on most points of sailing. This is the cut which is used for the majority of spinnakers in use in the offshore fleet today.

RADIAL HEAD ($\frac{1}{2}$ to $1\frac{1}{4}$ oz)

As its name implies, this spinnaker has the advantages of cloths radiating from the head; Fig. 13.1 (f) and 13.5 (c). It is a cut used where the loadings will not be too great in the sail (because of its size, of the prevailing winds, or perhaps because a couple of reachers are already in the locker and this one will be used down wind only), so there is no need for special attention to the stresses in the lower half of the sail, which can be made entirely with horizontal cloths.

SUPER STAR-CUT ($1\frac{1}{2}$ to $2\frac{1}{2}$ oz)

This is not a specially large star-cut spinnaker, but one which is, in fact, somewhat smaller. It is designed as a heavy weather reaching sail, so is made of appropriately stronger cloth; it also has the narrow head and flat section of all heavy weather spinnakers, with extra strong rings and reinforcement

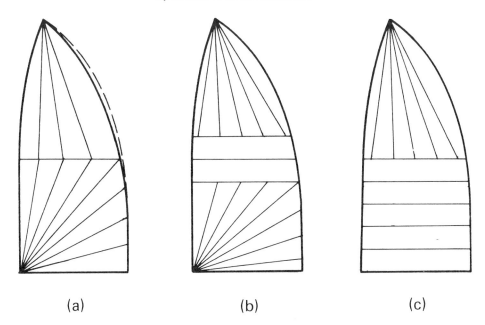

(a)　　　　　　　　　(b)　　　　　　　　　(c)

Fig. 13.5 Development of the Star-cut
In the beginning was the star-cut (a); this has a slightly narrower head than a general purpose, or running, spinnaker (pecked line) as befits a reaching sail. Because it was seen to be good, it quickly begat the tri-radial general purpose sail (b), which was slightly fuller in the head. This in turn was followed by the radial head (c), designed for running down wind, and therefore with a full head and of slightly lighter cloth (due to its lower relative wind speeds).

patches. This is a sail which responds well to being made from Mylar or Melinex.

CENTRE OF EFFORT

It is sometimes useful to shift the CE nearer to the outer end of the spinnaker pole. This can be done, as I suggested in earlier editions of this book, if a small amount of area is surrendered at the clews. To illustrate the idea, I have to revert to showing the sail in full frontal elevation as in Fig. 13.6.

Area. The area of a restricted rule spinnaker can be taken as that of the full rectangle formed by the stays and the foot, minus 10 per cent if the sail is narrow and flat at the head. This is very approximate, because it is hard to measure a concave area; see end of Chapter XII.

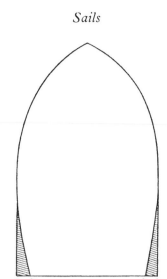

Fig. 13.6 Centre of Effort

It is sometimes efficient to shift the spinnaker away from the mainsail, so that it operates in less disturbed air. If the sail is cut away at the shaded area, it will move its clews from A to B; this will mean that the whole sail will move that much further outboard on the pole, which will disengage it from the mainsail. The slight loss in area is more than offset by greater efficiency.

ORBITAL SPINNAKERS

Orbital or spherical spinnakers are the result of the free rule, which does not limit the cross-measurement of the sail above the foot; see Fig. 13.1 (c). The rule sometimes restricts the length of the stays and the foot, but in any case a practical limit is imposed by the length of the sail which will set from the spinnaker halyard sheave without falling in the water in light airs, and by the width of foot which can conveniently be set on a particular pole. The effective limits for these two distances are approximately the same length as the I measurement for the stays, and two and a half times the spinnaker pole length for the foot (although dinghies can go up to about three times the spinnaker pole for the foot of a spinnaker, where the pole is not longer than about 5 ft). Once the foot is under control on the pole, however, the sail can widen out above it to achieve greater area, providing it is cut correctly. Hard Sails Inc. pioneered the way in 1955, and most free rule spinnakers have been cut that way ever since; Fig. 13.7.

Area. The area of an orbital spinnaker is hard to assess, as it depends so much on the mid-girth width. A rough guide is to take the area of the rectangle which would be formed by the stays and the foot, and then to add 20 per cent for the extra area plus another 10 per cent if there is a skirt; see the end of Chapter XII.

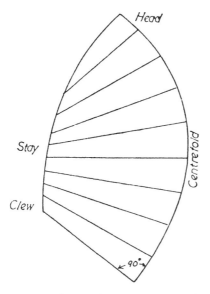

Fig. 13.7 Orbital or Spherical Spinnaker

The centrefold of an orbital spinnaker forms the arc of a circle, whose radius is found by an exact calculation which is the secret of each Sail Maker. Some modification may be made to this rule of thumb, such as flattening the curve at the head, but the sail is based on the circle conception. The cloths strike the centrefold at right angles, so that the central seam is superfluous (because the cloths can be folded back on themselves during the cutting out stage, to form the other half of the sail). This in turn means that the angle formed by the foot and the centrefold in the middle of the foot must be a right angle, if the foot is to be kept on the threadline. The cut has the same suitable panels for shaping by broad seam as the horizontal spinnaker.

CLOTH WEIGHT

Once again I must emphasize the importance of a proper appreciation of the limitations of various cloth weights. It has taken a long time for a true realization of the part played by sails to become widespread; too often the spinnaker lags behind.

A heavy weather spinnaker may weigh three times as much per square yard of cloth as a light weather sail, so the former should not be expected to fill in a force 1 wind. Perhaps more important, a light weather spinnaker should no more be used in a force 4 wind than should a light genoa; unlike the light genoa, which might only blow out of shape, the spinnaker will almost certainly burst. This is particularly true if it is used on a reach, where the relative wind is greater than on a run. Reference to the formula $W = 0.004V^2A$ at the end of Chapter II will show that an apparent wind of 25 m.p.h. will exert an average pressure of 2·5 lbs per sq ft on the effective sail area presented; this means over a ton in a sail of 900 sq ft. A wind of 35 m.p.h. will produce the same weight in a sail half the size.

251

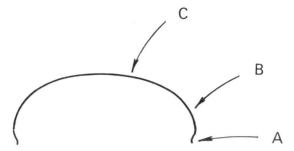

Fig. 13.8 Slack Luffs
Any spinnaker runs the risk of the cloth at the luffs/leeches stretching more than the reinforcing tape which runs along them. This is particularly true of the orbital spinnaker, where the cloths strike these free edges at a marked angle as the head is approached, so that bias distortion is likely. Steps have to be taken to tighten the necessary seams to control this, or the very edge of the sail would not stretch due to the tape (A), but the cloth immediately inside it would do so (B); this would be exaggerated by the broad seam incorporated to flatten the sail in the middle (C), so that we get a section as shewn above.

GEAR

Spinnaker gear must be studied carefully if the foredeck gang is expected to put up fast times. The gear itself must be simple and strong, and must be partly tailored around the gybing technique. This in turn may be influenced by the preference of the owner and the hand in charge of the spinnaker, if the boat is lucky enough to have a permanent man.

Pole. The advantage of a double-ended pole is that it can be plugged in either end. Its disadvantage is that it cannot therefore have the ideal outer end fitting, which would make it too bulky to go into the spinnaker cup. The final selection will be influenced by the gybing technique and the rig, as we shall see later, because a single pole gybe on a cutter demands a double-ended pole, while a similar gybe on a sloop allows a single-ended pole to be used. At all events, take care to see that all end attachments are sufficiently robust for their task and simple to operate (they may have to work under pressure in the dark).

Hoisting. Spinnakers always used to be hoisted in stops, or straight from the deck if the weather was light. These are still good methods, and a stopped sail is often used in large yachts, particularly in heavy weather, as it keeps the sail under full control as it goes up. The modern drill, however, is to hoist from some sort of special bag or sheath made for the purpose. I shall go more fully into various forms of spinnaker stowage in the next chapter. It is enough here to say that some device is needed for stowing the spinnaker

Plate 13.3 Spinnaker Testing (2)
A major part of the Sail Maker's task is to evaluate his products, to stay in touch, and to be familiar with all kinds of craft. Here my step-brother Stephen Ratsey and I are sailing a GP 14 in the early days of developing its spinnaker (note that we haven't even got a second fairlead for the spinnaker sheet, which has been doubled up with the jib).   *Ratsey & Lapthorn*

neatly, while at the same time having it ready to hoist at a moment's notice. The secret in most systems is not to waste time while it is going up, but to haul away with a will. The sheet should be trimmed as the sail goes up, but not too much or too soon, or else the spinnaker will fill early and be hard to get up the final few feet.

Winches. Winches must not only be powerful enough for their task, but they must also be sited where they can be brought into use without interfering

253

with the smooth running of the boat. Considerable thought is needed in this planning, which is closely linked with the system of gybing which it is proposed to adopt. Let me merely say here that winches should be powerful enough to wind the pole off the forestay in a stiff reaching wind, when the mechanical advantage is low due to the narrow angle of the guy. It is also useful if the spinnaker does not have to rely entirely on both genoa winches, as the leeward one may certainly be wanted while the spinnaker sheet is on it; this becomes progressively more important with size, and at 30 ft LOA and over it is essential to have a total of four sheet winches on any boat which races seriously.

Sheets and Guys. On boats up to 30 ft LWL, both sheets and guys can be of three strand non-stretch rope. Above this size, if the boat is raced hard, the spinnaker boom guy should be of wire with a rope tail, because the stretch in a rope will allow the pole to move forward too much under pressure — particularly on a reach when this movement is most likely to spoil the set of the sail. Generally speaking, the sheet should be led through a fairlead no further aft than level with the outer end of the main boom when it is sheeted amidships; the fairlead should be forward of this when close reaching, particularly in light winds. This is because the foot of the spinnaker must not be stretched too tight, or there will be no flow in the sail and a choked slot. The guy should lead somewhere forward of the sheet (except that it will, of course, go to the sheeting point when one line doubles for both sheet and guy). A good tip for star-cut spinnakers, is that the sheet should point directly at the middle of the star when reaching[47].

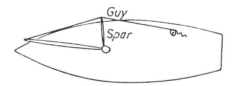

Fig. 13.9 Jockey Pole
A jockey pole or bearing out spar is used when the spinnaker is on a close reach. This props the guy outboard to a position of better mechanical advantage, and also frees it from chafe on the main shrouds.

Bearing-out Spar. Many rules, including the IOR, allow a short spar or reaching strut to be used to bear out on the guy where it rubs the shrouds when reaching. This not only frees the guy from the effects of chafe, but also increases its mechanical advantage, and is thoroughly recommended.

Chapter XIV
Using a Spinnaker

When sailing dead before the wind, the object of a spinnaker is to present the greatest area of sail to undisturbed wind, so that maximum drag is achieved; the boat will thus be blown down wind. To do this, sufficient cloth must be in the sail in the first place, and it must be so shaped that the air flows outwards from the middle to spread the luffs as far apart as possible. So we are not entirely concerned with drag pure and simple, even when the wind is right aft[48].

When sailing on a reach, the airflow round the spinnaker changes from one which blows into the middle and out of each side, to one which passes horizontally across the sail from luff to leech. The object here switches from the dead run case to one more allied to the function of a headsail: the airflow must be changed into forward thrust through the pressure differential pattern we examined in Chapter II. The spinnaker's principal advantage over a conventional headsail in these circumstances lies in its greater area. Although it is acting exactly like a headsail, it does not have the advantage of a head-sail's straight luff, flat flow or straight leech; quite the contrary, it has a sagging luff, deep section and a leech which returns to windward to a marked degree when judged by headsail standards, even if the spinnaker is flat by its own criteria. We have to be more than ever on our guard, there-fore, to see that the wind is not deflected too much into the lee of the mainsail, and that the component of the spinnaker's thrust is as forward acting as possible.

We should remember, therefore, in reading the rest of this chapter, that for most of the time a spinnaker is set we are dealing with the equivalent of a very large, full headsail which is set without the advantage of a straight luff. Only on limited occasions when the wind is within a 5° to 10° arc either side of dead astern are we concerned with drag as a prime requirement.

The first consideration with using a spinnaker is often whether to use it at all. There are occasions, particularly on a close reach, when the sail will fill and draw, but when another sail would be more efficient. The governing factors are apparent wind angle and strength, and the type of sail which is available as an alternative. If the spinnaker is strapped alongside, so that there is almost as much thrust aft as forward, it will only serve to heel the boat and slow her down, possibly giving rise to a broach. On the other hand, it may be that the sail is contributing to forward speed, but only marginally. In this case it would possibly not pay to take off the sail in, say, a Soling where the alternative is a headsail which is less than a sixth of the size of the spinnaker, yet it might easily pay in one of the offshore racing fleet, where the spinnaker is only two to two and a half times the size of the largest headsail.

As a rough guide we can make a quick rule of thumb, for use in medium winds, which says that a properly cut spinnaker can be carried with advantage in apparent winds five degrees forward of the beam, for each amount by which the spinnaker is larger than the headsail which would replace it. Thus, if the spinnaker to headsail ratio is six or seven to one (as large a difference as is usually met), the larger sail will pay dividends with the apparent wind up to 35° forward of the beam. As the wind strength increases, the headsail's advantage is correspondingly increased also. A

Plate 14.1 Spinnaker Stopping – Elastic Band 'Magazine'
A plastic bucket with the bottom removed (and smoothed off). The strip of wood under the bands is a refinement to make it easier to pick up a single band.
Roger Marshall

star-cut spinnaker gains another 10° to 15°. A ratio of three or four to one brings the angle down to 15° or 20°, because anything further forward would mean that the moderately large headsail could drive her better.

PACKING

Some method of preparing a spinnaker for use is obviously necessary, and the system must be one which can be got ready when beating to windward after the off-wind leg, and which can be stowed ready for use some time later.

STOPPING

A spinnaker can be quickly stopped by using elastic bands and a short length of plastic drainpipe; from about One Tonner size upwards, a plastic bucket with the bottom cut out is used; see Fig. 14.1. If stopping cotton has to be used without the help of a feeder pipe, the head of the sail should be made fast and the luffs pulled out so that they are free from tangles. The sail

Bucket or pipe

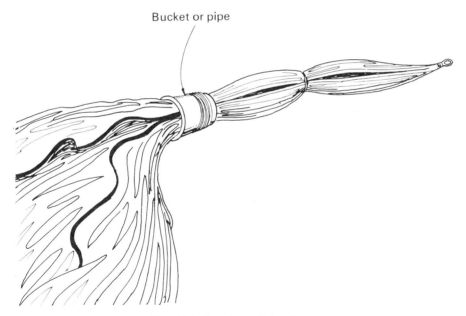

Fig. 14.1 Stopping a Spinnaker

Elastic bands are placed round a short length of plastic drainpipe, or round a plastic bucket whose bottom has been cut out and smoothed off carefully. The diameter of the pipe should be about one inch for every ten feet of height of spinnaker, or I measurement. The spinnaker is then drawn through the drainpipe or bucket, while care is taken to see that the two luffs are free from twists and side by side; the rest of the sail follows as it may. An elastic band is slipped off the pipe or bucket, at intervals of 3–6 feet depending on the size of sail.

257

Plate 14.2 Spinnaker Stopping – Frogleg Pattern
A spinnaker stopped in the frogleg manner, so that the two clews may be separated
before the sail is broken out.   *Roger Marshall*

should be gathered together from each side, starting at the head, so that it is
flaked and not rolled towards each luff. Make sure that the bunt of the cloth
is pulled towards the foot all the time, and increase the number of turns of
cotton towards the clews, where the strain will be greatest. In both forms of
stopping, as the foot is approached, the clews may be divided so that two legs
are formed; this will allow the tack and clew to be separated during the
hoisting process, without the sail accidentally breaking out.

SHEATH

For this method, the two luffs of the sail are traced through and pulled out
side by side; the sail is gathered together between them. This is then enclosed
in a lightweight nylon sheath, with its two sides held together by an open
ended zipper or by velcro. The resulting snake is hoisted to the mast head,
whereupon the pull of the sheet separates the velcro or causes the zipper to
disengage, allowing the sheath to fall clear so that the sail may open. A
safety line should be fitted to avoid loss.

TURTLE

The spinnaker turtle was reported by Corny Shields to have been invented in
the early fifties by Philip Benson of Marblehead[38]. Owen Parker was using

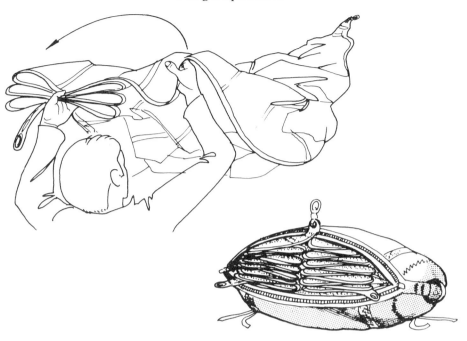

Fig. 14.2 The Spinnaker Turtle

First developed in the 1950's, the turtle offers a convenient way both of preparing the spinnaker for hoisting, and of stowing it compactly for moving it around the deck. The important point is that both luffs should be carefully traced through and stowed in last, in an untangled condition. In an emergency, even a cardboard box will do the job.

one in England in 1955 and says that he introduced it into Newport RI the following year[49]. At all events, it is certainly a wonderful idea, and must have saved more time for harassed crews all over the world than almost any other single gadget. There are many variations on the theme, from the converted plastic trash bucket to the specially tailored knapsack with press-stud fasteners and shock cord all over it. They all achieve the same end: a spinnaker which is neatly stowed into a small compass, with its luffs checked for twists, and with head, tack and clew protruding ready for attachment to their various fittings; see Fig. 14.2.

A spinnaker up to about 30 ft on the luffs can be bagged into a turtle by one person. Starting at either clew, one luff is traced along its length and flaked back and forth into one hand. This process is taken past the head and down to the other clew, so that both luffs are then securely held in a bunch in one hand. The main bunt of the sail is then thrust into the turtle, preferably with the foot going in at the bottom, although this is not essential. Finally, the luffs are pushed in last, with the head and clews carefully protruding in the middle and either side respectively.

Plate 14.3 Spinnaker Stopping – The Turtle
A neat turtle tied to the lifeline. The halyard, sheet and guy are already clipped on,
and the bag will break its velcro fastening open as the sail is hoisted.   *Bunty King*

The same result can be achieved on smaller sails by starting at the head and working down both luffs simultaneously. The object in both cases is to see that the luffs are free from twists and turns, and that they go into the bag last with the head and clews where they can be hooked on, to come away cleanly when hoisting sail. A larger spinnaker will take two people to bag, because the whole length of both luffs cannot be held in one hand. If the sail has to be got ready in a real hurry, hold the three corners and ram the rest of it into the turtle willy nilly; nine times out of ten it will come out all right. In light winds, small sails can be launched direct from the arms of a crewman stationed to leeward.

LAUNCHING TUBE

The launching tube originated in the dinghy fleet, and has spread to the keelboats. The spinnaker is drawn into the tube by a retrieval line which is attached to its mid-point; when stowed, the centre of the sail is pulled in first, followed by the rest of the doubled sail, leaving the head and two clews exposed at the tube mouth. Hoisting is a matter of seeing that halyard, sheet and guy are attached, slackening the retrieval line, and hauling on the

Plate 14.4 Spinnaker Stopping – The Chute
The simple spinnaker chute of *Quarto*, the Quarter Tonner of the late Jack
Knights. Note the feed rings attached to the hatch tops.   *Author*

halyard. The disadvantages for the offshore fleet are the problem of keeping
the hull watertight with a large hole on the foredeck, and the fact that one
tube can only operate one spinnaker (many boats have three or more
spinnakers, but only room for two tubes).

SPEE SQUEEZER
The Spee Squeezer® was first thought of by Chris Hall of the Isle of Wight.
The principle is that the spinnaker is encased in a nylon sheath and hoisted
to the masthead. The lower end comprises a funnel or bell mouth moulding,
which can be drawn upwards to compress the sheath and unfurl the sail; it is
on an endless line so that it may be hauled down again to furl the sail when
desired – indeed, it can be used at the half way position for short periods as a
sort of reefed spinnaker. It is invaluable for shorthanded boats, and has been
used with success in OSTAR, AZAB and Round Britain races; there seems to
be no limit to size, and one is fitted to *Shamrock*, the ex J-class racer. Similar

(a)

(b)

(c)

(d)

Plate 14.5 Spee Squeezer
In (a) the spinnaker is at full hoist, but still encased in its nylon sheath. The bell mouth is hoisted upwards to release the sail (b) by pushing the sheath into a concertina. The spinnaker can be set reefed in this manner. At (c) the bell mouth is fully hoisted and the sail deployed. The basic equipment of bell mouth funnel, nylon sheath and halyard/downhaul is shown at (d).

devices are available under other trade names, some of them using rings (Spinnaker Sally®) or some of them a long wire coil (Spiral®) instead of the nylon sheath. The Spee Squeezer's continuous sheath makes for easier one-man operation, and there is no practical limit to the wind strength in which it can be used. Unless they are tended carefully, rings can allow the spinnaker to balloon between them in strong winds, with attendant problems.

HOISTING

The spinnaker is usually hoisted from the leeward side of the foredeck or from directly in front of the forestay. This is not the place to go into all the different methods in detail, and I refer the reader who is anxious for full information to *Spinnaker*, by my good friend Bunty King. Let me merely repeat here that the secret lies in getting the thing up quickly, so that it does not start to fill before it is at the mast head. A second important point is that whatever stowage you use should ensure that the sail deploys from the foot upwards; in this way you will avoid many snarl-ups and figure-of-eight wraps, because twists will tend to unwind on the head swivel. Finally, timing of the break-out is important. If the sheet is pulled tight too early, the sail will fill before it is right up; if it is left too late, the danger of a wrap is increased as the sail flaps idly at full hoist near the forestay.

TRIM

'The most important single factor in proper spinnaker trim is the positioning of the spinnaker pole.'

This was said by Stephen van Dyck, spinnaker trimmer for the America's Cup defence[50]. There are not many who would disagree with him.

POLE ANGLE

The object of trim is to get the spinnaker to spread as broad as possible, high and wide into air undisturbed by other sails or spars and rigging, and to develop maximum forward thrust. To achieve this the sail must be extended as far from the mast as possible across the direction of the apparent wind, when seen in plan view.

This means that the pole should normally be at rightangles to the apparent wind, as Fig. 14.3 will show. A vertical elevation of the pole under the same conditions shows that it should also be at rightangles to the mast to achieve the same effect in this plane; Fig. 14.4.

In both cases the tack is then allowing the sail to stand as far as possible from the mast, in order to collect the most undisturbed air. Naturally, a

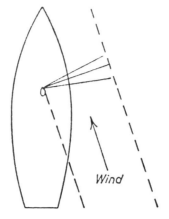

Fig. 14.3 Pole Angle – 1
If the spinnaker pole is trimmed at right angles to the apparent wind, it will
project maximum area of the sail across the wind.

small angle of difference from the optimum will not affect the issue very
much, and other considerations of trim may require a slight deviation from
90°. As soon as the pole strays from the rightangle by more than about 15°,
however, the percentage loss of tack offset goes up rapidly.

I recall racing a Dragon in Cowes Week one year. I was fortunate enough
to have the spinnaker hand from the American yawl *Bolero* on board, while
the latter was undergoing repairs after hitting an uncharted underwater
obstruction. Needless to say, I gave him charge of the spinnaker, although
he assured me that he had never been in a Dragon before. We were running
eastwards up the Solent in perfect conditions lying third about twenty-five
yards behind *Nortic*, where we had been keeping exact station for about five
minutes.

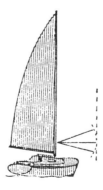

Fig. 14.4 Pole Angle – 2
The spinnaker pole should be at right angles to the vertical plane of the mast, if it
is to keep the tack as far from the mast as possible.

'Give me an inch of pole,' called my spinnaker trimmer, and we gave him exactly that. Immediately the relative speeds changed and we slowly started to creep up on the boat ahead. I am afraid that I cannot recount a tale of crushing victory, for *Nortic* soon spotted us and restored the *status quo*, but the lesson was graphic.

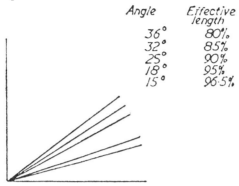

Angle	Effective length
36°	80%
32°	85%
25°	90%
18°	95%
15°	96·5%

Fig. 14.5 Pole Angle – 3

This drawing shows the effective length projected by a spinnaker pole which is allowed to stray too far from the right angle. Anything more than 20 degrees off line, starts to reduce the effective length quite considerably – in fact by the cosine of the angular displacement.

The illustration at Fig. 14.5 shows how the effective length of the pole varies according to this angular displacement from the optimum. In fact, the effective length lessens by the cosine of the angle of displacement.

At 18° up or down from a rightangle, or aft or forward for that matter, the pole is 5 per cent in from its maximum; at 25° this increases to 10 per cent, and at 36° it is as much as 20 per cent. The moral of this is obviously not to let the pole be more than 20° off the rightangle at any time.

POLE HEIGHT

The height of the pole must also be settled. Basically, the aim is to see that the tack and clew of the spinnaker are the same height above the water; this will ensure that the sail, being symmetrical, is not twisted into a poor aerodynamic shape. The outer end of the pole must therefore be hoisted to the position where it is estimated that the tack will have to go to keep level with the clew; the inner end should then be raised to ensure that it is at right-angles to the mast, and the pole squared to the apparent wind. The sheet may then be adjusted until the luff is on the point of falling in (more on this later) and the tack and clew compared for height. Any difference should be adjusted by raising or lowering the pole bodily. If the tack is allowed to rise higher than the clew, the leech will tend to twist inwards, close the slot, and backwind the mainsail.

The spinnaker is now in basic trim, and fine adjustment must be made on the sheet.

EXCEPTIONS

There are, of course, exceptions to such a broad generalization. In light winds the pole should be squared aft an extra 10° or so, to prevent the upper part of the spinnaker from falling away too much. In heavy winds, the converse is the case, in order to reduce the tendency to roll and to aid in control: it may not always be possible to trim the sheet quickly enough to stop the sail falling in, so a little in hand will help here. Equally, because the star-cut is so flat, flow is given to the middle of the sail by having the pole lower and the sheet lead further forward than normal when using this type of spinnaker. Similarly, the pole should be kept low in winds of force 2 or less, in order to straighten the luff and to reduce the amount of sail which has to be lifted before it fills. It may then be slowly raised as the sail fills and the free clew lifts. In these conditions pole angle is important, in order to catch as much air as possible, but height of pole (and thus aerodynamic shape) takes second place to the importance of getting the sail to fill at all.

A final exception concerns the height of the inner end of the pole in large yachts when close reaching. If it is allowed to be lower than the outer end (which will be near the forestay), a reduction in strain will result, as the pole will be more nearly in the same plane as the afterguy. The topping lift will then only have to counterbalance the foreguy, and will not be fighting the afterguy as well.

SHEET

We have already seen that we want the spinnaker to develop as much forward thrust as possible (F_T spin, to revert to the symbols adopted in Chapter II). This means that the sail, regardless of the pole position, should be trimmed so that it presents its arc facing as fully forward as possible. To achieve this the clew should be abreast of the tack when reference is made across the boat; Fig. 14.6 (b).

Naturally, it is not possible to achieve this neck and neck situation when the boat is other than on a broad reach or run. A simple rule can be stated for sheet trim: ease the sheet until the luff starts to fall in at the head, then harden it so that the sail is just on the quiver; Fig. 14.7. In very light winds it seems to pay to ease the sheet rather more than usual; in heavy winds it may be better to harden it a little more, so that sudden puffs do not cause the sail to fall in. This knife edge balance demands the utmost concentration and speed on the sheet. If the sail collapses in light winds it may take quite a long time to re-establish it.

Here let me say that Stephen van Dyck's dictum that there should be only

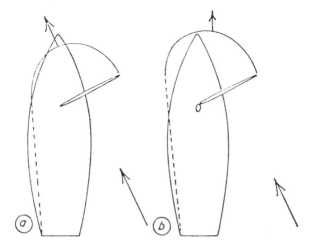

Fig. 14.6 Spinnaker Trim – Plan View
If the spinnaker is sheeted too hard as in (a), the sail is pulled to leeward, so that the total thrust (F_T) acts at an angle to the fore and aft line. Easing the sheet so that the clew is level with the tack (b), brings the line of thrust more efficiently back in line with the boat's direction.

one man in charge of trimming the spinnaker is worthy of more than the lip-service it all too often receives. A soviet of opinion is all very well, indeed it is to be encouraged for many a good suggestion will come of it, but there must be only one man who collates all the information, both visual and aural, together with the possible courses of action, and who then translates this into executive instructions to the crew.

Let me repeat here that the sheet should be led to the rail opposite the end of the main boom, in order to keep the leech of the spinnaker as far from the mainsail as possible. It sometimes pays to let the sheet pass over the outer end of the main boom on a broad reach, as this opens the slot still more, but take care not to let it ride too high or it will hook the mainsail to windward, and if you do it for long, be prepared for chafe on the mainsail, especially if it is Mylar or Melinex. Many boats have a travelling sheave under the main boom, so that the spinnaker sheet can be hauled out to the best position; this also helps to combat chafe.

Corny Shields has written some wise words on spinnakers[38], not least of which is his generalization on trimming. He said, quite rightly, that it is in light to moderate weather that correct trimming pays the greatest dividends. When the wind is really blowing, your boat soon reaches her maximum hull speed, so the finer points are wasted. He went on to say that a spinnaker should, however, be hoisted whenever practicable, because there are always lulls which would cause a drop below maximum speed without it. Most authorities are unanimous in recommending that the sheet be trimmed hard

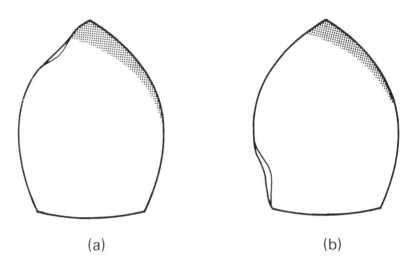

(a)   (b)

Fig. 14.7 Sheet Trim

Wind shifts occur just as much when a boat is reaching or running as when she is close hauled. The spinnaker trimmer's job is to see that pull from his sail is directed as much forward as possible and taking advantage of every freeing puff. Besides bearing in mind the overall shape of the spinnaker, as dictated by pole height and angle, he should ease the sheet until the weather shoulder just starts to fall in (a), then harden very slightly, before starting to feel for any improvement again; this is a constant search, demanding intense concentration. If the sail starts to break near the clew as in (b), the pole is probably too low, and there is a danger that the whole sail will fold in. Collapse is less likely with a high break because the foot is full and helping to spread the whole sail; if the break is low, there is no such support below it.

   If the sail is falling in repeatedly, there is a danger that the trimmer will have to sheet the sail too hard; it is better to make correction to basic trim by easing the pole. Conversely, if the wind frees through 5–10 degrees and holds, the pole should come aft to keep the clews level, rather than the sheet eased too much.

in hard weather because of the difficulty of reacting quickly enough in the gusts. In addition it can sometimes help to lessen rhythmic rolling if the sheet is hardened and led further forward in the boat, say to a strong point at the chain plates. I would like to add a warning here against strapping the sail too closely alongside, thus causing the boat to heel excessively to an inefficient underwater shape.

HALYARDS

In winds up to force 3, the spinnaker should be hoisted hard up. Above this, it may be eased at the head with advantage, particularly when reaching. The amount of drift varies with different boats, ranging from 6 to 12 in on a dinghy, to 5 to 6 ft on the larger yachts, depending also on wind strength.

This has the effect of disengaging the sail from the interference of the mainsail. An eye should be kept on the lower quarter of the sail, to see that it does not cause it to slope too much back towards the boat, thus burying her nose. Remember that, by virtue of two of its attachment points being at the stern and the masthead, a spinnaker has a natural tendency to push the bow down – despite what many people say to the contrary.

A slightly eased halyard will serve as a good indication of the direction of pull of the sail. If the head falls well off to leeward, the thrust is inefficient and you should start thinking in terms of a genoa if the spinnaker cannot be trimmed to better advantage. If the sail is pulling well forward, then you have done your job well. On occasions it can move out to windward, and this means that the sail is exposing more area to undisturbed wind, so it is also a good sign.

GYBING

I do not want to become too involved in spinnaker techniques, for the only way really to become proficient in handling them is to practise – first of all on a calm day, then in rougher weather, and finally in a good blow at night. Gybing, however, offers one of the more absorbing ways of losing or winning races, so a few words may be pertinent, particularly if an improved technique can save a sail being torn.

Dip-pole Gybe. This system uses only one spinnaker pole, which is left attached to the mast and dipped through the foretriangle. If the boat has a baby stay, it must be unfastened for the gybe, and transferred to the other side of the pole. Smooth passage of the pole past the forestay is important, and the topping lift should be marked at the point where the pole end just clears the pulpit as it swings across; the inner end will almost certainly have to be pushed up the mast on its slide, and here again the exact position should be marked. Both these marks should be detectable by touch for boats which race at night.

End-for-End Gybe. If the pole will not pass through the foretriangle while still attached to its mast cup (because of a permanent inner forestay, or perhaps there is only a fixed point attachment on the mast which doesn't allow the pole to clear the forestay), it must be unclipped from the mast and from the spinnaker before being transferred across the boat and reattached. The outer end should be snapped onto the guy before the inner end is engaged in the mast cup; it is best if the guy is free-running through the pole end fitting, so that the spinnaker shall not take charge before the pole is firmly attached to the mast; Fig. 14.8.

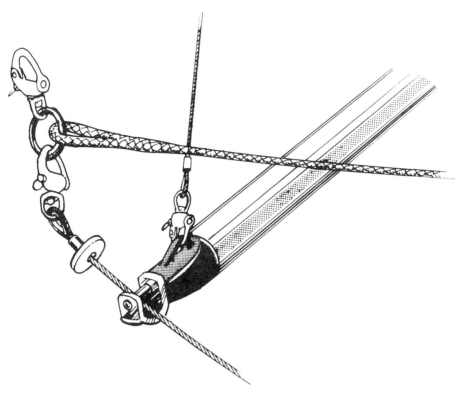

Fig. 14.8 Pole-end Guy Attachment
The guy is free to run through the jaws of the pole-end fitting. These are closed by
a spring plunger, which may operate via a trigger mechanism: the jaws may be left
open so that they can be placed over the guy, which then triggers the mechanism
to close them. This is a dangerous toy for the inexperienced, particularly at night,
because there is a lot of power behind the plunger, and fingers have been lost
before now.

Twin-pole Gybe. Both the dip-pole and the end-for-end gybes leave the
spinnaker without a pole at either corner for a short time. If the wind is
strong, or indeed the boat is large, there will be quite a lot of power in the
sail, which may get out of hand. The use of two poles ensures that the sail is
kept firmly in control at all times; in particular, at the precise moment of the
gybe, each clew is held firmly at the end of a pole which is locked in position;
see Fig. 14.9.

Single or Double Sheets/Guys. Most small boats use one line for both sheet
and guy. This is, of course, simpler but there is one main snag: at some time
during the gybe, the pole will have to be clipped to the sheet while it is under
strain, as it is about to become the guy. This can be difficult in a weight of

wind; it becomes impossible as the size of the spinnaker increases – we can say that 30 ft LWL is the sort of size where the change to twin sheets and guys should be made. This agrees with the size we have discussed for the guy to be made of wire.

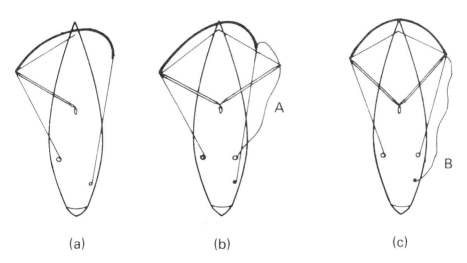

(a)   (b)   (c)

Fig. 14.9 Twin-pole Gybe Principles

A = Slack after guy, before being tensioned
B = Slack sheet, after being eased

While the boat is sailing normally under spinnaker, the pole is locked in position by three lines: foreguy, topping lift and after guy; there may also be a downhaul if this task is not fulfilled by the foreguy. The after guy renders freely through the jaws of the pole-end fitting, and is pulled hard aft to draw the tack of the spinnaker back and down to the pole end against the pull of the foreguy (a). Without changing this in any way, the new pole is clipped over the lazy guy (or over the sheet if this doubles as guy) and is then fastened to the mast (b). Just before the gybe itself, the boat is run off dead before the wind, and the sheet is eased gradually, while the lazy guy is pulled in to draw the other clew/tack back and down to the end of the second pole, against the pull of its own foreguy. The spinnaker is now locked in position by two firmly stayed poles (c). When the boat has been gybed, the old guy is released from the old pole, which is then stowed.

PEELING

So that the boat shall not lose drive while spinnakers are being changed, the peeling process has been evolved. This involves hoisting the replacement sail on a second halyard, either inside or outside the spinnaker which is to be taken in. When the new one is up and trimmed, if the old one is now on the outside, the tack is allowed to fly free so that the sail peels away ready for pulling into the cockpit via the sheet; if the old one is on the inside, the sheet is released and the spinnaker is gathered onto the foredeck inside the new sail.

Plate 14.6 Lowering the Spinnaker – Cockpit Takedown
Tina lowers the sail conventionally (a), and pulls it in under the boom (b).

John Driscoll

The intricacies of the peel itself are well explained elsewhere[51], and need not be detailed here, where I shall stick to a few general tips and hints. Suffice it to say that the question of whether to peel inside or outside is not a matter of the chief foredeck gorilla's whim, but of how the two spinnaker halyards will be left afterwards – for the process puts half a twist into them, or takes it out, depending on which halyard is used on which tack. Have a look, therefore, before you make the decision, or you may finish up the day's peeling by having to send a man aloft to unwind the halyards.

LOWERING

A basic rule when lowering a spinnaker is to get it into the lee of another sail or sails – the mainsail, a genoa or, when peeling, another spinnaker. This ensures that the empty sail is more controllable as the wind tries to blow it hither and yon. A second sound principle is to steer a steady course, so that the foredeck gang know where the wind is coming from all the time; now is not the time to put on the wheel a helmsman who is easily distracted by outside influences. Finally, make sure that the man on the main halyard can see how the crew is coping.

Cockpit Take-down. This is the most easily learned take-down procedure. The clew is taken in hand (if it can't be reached directly, the sheet is grabbed forward of the fairlead), and then the tack is unshackled so that it flies free to leeward like a flag. With no weight now in the sail, it can be pulled into the cockpit as it is lowered. The man on the halyard can easily drop it in the water if he lowers more quickly than the crew can gather it in.

Foredeck Drop. The pole is eased to the forestay and a hand goes to the tack. The sheet is then allowed to run free, so that the sail blows out ahead, to be gathered from the tack as the halyard is lowered. This keeps the action out of the cockpit, but usually means having the weight of two men on the foredeck – not always desirable.

The Big Drop. This requires a retrieval line which runs up to the head via a couple of rings in the middle of the sail; its tail is held by a crewman somewhere aft of the mast. The pole does not need to be eased onto the forestay, so the genoa has plenty of airspace to be hoisted and trimmed as the leeward mark is approached. At the mark, the guy is eased and the spinnaker halyard let go with a run; the sail is pulled in under the genoa by vigorous hauling on the retrieval line. This system keeps weight aft but clear of the cockpit, and allows the spinnaker to be kept up and trimmed until the very last moment.

273

Plate 14.7 Lowering the Spinnaker – Foredeck Drop

Uin-na-Mara (KH 9) holds the inside berth on *Vanina* (I 8188), who has allowed her main boom to gybe (a) as they were both running by the lee for the mark (left foreground). As the boats round the mark (b), they drop their spinnakers on the foredeck under the lee of the genoa, and *Uin-na-Mara* profits from her inside berth. If either boat had dropped early, she would have lost crucial yards, but their proximity to each other has obviously ensured that the both held on until the last second. This is a discipline which has to be cultivated even when there is no rival breathing down your neck – because the yards lost by a lazy drill could be just as important at the end. *John Driscoll*

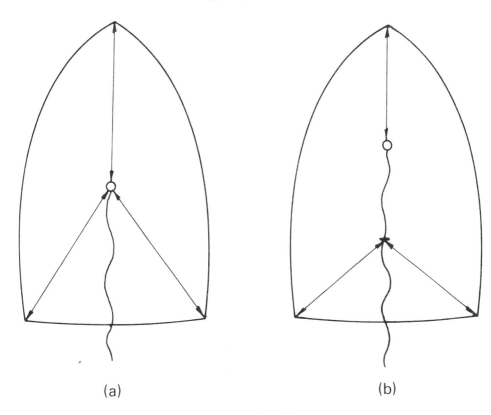

(a)   (b)

Fig. 14.10 Retrieval Lines
In (a) the retrieval line is attached so that it is equidistant from all three corners of
the spinnaker. For a faster stow, the line is taken through a fairlead to an attachment point further up the sail (b); from clews to fairlead and from patch to head
need to be the same distance. Retrieval lines used with a chute are rather harsh on
the sail; when used on the open foredeck of an offshore boat, they can save snags.

Launching Tube. Recovery into a launching tube is similar to the big drop,
except that the retrieval line is attached to the middle of the sail rather than
the head. Sheet and guy need to be eased as the sail disappears into the tube,
so that all three corners are eventually left at the mouth. It is quick and
efficient, but one tube can only cope with one spinnaker.

Floater Take-down. This is only used when on a dead run before a light
wind. The pole is left square and a hand grasps the spinnaker by the middle
of the foot, which is then drawn aft towards the mast while sheet and guy are
allowed to run, so that wind is spilled from the sail. The halyard is freed, so
that the spinnaker drops to the deck. This is as good a method as any if the
conditions are right; one of the benefits is that it takes no special gear,

Plate 14.8 Lowering the Spinnaker – The Big Drop
The retrieval line for the spinnaker of *Aries*, here (a) leading *Williwaw* to the lee
mark, can be seen running from inside the sail, down the luff of the genoa and
under the tack. It enables her to keep her spinnaker pole topped up and aft until
the last second, while *Williwaw* has a man already on the foredeck (she also has a
retrieval line, running down the outside of her spinnaker); *Aries* must be gaining
yards at this moment. The Swedish boat lying third will have lost even more
ground by her early drop.

another is that it is practised in light winds, so little harm can come of it if it
doesn't go quite right first time.

Aries lets her halyard run (b), relying on the lee offered by the genoa to control the spinnaker as the retrieval line is pulled in, while the boat rounds the mark (seen over the cockpit).   *John Driscoll*

Chapter XV
Care and Maintenance

LAYING-UP

You will only get the best use from your sails if you lay them up for the off-season period carefully. Briefly, they should be repaired, cleaned and stored, in that order. A Sail Maker will usually reverse the first two, because he has clean premises in which to do his repairs and he wants to keep them that way; the amateur sailmaker will probably get some dirt on to the sail he is repairing unless it is done in the drawing-room.

CHECK

It may sound obvious, but you should start by finding out what has to be done; a little method will save hours in the end. Spread each sail where it won't pick up grease or dirt, and put on your sailing shoes – for you are going to walk all over them. Arm yourself with a needle and thread, so that you can mark each job with a short length of contrasting colour. Start at the head and work round the luff, foot and leech, looking for problems before going onto the sail itself.

Head. Headboard (eyelets and stitching), roping (chafe and security), head eye of jibs, reinforcing patch.

Luff. Boltrope, luff tabling (stitching and delamination), slide or hank attachments, reef cringles, luff wire.

Tack. Tack eye, Cunningham hole, boltrope (chafe and security).

Foot. Boltrope, foot tabling, slide attachments.

Clew. Clew eye, clew patch, boltrope (chafe and security).

Leech. Tabling for chafe and creases, leech line, reef cringles, batten pockets (chafe and security).

Bunt. All seams for chafe, reef points, insignia and numbers, delamination of Mylar/Melinex.

Battens. Cracks in the ends, correct length, markings (*inner end, outer end, top, bottom* etc.).

278

Plate 15.1 Looking for Trouble (1)
Maintenance starts with spreading the sail on a clean surface, prior to going over it systematically, looking for trouble. Mark any job with a short length of contrasting thread.   *Author*

Sheets. Chafe, weakness, whippings.

Sailbags. Include these, largely because a repair to a bag can give the virgin sailmaker confidence to tackle the real thing.

Spinnakers. Tie the head or one clew about ten feet up, and hold the sail up to the light when checking for small holes.

STITCHING

Chafe is the bugbear of synthetics, so look carefully at all stitching. Use the flat of a knife point and really pick at it hard; you want to find any weakness

279

now, not when you are fifty miles off shore. You may only find one or two stitches gone, but this would spread rapidly the following year, so stop the rot immediately. In bad cases a chafing patch may be needed. The points to watch are where the mainsail bears on shrouds or lee runners, the leech of the mainsail if the topping lift has been allowed to rub against it, headsail leeches and clews in way of shrouds, jumper stays, spreaders and sundry projections on the mast, such as the spinnaker track, as the sail comes about. Batten pockets tend to go at both ends: at the leech it is the stitches where the batten end stretches the hole as it is pushed home; at the inner end it is the padding effect caused by the extra thickness of the elastic in the end which makes the batten chafe through the cloth. Take care not to sew in the leech line as you repair leech tablings and batten pockets. See that the protectors on the ends of full-length pockets are doing their job properly. Finally, do not forget the spinnaker, particularly if the head swivel is shackled on, thus giving it play to work from side to side and attack the stitching around it; check the clew rings and look also at the foot tape where it bears against the forestay from time to time. Try to establish the reason for any chafe you find, and see whether you can eliminate the cause, perhaps by re-siting a mast cleat or other projection.

FITTINGS

Check on the rope around the *headboard* and *clew eye*. This can sometimes start to pull away, and should be resewn by hand. Remove the hide casing, if fitted, and pass the needle between each lay of the rope, using four parts of waxed thread; the hide casing can be softened for easy sewing by soaking it in water for half an hour or so. On a grooved luff mainsail, the cloth between the rope and the headboard may show signs of chafe. A patch would make the sail too thick to pass in the groove, so about all that can be done is to sew by hand four or five rows of stitching up and down the affected part, to give it more strength; the finished job should be beaten as flat as possible. *Cringles* and *eyelets* should be examined for distortion. See that all *slides* are at an even distance from the bolt rope and that seizings, as on *snap hooks* or *piston hanks*, are firm. Check the latter to see that they are good and tight (or they may jam on the way up or down the stay) and apply not more than two drops of oil on the piston. Where slides are shackled to the sail, see that the bolt rope is cased with hide or cloth to minimize chafe. All *lashings* and *lacings* should be properly whipped at the ends, and do not forget the *reef points* under this heading. If your *battens* are wooden, they should be rubbed down with sandpaper, and given a couple of coats of varnish. Split a short length of plastic tubing and fasten it to the inner end of a full-length batten if you do not have external protectors; tape the ends of thin battens to help stop them splitting. You should also look at your *sheets* and *halyards*

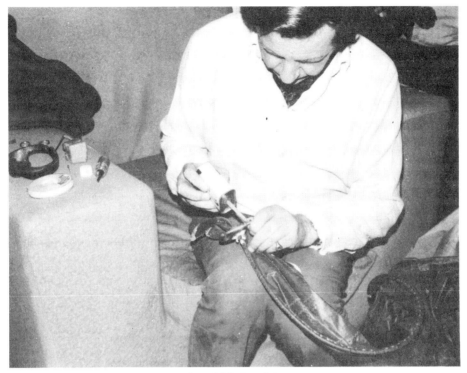

Plate 15.2 Servicing
Not more than two drops of oil should be put on the plunger of each piston hank or
snap hook, or it will spread to the sail.   *Author*

while you are about it, for you will get chafe where the same part of a rope or
wire always bears on a sheave. Switch them end for end to change the point
of stress, renew whippings and throw away suspect wire and shackles. You
will probably do these two items at the same time as the rest of the running
and standing rigging. Have a really close look at all *luff wires*. Stainless steel
does not always live up to its name and, while it will not necessarily rust, it
reacts chemically with polyester to produce a discolouration of the cloth
which will eventually start to weaken the cloth. Galvanized wire will rust or
corrode away unless it has been properly protected. Most Sail Makers in
Europe use plastic-coated galvanized wire for temperate climates. Pay
particular attention to the tack, for this is where the wire gets wettest and
where the coating has been disturbed in making the tack eye; flex it back and
forth, and listen for the tell-tale rustle which will reveal any stranding. Pull
spinnakers out by their clews from the head, and compare the length of the
luffs. If a sail is symmetrical and if it is fitted with wires which differ in
length, one of them is probably broken and its repair is a job for the Sail
Maker.

Fillers. The chemicals which are put into some synthetic cloths will eventually work their way out of the weave, to the detriment of the performance of the sail. As these fillers have been forced under pressure into the material between heated rollers, they cannot be put back again once the cloth has been made into a sail. There is nothing, therefore, which anyone can do – professional or amateur – to restore the filling to a Terylene or Dacron sail.

CLEANING

A dinghy mainsail once came into the sail loft where I was working with a letter from an irate owner complaining about the set of the sail. When we put it on the test spar, it looked like a badly-made accordion; the owner was right, it certainly did not set well. We knew that it could only have been made to look like that with some very harsh maltreatment, so I wrote to the owner and suggested that he might have boiled it in a machine, or put it through a rotary ironer. It transpired that he had done both, so there *are* those who will do the strangest things to a sail and expect it to stand up to it.

Dacron or Terylene sails small enough to go comfortably into the bath – anything up to 120 sq ft – may be washed that way; see below for the special care needed for film laminate sails. If the sail is too big for the bath, find a stretch of clean concrete or tarmac where you can spread the sail and hose it down. If you use the garage apron, be sure first that it is clear of oil. Use a scrubbing brush – Sail Makers often use an industrial rotary scrubber – and any mild household detergent. Stubborn stains may be attacked with a proprietary brand of chemical cleanser, without harm to the cloth. Remember to rinse the sail in fresh water afterwards to remove any trace of a 'high-water mark'. Terylene and Dacron are resistant to chemicals, and I am indebted to Imperial Chemical Industries Ltd for the detailed instructions about removal of different stains from polyester, which will be found at Appendix B.

Mylar/Melinex. It is known that polyester becomes more susceptible to ultra violet degradation if subjected to alkalis, while acids do the same for nylon. Any washing of Mylar or Melinex with detergents should therefore be extra thoroughly rinsed to remove all traces, because the light nature of the woven polyester or nylon substrate in laminated sails makes them specially vulnerable. In addition, the precise nature of adhesives used in various cloths is a secret closely guarded by each manufacturer, so you will never be entirely sure what effect bleaches or detergents may have. Some authorities go so far as to say that film laminate sails should never be washed at all, others that only very recent soiling should be tackled. At all events take care with the use of chemicals.

Plate 15.3 Drying a Sail

Any sail left to dry in the garden (a) should be hung up by the luff, so that the strain is taken on a part of the sail which is strong enough to avoid stretching. If it is dried on the mast (b), be prepared for a lot of chafed stitching.　　　*Author*

283

Ironing. Ironing synthetic sails, as I implied just now, is not recommended. There are, however, people who do so, and who do so successfully. If you are tempted to follow their example, be prepared for isolated patches of the sail to be overheated. This will cause localized fusing of the filaments and distortion of the cloth which can never be cured. In addition, a heat of 160°F causes shrinkage, so you must be careful even if you are satisfied that you will not overheat the cloth. I would be failing in my duty if I did not advise against ironing. If, despite this warning, you are determined on this course of action, use a heat controlled iron on the coolest setting. Switch the iron off before using it, and do not leave it in contact with one part of the sail for more than one or two seconds. The safest treatment for sails which are badly creased is to wash them and then spread them in the open air to dry. If you are going to hang them up to dry, never hang them by the leech; hoist by the head and then hold the other end up by the tack, so that the strain comes on the luff wire or rope. Do not iron Mylar or Melinex.

If you are going to ask your Sail Maker to do any or all of these tasks, do it early in the slack season so that he can fit it into his quiet period. You will acquire merit, and get better attention and service.

Mildew. While mildew cannot attack synthetic cloth itself, it can form on any dirt or moisture left on a sail, as indeed it can on a moist piece of glass. This will leave an unsightly stain which it is difficult to remove, although a weak solution of bleach will do a fair job.

STORAGE

Sails should be stored loosely flaked in a clean, dry attic or garage, so that air can circulate freely; the truly conscientious will turn them over once or twice during the winter. These conditions, however, are the ideal ones and I am aware that they hardly ever occur. The main thing to remember is no damp and no creases, therefore any dry place will do, and the sails may be stored in their bags if the latter are big enough to avoid having to cram the sails into them. Dinghy sails can often be stored rolled round the main boom and hoisted on to the rafters of the garage. At all events, avoid folding or bunching the sails too tightly, and do not put heavy weights on top of them. Avoid creasing windows.

FITTING-OUT

If you have done all that you should have done at the end of the season, your sail problems regarding fitting-out should be minimal. If you did not do a thorough job of laying-up, get out your sails as soon as you can and go through the items listed at the beginning of this chapter. In any event, put a second drop or two of oil on all hanks, snap-hooks and shackles, and a light coating of grease on slides if they are not nylon or nylon coated. You then need only to check that mildew has not managed to start, and that the sails have not been eaten by rats or mice (whether they actually eat the cloth, or merely use it to make their nests, they seem to have a liking for synthetics, and the result is the same whatever they do with it), and you are nearly ready to go.

Rigging. I say nearly, because you should first check that your rigging is properly cleaned down and free from chafe-promoting stray barbs of broken strands. A newly launched boat in particular will have dirty wires, and light alloy spars have an amazing propensity for picking up dirt as well. A clean rag on wires, with some petrol or gasoline for bad patches, and a Brillo® pad and warm water for metal spars, will work wonders in a short time. Be careful if your spars have a protective coating: Brillo may take some of it off so only use a clean rag soaked in fuel in this case.

Decks. Do not forget to see that your decks are clean as well, because the sails will spend a certain amount of their time lying on them.

Spars. The grooves of wooden spars in particular should be inspected for splinters or other snags; some alloy spars can also become rough in the groove if they are not anodized and salt is allowed to gather. A fine sandpaper or emery cloth followed by a light coating of paraffin wax should be used in both cases. See that screws holding tracks to spars are fully home and secure, so that their heads will not catch on the slides; check the easy operation of any second track reserved for a trysail, and also the gate if one is used.

BREAKING-IN NEW SAILS

Gone are the days of slow stretching of new sails. Synthetics come out to their marks almost immediately, and new sails can be used without any preliminaries. Ideally, it is best to sail on a broad reach in light winds for about half an hour while the canvas settles down, but you can race as soon as you bend the new sails if it is essential (it never should be, for it only needs a start to the day's sailing thirty minutes earlier than usual). You should not criticize new sails for faults, however, until they have been used in something stronger than light airs for three or four hours. Leeches of headsails, in particular, may judder a bit until the sail has stretched out to allow the clew to draw back and down, thus putting more tension on leech and foot.

I would advise against reefing a new sail in its first four or five hours of sailing.

CARE IN USE

There are some general points which apply to the use of both new and old sails, if they are to give long service. The overriding precept is to use your sails with care. There naturally comes a time in every boat when consideration for the equipment has to take second place, and your sails should stand up to limited misuse from time to time, but they will react unfavourably to prolonged or repeated mishandling, so watch the following points.

BENDING THE MAINSAIL

I have already gone fully into the question of setting and sheeting sails from the trim point of view. The only aspects which concern us here are those which apply to the proper setting of the sail at rest. The main halyard should lead off the sheave fairly on to the head; the most common fault is for the lead to be too close to the mast, which will cause the headboard to pull over towards the mast thus creasing the upper part of the sail.

The tack-pin should ensure that the foot rope runs in a straight line all the way. If the boom is not a roller reefing one, the tack-pin will normally be between $1\frac{1}{4}$ and $1\frac{3}{4}$ in away from the mast, and the Sail Maker will allow for this; if it is any different, he should be told to an accuracy of half an inch. The clew should also leave the foot rope in a straight line, and it is best to have a slide fitted at the clew eye, unless it fastens to a proper clew outhaul slide. A grooved foot on a cruiser (i.e. one which will not be subjected to regular adjustment while sailing) may have a lashing round the boom at the clew when it is hauled out, to take some of the weight transmitted through the leech. This will help prevent the sail pulling out of the groove, or the groove itself splitting if it is of wood. This clew lashing should be tight enough to cause the clew eye to lie over sideways slightly with the sail at rest, because the strain along the leech will soon pull it upright when you start sailing.

BENDING THE HEADSAIL

The tack of a headsail should ensure a straight luff, so it should not be too far from the foot of the stay concerned. If the sail is set on a tack span, have a snap hook or hank near the tack of the sail to prevent it sagging away from the stay; similarly there should always be one near the head. It is good to have a snap or hank on any head pendant, to stop it winding around the stay before the tension is fully on it. If you are bothered with the bottom hank riding down over a turnbuckle or swaging when the headsail is lowered, try putting a small disc or ball of wood or plastic round the stay immediately above the offending fitting, so that it acts as a buffer to the lowest snap hook or hank. A boom staysail foot should obey the same rules as a mainsail as regards tack and clew fittings.

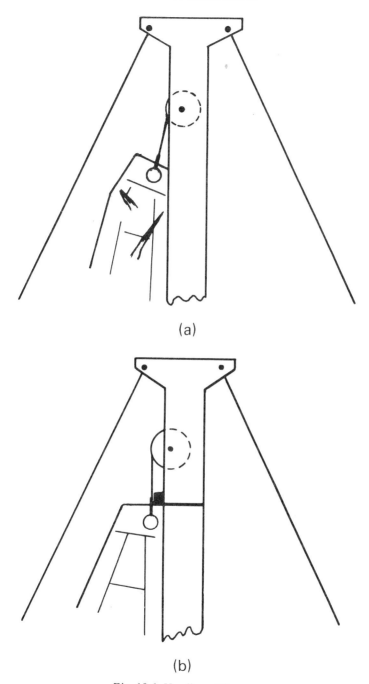

(a)

(b)

Fig. 15.1 Headboard Creases

If the halyard is pulled over towards the mast as in (a), creases will run from the headboard. These can be avoided by fitting a sheave which projects further from the aft face of the mast to give a fair lead to the headboard as in (b).

HOISTING SAIL

Always take the weight of the boom when hoisting the mainsail, either by holding it up or by taking up the slack on the topping lift. A sail which is flogging head to wind and trying to pull up the weight of the boom by its leech will soon stretch the leech and become inefficient.

CHAFE

I have already said enough to make the reader aware that stitching sits on top of synthetic sailcloth, so chafe is a bugbear; this is doubly true when you remember that most synthetics suffer from ultra violet degradation, that synthetic thread is thin, and that it is fully exposed to sunlight where it lies on the surface. Lee runners should always be allowed to go right forward, and should be lashed there if necessary. Anti-chafe measures at the ends of spreaders are worth their weight in gold, the topping lift should be removed on long voyages, and the spinnaker foot should never be allowed to bear against the forestay for any length of time. There are many anti-chafe precautions which can be taken, and they are more important to the modern boat than they were in the days of hand-sewn cotton. Sheets and guys should not be forgotten, particularly where they bear against the boom or shrouds.

Minor Repairs. Minor repairs should be attended to right away, particularly those resulting from snagged sails or chafed stitching. A job which would take half an hour can quickly get beyond the resources of the crew if the sail is used without repair, even if it is only a few hasty stitches or a piece of sticky tape. Adhesive backed spinnaker repair tape can be obtained from most Sail Makers, and no yacht should be without a roll or two, especially as it will hold on a mainsail for a surprising length of time as well. Ordinary sticking plaster from the first-aid box is better than nothing. Immediate steps should, of course, be taken to locate the cause of a snagged sail, in order to eliminate it if possible.

USE OF LEECH LINES

The correct use of leech lines is so rare that they should be abolished. They are a tacit confession of failure by the Sail Maker, for their role is to steady a drumming leech, which should be corrected permanently in the sail loft. The right way to use one is to pull gently on it until the vibration partly settles down, and then to make it fast. If the line is pulled until the drumming stops completely, it will almost certainly cause the leech to curl to windward. This is the worst possible leech shape, and there are enough troubles with sails without producing any more deliberately. It is far better to have a slight vibration and free run-off for the wind, than a quiet leech which is hooked. The best job the leech line does is not to the efficiency of the sail, which is not

288

seriously impaired by so-called motorboating, but to the morale of the helmsman. If you find it hard to tie off the line when it has been pulled to steady a leech, try sewing a button in a handy place so that the line can be wound round it. At all other times the line should be left completely free.

TIED REEFING

Not only is it important to reef a sail properly to get the best out of it, but also so that the set of the sail shall not be permanently ruined by uneven stresses along the foot. Take care that the tack cringle is lashed firmly so that it is in line with the new foot of the sail. The reef ear-ring on the leech of the sail should be pulled out hard, so that the foot is well spread; it must of course be tied down securely. Individual reef points should be tied with the same tension throughout, so that the sail sets well; a continuous lacing should not have any hitches at each reef eyelet, or it will not be able to render and thus equalize the strain along the foot. It is preferable to tie under the foot rope, but a grooved boom effectively prevents this; in this case the line has to be passed right round the boom. Jiffy reefing, as described in Chapter VII, makes the operation easier, and thus reduces the chances that the sail will be damaged in the process.

MYLAR/MELINEX

The advent of film laminated cloths has not changed the fact that sail care is important to long life of the wardrobe; but it has altered the emphasis slightly.

Delamination. Delamination is the breakdown of bonding between the film and the woven substrate. Due to improved adhesives, it is not quite the problem it was in the early stages, but the danger is always there. Delamination can be started in a number of ways, which include overloading to the yield point, flogging, point loading, repeated flexing, and rips or tears.

Yield Point. I have already said enough about not using any sails in wind strengths above their designed range, to make it obvious that this is a crucial factor in sail care; it is doubly important with film laminate sails. Make sure that your Sail Maker tells you the upper limit of each sail, and make sure that you pass this on to the crew by using an indelible marker to put this wind speed on the clew and the sailbag, and then invest in a good anemometer.

Flogging. If laminated sails are allowed to flog head to wind, possibly aback on the rigging, they will respond by chafing (as will polyester sails) and delaminating. This not only means care in use, but also not hoisting them by the tack to dry, so that they flap in the wind (if you want to dry them, take them sailing in a light breeze or spread them on the lawn). A good deal of wear and tear can be avoided by fitting a tacking line. This is a line spliced into an eye half way along the foot of the genoa, led through a fairlead at the bows, and brought back to the cockpit. When changing tacks, the line is used to haul the sail forward as the boat passes through the eye of the wind, and thus clear of the mast.

Point Loading. Even if you are careful not to overload your sails in strong winds, you can still cause point loading if you hoist them wrongly. If you have a film laminate sail which is fitted with hanks or slides and you hoist it too slackly, each slide will pull a crease from the luff as the sail strains unevenly; equally, there is a danger of the luff tape being overstressed if the sail is hoisted too hard on the winch. Haul them up, therefore, until the small wrinkles at the luff are pulled out, and then don't haul any more, or you may get local delamination.

Flexing. Flexing does not cause quite the trouble you might imagine, because the film will blow back into shape in use, and the woven substrate is so light that it does not take up permanent creases easily. This is not to say that film laminates should be stuffed willy nilly into sailbags, because repeated creasing will eventually cause problems. It has been said that Mylar sails are like omelettes: they are better folded than scrambled. If sails are folded as described later in this chapter, creasing will be kept to a minimum not only as sails are bagged, but also while they remain stowed and later get dragged on deck for the crew to find the head, tack and clew for re-setting.

Tearing. There are enough spectacular tears each season to make every owner nervous of this problem with film laminates. But it is not so bad as it may at first seem for, like most tears, it usually starts as the result of thoughtlessness – the tear, however, is sometimes dramatic. It is important to ensure that all snags and sharp points are removed or fitted with anti-chafe tape or boots. The sails themselves should be protected from permanent snags such as spreader ends or shrouds, by incorporation of sacrificial patches; these are often best fitted after the new sail has been hoisted, and the danger area identified and marked on the sail with a pencil. If a hole is caused in a sail, it should be patched immediately with repair tape and then returned to the loft for permanent repair depending on size: anything under quarter of an inch in diameter may be safely left, providing there is no further delamination and the repair tape is adhering well (it sticks better to the film rather than the woven substrate).

Owners should be aware that film does not adjust itself around any hole, in the way that woven cloth tends to. Therefore any puncture will remain open, and this extends to those holes caused by a sewing machine. Too much sewing with close spaced stitches will therefore result in a weakness somewhat similar to the perforations on a breakfast cereal packet where one is encouraged to 'tear along the dotted line.' It is sometimes better to be content with iron-on sticky tape in preference to sewing.

Seams can give trouble for this reason. This is especially true where, as in the leech, they are subjected to extra stress without the support of a boltrope. This is why you will sometimes see mainsails with taped seams for some distance inside the leech. This is largely a matter for the Sail Maker, but it is something an owner may add for himself if he wishes. The Sail Maker may additionally protect this vulnerable area by doubling the cloth all the way up the leech and, in the case of genoas, along the foot.

BOARD SAILS

Besides all the problems which any sail is heir to, a board sail has one or two of its own. To start with, it gets wet from top to bottom every time it is taken out – even on fairly calm days. Secondly, at the end of the day there is a temptation to roll it round the mast, put it on the car roof rack, and drive home with attendant buffeting.

Washing. Rinse all salt out of the sail by hosing down with fresh water. Too much scrubbing and detergent may affect modern materials, so don't worry too much about the odd stain.

Folding. Anyone who races at all seriously will be advised to reserve his or her racing sail for racing days. This will be kept off the mast, rolled horizontally (with due regard for the large window), and preferably stowed in some sort of plastic piping of 6 ins diameter, such as that used by plumbers; this protects the leech and batten pockets in particular. A board sail and leisure use may, indeed, be rolled round the mast but, if it is transported on top of the car, you should keep the whole thing in a special stocking.

LOWERING SAIL

There is no excuse for pulling a sail down by its leech. This is sheer laziness and will ruin a good sail in short time.

STOWING SAILS

The dinghy man will always remove his sails from the boat after sailing, and so will the small keelboat one-design owner. For best results the sails should be hosed down with fresh water to remove salt, then dried and carefully

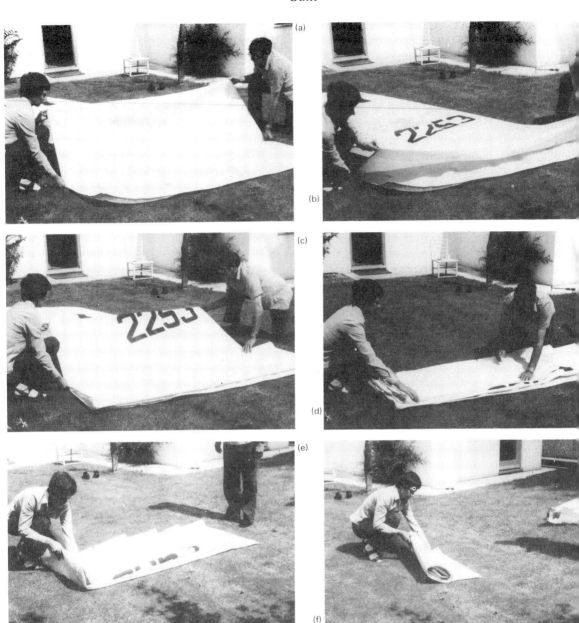

Plate 15.4 Folding a Mainsail
With the sail laid out on the ground (a), one person goes to the luff (the lady in this case) and one to the leech. The first fold is laid down on the foot (b), with the luff superimposed on itself; the line of the leech moves slowly towards the luff as progress is made up the sail. The second fold (c) follows the first, and so on until at (d) the head of the sail is reached. The sail is rolled from the luff at (e) until the job is finished at (f).   *Author*

rolled or folded so that multiple marble crazing does not occur in the cloth. A sail of under 4 or 5 oz weight which is rammed into a bag, be it twice as large as necessary, will undoubtedly crease after a time. Besides causing breakdown of the chemical fillers in the cloth (this danger recedes as sail cloth improves in quality, thus doing away with the need to add too many chemicals in the finishing stage), creasing will tend to settle in one particular place; if that place should happen to be the leech of the sail, it will seriously interfere with the set. There comes a time when the leech has places on it which sit at rightangles to the main plane of the sail, due solely to repeated casual creasing in the same spot. Even ironing, which no true Sail Maker would ever recommend to an amateur, will not remove this sort of stubborn fold, and the only remedy is to trim off the offending cloth.

Folding a Mainsail. A mainsail which is taken off the boom may either be folded with the folds running vertically or horizontally. If the same folds are

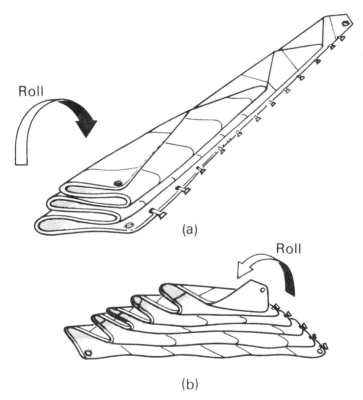

Fig. 15.2 Folding a Mainsail
In (a) the creases will be vertical, whereas in (b) they will be horizontal. Most people prefer (b) on the grounds that airflow is less disturbed, but there isn't much in it.

always taken, they will soon become creases, so different points should be chosen each time. It is not a bad idea to fold horizontally and vertically alternately.

Bear in mind that a horizontal crease will disturb the airflow less than a vertical one, but the former method causes sharp bends at the leech itself. A better system is to roll the sail round the boom, thereby eliminating all creases.

Folding a Headsail. A headsail up to about 100 sq ft can be stowed without folds at all. The luff should be rolled from the head towards the tack, thus making a tube stretching towards the clew. This is then stowed in its turn by

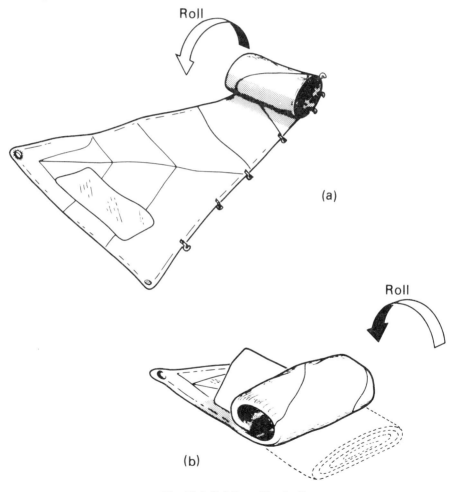

Fig. 15.3 Folding a Headsail
A small sail is rolled down its luff (a), and then rolled again from luff to clew (b).
Larger sails may be folded in concertina fashion like a mainsail; see figure 9.6.

294

(a)

(b)

(c)

(d)

Plate 15.5 Folding a Headsail

Roll the jib down the luff from the head (a). Adjust the size of the roll (b) so that any window finishes at a place where it won't get creased. When the roll is complete (c), check that the window is OK and then fold in half to finish the job (d).

Author

rolling from the tack to the clew. If care is taken, any window can be arranged so that it does not have to be bent too sharply.

Stowing on the Boom. A sail stowed on the boom should be bunched down, with the foot of the sail pulled out and wrapped round the main bunt of the sail; pull well aft as you bunch down, or the result will be too bulky forward. This method has the disadvantage that the same part of the sail is always on the outside – namely the bottom 2 or 3 ft. If a cover is not used, the exposed bottom portion will eventually be subject to weakening from sunlight or industrial smoke. It is possible to ring the changes somewhat by flaking the sail carefully from side to side as it is lowered, and leaving it balanced on top of the boom.

Battens should preferably be removed, but they may be left in their pockets if they are carefully ranged along the length of the boom. Ease the clew outhaul, not so much to compensate for shrinkage which is non-existent with synthetic rope (though it will help the footrope to retain some of its springiness), but to encourage proper setting up of the foot tension next time out.

FURLING GEAR – MAINSAILS

Sail Tiers. The normal sail tie is a simple and effective way of lashing a correctly stowed mainsail (see Fig. 15.4) to its boom when in port. Short

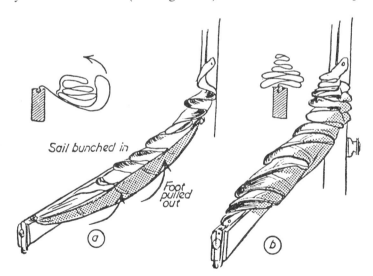

Fig. 15.4 Stowing a Mainsail
The sail is stowed inside the foot, which is pulled out and then folded over to present a neat appearance (a); be sure to pull the sail well aft while this is going on, or it will bunch forward. Alternatively, the sail may be flaked neatly from side to side on top of the boom (b).

lengths of shock cord with hooks or toggles are quick in use, but they tend to release with a snap, so take care not to get one in the eye. Conventional sail tiers should be of adequate length, and should be prepared before lowering a mainsail with slides on its foot. They are passed between the footrope of the sail and the boom, but you should not forget to tie the ends loosely together, in case they work free and go overboard before the sail is lowered.

Shock Cord Furling. The Americans, in the person of Ralph Wiley, introduced the shock cord system to the yachting public in November 1951[52]. Basically the original conception was to have a length of shock cord stretched down one side of a rectangular boom under light tension. It was held fast at intervals of every 4 to 5 ft, and hooks were provided on the opposite side of the boom exactly half-way between these anchorages. When the sail was stowed on the boom, the shock cord was taken across the top and hooked on the other side, thus forming a zigzag of restraining elastic.

It has since been found that a better job can be made if a length of shock cord just under double the length of the boom is taken, and formed into a loop. A stout eye or snap hook is attached to each end so that the loop may stretch double under the boom. A hook is attached about every four to five feet to one side of the loop, and the two sides are seized together midway between each hook. When the sail has been furled and stowed on the boom, simply take one length of shock cord either side of the boom and hook together on top.

This system has the advantage that it can be removed while not in use, thus prolonging the life of the shock cord, and also getting it out of the way if a reef has to be rolled down. For those who want to have it permanently rigged on a roller boom, grooves can be cut in a wooden boom, so that the shock cord and hooks are recessed. Metal booms should use a system which can be removed easily, such as the double length method described above.

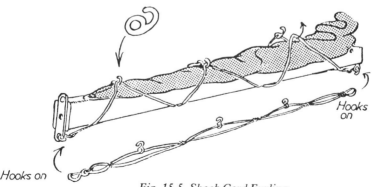

Fig. 15.5 Shock Cord Furling
A doubled length of shock cord is hooked onto each end of the boom, with hooks midway between seizings.

Roller Reefing. Many boats are still fitted with roller reefing, either conventional or through-mast; the latter is so quick that it is often used as a means of stowing the sail when in port. Check all gear wheels and handles for free operation, and grease lightly if necessary. The sail may chafe on any projection on the boom, so look for signs of wear and fit protecting patches if necessary. Now is the time to buy that spare reefing handle.

Rolled Luff. A mainsail may also be rolled about its luff to furl inside the mast. There are various proprietory systems, one of which is the Stoway Mast® of Hood Yacht Systems. The sail is hoisted and lowered on a rotatable rod which rides within the mast groove, so it acts like a boltrope and keeps the luff from sagging. Used on the largest cruising boats, it cuts down labour, acts as a rapid reefing system, and furls in seconds. The IOR requires mainsails to be reefed along the foot only, unless the sail has no battens and can be completely roller furled along the luff[53].

FURLING GEAR – HEADSAILS

Roller furling headsails are popular on cruising boats because of their simplicity of operation. Things have improved since Major Wykeham-Martin

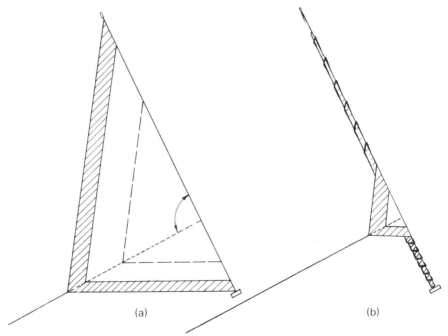

(a)   (b)

Fig. 15.6 Roller Headsail
The sheet angle must run at right angles to the luff, if it is not to change as the sail is reduced (a). The protecting strip of cloth at leech and foot is often of darker material, and it lies on the outside of the roll to guard against ultra violet rays (b).

gave his name to the idea, so that the system is now strong enough to be used as a method of reefing; make sure that your headsail is so shaped that there is no need to alter the sheet lead as the sail is rolled about its luff (Fig. 15.6).

There should be panels of cloth along the leech and foot which are not sensitive to ultra violet rays, because that is the part of the sail which is permanently exposed to the elements when the headsail is fully rolled. The sail should be hoisted in a grooved rod, so that it may be removed for repair or storage without dismantling the entire forestay.

SAIL COVERS

Sails which are left on their spars will deteriorate if they are not covered. Not only will they get dirty, but industrial smoke and sunlight both attack synthetic cloth and stitching. When I was at Cowes, the owner of the veteran sloop *Cynthia*, built at Falmouth in 1910, brought her six-year-old Terylene mainsail into the loft just after the Round the Island race. It had blown fairly hard at the start of the race and a number of boats had been dismasted, including I may say, the one I was in; *Cynthia* had torn her 11 oz mainsail along the foot and the question was could it be repaired? It soon transpired that the cloth and stitching were rotten for the whole of the bottom 2 ft 6 in of the sail, where it was always flaked on the outside of their boomtop stow without a cover; the rest of the sail was in good heart. We cut a parallel piece 3 ft deep off along the foot, thus also shortening the foot length by 11 in, and the owner had her re-rated forthwith. Despite the fact that we had cut out a good deal of the broad seam originally put into the sail, the result was good enough for *Cynthia* to win the Albert Gold Bowl at Ryde the following Saturday. None of this would have been necessary, however, if a good cover had been used regularly.

To be good, a cover should be water- and light-proof, yet should allow the sail to breathe to avoid condensation. This means that it should not be too tight fitting underneath. There are several synthetic materials which are good for this purpose. The cover should go right round the mast at the forward end, with a tight collar at the top. A lacing is probably best for the attachment at the mast, as it can be got really right; shock cord and hooks are the quickest way along the underside of the cover. The inconvience of catching lines and clothing on hooks if they are placed on the outside, should be weighed against the way they will scatch the boom if placed inside. I prefer the former, but there is not a great deal in it, particularly if the cover is nice and free hanging underneath the boom.

Bagging Sails. Large sails taken off the spars or stays usually have to be stowed in bags. Synthetic sails do not like being crammed into too small a compass, so see that the bags are plenty big enough, and that they have enough room in the locker. It is no good having a big bag, which then has to be jammed into a small sail bin. If you have a boat where the ability to roll or fold your sails, as compared with putting them into bags, is marginal, the most important sail to preserve is the light genoa. The cloth will be anything from $2\frac{1}{2}$ to 5 ounces and this is a range which will crease more readily than a heavy one and yet not be light enough to blow out again. Accordingly fold your light genoa if you can, even if you do not bother with the other sails.

Stopping Headsails. Headsails should be put in stops by holding the head and pulling the luff and leech out straight, side by side. The rest of the sail may be taken at the fold thus produced and rolled towards the leech (which should be kept close alongside the luff). An elastic band is then looped over each hank or snap hook, round the rolled sail and over the hank again; the size of band will be found by trial and error, but don't go too small or narrow except possibly near the head. Work along the sail by sections, from hank to hank towards the tack, and take care to see that the clew sticks out ready to receive the sheets. If you use stopping cotton instead of elastic, put only one turn near the head, but up to five or six at the clew, which should ideally have a stop each side of it.

Stopping Spinnakers. A spinnaker can be quickly stopped by using elastic bands and a short length of plastic drainpipe; see Chapter XIV.

Chapter XVI

Repairs

EQUIPMENT

Every yacht's crew should have the ability to undertake the sail repairs which may become necessary during its voyage. This will vary from the emergency taping of a spinnaker rip on a Soling, to fitting a new clew cringle, or repairing a torn seam, on a trans-atlantic crossing. The rest of this chapter gives the necessary basic information, but practice is important and the amateur should take the opportunity to try his hand from time to time on a piece of old Terylene or Dacron cloth and a short length of rope. This chapter cannot hope to cover all the various aspects of home repairs fully, and the reader interested in getting more involved is referred to my book *The Care and Repair of Sails*.

Sewing Machine. It is usually only the largest yachts which have room for a sewing machine on board. If a seam should go from end to end, however, a machine can quickly repay the stowage space it occupies. What would be a long chore by hand, can be repaired in minutes with a machine. It should preferably have the ability to sew a cross-stitch, or zigzag as it is also called; Read's of Southampton make an excellent model.

Machine Thread. The best thread for sewing synthetic sailcloth is synthetic, both for machine and hand work. Machine thread is finer than hand-seaming twine, and it comes in many styles and weights. Two weights, a light and a heavy, are enough for the best equipped boat. The light machine thread would be used with a sewing machine for all sails up to a cloth weight of about 4 ounces; the heavier thread would be used on the machine above this weight. Either thread can also be used for any light hand-sewing which might be needed, say, on a spinnaker.

Hand Twine. In England Terylene hand twine is graded by breaking strain, and is graduated in even pounds from 2 to 8. A comprehensive table is given at Appendix C, showing which weight of twine and which size needle should be used for most cloth weights. However, the average boat will not normally carry a full range of twines, and you will want to know the minimum which will see you through. The answer is to have two: one fairly light and one reasonably heavy. A rough guide to the proper twine to use with a particular cloth is to halve the cloth weight in ounces to find the breaking strain of the twine in pounds. Thus a 4-oz cloth should be sewn with a 2-lb twine. Therefore, you should have available at least one twine for the working canvas and one for lighter headsails, in addition to the machine thread for hand-sewing spinnakers and ghosters. If you are working on parts of the sail which have three or four thicknesses, such as the head, tack and clew patches, or on the rope, or on a worked eye, you should ideally use a size heavier twine, but extra strength may be given by using four parts instead of the more usual two. The twine should be waxed before use, not only for added protection but so that it will lie together and not unravel and snag in use. If beeswax is not available, a candle will do; even soap will help hold the twine together for easier sewing. But most hand twine is pre-waxed these days.

Needles. Sailmakers' needles are graded to conform with the standard Wire Gauge. Sizes most commonly in use in the loft range from number 13, which is used for the heaviest work connected with a sail of about 10 or 12 oz cloth, to number 19 which is used for hand work on dinghy sails. Most Sail Makers have larger needles, in case they have to rope a really heavy cotton sail for a schooner, but 13 to 19 are the commonest in use. The larger the needle, the easier it is to thread and hold, so the temptation is to employ too big a needle for each job. But the larger the needle, the larger the hole it makes in the canvas, sometimes to the detriment of the task. The table at Appendix C gives the ideal size of needle and twine for each particular task. As with twine, however, you will want to know which three or four needle sizes will suffice for most jobs. If you have numbers 18, 16 and 13 on board, plus an ordinary domestic needle, you should get by on most occasions. It is a useful dodge to blunt the point of any needle which is used for roping, so that it passes between the lay of the rope more easily.

Sewing Palm. A sewing palm is not difficult to get used to, and should form part of the kit of every yacht. It takes practice to become really proficient, however, so do not wait until a repair is required before you try it out. There is a minor difference between a roping palm and a seaming palm, but only in the needleguard and the thumb piece. The roping palm has larger indentations in the needle guard which is deeper set, because a roping needle is usually one or two sizes larger than the sewing needle for a given sail; it also has a raised portion round the thumb, designed to allow the thread to be wrapped round it and pulled tight at each stitch. A roping palm is not really suitable for the amateur, because the deep-set needle guard means that it may be difficult to hold the shorter needles when they are back against it.

Other Equipment. Serving mallets, stitch irons and the like are not necessary unless you intend shipping as sailmaker on a schooner (in which case you will need more training than can be learned from this book). A sharp knife is essential, and a short school ruler will often be found useful. It may be as well to have the cutters, punches and dies for two or three sizes of rings, together with the necessary brass rings and turnovers, if it is thought that this sort of work will be undertaken. There are many sizes and they are heavy and bulky, so specialist advice should be sought before purchase. A bench-hook takes up little room and can help with hand-sewing. The hook goes into one end of the work, and it is tied by a line away to one side. One hand then tensions the cloth against the pull of the bench-hook while the other does the sewing. A marlin spike is a usual item on board most boats, and an extra big one is useful as a fid for reaming eyes and cringles. Any blue-water cruising boat should carry an electric soldering iron for heat cutting and sealing. The whole collection should go into a convenient hold-all after anything metal has been lightly greased to prevent rust. The hold-all makes an admirable item on which to get some practice sewing, if it is made by yourself.

TYPES OF STITCH

MACHINE SEWING

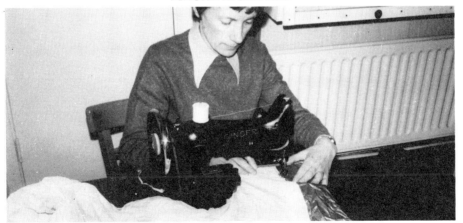

Plate 16.1 The Domestic Sewing Machine
Sails up to about 150 sq ft (250 sq ft in the case of spinnakers) can be handled on the average domestic sewing machine, but many of them won't tackle more than a couple of thicknesses of 5 oz cloth at a time. The Read 'Sailmaker' will take five thicknesses of 7 oz Terylene.   *Author*

A zigzag stitch is usually best for machining sails, and there should not be too much tension. This is so that there shall be room for a certain amount of movement without stressing the thread. This is not to say that a straight stitch is no good at all – it is certainly better than nothing, and may even be best on spinnakers. Be sure that the thread tension is the same on both sides, so that the interlocking part of the stitch is in the middle of the cloth and not lying exposed on one side. You will need a certain amount of room round the machine in order to work on a large sail; one of the governing factors will be whether the sail will manoeuvre under the arm of the machine, or whether there is too much cloth to go through. Try to keep the work spread flat, but without tension. It helps considerably to tack or pin the work before sewing.

HAND-SEWING

The twine should normally be used doubled or even quadrupled, because this will mean fewer stitches for a given strength factor. This advice extends especially to working eyes, which should have well-spaced stitches using at least four parts of twine. The fewer stitches, the less likelihood of wrinkles being caused. To wax the twine, draw it across the beeswax block so that it cuts into the surface; four passes should be enough to do the job properly.

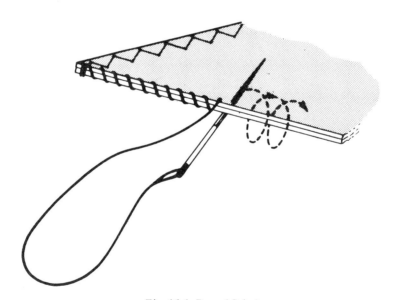

Fig. 16.1 Round Stitch

As with most other stitching, a start is made leaving an inch of the end of the doubled twine protruding from the work. This should then be laid along the cloth in the direction of sewing, and the first five or six stitches should be made round it, to form a solid anchor. Then it is a simple matter of up through the sail, back towards the worker, and down to repeat the cycle. It is finished off by passing the needle under the last few stitches and then taking a final tuck into the canvas.

Most hand-sewing should aim at five to six stitches per inch, and the following three basic stitches should prove enough for most tasks.

Round Stitch. If the edge of a sail has to be sewn, as when a turned tabling is joined at the very leech or when the outer end of a batten pocket is sewn to the sail, the round stitch is used. It will usually be found best to sew from left to right, pushing the needle up and away from you; Fig. 16.1.

Flat Seaming Stitch. If a seam or patch is involved, or the inner edge of a tabling for that matter, it will not be possible to push the needle repeatedly up through the work. It must therefore be pushed down through, and then up again all in one movement. This is the flat seaming stitch, also known as the tabling stitch; Fig. 16.2.

Sailmaker's Darn. This stitch is useful for gathering the two sides of a tear, either temporarily or as a permanent repair, and is the same as the domestic herringbone stitch; Fig. 16.3.

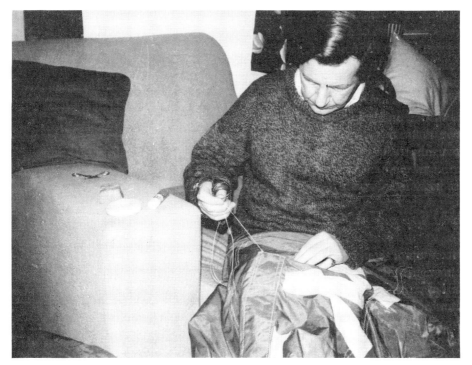

Plate 16.2 Repairs to Batten Pockets
Batten pocket ends are strong candidates for a few reinforcing flat seaming stitches during the winter (the lady in Pl. 16.1 was not best pleased with my beeswax on the chair arm . . .)   *Author*

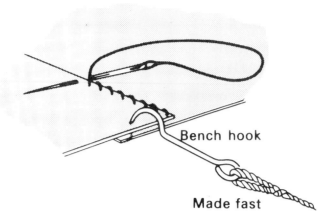

Fig. 16.2 Seaming Stitch

It is easiest to work from right to left, pushing the needle back towards the left shoulder as it enters the canvas. See that the needle emerges at a uniform distance both along and across the work, and do not pull the stitching too tight, or it will pucker. A bench hook, attached away to the right, will allow the left hand to hold the work together and pull it to the left while stitching with the other hand, thus ensuring steadiness. Often the seam to be sewn will be in the middle of the sail, and this means that a bight of the sail must be doubled towards you over your knee while sewing. This being so, care must be taken to 'skin' so as not to catch the bottom layer in what sailmakers know as 'catching a crab.'

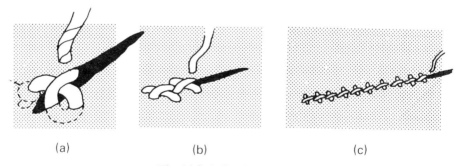

(a) (b) (c)

Fig. 16.3 Sailmaker's Darn

This is one of the few occasions when the doubled twine can be knotted at its end to form a stopper at the beginning of the work, which is sometimes rather looser than other sewing. Stitching is from left to right, and the start is made by pushing upwards through the far side of the tear. The needle is then brought back over the tear and passed down through the near side, to be brought up on the *left* side of the stitch thus formed (a). After crossing over the top of this stitch, the process of sewing up through the far side is repeated. Each stitch should not be pulled tighter than is necessary to hold the two sides of the tear together, or wrinkles will result. This is not to say that they should be slack, for their very job is to draw two pieces of canvas towards each other. To finish the job, the twine is usually tied off in a half hitch and tucked under.

306

PRACTICAL WORK

ROPING

Twists must be eliminated from the rope before it is sewn to a sail, so that it lies naturally. Repair work usually involves putting a short length back on the sail, so it will probably already be attached for most of its length. If, however, a complete new rope has to be put on, it should be carefully checked for twists and then held out taut while a pencil line is marked along it as a reference while sewing. Rope has a tendency to shorten up during sewing so, if a specified length is to be sewn to a sail, it should be struck up at intervals of about 1 ft, so that the length is shared evenly and the rope is not sewn on tight at any particular point. It is an interesting fact that most hand-sewn rope will lose some of its length during the sewing; an exception is some soft spun rope. If a sail has 25 ft of rope sewn to the luff and the rope is then taken off, it will be found to measure about 6 to 9 in short. It is for this reason that a sail cannot have its rope taken off during adjustment, and then the same rope put back – there would not be enough. If for some reason the same rope has to be used, it is best to use a fairly light twine and not pull the stitches too tight in order to reduce shrinkage. Conversely, if a sail is roped too slackly and stretches too easily on the spars, it can be made tighter by sewing over the roping a second time and pulling each stitch tight.

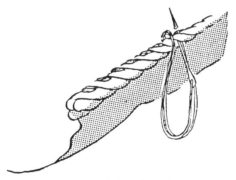

Fig. 16.4 Hand Roping

The edge of the sail should be towards you, over your knees, and the rope laid just under the edge, which is then turned up through 90 degrees for convenience of sewing. A bench hook, tied away to the right, is useful for steadying the job. Start at the left and, pushing away from you, pass the needle between the strands of the rope and then through the edge of the sail, in what is virtually the same movement as the round stitch described above. It will make things easier if the point of the needle is dulled first, to stop it going too readily into the actual strand itself. Pull the stitch tight and bring it back over the top towards you, and repeat the process between the next two strands. It is important not to sew through a strand thus weakening it and causing irregularities in the lie of the rope. It is also important to pull each stitch with the same tension. You will find that you have to make a conscious effort to use up all the sail before the next set of match marks is reached, and it is usual for the beginner to reach the rope mark before the one on the sail.

307

The actual process of roping can be fairly quickly assimilated as far as the beginner is concerned (Fig. 16.4), for he will not normally be required to rope a sail from top to bottom, but rather to renew a short length which has pulled away. The finer craft of full-scale roping takes a good deal of practice to learn, because consistency is important if wrinkles are not to appear from a rope-bound sail. Practise on a spare length for an hour or so before tackling any important job.

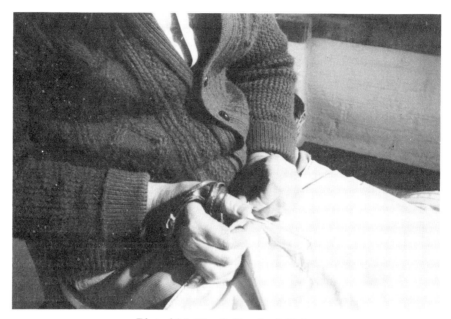

Plate 16.3 The Sailmaker's Palm
A sailmaker's palm takes very little getting used to. Practise on some old cloth or a sailbag before starting to rope a sail. *Author*

WORKED EYE

A hand-worked eye (Fig. 16.5) or one put in by hydraulic press has two or three times the strength of one stamped in with a hand punch. If the eye is going to be subject to chafe on its inner surface, a liner or turnover should be clenched over the stitching as a protection.

CRINGLE

It is sometimes necessary to work a cringle in a sail, either for an external tack eye or for a reef cringle. This is a rope loop attached to two small eyes on the edge of a sail, and it usually has a metal thimble wedged into it to protect it from chafe. Details of how to work one of these are in *The Care and Repair of Sails*.

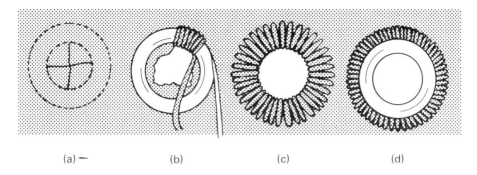

(a) —   (b)   (c)   (d)

Fig. 16.5 Hand Worked Eye

Lay the brass ring at the desired place, and mark its inner and outer circumference
on the sail in pencil. Make a cross-shaped cut in the inner circle (if the full circle is
cut away, the final job will not be strong enough), as in (a). The brass ring is then
laid on the cut-out, and the needle passed down through the canvas outside the
ring at any point on the outer circle, usually on the side away from the worker.
The twine is pulled through downwards, leaving a tail to be sewn over by the first
four or five stitches as a stopper, and the needle then brought up through the
cut-out and centre of the ring (b). It is then passed over the top of the ring and
sewn down through the pencil line again, moving slightly round the circle each
time, for the process to be repeated (c). Ideally, a fid or spike should be reamed
through the partly worked ring at intervals, to keep the canvas spread and the
stitches even. Each stitch should be pulled really tight, and modern practice is to
use four parts of twine, spacing the stitches rather wider apart than used to be
customary, to reduce the risk of wrinkles. The brassy is then punched into the
sewn ring to protect the stitching against the chafe of shackles etc, and the job is
done (d).

PATCHES

A clean cut of about an inch in length may be sewn together with a sailmaker's darn, providing the cloth is in good heart; anything larger should
have a patch. The tear should be trimmed square with the warp and weft,
and a patch cut in similar cloth (with its warp and weft lined up with those
of the sail) plenty big enough to overlap the squared off hole. If the two
threadlines are not lined up, uneven stretching may result, causing wrinkles.
Many authorities advise turning the edges of the patch under, but synthetic
cloth can be sealed at the edges if it is cut out with a fine electric soldering-
iron: the heat will melt the threads to cut out the patch, while at the same
time causing them to fuse together so that they do not fray. The tear in the
sail may be trimmed in a similar manner. Of course, if you are on board and
do not have a heated iron, the edges of the tear and the patch will have to be
turned under to avoid fraying. In any case, the patch should be put on slack,
or it may tend to gather the sail into small puckers. It may help to keep the

whole thing in shape if any trimming of the tear is left until after the patch is put on one side; Fig. 16.6.

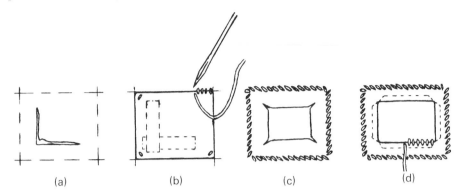

(a) (b) (c) (d)

Fig. 16.6 Patch
The two sides of the tear should be cobbled together temporarily or stuck with repair tape (even sticking plaster will do), so that the sail is not distorted while the patch is applied (a). The patch should be pinned, stuck or tacked in place (b), and then sewn round from right to left using the seaming stitch described in figure 16.2. When the patch is in place, turn the work over and square off the tear if this has not been done already (c). Mitre-cut into the corners and turn the edges under, so that they lie between the new patch and the original sail. Sew round again from the second side and the job is done (d).

DARNING

Darning should be restricted to very small cuts and holes no bigger than the end of a cigarette, and should never be used where the canvas is known to be weak. Use a double, or even quadruple, seaming twine, and pass the needle under and over the first layer of stitching you put in, in the usual domestic manner.

SEAM PROTECTION

There are some very good liquids about which are designed to be painted onto seams in order to protect the stitching. They penetrate and bind the materials together, so that a stitch may be worn completely away on the surface, but the remaining stub stays firm in the cloth acting as a kind of rivet. It is important that a sail should be thoroughly cleaned of all salt particles and heavy soiling before treatment, and advice should be sought from your Sail Maker before trying it on film laminates, in case it has an effect on adhesives. Many of these preparations are evil smelling, so that Sail Makers don't like them, but they are worth having in the repair kit.

310

Plate 16.4 Repairs in the Loft
A part-width panel being inserted in Gowen's loft, either to repair a rip, or to make a sail longer on luff and leech. Judging by the fact that the bolt rope does not seem to have been removed, this is a repair job. *Hare*

REPAIR TAPE

An excellent repair tape is available from most Sail Makers for repairing spinnakers. It comes in a variety of colours, so a multi-hued spinnaker need not be disfigured. The tape is self-adhesive, with a waxed paper backing which has first to be removed. It is about 2 in wide, and usually comes in rolls of 25 ft so that quite long tears can be most effectively mended. It will hold in place for a long time, indeed will certainly last a season's normal use, so it tends to make the lucky owner rather lazy regarding his repairs. In addition it will hold on Terylene or Dacron sails quite well, so do not hesitate to use it if you cannot patch a mainsail; it sticks particularly well to the film side of a laminated sail. Insulating tape from the engine kit and sticking plaster from the first aid box both offer an emergency alternative.

SAILMAKER'S WHIPPING

An ordinary whipping will quickly come undone in the normal wear and tear of working the ship, thus promoting frayed ropes ends; the sailmaker's whipping is much more resistant. Thread a fine needle with seaming twine so that two parts are put on at one time. Most sailmakers will scorn to knot the

311

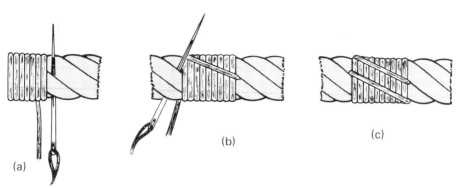

Fig. 16.7 Sailmaker's Whipping
Whip in the usual way (against the lay of the rope), then sew between the strands
of the rope and out the other side (a). Lead the twine back over the whipping along
the line of the lay of the rope, and sew again between the lay at the other end of
the whipping (b). Lead the twine back over the whipping, again along the lay, and
repeat once more until three passes have been made (c). Sew through the rope to
finish off securely. The length of whipping should never be less than the diameter
of the rope in question.

end, preferring to leave a small tail exposed to be sewn over at the start to
make an anchor; but you and I are not shipping as sailmakers, and we wish
to know the simplest secure system, so we start with a knot.

MYLAR/MELINEX

Repairs to film laminates which are open to the amateur are fewer than with
polyester, and depend largely on the nature of the damage. If the sail is torn
or has started to delaminate, the affected area of cloth must be replaced, and
this is a matter for the Sail Maker. On the other hand, all the usual minor
attentions such as boltrope resewing, working an extra eye, or darning a
small hole, may be attempted by the competent owner. Remember my
remarks in Chapter XV about lines of weakness caused by over-enthusiastic
use of the sewing machine, and make use of more widely spaced hand
stitches or repair tape.

Chapter XVII

Faults and Creases

A Sail Maker sees more bad sails set up in his loft than good ones. If his production is anything more than a few sails a week, he does not have the time or manpower to test every sail he makes, so he does not see the hundreds which go out to all parts of the world which are satisfactory. All too rarely does he get a letter back from the satisfied owner. He does, however, hear the complaints, although here again he sometimes does not hear straight away. The average Sail Maker considers that he has to make a dozen winners to wipe out the effect of one bad sail caused by its dissatisfied owner complaining in the clubhouse. To this end he usually has an alteration service designed to bring speedy attention to a faulty product, so that the disgruntled owner realizes that he gets the best and quickest remedy.

A sail will often only show its faults when set on the boat, with its attendant mainsail or headsail, and using its normal spars. Sometimes the faults will not appear unless the boat is actually sailing. It is therefore important for a Sail Maker to be a practising helmsman, and to be able to go afloat to examine his products. Often he can decide on remedial measures on the spot. At other times he can determine what is wrong, but needs a closer examination before making up his mind what he will do to cure it. He will then take the sail back to the loft for further attention on a test rig.

Test rigs can either take the form of a mast and forestay rigged on land in the open, where the wind is not disturbed by buildings and trees, or else the sails can be set up horizontally in the loft. In the latter case, a series of different sized tracks may run along a wall, with a gooseneck fitting on to which a boom can be fitted, again with a number of different sized tracks on it. This, of course, is so that various types and sizes of slide can be accommodated. A groove will also be needed, and this can often be made, as Bruce Banks has done, with a slot large enough to take most types of slide, thus doing away with the need for a multitude of different tracks. Smaller mainsails, used perhaps on bendy spars, will be set on a horizontally rigged grooved mast and boom, arranged to that they can be bent at will in the

313

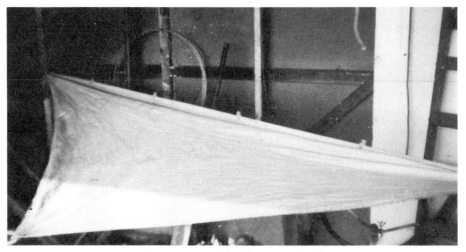

Plate 17.1 Looking for Trouble (2)
If a headsail needs looking at for flow troubles, set it up horizontally by pulling
head and tack apart to tension the luff; the clew should then be held off to one side
so that gravity lets the sail take up a natural curve. This woven jib has uneven flow
at the tack, almost certainly caused by the seizings which hold the luff close to the
wire shifting up or down. They may push back into place to give a more even flow,
or they may have to be cut away to do it; in both cases, reseize when all is in place
again.   *Author*

right place.

A headsail can be set up horizontally by fastening it at the tack and
pulling out the head on a tackle to stretch the luff taut; the clew can then be
pulled out on one side. In both cases, mainsail and headsail will take up their
designed shape under the influence of gravity.

When a sail is set up like this in a loft, the Sail Maker can walk all round
it. He can then examine at close quarters those parts of the sail which are
suspected of giving trouble; he can also try pinching and pulling the cloth
with his hands, to see what effect tightening a seam or pleating the luff or
foot will have. I do not say that an indoor horizontal rig will always provide
the answer, but it is an invaluable adjunct to the Sail Maker's armoury in
the fight against sail faults.

Many sails are returned to their makers for attention because of faults
which are imagined or induced by their owners. On the other hand, a sail is
like a suit of clothes and has to be individually tailored to the boat on which
it will be used, if it is to give of its best. Something 'off the peg' will very
often set well, but as class competition becomes hotter special needs require
special attention, and it is often necessary for minor alterations to ensure a
perfect fit. It is important to give the Sail Maker the chance to make those

alterations, because he cannot do anything if he does not know about it, and a poor-looking sail may only need a few touches here and there to turn it into a potential winner. It is equally important to give a sail a fair trial. By this I mean that it should not be condemned too quickly, nor should it be refused a second chance after alteration. I have known sails brought into the loft by very angry owners, when it has been most difficult to persuade them to give another chance to what they considered a hopeless case. In most instances the problem has been cured, and in several the sail has proved to be a favourite thereafter. In some, I regret to report, the owner has been too stubborn to try again, so both sides are the loser.

It is, of course, important to be frank with your Sail Maker, and not to expect the impossible. He cannot cut a sail if he is not given all the pertinent facts, nor will it set well if it is hoisted badly, used under different conditions from those given to the Sail Maker (different spars or winds), or maltreated in use.

You would be surprised at the number of sails returned under complaint by owners who have only themselves to blame. A Sail Maker quickly learns to spot this sort of thing, although he is not always able to accuse the owner outright for fear of giving offence and acquiring bad publicity. It is a cross which has to be borne, but not borne willingly.

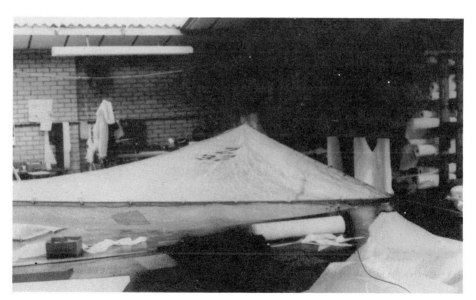

Plate 17.2 Looking for Trouble (3)
If a mainsail has to be checked for one small point of flow, it does not have to be tediously fitted to the test rig as shown in Pl. 4.4. It may be pulled out under tension on the luff and treated exactly like a headsail, as shown in this shot of W G Lucas' loft at Portsmouth. *Author*

315

MAINSAIL FAULTS

The principal faults which affect mainsails, in order of frequency, are as follows:

1. Leeches: slack (motor-boating or falling away) or tight.
2. Creases: wrinkles, pleats and hard spots.
3. Fullness: too flat or too full; fullness in the wrong place; back-winding.
4. Size: too small or too large.

MAINSAIL LEECHES

Motor-boating. If the leech is slack at its extreme edge only, that is to say at the tabling, it will vibrate for its last two or three inches. This is known as motor-boating because of the noise it makes. The cause is often to be found in the way the tabling is put on: it is probably a little on the slack side and needs removing and shortening slightly. Care should be taken not to overdo it, or the reverse will occur and the leech will curl. This in itself may also cause the same effect, as the part of the sail which sits tight up to windward will vibrate in the airflow. If the tabling is not a turned one, but has been merely rolled over, the fault may be in the way the cloths are joined together at the very leech: they may have been allowed to wander apart at the leech end of the seam, thus slackening the edge of the sail. In addition a cupped leech may give the same effect, and this fault is treated separately below.

It is also possible for a leech line to be the cause of the trouble, not because it is too loose, but because its weight and bulk cause a disturbance to the airflow. This is particularly true if the leech tabling is narrow and thus gives little room for the line to pass along it, because the cloth will then strain at the stitching and cause wrinkles which in turn will cause the airflow to vibrate the slight extra weight of the leech line. It is also possible that a slightly rounded curve to the leech between the battens will flutter in the wind, so the sail should preferably be straight between batten pockets as in Fig. 17.1.

The foregoing are all the responsibility of the Sail Maker, but there are two more possible reasons for motor-boating, both of which occur as the direct result of mishandling by the owner. First, the leech may become creased parallel to its length, thus causing a short length to sit up at an angle to the main plane of the sail; Fig. 17.2. The cure is either to try and smooth out the crease (which is not easy), or to cut off the offending cloth if this is feasible.

The second fault in the power of the owner to avoid is local stretching of the cloth. This is most likely to occur through hauling the sail down by the leech. This cardinal sin is so frequently committed, even by the top

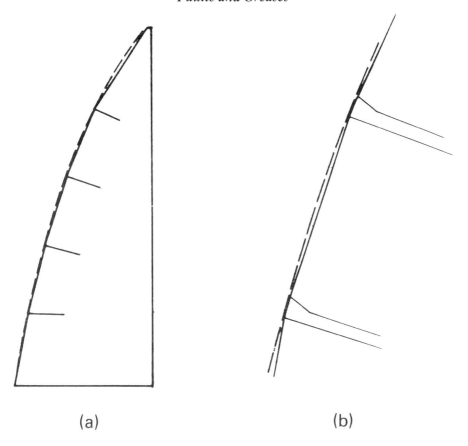

(a)   (b)

Fig. 17.1 Mainsail Leech Flutter (1)

If a leech is curved for the whole of its length, there will be a very small roach between each batten. This may be enough to 'motor-boat' in the wind, the cure is to trim the offending cloth away to a straight line between each pair of battens, and to the head and clew. The scale of (a) is not large enough to show the effect properly, so (b) represents a section of leech between one pair of battens.

Fig. 17.2 Mainsail Leech Flutter (2)

If the edge of the leech gets creased, probably through careless stowing, it will stand up to windward as shown by this section through the sail. It may be possible to iron out the crease very carefully; failing this, the flap may be trimmed off, even if it means a hollow curve between the battens. The best cure is to avoid the problem in the first place by folding the sail properly, as shown in figure 15.2.

helmsmen, that it is hard on the nerves of a Sail Maker to attend the dinghy park as the boats come ashore at the end of a day's racing.

Most of these faults show on the horizontal test rig, but there are some which do not, and the proper course is to take the offending sail on to the water. Sometimes an intelligent guess can be made, based on probabilities, but no Sail Maker likes to have to do this.

Cupped Leech. A cupped leech is one which has a good flow to within 6 or 8 in of the tabling, then falls away to leeward in a slight pocket which returns to the correct position at the tabling; Fig. 17.3.

Fig. 17.3 Mainsail Leech Flutter (3)
A cupped leech is caused in woven sails by the cloth at the last 6 inches of the leech being too much on the bias, with resulting distortion; but the leech itself doesn't stretch because of a stout tabling. The result is shown in this section through the sail, and will need very careful attention to the seams.

The cure lies in the cut of the sail, but this cannot be altered once the sail has been made. Either a narrower tabling should be fitted, or else a few seams tightened inside the tabling, just enough to take up the slack; this will mean tightening about an $\frac{1}{8}$ in for a distance into the sail equal to the amount of the cup, say 6 or 8 in.

Leech Falling Away. If the whole leech of the sail, or even part of it, falls away, then there are again several possible reasons. All of them promote a slackness right down the leech, well into the sail, and not just at the tabling. It is necessary to find the cause of the slackness in each particular case.

1. *Halyard.* If the halyard of a woven sail is not pulled right up, the luff will not be set up hard and the flow will not be drawn forward; this means that the leech will have a hard line along the inner ends of the battens, which will fall away. The same thing can be caused to a lesser extent by not pulling the foot out hard. The cure may not always be easy, because the sail may already be out to its marks, or the halyard purchase may be insufficient. A quick check can be made by pulling down on the Cunningham hole if one is fitted, or on the lowest slide eyelet, which should show whether there is any slack in the luff. I went on board a large sloop some time ago, where the mainsail luff was over 65 ft long and the owner was complaining of a slack leech. A quick tug at the luff rope showed that the sail was not pulled up

sufficiently. I pointed this out, and that there were 2 or 3 ft of track still clear at the head, but he would not believe that his halyard winch (which he had selected himself, and not through a Naval Architect) was not man enough for the task. Because the winch could not get any more tension on the luff, the owner claimed that the sail was hauled up properly. Unfortunately there was no downhaul to the boom, so that could not be used. I rigged a four part purchase handy billy on the bottom slide eyelet and pulled it down over a foot with little effort. The crease at the leech disappeared instantly.

2. *Stretched Leech.* The Sail Maker cannot always lay the blame for slack leeches at the owner's door. The second most common cause is that woven cloth has stretched too much for some way inside the leech of the sail – usually at least in to the ends of the batten pockets. This can be caused by

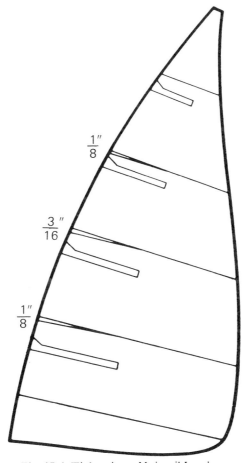

Fig. 17.4 Tightening a Mainsail Leech

Where a mainsail leech is too slack, usually one seam is tightened between each pair of battens. The amount which the seam is taken in is in the order of $\frac{1}{8}$ in or $\frac{1}{16}$ in, from the very edge in as far as the end of the battens.

one of two things: either the cloths have been laid at such an angle that the pull comes too much on the bias and so distorts the cloth, or else too light a cloth has been used to make the sail, and it has not been able to stand up to the forces imposed upon it. Both these reasons are the fault of the Sail Maker (for even if he is given strict instructions to make a sail from a cloth which he considers too light, he should inform the customer of the dangers). The cure lies in ripping open some of the seams at the leech, and tightening them by increasing the overlap of one cloth upon the other, in a tapering nip, going at least in to the ends of the batten pockets; Fig. 17.4. The number and distribution of seams, and the exact amount of tightening (in the order of $\frac{1}{8}$ in or so per seam) will depend on the gravity of the trouble; they are decided by the Sail Maker as a result of observation.

3. *Bendy Mast.* The third reason for a generally slack leech is a mast which bends aft at the head more than the Sail Maker was informed, or for which he did not make proper allowance; Fig. 17.5. If not enough round has been built into the top of the luff, and the masthead comes aft, the sail will

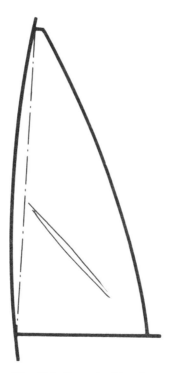

Fig. 17.5 Excessive Mast Bend
If the mast bends more than the Sail Maker was informed, there will not be enough cloth at the mainsail's luff to take up the curve of the bend. As the sail is pulled forward willy nilly to conform to the shape of the mast, so it will strain from the clew and produce creases.

be held on a line from the clew to just below the head (at the point of maximum forward curvature), yet the head itself will come aft, thus slackening the leech. The cure is either to stiffen up the masthead, or cut more round into the upper luff – an alteration which is not possible without shortening the luff and leech slightly.

4. *Roach.* The final reason for a completely slack leech is a roach which is too large; Fig. 17.6. If the Sail Maker puts on too much, he is asking for trouble, and the only certain cure is to remove the extra inches. A stop-gap

Plate 17.3 Excessive Mast Bend
This OK sail has not had enough round built into its luff to match the rather marked bend of the mast. The result is the series of creases radiating from the clew, as the mast bows forward, dragging the sail with it.   *Yachts & Yachting*

321

Plate 17.4 Batten Pocket Poke

Classes like the 14 ft International and the 12 ft National (shown here) are prone
to leech problems which stem from their over-generous cross-measurement limits.
If the girth is permitted, the owner insists on having it; the battens then have to
support a greater roach than will stand properly. This typical ridge can only really
be eliminated by trimming two or three inches off the roach (any attempt to
tighten seams would probably only close the leech).   *Yachts & Yachting*

palliative can be provided by tightening some seams at the leech, but this
may lead to the whole leech being closed rather than open. This, coupled
with the typical ridge along the inner ends of the battens, will stop a boat
more quickly than almost anything bar an anchor.

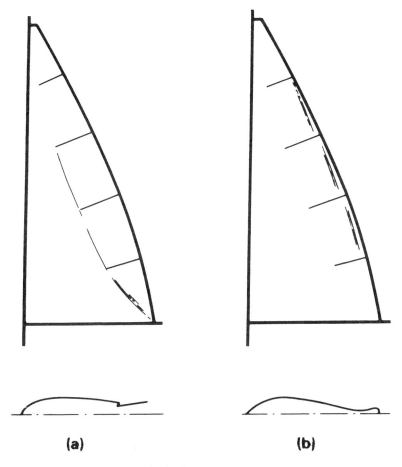

(a)   **(b)**

Fig. 17.6 Leech Problems
If the whole leech area has been pulled out of shape by misuse, a crease will run
from the clew up and along the ends of the battens (a); a cure can be attempted
along the lines of figure 17.4 above. If only the outer half dozen inches of the sail
have stretched, while a tabling holds the very edge in check (b), there will be a
cupped leech, with the familiar 'motorboating' noise as the sail flutters when on
the wind; the tabling may have to be removed before adjustment is attempted.

Tight Leech. A tight leech to a mainsail stops a boat even more effectively
than a slack one, because of the rear component of the wind force which is
generated, and the energy dissipated in disturbing the airflow unnecessarily.
The only possible exception to this is an extremely full mainsail under
ghosting conditions, because the forces involved are so low that only that
portion of thrust which is generated at the powerful forward part of the sail
has any effect. Tight leeches can be subdivided in the same way as slack
ones:

1. *Leech Tabling.* If the tabling has been put on tight, it will draw the

after end of the sail together and will feel drum hard to the touch when the sail is sheeted home on the wind. The cure is to ease the tabling in the sail loft, which may involve adding a few inches of new tabling and sharing it out evenly.

2. *Whole Leech.* Here again the Sail Maker is at fault. If he has either laid woven cloths without any bias on the leech so that it has no give, or if he has tightened one or two seams in the wrong place, the whole leech area at the battens will hold too far to windward. The wind will not get a free run off, and the boat will slow appreciably. The cure lies in easing some seams in the sail loft.

3. *Too Full.* A very full mainsail must, of necessity, fall well away to leeward from the luff to achieve its fullness. The sail eventually has to return to the boom, and this means that the leech has all the characteristics of a tight one. The solution is not to use such a sail in anything other than drifting conditions, or it will knock the boat down and hold her back. Failing this, the after end of the sail may be flattened by tightening some seams inside the tabling as described below under the heading *Too Full Aft.*

MAINSAIL CREASES

I have put creases second in order of frequency of mainsail faults, because I am not counting those creases we have just dealt with under slack and tight leeches. I am more concerned here with smaller creases emanating from various points on the sail for no apparent reason. It will be found in general that most faults with a sail will lead to creases of one sort or another, and we shall overlap slightly here on what I have just written and what is to come.

Clew. Creases at the clew form the most widespread complaint with Terylene or Dacron mainsails. A hard line from the clew to the inner end of the bottom batten is often a sign of a slack leech in the lower half of the sail, and the cure lies in one of the solutions I have put forward above: hoisting harder, tightening one or two of the lower leech seams, or reducing the leech round. It may, however, stem from a tight leech, in which case the kink will be to windward and not to leeward, and the solution is to ease a seam or two. Equally, the sail may be too full along the foot in the clew area, in other words the fullness has been taken too far aft. If some of the foot round is rubbed away from the after part of the sail, the leech will be flattened at the clew and the sail thus drawn up to windward to take away the crease.

On the other hand the leech itself may be good, and yet the clew area may have creases radiating from it. This is an unfortunate failing of synthetics, and one for which there is no immediate solution. Its origin lies in the hardness of the cloth, which will not give like cotton when it is confined or crimped up as when sewing an eye. These radiating creases, therefore,

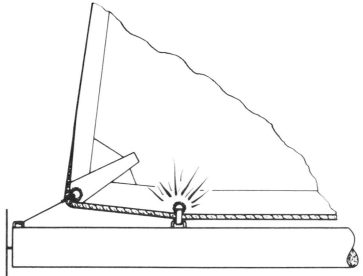

Fig. 17.7 Clew Creases
Apart from the various causes outlined in the text, a clew may show creases if the
foot of the sail is not in a straight line at the outer end – so look to this before
imagining other, and more serious, causes.

originate from the clew eye itself, and there is little that can be done, save
perhaps fitting a heavier clew patch, to try and alleviate the trouble. The eye
should have been worked with fewer stitches, and perhaps not pulled quite so
tight as they were. As cloth becomes softer, this danger recedes.

There is also the crease which runs from the clew towards a point about
half or three-quarters of the way up the luff, and having no relation to the
batten pockets. This is usually the result of a sail which does not have
enough round to the luff for the amount that the mast bends. The cure is
either drastic surgery to the sail to increase its luff round (a difficult and
costly business), or else stiffening the mast so that it does not bend so much,
perhaps by tightening the jumper stays.

Head. Creases from the head are usually caused by the way the headboard is
sewn into the sail. Too many, or too tight stitches can cause this, as can an
irregularly shaped headboard, or faulty cutting of the cloth at the head. The
cure lies with the Sail Maker, and is not always easy. It explains why headboards are put in in a variety of ways these days: plastic boards riveted either
side of the sail on the outside; plastic boards sewn into a pocket at the head,
without any stitching going through the board; or metal boards with the
minimum of stitching. Check also that the halyard leads fairly off the sheave
and does not pull the headboard over towards the mast as shown in Fig.
15.1 (a).

Tack. If creases run from the tack they may be caused by a badly sewn tack eye, as with the clew. This is not usual, however, as a mainsail is under sufficient tension on both luff and foot to eliminate most wrinkles of this origin. A more likely cause is that the sail has not been cut back at the tack by the right amount to lead straight to the tack pin, which is why the distance from the pin to the aft face of the mast is so important to the Sail Maker; alternatively the tack pin may be out of horizontal line with the foot of the sail, which is thus being pulled out of its true direction. Another reason can be the cut of the sail itself, for which there is often no cure, unless the fault is that there is too much round to the lower luff, in which case the sail can be flattened. This is a fairly common fault with fully battened mainsails, which need fullness in this area yet cannot accept very much round due to the way the battens restrict the movement of the cloth. A crease which runs more as a fold along the length of the luff or foot is the result of too much tension on the halyard or outhaul. It is manifestation of the flow in a sail, and a good breeze will soon blow it into shape – as, if you are lucky, it may with many other creases mentioned in this chapter, so do not rush into remedial action until you have given the sail a good chance to settle down.

At the Rope. A multitude of small creases emanating from the rope is a sign that the sail has not been hauled up or out hard enough. If it is already at its marks, Cunningham holes should be fitted to a woven sail as an immediate measure; the sail can be shortened slightly if a permanent cure is sought.

On the other hand, the rope may have been sewn too tight all along its length, and will not allow the cloth to stretch as it should. Re-roping is the only cure. It may, however, only be tight at one spot, in which event 'crow's-foot' creases will be evident over a short distance, say 6 to 12 in, of its length. It may be that the roping is tight at this particular spot, or that the rope has been allowed to twist as it was put on. Again, re-roping is the cure, and it is normally a job for the Sail Maker.

Hard Spots. A hard spot can be caused in a sail if the cloths are not over-lapped exactly parallel with one another (allowing for any broad seam involved). If one cloth is pulled over or eased away from the other, local areas of tightness or slackness will be caused, and the cure is to rip the seam and re-sew it. Similar puckers can come from racing numbers, insignia or windows which are not lying exactly flat when they are sewn, or sometimes if they are sewn on with too small a stitch or too tight a tension on the sewing machine.

MAINSAIL FULLNESS

Fullness is a question of relativity. What one man may consider full, is medium for the next; one helmsman may want more fullness from a heavy weather sail than the next. The only way to be fair to a Sail Maker when specifying fullness is to refer as a yardstick to another suit of similar sails he has made himself.

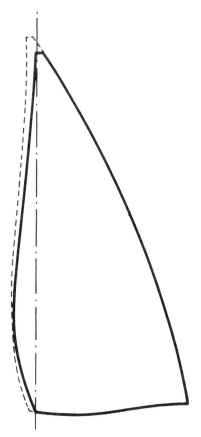

Fig. 17.8 To Increase Mainsail Fullness (1)
If the upper luff is cut back from the dotted line, there will be more luff round, and hence a fuller sail. Note that both luff and leech will be reduced. Shortening the foot slightly at the tack will give further scope for adding round to the lower luff. With luck, this modification will only require the headboard to be refitted, while batten pockets and sail numbers may remain.

Too Flat. A mainsail which is too flat is difficult to cure without major re-cutting. More cloth has to be found from somewhere to give the extra flow, and it cannot satisfactorily be put in one long strip up the luff. There are two ways in which the job can be done properly. The first, and easiest, involves moving the headboard slightly over towards the leech to allow the luff to be re-rubbed with more round; Fig. 17.8. This is not always practicable, because it means reducing the length of the luff and leech slightly.

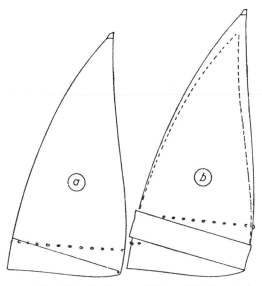

Fig. 17.9 To Increase Mainsail Fullness (2)
If the sail is to remain exactly the same dimensions, a new cloth must be inserted. The rope or tape has to be taken off the luff and from around the tack, and the sail separated along the tack seam (a). When the new cloth has been added (b), the luff and leech must be cut back to the original (dotted) dimensions, allowing extra luff round for the required increased fullness. Headboard and batten pockets must be lowered, and possibly the sail numbers and reef points moved.

The second method is more complex, and involves taking the sail to pieces and inserting a new cloth as shown in Fig. 17.9. The new cloth should be well crumpled before going in, otherwise it may sew tight on to the old cloths. If there is a row of reef points crossing over the ripped seam the result may be slighty bizarre, but this must be accepted. This method may bring trouble from the phenomenon of the vanishing rope which I mentioned in Chapter XVI. When the luff rope comes to be sewn back on to the sail, it will almost certainly be found to be too short; depending on the deficiency, the sail may have to be re-roped; all this makes for a lot of expense. It is also sometimes possible to rip the luff end only of a few seams, and to build in more broad seam. This, of course, shortens the luff by the amount of extra broad seam (not normally significant) but cannot, by itself, produce extra fullness if the cloth is not there in the first place.

A third, do-it-yourself, possibility exists for dinghies, which has an air of desperation about it. I do not recommend it unless all else has failed and you are prepared to see the worst come to the worst. The boat can be laid over on her side with the mainsail hoisted, and wet sand shovelled into the sail. If this is left for several days some stretching will certainly occur, even if it is in the wrong place. It has been done successfully, however, but do not do it to your best sail. It is not good sailmaking to say the least.

Too Full Forward. A sail which is too full forward can easily be flattened by pleating along the luff or foot, as appropriate. This does not harm the aerodynamic qualities of the sail, and has the advantage that it can always be released again with no more harm than a row or two of stitch holes.

Too Full Aft. If the mainsail is too full aft, the boat will go badly, except in light winds. The cause of this trouble lies in one of three factors: the cloth is poor; the sail was made that way; or it has been used in winds too strong for it. Whatever the reason, there is not a great deal which can be done without considerable re-cutting, if the problem is serious. We know, however, that more tension on the luff of a woven sail pulls the flow forward, so the first step is to do this. Either pull harder on the halyard, or fit a Cunningham hole and pull down on it. If the sail will not stretch more on the luff, it can be re-roped with a slacker rope, at the same time possibly dropping the headboard so that it stays within the black bands when fully stretched. The final measure is to rip apart several cloths and re-design the broad seam in the sail, removing any tightening at the leech and increasing it forward. This, however, is a costly remedy for what may be a bad sail not worth further expense. First-aid along these lines can be administered, however, by tightening some seams along the point of greatest fullness at the roach. This should not be carried right to the tabling, or the whole leech will come up to windward, whereas if it is stopped about 6 to 12 in short, it will be the equivalent of easing some seams at the leech, thus freeing the whole area. An additional remedy is to pleat out some of the foot round towards the clew; this must not be overdone, however, or a hard spot will result.

Fig. 17.10 Mainsail Too Full Aft
If a few seams are tightened from a short distance forward of the leech, on to about half way from the luff, the belly in the aft part of the sail should be reduced. The result may just be a worse mess, so be prepared for disappointment.

Backwinding. I have separated backwinding from a sail which is simply too full because, while the mainsail may indeed be too full, the fault is often to be found in the headsail. If the headsail leech curls to windward, or if there is not enough hollow in it to allow free passage to the airflow, the wind will be deflected into the lee of the mainsail. The best cut mainsail will backwind in these circumstances, so the two sails should be examined in conjunction. I shall deal with headsail leeches later in this chapter.

MAINSAIL SIZE

A sail which is too small or too large has to be altered by the Sail Maker. Sometimes the owner of an offshore racer would rather alter his black bands to conform with the sizes as found, rather than risk deforming his favourite sail through surgery. It is, of course, easier to reduce a sail than to make it larger, but I go more fully into this question towards the end of this chapter. Let me just say here that it is very seldom that a mainsail is as much under size as some owners think. A Sail Maker is used to working in his material, and knows how much to allow for stretch, so it is rare that he makes such a large allowance that the sail is as much as 1 per cent short of its marks. Yet most Sail Makers have had complaints of this nature from time to time. They mainly stem from incorrect measurement. Many a sail has been condemned as too small because it fails to show the full luff length when spread on the lawn. It must be set under normal halyard tension on its spars before a fair assessment can be made. I grant you that a sail which is roped tightly will be under size, and will never get out to its marks, but re-roping should not only solve the problem, but make the sail set in the way it was intended.

It is, of course, more common for a sail to be under or over the cross-measurements in a closely controlled class. In this case inches, and even parts of inches, count, and the Sail Maker is often at fault. This mostly concerns the dinghy classes, although keelboats like the Dragon also bring their problems. In defence of the Sail Maker, I would mention that he is working to fine tolerances. The rules will outlaw any sail which is the smallest fraction of an inch over the maximum; the owner will sometimes refuse any sail which is more than half an inch under, because he is losing area. Add to this that different measurers in different clubs can get the same sail to produce many different answers for the same measurement, and you have a nice problem in compromise. I remember one owner calling at the loft in Cowes with a 5–0–5 mainsail which he said his Measurer made two inches under on the half-height; he felt that this was losing too much area. I measured the sail in his presence, and make it half an inch under. He went off a happy man, but returned next day, saying that his Measurer would not believe my figures. We measured it again, with the same result. This happened no less than four times, when finally the owner telephoned to say the club Measurer had decided that he was not getting very accurate figures spreading the sail on an uneven lawn, so he had taken it to a gymnasium and that he now agreed my figure. Mark you, not many Measurers have the perfect facilities of a sail loft for their difficult task, and full allowance must be made for this. Which is why the average Sail Maker errs slightly on the small side when he is making a sail to a specific rule.

HEADSAIL FAULTS

The headsail is prone to similar faults to the mainsail, with the addition of a slack foot. Once again I have listed them in the order which I have found most frequent. It may well be that other Sail Makers find a different frequency, but there is nothing significant in it, and I only mention it for the sake of interest.

1. Leeches: slack or tight.
2. Fullness: Too full aft; too full foward; flow too high; too flat. I refer here, principally to headsails with luff wires, not tapes.
3. Foot: slack or tight.
4. Creases: wrinkles, pleats and hardspots.
5. Size: too small or too large.

HEADSAIL LEECHES

Slack Leech. A slack leech is a sign that the wind is escaping from the aft end of the headsail, and is thus not a particularly bad fault. The sight and sound of it, however, have a poor effect on morale, so it should be attended to if for no other reason. Check first that the sheet lead is not too far aft, then the leech line may be gently tightened so as to alleviate the flutter to a more acceptable movement, but it should never be tightened so that the leech curls. The real remedy lies in the sail loft, where a few seams and/or the tabling should be tightened $\frac{1}{8}$ in or so each. On the other hand, the leech may show fair on the test rig, but there may not be enough hollow to it, and it can then be hollowed some more. See also my remarks about mainsail as regards *creased, cupped* and *stretched* leeches. The most common single fault with a headsail is the cupped leech, and it requires the most delicate attention. If the worst comes to the worst, increase the hollow to cut away the stretched portion of cloth, but care must be taken not to set the new leech too much on the bias as a result.

Tight Leech. A tight leech on a headsail is one of the worst faults which can occur. Not only does it affect the flow over the headsail, but it also badly disturbs the air over the lee side of the mainsail, thus causing a major breakdown in thrust. After checking that the sheet lead is not too far forward, this important part of the sail should have immediate expert attention from the Sail Maker. The individual breakdown of the reasons for a tight headsail leech is exactly the same as that for the mainsail as shown above. An additional remedy available to the headsail once again is to hollow the leech further, thus cutting away the offending cloth. This is easy on a sealed leech without a tabling (which is only really suitable for dinghies and day-sailers) and a most unlikely fault on a horizontally cut headsail. If it does nothing else, it will make the Sail Maker take off the leech tabling and put it back on again, with the chance that he will tension it better the second time.

HEADSAIL FULLNESS

Too Full Aft. The flow in a headsail should be more forward than a mainsail. It will move aft for the same reasons as in a mainsail, and the corrective measures are the same. Where a woven mainsail is pulled harder on the halyard, a similar headsail is pulled more on the wire. This means that the

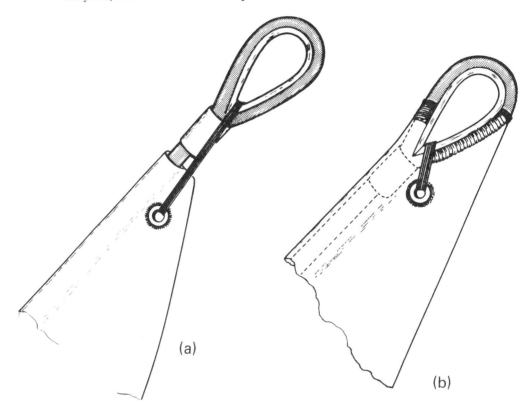

(a)

(b)

Fig. 17.11 Headsail Luff Fullness
On a conventional headsail with a luff wire, the head eye usually runs out of the sail (a). If the luff seizings are cut (and those holding any hanks to the sail), the sail can be pulled harder on its wire and right out over the head eye, which is then worked into the sail; this induces more flow up the luff and flattens the leech. If the head eye does not run out to start with, so that it is already worked into the cloth, the luff of the sail must first be shortened to allow it to be pulled more on its wire.

luff seizings and hanks have to be cut away, the luff shortened slightly if there is not already some excess wire available, and the luff of the sail stretched more along its wire, to draw the flow forward. Adjustable luff headsails of woven cloth may be treated like mainsails.

This will not always work completely satisfactorily, but it is surprising what a new lease of life it can give to a woven sail which has been blown out of shape by heavy winds, providing the cloth was initially a good one. Ghosters and drifters are constantly being subjected to wind strengths far in excess of those for which they were designed ('The wind got up, but she was going so well that I didn't want to change to the genoa'); even these can be helped a lot by pulling more on the wire if the maltreatment has not gone on too long. Film laminate sails cannot be resuscitated in this manner, and over-stressing will ruin them.

Too Full Forward. If the headsail is too full forward, it may be because it is, indeed, cut too full, but it may also be because the stay sags too much. In either event the luff should have some cloth removed, and this can be done by pleating. An alternative reason is that a woven sail may be pulled too much on the wire; it should be eased back a $\frac{1}{4}$ in or so (rather more in large

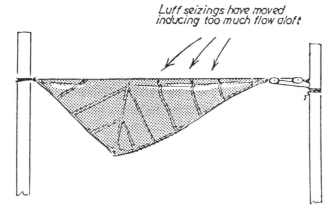

Fig. 17.12 Checking a Wire Luff Woven Headsail for Flow

Make the head fast to a strong point on the wall or to a tree, and pull out the tack on a handy billy or purchase, so that the luff wire is horizontal and tight; hold the clew out to one side and the sail will take up its aerofoil shape. If the sail is held to the luff wire by seizings, it will then be possible to see whether these have moved up or down the wire, causing the luff of the sail to be locally pulled too much, thus distorting the flow. The seizings of the sail in this drawing have slid down towards the tack, causing slackness in that area and too much tension at the head. All seizings, including those which hold any hanks in place, should be cut away, and the cloth allowed to settle to its natural position, evening out the tension. The seizings and hanks should then be replaced firmly, taking care not to pass the needle through any protective covering on the wire. While the sail is set up, take the opportunity to examine the leech critically for any slackness.

boats), until the sail takes up a better shape. Remember though that a heavy weather headsail will need to be pulled rather more than one for light weather, so it should have a deep fold down the luff in light airs; this will blow aft in strong winds. Film laminates apart, it is only the light weather headsail which should have a smooth curve preset to the one third position in conditions of little or no wind.

Flow Too High. After a certain amount of use a wire luff woven headsail may end up with its flow too high (or, indeed, too low or just badly spread over the luff). This will almost certainly be because the luff of the sail is seized at intervals to the luff wire, and these seizings have moved on the wire, causing the sail to be stretched more at one point than at another. The solution is to set up the headsail in a horizontal position and share out the luff tension more evenly.

Too Flat. The rear half of a headsail should always be pretty flat so, if the sail is said to be too flat, it usually means that there is not enough flow forward. This can usually be cured by pulling the cloth more on the wire, to induce a fold in the cloth up the luff, from where it will be blown back into the sail when the wind acts on it. In extreme cases the sail may have to be taken to pieces and some broad seam put into the mitre, but this should not normally be necessary.

HEADSAIL FOOT

Slack Foot. Apart from a sheet lead which is too far forward, a slack headsail foot is usually the result of too much round being built on to the foot in an attempt to gain free area. A conservative guide to the correct amount of foot round is 1 in for every 3 ft of foot length. Foot round, however, not only represents free area, but it also keeps a genoa or genoa staysail near the deck. This acts as an endplate and prevents too much wind escaping under the foot.

A slack foot can also be caused by woven cloths lying too much on the bias, and thus stretching. The remedy in both the above cases lies in tightening a few seams into the sail for about 5 per cent of the foot length; i.e. a genoa 20 ft on the foot should be tightened into the sail about 1 ft, a working jib with a foot of 10 ft should go in 6 in and a dinghy jib of 5 ft length should be tightened in to 3 in.

Tight Foot. It is rare to have a tight foot to a headsail, and not particularly detrimental to performance; in fact it can be advantageous in reaching conditions, and I have sometimes wondered why a drawstring along the foot tabling has not been tried more often, with a view to tightening the foot off

Plate 17.5 Shifting Jib Luff
The jib on this Lazy E is suffering from shifted seizings as shown in Pl. 17.1 (it also looks as if the sail needs shortening on the luff and pulling more, in accordance with Fig. 17.12). Incidentally, the mainsail needs more tension on the foot, and would be better off with a softer top batten. My guess is that the sailcloth is of indifferent quality and has over-stretched.   *Yachts & Yachting*

the wind. If the foot is, in fact, too tight for windward work, one or two seams should be carefully eased an $\frac{1}{8}$ in or so. Before doing so, however, check that the tightness is not caused by the sheet lead being too far aft.

HEADSAIL CREASES

General creases occur in a headsail for more or less the same reasons as they do in a mainsail, and my previous remarks concerning the latter should be observed where they apply.

Tack. Probably the most common crease in a headsail is the one which runs up from the tack. This is caused by the shape of the tack eye, which is usually worked into the sail so that the foot shall be as low as possible, and the tension which is always on it due to the luff being stretched on the wire.

The cloth has to be shaped round the eye at the bottom of the wire, which is then sewn into the sail. The sail is next pulled on the wire so that the canvas is stretched from the small arrows. Sewing the shaped sail tightly to the tack eye can cause wrinkles on its own; when the cloth is subjected to tension in addition, the risk is greater. Apart from letting the tack eye run right out of the sail, so that it does not have to be shaped, the cure for this fault is not easy. If a tack board is allowed, a small piece of Perspex can be slipped under the tack patch, and this should do the trick. Not many rules allow this, however. A second possibility is to sew a length of webbing through the eye and up into the sail, so that some of the stresses can be absorbed; Fig. 6.3. This should be taken 6 to 18 in into the sail and sewn with broad stitches, care being taken to see that there is room in the eye for the tack shackle or pin. Check also that the sail is hoisted right; Fig. 17.13.

Clew. All the stresses of the sail concentrate at the clew when hard on the wind. It is natural that a certain amount of creasing should be set up in this area. The clew eye itself may encourage this, in the same way that any eye will do so; the stainless steel D-ring type clew, with tapes radiating into the sail will do a great deal to spread the load, as will a large and heavy clew patch with plenty of under-patching.

Head Eye. The head eye usually runs out, so is not so prone to creases. Where they occur, they most likely originate from the small eye at the head so that the sail may be pulled on the wire. A length of webbing tape is the best hope of success.

Piston Hank or Snap Hook Eyelets. Piston hank or snap hook eyelets can cause creases if the hank itself is seized so tightly that it folds the eyelet over against the luff wire; this is aggravated if there is too much distance between the eyelet and the wire. In addition, the sail may have moved on the wire through the seizings pulling up or down, as explained above; this occurs if the headsail is lowered by pulling too hard on the cloth and not on the wire. The answer is to regulate the cloth on the wire as described above. If a

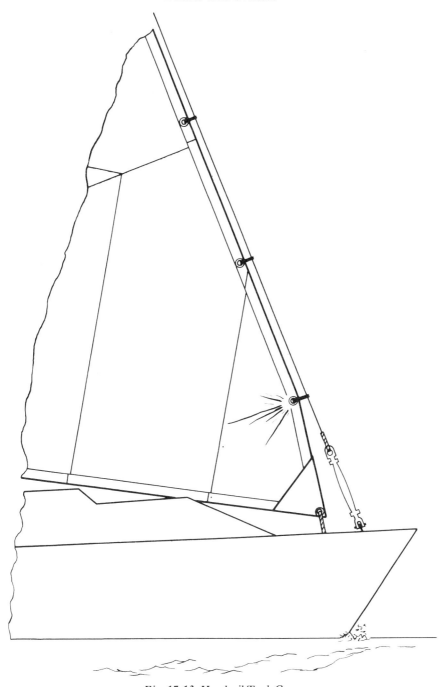

Fig. 17.13 Headsail Tack Creases
If the tack of a headsail is made fast too far aft of the forestay, creases will run from the first hank up. So check this, before you condemn a sail out of hand for tack creases.

337

hanked film laminate sail is hoisted too slackly, small creases will run from the hanks, and lead to local stressing with possible delamination. The solution is correct hoisting: not too little and not too much.

Hard Spots. Treatment for hard spots in a headsail is exactly the same as for a mainsail; see page 326.

Tight Mitre. A tight mitre is sometimes evident in light winds. This results from shaping of the mitre seam, and will almost certainly blow out in stronger winds, to leave a nice flat leech. If the crease persists, and cannot be cured by pulling more on the wire as described under *Too Flat* above, the seam must be eased slightly in the middle.

HEADSAIL SIZE

A wire luff headsail lies on the ground the same way that it is made. By this I mean that there is no rope to gather it up so that it looks short, and there is little broad seam to the average headsail so it will lie fairly flat. There is thus little scope for error or misinterpretation of the facts, so that relatively few headsails are found to be the wrong size.

The principal source of misinterpretation is on the luff, particularly where the sail is not seized to the luff wire but is left to 'float' and find its own level. We have already seen that a wire luff woven headsail is made short in the luff, so that it can be stretched on the wire to induce flow in the luff. If the wire is loose inside the luff tabling and the sail is laid on the ground, it will appear short unless the wire is pulled straight (thus stretching the cloth). A sail which is seized at regular intervals to its luff wire will show clearly if the wire is not straight, because it will lie in slight twists under the tension of the already stretched cloth. In either case a firm pull is required, particularly if the cloth is fairly heavy; see Fig. 4.4.

SPINNAKER FAULTS

Spinnakers are not such special sails that diagnosis and treatment of their troubles merit a special chapter to themselves, even though I have accorded that honour to making and setting them. They suffer the same sort of faults as mainsails and headsails, but to a lesser extent because the springy nature of their canvas tends to allow creases to dissipate throughout the sail. I propose to deal here only with those faults which are peculiar to spinnakers.

Narrow Head. The most common fault from which nearly every spinnaker suffers is that it is too narrow in the head. The cure for this is to get off your boat and on to somebody else's, where you will find that his high shouldered, bursting beauty which you were admiring from afar, looks just as narrow gutted from close behind as your own sail now looks broad in the head.

The two photographs in Plate 13.2 were taken in 1965 in the Ratsey & Lapthorn wind tunnel at Cowes, and are of the same spinnaker within seconds of each other. If, in fact, your particular spinnaker is narrow in the head, there is little the Sail Maker can do about it. You should resign yourself to the fact, and take what profit you can: it will knock the boat down less in a strong beam wind; it will probably be flatter aloft, and so you can use it with the wind well forward; there is not so much weight of canvas aloft, and therefore less total weight to lift if conditions are very light.

Tight Luffs. Many spinnakers suffer from tight luffs. They curl in, particularly near the head, and make the sail a poor performer on a reach because the luff collapses before it should.

This is caused by the tapes being too short for the sail (which has been caused in its turn by the sail stretching and the tapes staying their original length). The cure is to ease the tapes, taking care that they do not exceed the maximum allowed by the particular rule under which the sail is measured. If they do, then the sail will have to be shortened by the appropriate amount.

Head Creases. Two major creases radiating down from the head for about one fifth of the way into the spinnaker are a sign that the head is too full or the sail has been badly designed. The Sail Maker has tried to fit too much cloth into the top of the sail, and it will not stand unless the wind is dead aft; Fig. 17.14. Either the sail must be made narrower aloft, or else the head

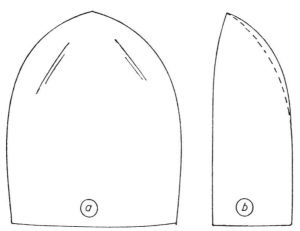

Fig. 17.14 Spinnaker Head Girts
Girts from the head (a) betray the fact that the Sail Maker has tried to get too much cloth into that part of the sail. When folded in half about the centre seam and laid on the floor (b), this excess cloth is revealed as too bosomy a curve, and it should be cut back to the pecked line.

seams should be completely unmade and and tightened considerably more
– probably a little of both. This is not an easy fault to cure without cutting
away a good deal of cloth.

Loose Foot. A spinnaker which has too large a skirt on the foot will set badly
in that area on almost all points of sailing. The solution is to remove the
offending extra cloth, and/or to tighten the foot by inserting some vertical
darts in the bottom cloth as shown in Fig. 17.15.

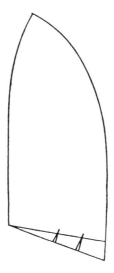

Fig. 17.15 Slack Spinnaker Foot
Slackness is sometimes caused by too deep a skirt. Remove the wedge at the foot,
or else tighten the foot by means of vertical darts as shown.

Chapter XVIII

Design and Rating

Speaking of the IOR formula (and other similar handicap rules), a yacht designer's task is to integrate the hull he has in mind with the sail area necessary to give the boat a good performance in light winds; fresh wind performance follows provided that he keeps his stability sensible. He will have to adapt and compromise here and there, so that the resulting combination rates well under the rule, and is efficient over a wide range of wind and sea conditions. An inch or two less on the beam may have to be paid for in the sail plan; a gain in sail area may be at the expense of a compensating loss in the centre of gravity factor.

RIG

In the old days of the RORC and the CCA, a designer could often draw plans to the same area for a ketch, a yawl, a sloop and a cutter, and there might not be much in it as regards advantages and disadvantages. Indeed, John Illingworth is on record[54] as having done precisely that. But modern hulls are so efficient in their underwater shape, and the IOR is so comprehensive in its measurement of all the factors which help or hinder a boat in her progress through the water, that the sloop has emerged as Best Buy. There are, of course, occasions when other considerations apply, such as prevailing winds or sea states, so that a low sail plan is preferred by the owner (in which case a yawl might be desirable) but, by and large, we get a single mast with overlapping genoa. We shall see shortly that discussion is more likely to centre around the pro's and con's of masthead versus fractional rig, rather than one or two masts; lovers of yawls, however, should not despair, because the rule is not too harsh on their preference – a mizzen can be almost tax deductible as far as the rating goes, and I don't by any means rule it out of court.

341

LUFF/FOOT RATIO

The ratio of the luff of a sail to its foot is sometimes incorrectly called the aspect ratio. Tony Marchaj in his book *Sailing Theory and Practice* correctly defines aspect ratio as the ratio of the height of the sail to its *mean* width. Worked out mathematically, so as to allow for leech round, this is represented by the formula which gives us:

$$AR = \frac{L^2}{SA} : 1$$

where AR = aspect ratio, L = luff in feet, and SA = sail area in square feet; both L and SA may be expressed in metric terms.

On the other hand, a simple relation of the length of the luff to the length of the foot is more readily grasped by the average owner, and that is what I propose to use in this book. Note that this will give a value of just over half the mathematical aspect ratio. I shall use this relation of luff/foot for mainsails, headsails and spinnakers.

Beating to windward is the most inefficient condition as far as making ground towards one's objective is concerned. On all other points of sailing one is heading towards his immediate goal. In addition it is the condition where races are often won and lost, so the close-hauled situation is the one we should seek to improve, at the expense of reaching and running if necessary.

MAINSAILS

A mainsail produces less induced drag per square foot of its area as its luff/foot ratio increases, though the relative disturbance caused by the mast increases, and some say that an elliptical form is desirable. There are, however, practical reasons at present why a permanently bent mast is not used on anything other than an extreme boat, such as some 30 sq metres (the IOR forbids a permanent bend), but Tony Marchaj certainly started something with *Lionheart's* bendy topmast in 1979, and we haven't heard the last of this yet. The 12-metre rule used to allow this, and the IOR (correctly worried about the possibility of extreme boats going for too much flexibility at the expense of strength) effectively limits bending by more rigid mainsail girth restrictions at half and three-quarter heights; indeed, a rating bonus is available where bending spars don't effectively add to leech roach. The elliptical theory, however, may help to explain the undoubted efficiency of the headsail in its own right, due to its luff being slanted towards the rear in an aerodynamic imitation. We have already seen in Chapter II the main reasons for a headsail's efficiency. Its slanting luff is a possible extra advantage, because sweep-back also has a beneficial effect on efficient loading.

There are, however, practical limitations on the maximum value of the luff/foot ratio which can be used, particularly as the boat gets larger. These are almost all connected with problems of staying the mast, and also the attendant increases in hull size and weight to avoid excessive heeling with a tall rig, if a reasonable area is to be maintained. Marchaj originally gave this limit as 2 to 2·2:1 (his actual figures were an *aspect ratio* of 4 to 4·5:1), but there are plenty of yachts which exceed this figure today. The 30 sq metre in its heyday went as far as 3·5:1, a Dragon is about 2·7:1 and the Soling is nearly 3:1. Speaking of the offshore fleet, John Illingworth gave his opinion of the upper limit as 3·2:1 for straight spars, but modern technology has enabled this figure to be exceeded by most of the racing fleet, large and small, medium and light displacement, as we shall see below, so that 3·5 or 3·6:1 is quite common.

HEADSAILS

The optimum luff/foot ratio of a headsail is not normally a factor which influences the size of the sail significantly. This will be governed largely by the foretriangle within which the sail must be set, and the rules it must obey in doing so.

Where either an offshore racer to the IOR, or a new class of boat is being considered, the question of masthead or fractional rig is more likely to be dictated by rating considerations than headsail luff/foot ratio. The base of the foretriangle will establish this ratio for the offshore racer, because the sail may not have a longer perpendicular from the clew to the luff (LP) than $1·5 \times J$ without penalty. Under this rule of measurement, therefore, a maximum size headsail will be a genoa of relatively low luff/foot ratio. Another way of looking at it is that the maximum luff of the headsail is fixed by the length of the forestay. To achieve a sail of 3:1 would mean having a foot shorter than the rules would allow, so that free area would be needlessly sacrificed in a search for aerodynamic efficiency; this is even more true on a fractional rig.

The Naval Architect, however, may vary the foot length of the headsail of a new one-design boat at will — although he is more likely to draw it so that the leech will coincide with the line of maximum camber of the mainsail, as we saw in Chapter II[22].

An offshore boat's I measurement is likely to be decided, therefore, by the luff/foot ratio of the mainsail (which will dictate the height of the mast), and a preference for either masthead or fractional rig. The J measurement can be influenced by the luff/foot ratio desired for the headsail, but it is more likely to depend on the need for a suitably proportioned spinnaker. We shall examine this factor shortly.

Only where a Naval Architect is designing a new class of boat and making up his own rules, therefore, is the luff/foot ratio of the headsail likely to be of more than academic interest. In practice, a headsail which has a ratio of about 2 to 2·5:1 seems about right. This is produced under the IOR by a foretriangle I:J ratio of 3 to 3·75:1.

A further point which has to be considered when deciding the J measurement of a boat to the IOR, is the sheeting base of the genoa. Ideally this sail should be able to sheet between 7–10 or 11 degrees to the central line, with a fairlead somewhat in from the toe-rail, although a narrower angle can sometimes be accepted in light airs and smooth water, as discussed in Chapter VIII under *Barber Haulers*. The same general effect holds good for a cutter, but the jib will, of course, be high cut to clear the staysail as discussed earlier in this book. This means that it will sheet right aft, but it should be cut low enough to bring this position sensibly forward if the stern narrows unduly, as with a double ender.

SPINNAKERS

The foretriangle does, however, often affect the proportions of the spinnaker. There is no doubt that a spinnaker with a luff/foot ratio which approaches even 2:1 is a narrow gutted affair which will not set very well in practice. Experience has shown that a ratio of somewhere between 1·6 and 1·8:1 will give a reasonably proportioned spinnaker. A low figure of 1·4:1, while giving a sail which sets well, does not have a big enough proportion of its area aloft where the wind will do most good, other than close reaching. When we turn to orbital spinnakers, the ratio goes down again, not because the height needs to be less, but because the width can be more without infringing the rule. A Soling orbital spinnaker is about 1·3:1, while one for a 12-metre or a 14 ft International can be as low as 1:1 – and these measurements compare the luff to the foot of the sail only, not to the half-height width, which greatly exceeds the foot, thus reducing the effective ratio to considerably less than 1:1.

Let us turn now to the specific case of the IOR spinnaker, which is limited in width to $1 \cdot 8 \times J$ all the way from head to foot. We find that a foretriangle ratio of 3:1 (i.e. I:J) will give a spinnaker luff/foot ratio of $0 \cdot 95\sqrt{3^2 + 1^2} : 1 \cdot 8$, which is 1·76:1, or near the top end of our ideal range. Where the I:J ratio is increased beyond 3·3:1 the spinnaker rapidly becomes too narrow, unless some penalty is taken on the width of the sail. As we have seen, 3:1 is also the low end of the I:J range for a well shaped genoa.

MASTHEAD OR FRACTIONAL RIG

In an attempt to discourage the evolution of boats with large genoas and token mainsails, the current IOR slightly benefits mainsail area, in that RSAF is weighted about 1·43 times RSAM. Some time ago, Camper & Nicholson decided to see how this might affect the sail area and performance of their latest Half-Tonner, one with masthead and the other with fractional rig, and both still meeting the same rating[55]. Based on a constant RSA of 480 sq ft, the vital statistics of the two sail areas were as follows:

	Masthead	*Fractional*
P	32·65'	37·5'
E	10·0'	12·0'
Luff/foot ratio	3·27:1	3·13:1
Mainsail area (sq ft)	163	225
I	38·5'	34·5'
J	11·6'	11·5'
I/J ratio	3·3:1	3:1
Fore △ area (sq ft)	223	198
Fore △ area : total area	58%	47%

This represents an extra 5 per cent area for the fractional rig when the genoa has been taken into account going to windward; down wind the advantage is reversed, with the masthead boat carrying over 20 per cent more area (largely based on the assumption that a big boy would not be carried in the fractional boat, because the rather small sail would be blanketed by the large mainsail; in any event, the difference in mainsail and spinnaker would not be enough to require balancing out with the blooper's area opposite the spinnaker). The fractional rig was reckoned to gain on the reach (larger mainsail of lower aspect ratio), to benefit more from a double head rig, and to be better in strong winds, when the lower aspect ratio should mean less heel, and the smaller spinnaker ought to be easier to handle and control. The masthead rig was reckoned to gain down wind in light weather (larger spinnaker and use of big boy), and in ability to point.

The theoretical analysis concluded that light displacement boats, with their easily driven hulls requiring a relatively small sail area, should profit from the fractional rig; otherwise the choice was thought to be marginal. After the report was written, comparative trials were conducted with the two Half-Tonners in question, and these largely bore out the findings.

It is worth recalling here that, in 1960, the same firm put a masthead rig on their successful fractional rig *Jolina* – a heavy displacement design. Two otherwise identical boats were built (in wood) in the same yard that winter: one was *Sunmaid III* (fractional rig) and the other *Jolina II* (but masthead this time). There was much speculation as to what would happen when they raced against each other, and the result was not long in coming. The masthead *Jolina II* knocked six bells out of *Sunmaid* under the existing RORC rule[56]. But these were relatively heavy boats, so this is a big factor in making the choice between rigs.

THE YAWL

The yawl rig has many things going for it. To start with, it reduces the size of the mainsail, by splitting part of it off to form the mizzen. If in addition the foretriangle is double head rigged, a young family can easily work the boat. Thirdly, the area of the mizzen-staysail is a very lightly taxed bonus when off the wind. Fourthly, the mizzen sail itself can be used to increase area at less cost to RSA than a sloop (because in a yawl, RSAM is replaced by RSAC, which includes the mizzen at a reduced rate).

Against these supposed advantages must be set the facts that, when the wind is forward of the beam, the mizzen is acting in turbulent airflow downstream of the mainsail; that conditions favouring the mizzen-staysail are limited to beam reaching; that dead down wind, the mizzen does little more than disturb the airflow over the mainsail (it has every right to, considering what the mainsail does to the mizzen when close hauled). But the IOR recognises these disadvantages, and the formula nearly compensates – it doesn't quite, but throw in a bit of race luck (a lot of reaching, or a good wind shift at the right moment), and the yawl can be up there on the winner's rostrum.

PROPORTION OF FORETRIANGLE TO TOTAL AREA

We have seen that a headsail is a highly efficient sail in its own right, partly because it carries the main driving force of the combined aerofoil, and partly because there is no mast in front of it to disturb the airflow.

It is interesting to note how the foretriangle's share of the total sail area has changed over recent years. When John Illingworth first wrote *Offshore* in 1949, he suggested that the foretriangle should represent somewhere between 40 and 50 per cent of the total area of the mainsail and foretriangle combined. An increasing tendency towards masthead rig, coupled with a general awakening to the efficiency of the genoa, caused the figure to rise to 55 per cent when this book was first published in 1967. The change to the International Offshore Rule caused further rethinking, because the effect on rating of the split of area behind and in front of the mast had once again to be reassessed against its efficiency and cost. The result was a further increase in the foretriangle, until the point where it was more than half as big again as the mainsail. Sparkman and Stephens' design for the second *Morning*

346

Cloud had a foretriangle of just over 61 per cent of the total area in the early seventies. Camper & Nicholson's then went as high as 63 per cent, while Angus Primrose fixed the level at 60 per cent, designed for the first full IOR year.

Five years later the pattern had not changed a great deal, as we find German Frers designing *Scaramouche* in 1976 with a foretriangle of 60·5 per cent of the total area. All these vessels were heavy displacement and masthead rig; the swing to fractional came about with increasing popularity of Quarter- and Half-Tonners and other small boats in the light displacement vein, so that foretriangles could expect to be a lower percentage of the total. Typically, this proves to be something like 40 per cent (so we are back to John Illingworth and 1949 again), but the hulls are so easily driven that any reduction in area off the wind is no great disadvantage – indeed, fractional boats are less difficult to control than their masthead sisters. The appropriate figures are as follows:

	1971 *Morning Cloud* (masthead)	1976 *Scaramouche* (masthead)	1983 Marshall Half-Tonner (fractional)
P	45·04'	56·7'	36·5'
E	12·4'	14·75'	13·5'
Luff/foot ratio	3·6:1	3·8:1	2·7:1
Mainsail area (sq ft)	280	418	246
I	51·04'	62·5'	33·0'
J	17·44'	20·75'	10·0'
I:J ratio	3:1	3:1	3·3:1
Fore △ area (sq ft)	445	640	165
Fore △ area : total area	61·4%	60·5%	40·1%

To summarise, a mainsail luff/foot ratio of 3·5:1 and an I:J of 3:1 are common on masthead rigs, and are by no means incompatible with a 60 per cent foretriangle proportion; they give reasonably shaped genoas and spinnakers. The fractional rig usually has a lower aspect ratio mainsail and, if the hull is easily driven, what it suffers from any loss of slot effect over the upper part of its mainsail is more than made up by other gains: the CE is low, so that the boat is more easily controlled; spinnaker efficiency is good; there should be no need for a blooper; and there is more area up wind.

RATING

When cruising yachts of different size and shape race together, they have to be handicapped with the object that all shall have an equal chance of

347

winning. The two clubs which cover most of the world with their rules are the Royal Ocean Racing Club and the Cruising Club of America, and they sensibly combined their different formulae for handicapping into the International Offshore Rule some time ago. In addition to this rating rule, there are many, more parochial, rules for cruiser/racers which have come into being due to the rather complicated (and expensive) nature of measuring a yacht under the more senior clubs. All aim at encouraging seaworthy boats, rigged sensibly, and at penalizing extremes which might lead to an unsafe vessel. Many of them have been going long enough to ensure that any attempt to gain unfair rating advantage attracts a sufficient penalty to make it not worth while; but within the rules there is usually scope for intelligent experiment. Others, however, are drawn up not to have boats designed to them, but to evaluate existing boats. This may equalise the chances of an existing fleet, but a bright Naval Architect will often detect a loop-hole and drive a metaphorical coach and horses through it. This means that the rule has to be rapidly re-written to close the gap; whereupon somebody spots another flaw, and the process continues. Many of us can think of examples. This is all really the sphere of the Naval Architect, but it may be interesting to examine superficially one or two of the more usual facets which interest the Sail Maker.

HEADSAIL INCREASE

Perhaps one of the most common questions a Sail Maker is asked is whether it pays to take a penalty on a headsail. While it is convenient to use the phrase, it is in fact really a misconception to talk about a headsail *penalty*. The IOR fixes a lower limit to headsail size, and $1 \cdot 5 \times J$ is used as the LP even if the largest sail is smaller than this; the rating then pays in proportion as the headsail gets bigger.

The following factors should be remembered when considering a headsail penalty for a particular boat:

1. The penalty operates all the time, even when overlapping sails are not being used (in heavy weather, or down wind).

2. If a headsail penalty is being taken, the spinnaker and its pole can also be increased in similar proportion (through adopting an oversize J measurement) without costing too much further increase in the rating. This will allow advantage to be taken of greater sail area off the wind as well as to windward.

3. There are occasions, particularly offshore, when a boat carrying a penalty is able to complete a race before an adverse change in the weather or a turn of the tide. It is no good having a lower rating than a penalized sister ship, if the latter is snug in port saving her time while you are jilling

about looking for wind half a day short of the finishing line. This factor can of course, also work in reverse.

4. The IOR penalizes oversized genoas rather more heavily than did the old RORC rule, and the gain in area seldom enables a boat to sail to the higher rating involved these days.

Close analysis of the rule and improved sailcloth and sailmaking have revealed the efficiency of the modern genoa. In the particular case of a boat being a poor performer in light winds, off the wind as well as to windward, it is worth considering the LP as a variable up to a value of about $1 \cdot 60 \times J$. In terms of cash, this is a simple and relatively cheap way to raise a rating to reach, say, a fixed Half-Ton or One-Ton level (but increasing the mainsail is often a better bet, as discussed below).

When I was racing in *Gitana IV* during the 1965 Fastnet, we had a huge quadrilateral which not only carried the quad penalty (quadrilaterals were allowed, but penalized, by the RORC in those days), but it had a foot in excess of $1 \cdot 5 \times J$ as well. We were fortunate in that race, because we were able to make good use of the sail, but there were plenty of times when we were under jib and staysail, or spinnaker, yet we still had to carry the crushing penalty bestowed by the quad (our time correction factor was slightly over $1 \cdot 1$ so, as *Yachting World* put it, we were giving ourselves time). Incidentally, we only took 3 days, 9 hours and 40 minutes, which was a new elapsed time record. Not many yachts have finished the course in under four days, *American Eagle*, the modified 12-metre, beating our record in 1971, to be followed by quite a number of the maxi-raters later.

If the boat goes well under normal canvas in all but the lightest winds, therefore, it is not worth taking a J penalty to improve performance in the few races which are completed in light airs. If, however, she is a poor performer on and off the wind, up to and including force 3, she might just profit from the increased area on more occasions, and thus sail to a higher rating. A final decision should be taken with the advice of a Naval Architect who has experience of sailing in the boat concerned. This, of course, is not always possible and, if the experiment is tried and proves a failure, the larger headsail can usually be cut down, so all is not lost.

MAINSAIL INCREASE

Because of the lower tax on mainsail area under the IOR, an owner who wants to raise his rating may be better advised to look to his mainsail rather than his genoa. At Appendix E is a graph kindly produced for me by my old friend Roger Marshall, a Naval Architect from Rhode Island. This shows the amount of actual area gain plotted against Rated Sail Area when P, E, I and J is each increased. It will be seen that E is the most cost-effective as far as the rating is concerned, followed by P; thus the mainsail attracts a lower penalty than the foretriangle. But it may upset the balance of the helm, necessitating moving the mast – possibly the most expensive of all these possible modifications in cash terms. A larger P, of course, means re-rigging the boat with a taller mast, unless the increase is minimal and can be accepted on the existing spar; it may also invite an increase in I.

But a larger sail area is no good if it doesn't improve performance more than it costs in the rating. So the designer must carefully consider where that area is to be applied, how it will affect speed, and whether it will be usefully employed throughout the average race (an increase in the mainsail will be of no use as soon as a reef is taken in; a headsail-only penalty doesn't help down wind). Displacement and stability play their parts in the final analysis, as well as how the airflow will be affected. All the factors need ideally to be fed into a velocity prediction programme (VPP), which will evaluate changes in rig (and hull shape) against rating. The process is not all that expensive and, at Grand Prix level, is a Best Buy when compared with tank testing or with trying the changes full size only to find that they aren't a success.

LOWERING THE RATING

Most owners at some time or other have worked out that they would have won a coveted cup if only their rating had been just a little lower. You can easily drop any rating by cutting off the mast at the deck; the problem is to reduce it without impairing speed more than the lower rating allows. This can sometimes be done without interfering too seriously with performance, by a reduction in the size of the mainsail. There are plenty of other ways in which it can be attempted, but I am only considering sails. If the boat carries too much weather helm, it is possible to reduce the rating and actually make her go faster in the process, if the foot of the mainsail is shortened; this will reduce weather helm, thus increasing speed whenever the wind is forward of the beam, and lower her handicap. Heavy displacement boats can sometimes make a useful reduction on the luff – if the sail is made shorter, it will then be more completely covered by the headsail with resulting improved efficiency to windward, particularly if the boat is fractional rigged, because she will tend towards masthead, which we have seen is better for heavy boats. Care must be taken not to reduce the mainsail below the minimum rated area as represented by $0.094 \times IC^2$. This sort of alteration is a fairly major affair, and it would be unwise to undertake it without expert advice; for one thing, the mast will need different staying arrangements as a result.

RAISING THE RATING

It is sometimes desirable to increase a rating by a small amount, perhaps to move from the top of one class to the bottom of the next, or else to sail to the

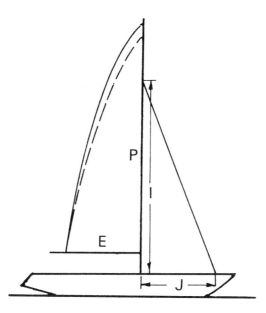

Fig. 18.1 Lowering the Rating

If a fractional rig yacht wishes to lower her rating by a small percentage, reducing the I measurement gives the greatest reduction in rating for the smallest loss of area; the next most efficient method is to reduce the J measurement. Both these, however, involve moving the forestay and are thus expensive and fairly permanent, unless some sort of adjustable forestay has been foreseen in the design stage. A reduction in P or E can be achieved with little modification other than to the size of the mainsail; reducing P offers slightly less loss of area than reducing E, but both can be restored by putting the black bands out to their original positions again (but the new smaller mainsail would have to be set aside, or expensively enlarged). At all events, the area loss comes from a low-efficiency part of the sail plan.

maximum rating permitted by certain regulations, such as the One-Ton Cup. There are, of course, many ways of getting a higher rating (some would say too many) but, if it is to be achieved by means of sails (which, like changing the propeller, has the advantage that it can be undone again quickly), the choice lies between increasing the mainsail, or the headsail (and spinnakers). Increasing JC used to be a popular method of doing it, because it confers larger genoas, larger spinnakers, and a longer spinnaker pole – all of which are readily noticed from the helm. But few IOR owners go for oversize genoas these days because, as will be seen from Appendix E, the increase in sail area from a larger E measurement can be three times what it would be for the same rating increase through a larger J. The snag is that the former puts it on in a relatively inefficient manner, whereas the latter gives it to the thrust-producing genoa. The genoa is not, however, three times as efficient as the mainsail, and you have to make up your mind whether you want a lot

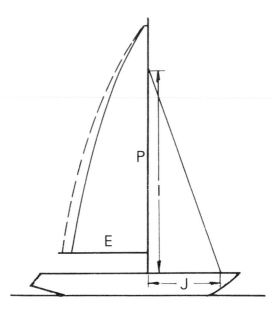

Fig. 18.2 Raising the Rating

If a fractional rig yacht wishes to raise her rating by a small percentage, the greatest gain in sail area for a given increase in rating will accrue if the E measurement is increased; the next greatest gain comes from increasing P. Both these have the advantage that they only affect the mainsail, and the status quo can be restored by cutting the new larger sail back to its original size and restoring the black bands. The disadvantages are that new spars may be needed, and that the extra sail area is not being added at the most aerodynamically efficient place. We should, therefore, really only consider small changes to the mainsail foot, which may possibly be accommodated on the existing boom. See Appendix E for examples of the values involved.

of extra mainsail or a little extra genoa (and spinnaker). If the boat is a consistently poor performer both up and down wind, so that she will profit from larger spinnakers as well as larger genoas up to and including force 3–4, a penalty J might be worth considering. If it doesn't work, the larger sails can usually be cut down with little extra final cost, after which they will remain usable with the original rating.

The best way from an efficiency point of view is to raise the height of the mast, thereby increasing the relatively cost-effective P measurement, giving more area where it will do most good in the light conditions we are considering – aloft. But this is very expensive and should be run through a VPP first. Apart from anything else, it invites a corresponding increase in I, and the quantity SPIN in the IOR formula must be borne in mind – this is a spinnaker area which is used as the rated sail area (RSA) if found to be bigger than the latter, thereby effectively setting a maximum size to the spinnaker. Extra area at lowest cost to the rating can be obtained by increasing the E measurement, possibly even keeping the same main boom; but it will be less efficiently applied. Here again the increase can always be removed without crippling expense, because the oversize mainsail should cut down easily. In general, if a boat cannot fine-tune her rating simply by adjusting E, she will probably never be competitive at the highest levels, so that this becomes Best Buy when the rating has to be raised.

SAIL AREA/RATING

Owners usually want some idea of how much a particular change in sail measurement will affect their rating. The IOR is such a complicated formula, however, that a straightforward answer is not always possible, although a qualified Measurer can often give a fairly close estimate. Figures for an average yacht will give sufficient indication for this book, and I am indebted to Roger Marshall for the sail plan of his Half-Tonner at Appendix D, together with the graph at Appendix E showing how variation of certain sail measurements affects area and rating; precise values for the boat in question have been put on the four curves, so that an indication of the degree of alteration is given.

RATING EVALUATION

It is tedious to work through the IOR formula, in order to turn a set of measurements into a rating. It is equally tedious to work out what changes are required in variables such as sails to effect a particular change in the rating. Gone are the days when an owner could do his own calculations fairly quickly on the back of an envelope, and nowadays we have to resort to expert help for comprehensive reliability.

Using his own computer, Roger Marshall (of Box 127A, Jamestown, Rhode Island 02835 USA) specialises in these calculations, and the effect of sail alterations can be quickly evaluated (hull too, for that matter). The computer takes care of the pitfalls which lie in wait for the unwary, such as minimum mainsail size, upper and lower black band limits, maximum spinnaker area without penalty and so on. He tells me that all too many rating certificates which he sees are found to contain silly penalties, simply because the owner has battens which are an inch or so too long, an oversize headboard, a spinnaker which strays a few inches oversize – the owner waited until he had used it a couple of times before he had it measured, so it had stretched from its designed sizes – or perhaps no 'bale' position marked on the boom, so the outer end is taken as the datum. This is the sort of service which anyone who races seriously should consider, if he or she wants to avoid unnecessary penalties. I have only been able here to highlight a few of the factors which go into this fascinating part of the sport. The rest is up to you.

Chapter XIX

Chinese (Junk) Rig

The Chinese are reputed always to have a word for it – but in this case 'junk' stems from the Javanese 'djong', meaning a boat. Nevertheless, while Europe was slowly evolving top-heavy floating castles, designed (if that is the correct word) to give soldiers good platforms for land-orientated engagements, and which struggled to make progress whenever the wind was not aft of the beam, Cathay had long been operating a one-sail windward-going, easy-to-operate rig which can still teach us a thing or two today.

There is reliable evidence[57] to show that the junk originated while the Romans were still in Britain, and that 600 years ago ocean-going vessels of 300 tons or more were plying as far afield as Africa. Although the rig may look complicated at first glance, when all is set and drawing, control is simplicity itself – and very efficient. In broad terms there is only one sail per mast, which ideally takes the form of an unstayed spar supported only at the keel-mounted step and the partners (though the Chinese certainly stayed their sea- and ocean-going vessels, as American Naval Architect Tom Colvin tells us[58]); the sail is a fully-battened balanced lug, with anything up to one third of its area forward of the mast. Each batten is more like a boom than a batten, and is fairly robust in nature; this ensures that the somewhat primitive sailcloth (bamboo matting in many cases) remains flat in section in strong winds, and allows fine control of the sail by means of separate sheets which are attached to the end of each batten-boom. Twist can thus be eliminated altogether if desired, and old photographs of junks on a reach make an interesting comparison with those of European yachts of the nineteenth century similarly sailing with the wind abeam, their main booms strapped in and their gaffs sagging off to leeward. Small wonder that the racing cutter of a hundred years ago had to have such a deep keel, if leeway were to be held in check.

By the time the weight of a heavy yard, thick sailcloth and a multiplicity of robust batten-booms have been taken into account, a large Chinese sail is a formidable proposition, so that native craft often need more than one

Plate 19.1 The Real Thing
A Ha-Kau fishing junk from Hong Kong. The mizzen of Exeter Maritime
Museum's *Keying II* is little more than an aid to rudder balance; the vessel spins
on her keel like a dinghy if the helm is put hard down. In eastern waters, the sails
are often rigged on alternate sides of the masts, which in this example are stayed
(Museum Director David Goddard suggests that this is not only because she is a
sea-going vessel, but also because an unstayed mast in China has to be much
stouter, and therefore rarer and more expensive).   *Exeter Maritime Museum*

halyard. The rig's very weight, however, bestows another advantage, in that
reefing is a relatively simple matter of easing the halyard and allowing as
much sail as necessary to lower of its own accord, so that the batten-booms
stack up on the main boom, where they are maintained by their own weight
between supporting lazy-jacks. We shall go further into both twist and
reefing later in this chapter.

Colonel 'Blondie' Hasler was among the first to bring the qualities of the
Chinese junk rig to the notice of Western yachtsmen. In 1959 he designed a
junk sail for his 25 ft Folkboat *Jester*, and sailed her to second place in the
Trans-Atlantic race the following year. Use of modern materials encourages
reduction in overall weight of the rig, and Hasler was no exception. Writing
just after the race[59], he was the first to admit that he had made his battens
too light. They were tapered down in the middle, so that they proved too
flexible (two of them broke) and had to be replaced with stouter substitutes –
which even then allowed too much flow to develop in strong winds, so that
stiffer ones still were installed after the race was over.

PRINCIPLES

The principle of the rig as used by the Western world can be followed in Fig.
19.1. The sail is divided by battens into a number of panels, depending on

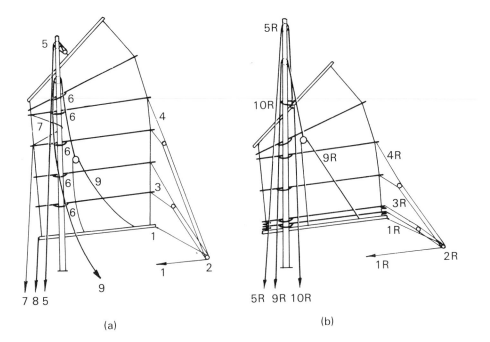

Fig. 19.1 Principles of the Junk Rig

1 = Mainsheet. 2 = Multiple sheet block at deck.
3 and 4 = Lower and upper spans to the battens.
5 = Halyard. 6 = Batten parrels. 7 = Luff parrels.
8 = Tack line. 9 = Lazy-jacks. 10 = Yard parrel.

In (a) the sail is fully hoisted. The lazy-jacks (9) are slack and the sheet (1) renders
between the blocks (2–4). In (b), two sections have been reefed out by lowering the
halyard so that the lazy-jacks are tight (9R); the sheet (1R) has to be overhauled so
that the leech is pulled in. The yard parrel (10R) and luff parrel (7) both have to be
tightened to keep the sail aligned to the mast.

size and shape, and is hoisted by means of a halyard (5 in the figure)
attached to the yard. The sail remains on one side of the mast regardless of
tack, and each batten-boom is held to the mast by its own parrel (6). The
batten-booms are usually paired by means of a sheet span (3 and 4) with
dead eye or lazy block, through which runs the single mainsheet running
from the main boom (1) via the lazy blocks and a multiple block at the deck
(2) to hand. An important part of the reefing system is represented by the
lazy-jacks (9), which support the main boom whenever the halyard is not
fully up, and which gather the sail neatly as each batten is lowered onto the
main boom; 9R in Fig. 19.1 (b).

There are further controls which can be seen in Fig. 19.1, designed to keep
the sail correctly aligned. A yard parrel (10) holds the yard close to the mast,
and is adjusted whenever the sail is partially lowered to reef, thus causing the

yard to want to swing aft and away from the mast. A tack line (8) is rigged to the forward end of the main boom to hold it down (this may need to be formed by a tackle, but usually a simple line made fast to a deck eye is enough – indeed, on a heavy rig, it may not be needed at all). A luff parrel (7) is not always necessary on a heavy native craft, but becomes important as more lightness is added; this pulls the battens aft against the pull of the yard parrel, and may be fitted to the upper battens only. Some control over the position of the CE within the scope of the batten parrels is thus available.

The Chinese often have each pair of battens controlled by their own sheet, which passes through a multiple block, which itself is on the end of a further sheet; some Western craft are similarly rigged, and the American Tom Colvin has used this system. This allows complete control of each part of the leech, but is rather lavish in the number of sheets which need tending. Some twist in a mainsail is advantageous, as we saw in Chapter II, so the somewhat simpler idea of one long-running sheet is probably preferable, even though it calls for a lot of overhauling at certain stages.

As I have said, all this may sound complicated, but in practice a Chinese rigged boat looks sparsely endowed with lines and rigging when compared with a modern sloop – particularly if the latter is a three-spreader cutter under spinnaker, with running backstays, babystay, and the rest.

DESIGN

Because a junk sail is nearly rectangular (and thus has as much area aloft as alow) and is rigged on an unstayed mast, it cannot be allowed to get too tall. Hasler's 25 ft *Jester* had a 240 sq ft sail with a mean hoist/chord ratio of 2:1 and five intermediate battens, and the successful Sunbird 28 is very similar (Fig. 19.2); the same firm's 32 footer in schooner form approaches 3:1 on its foresail. On the other hand, there are those who believe that 1·5:1 is a better ratio, particularly where ocean sailing is contemplated, and Tom Colvin is certainly one of these; the Kingfisher 20 was the first UK series production yacht to sport the rig, and this also had a low aspect sail, as has the 21-foot Coromandel, built by Newbridge Boats of Bridport.

SAIL PLAN

Selection of area, aspect ratio and number of batten-booms are important decisions in the overall design of the sail plan. As always, much depends on the shape of the hull and the intended use of the boat. Assuming a normally efficient cruising hull, intended for blue water sailing, the Naval Architect will decide on the sail area required to give the necessary mobility. In general terms, a Chinese lug needs about the same area as a mainsail/genoa combination for the same hull. This area should be turned into a sail or sails with

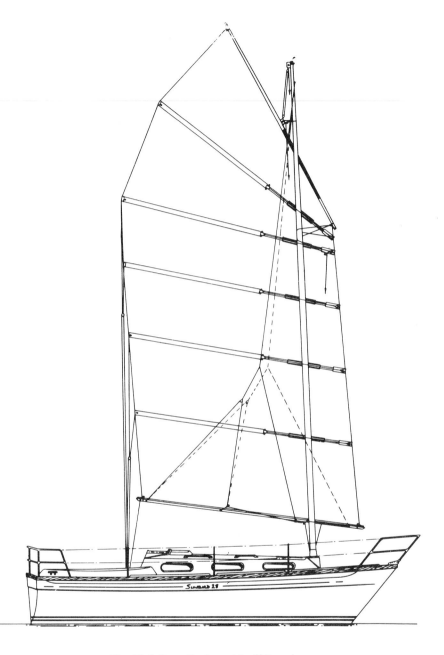

Fig. 19.2 Lazy-Jacks and Luff Parrel
This drawing of the Sunbird 28 shows something of how complex the lazy-jacks can become. Here they have spans and strops, and are carried forward to join together under the boom to form the fore lift. Note how the luff parrel only operates on the upper batten-booms (it is not shown right down to the deck for clarity). Drawing by courtesy of Sunbird Yachts.

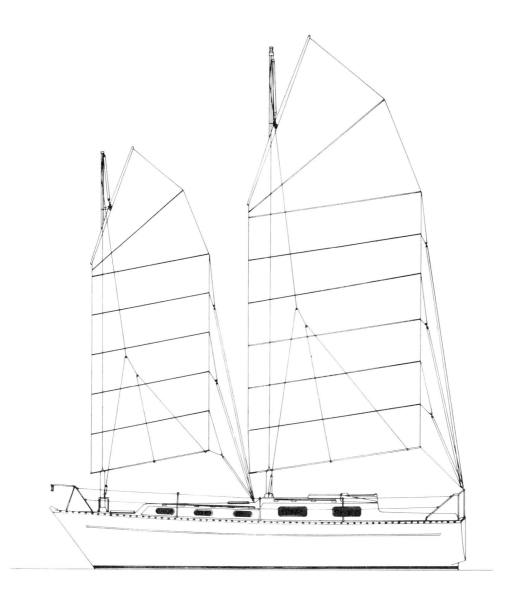

Fig. 19.3 Schooner-Rig Junk

The Sunbird 32 is available in schooner and single-masted junk rigs, as well as a conventional sloop version. In schooner form she has 186 sq ft in the foresail and 364 sq ft in the main. Neither sail has a sheet span to its top batten (because it would catch on the leech every time the boat changed tacks); this means that the main boom is not joined by a span to its neighbouring batten. In single junk rig, she carries 560 sq ft, while the conventional sloop has 198 in the mainsail and 375 in the genoa (total 573 sq ft). Drawing by courtesy of Sunbird Yachts.

359

a maximum ratio of mean hoist to mean chord of 3:1. If this results in too heavy a sail for the crew strength, the area must be split into two sails, and a schooner or ketch adopted (Fig. 19.3); this usually occurs around an overall length of 30 ft and upwards. In this connection, there is a tendency to canvas a boat for light winds, and rely on the very simple reefing to shorten sail as soon as medium conditions start to prevail.

The interplay between ketch and schooner affords interesting food for thought. A schooner may be considered superior up wind, where the foresail forms a slot but does not interfere too much with the mainsail; the ketch wins down wind, where the mizzen does not blanket the mainsail too badly. But reefing is so easy, as we shall see later, that the boat can be transformed from schooner to ketch and back again at the flick of a couple of lines. The choice is more likely to be dictated by balance of the hull, and the range of possible mast positions being limited by hatches, the engine and so forth.

Overall outline design varies widely in China, with only a broad pattern being evident. As might be expected, inland craft tend to have tall narrow sails, even broadening out at the yard to increase area aloft, and thus catch wind over the tops of river banks and low trees and hedgerows; these are also prevalent in the north (Fig. 19.4). Sea-going junks of the south usually have a lower aspect ratio, often with a more steeply angled yard and sometimes with a curved roach to the leech (but this brings its own problems as we shall

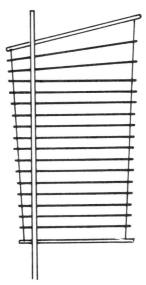

Fig. 19.4 Inland Junk Rig
On inland waters in China, the sail or sails may be tall and narrow, to catch wind over the surrounding hills and trees. Sails with as many as 30 battens have been observed.

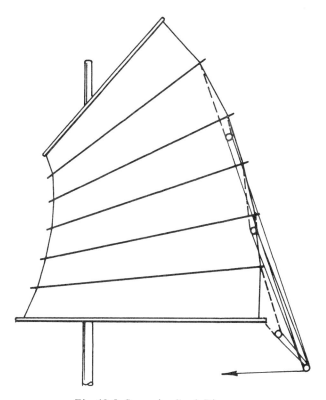

Fig. 19.5 Sea-going Junk Rig

For sea-going purposes, a much lower aspect ratio with fewer battens is preferred, sometimes with a hollow luff and a rounded leech. This leads to trouble with the lazy blocks (or euphroes, as they may be known) which catch on the batten ends when the boat changes tack, and have to be flicked clear; Chinese seamen become very adept at this process.

see later); Fig. 19.5. Within these generalisations, custom and fashion often dictate the final outline and, indeed, the number of batten-booms (as many as thirty have been reported).

BATTEN-BOOMS

Besides spreading the sail, an integral part of the batten function is to keep the sail flat at all times. This may not be ideal in light winds but, when the sail is on the windward side of the mast, stout battens prevent it bulging to windward where it presses against the mast. For this reason a junk rigged boat is never at her best when close hauled in Force 2. Thus, if only four batten-booms are used, they are particularly robust; in fact, traditional ideas about thickness and taper of battens have to be set aside, even where six or seven are incorporated. In China the stoutest bamboo is sought for sea-going craft, and it may well be that the wide variation in numbers which is seen, without any apparent rhyme or reason, is a function of the size and quality of bamboo available locally – flimsy bamboo means more battens; sturdy ones allow fewer sections because less of them are needed to hold the sail flat against the mast.

A particular sail may either be made up of individual sections, each laced to a batten-boom top and bottom or, more likely in the West, as a single unit, with battens attached to the outside between the sail and the mast. The battens thus take the chafe which must be ever-present as the sail pushes against the spar on one of the two tacks. It is a wise precaution to case the battens where this occurs (plastic hose pipe does a good job) and, of course, to have a cut-away in the pocket; some form of lubricant is useful, particularly if either batten or mast is wood (tallow, vaseline jelly, linseed oil and even beef dripping have been used).

SHEET

As we have seen, there are variations in the possible sheeting arrangements. I like the system adopted by Sunbird Yachts, whereby the boom and all the batten-booms except the top one, are controlled. If five batten-booms are used, the main boom has a single span or whip (or else the sheet starts at the boom end), and the bottom four battens are split into pairs, as can be seen in Fig. 19.2. A look at Fig. 19.5 will reveal the reason for a recurring problem with some junk sails – the leech roach causes the upper batten ends to catch in the sheet spans every time the sail is tacked or gybed, so that they have to be flicked clear. If the leech is vertical or even cut away, the spans are unlikely to get caught.

With local variations, then, on a sail with five batten-booms, the sheet may run in one part, starting at the main boom (1 in Fig. 19.1), to the multiple deck block (2), up the span joining the bottom pair of battens (3), then via the deck again to the next span (4), before leading back through the deck block to hand. In this way, the first pull is on the upper leech, so that twist can in some measure be controlled; in addition, there is direct control of the sail when it is reefed as shown in Fig. 19.1 (b).

LOADINGS

The subdivision of the sail into a number of panels, separated by the batten-booms, means that the boat is effectively setting six or seven (or more) individual sails. Because loadings are proportional to area, no single part of the sail has to withstand the full load of the rig at any time (though claims that each section only has to support the wind force on its own area are clearly misconstrued – stresses are imparted from one section to another via the battens). Equally, the balancing action of the area which projects forward of the mast, makes for lightness of control on the sheet.

HANDLING

No less an authority that Capt Joshua Slocum is on record[60] as considering the Chinese lug as 'the most convenient boat rig in the whole world.' He has been echoed by many others nearer our own times, and certainly the modern bermudan sloop is labour-intensive by comparison.

The two most obvious aspects for the newcomer to the rig are the silence and the easy motion of the boat. She is silent because the full length battens stop the sail flogging, even when head to wind. She is easy because the unstayed mast, rather than the boat, leans with the puffs, so that stresses are shed from the system. A rigid spar sends shock waves through the whole rig, which are transmitted to the hull and thence to the spinal cords of the crew. In aviation, who ever heard of a braced biplane in military service or on the air routes these days?

One of the less obvious aspects is the difficulty of knowing whether the sail is set to best advantage. The snag lies in the close-set full length battens (which make for such a quiet ride), because they don't allow any indication of too fine a β angle (or any stall warning). Thus it can be difficult for the newcomer to get the best from a Chinese sail, because it gives little indication of being at an inefficient angle. So we need one of the Best Buys I have advocated in this book: wind tallies or streamers are an important part of a junk sail (together with a knowledge of how to use them; remember TASTES from Chapter IX).

Colonel Hasler has said that the rig tacks and gybes more softly than anything he ever sailed with[59]; he likens the movement of the sail across the boat to the swinging of a barn door. All are united in praising the flat sail and flexible mast in a blow, so that heeling moment is reduced. There is, however, a qualification regarding the gybe. If the boat is rolling, or the sail is not controlled by the sheets in high winds, the main boom may sky so that the battens fold up against the mast like a fan. They fall back again (with a clatter) all right, but the sight is spectacular and, in high winds and seas, there is a danger of breakage. This must surely be the origin of the expression 'Chinese gybe' used in connection with a bermudan mainsail. In the case of the junk, there are no spreaders to get caught round, so (apart from any batten damage) it causes more harm to the ego than to the sail.

If anyone is worried about losing the unstayed mast itself, just remember that it is impossible to break it due to rigging failure or to compression loading; and a lot of F_H is shed through flexing and feathering at the head.

Plate 19.2 Sunbird 32

There are no headsails to change, and both sails always remain on their masts. Because of this, and the easy reefing, the crew never has to go on deck unless it be, to sunbathe. In a period of four months, David and Hilary Stookey covered over 4000 miles in their 20 footer, and never once had to put on wet weather clothing; all sail drill, including reefing, was carried out from the shelter of a sprayhood.

Alastair Black

Further information on the rig in general can be obtained in the UK from the Junk Rig Association, Forest View, Winston Avenue, Tadley, Hants.

CLOSE HAULED

If junks have a weak point of sailing, it is to windward in light weather. They are not quite so close-winded as a bermudan rig, but they do make up for a lot of this by their sensitive balance. In a breeze, they can be fine-tuned to feather the head and reduce heeling moment. Equally, ease of reefing and unreefing can gain a lot of time if conditions call for it. Thus, speed made good to windward (V_{mg}) is favourable in strong winds.

REACHING

On a reach, some control of twist enables maximum efficiency to be extracted (if the helmsman watches his wind tallies). The boat is particularly fast under these conditions, because the sail can be moved slightly fore and aft on the mast by adjustment of the luff parrel and the yard parrel or snotter. This moves the CE and alters the balancing effect of the sail, thereby affecting weather or lee helm.

RUNNING

A square sail, of course, is the most efficient shape for running down wind, and the rig's tolerance of running by the lee means that goose-winging prevents the aft sail of a two-master spoiling the airflow over the forward sail. Care should be taken to see that the two sails are square to the fore and aft line, as this takes out a lot of the rolling tendency; too far aft or forward will spoil the balance. A point to watch for when running is not to allow the sail to ease off too much, because this would put the battens into compression against the pull of the sheets, with attendant danger of failure.

The absence of shrouds means that the sail can be squared right off. Not only does this conform with what we have just discussed regarding rolling, but it also angles thrust at its most efficient. Secondly, as there is nothing to chafe on, the trade winds hold no terrors for the sailmaker on board.

REEFING

The joy of the Chinese rig is its simple handling (despite what seems at first blush like a formidable array of lines). The acme of this joy lies in the process of reefing. The very weight of the batten-booms (and, in native craft, of the heavy matting sail material) makes the process almost self-operating. Having been a bit of a handful to hoist in the first place, it may be expected that the whole lot will come down like a blind given the chance. And this is precisely what happens.

Let us say that we want to take out two sections of sail. The halyard is

(a)

(b)

(c)

(d)

Plate 19.3 Reefing
Release the halyard (a) and the yard is lowered (b) – it's as quick as that. The model in (c) shows how the yard falls away from the mast slightly; tightening the yard parrel pulls it forward again (d). The luff parrel can be seen curling round the mast. It used to be taken from one batten end, round the mast and back to the next batten end, and so on all the way down the luff. But its rearward pull is only needed on the upper luff, so it is usually seen only connected to the top two battens these days. *Author*

eased, so that the bottom two batten-booms are lowered onto the main boom, as shown in Fig. 19.1 (b); weight ensures that this happens, even when the sail is to windward of the mast and pressing against it, and there is no need to luff into wind to ease the pressure. As the yard comes down, the yard parrel, luff parrel and sheet all slacken automatically, and the main boom drops until it has taken up the slack on the previously set lazy-jacks, when it is held by them (9R in the figure) rather than the tension in the sail and main halyard. The yard and luff parrels (10 and 7) should be adjusted to draw the one forward and pull the other aft. Then the sheet should be trimmed and the job is done. It takes no longer to do than to read, and is just as easy.

Because the sail does not have to be actually touched in the process, and because the human forces are limited to those required to pull in the sheet and parrels, it is a simple matter to lead all these control lines through turning blocks to one position. Certainly this was done successfully in *Jester* back in 1959, and again in 1971 in *Ron Glas*, Jock McLeod's 47 ft Chinese rigged schooner on a motor sailer hull (where they terminated inside the wheelhouse). No longer does the crew have to go on deck to fight flogging canvas as he changes headsails in a seaway or pulls down a reef in Force 7 – he or she stands under cover and adjusts four or five lines. Oilskins become almost a thing of the past, used only when it is raining as you drop the anchor or go ashore, because the crew never have to go on deck unless they want to[61].

SAILS

We have already seen that Chinese lugs are pretty flat. Peter Lucas has probably made as many junk sails as any Western Sail Maker, and he tells me that they may be made without broad seam, as they rely on the battens to spread them but shaping is a bit of a lost cause. They are usually made in one piece, but they *may* be in sections between battens if desired. Cloths are laid vertically, to chop the area up into small sections; this means that the warp is parallel to the leech. A mitre is introduced near the head, to trip the cloths round so that the warp continues to follow the leech round the curve of the roach. The leech itself is usually cut slightly hollow between battens – up to 3 or 4 inches near the head, where the span may be anything from 6 to 10 feet; this prevents leech flutter through 'motor-boating'.

Battens. Batten pockets are best if they are closed at the front end, and the battens slipped in from the rear; this leaves a nice clean luff. They should have a cut-away portion in way of the mast, so that the batten itself can bear on the mast, rather than the sail taking the chafe.

Damage Control. Pairs of grommets, above and below the batten pockets, enable two battens to be tied together with a line right around in the event of a rip, thereby 'reefing out' the damaged section of sail. In this connection, the reason that sails are made with vertical seams is so that a tear will not run from luff to leech (nor from top to bottom, because the batten pockets chop the area up into small rectangles).

Bolt Rope. The head and foot are normally laced to yard and boom, but they may equally run in grooves (Sunbird designs are examples of this); the luff is normally taped. Strengthening is needed at the leech, where the sheet spans are joined; this is usually by means of webbing strops sewn to the edge of the sail.

DISADVANTAGES

As with any rig, there are advantages and disadvantages. Let us therefore first look at some of the drawbacks of the Chinese rig.

Weight. The sheer weight of the sail, batten-booms, yard and main boom makes the rig difficult to hoist. This is a question of fitting the appropriate purchase (tackle or winch); once it is up, it stays there until reefed (when its weight is a plus point).

Area. There is no means of increasing area in light winds, unless shrouds and running topmast backstay are added to support the loadings imparted by a spinnaker. This would negate a lot of the simplicity of the rig. A ghoster *can* be used without standing rigging, but self control is needed to take if off as the wind rises. Most junkies are too lazy for extra sails, and they tend to motor when in a hurry or, as Alan Boswell puts it, drink when not.

Efficiency. The Chinese rig is not the most successful design developed by man for going to windward in light airs.

Heaving-to. The rig will not heave-to properly. She will lie a-hull with or without some sail set.

Complexity. I have included this heading because the matter is often raised by those who have no experience of Chinese rig. What seems complex when described on paper is, in fact, remarkably simple when seen on board, and even more so when used afloat.

Trim. Correct trim is difficult, particularly for those with little experience of the rig, because the sail does not flog or judder when it is at an inefficient angle to the wind. Tell tales are an important aid to correct trim.

Plate 19.4 Sunbird 28
Note the absence of winches, shrouds, spreaders and forestay, also how the sail is
divided into small sections by its vertical panels. *Yachting Monthly*

ADVANTAGES

The advantages of the Chinese junk rig are such as to make one wonder why they haven't been exploited before. They have, of course, been evolved empirically over hundreds, not to say thousands, of years, and nobody really knows why some of them developed. Much depends and depended on availability of materials, local conditions and the task to be achieved.

Twist. Some control of the leech through sheet spans joining pairs of batten-booms ensures that twist can be kept in check.

Camber. Stiff full length battens means that the sail doesn't belly, even in strong winds. This makes for good aerodynamics in the higher wind strengths, reducing heeling moment while maintaining thrust.

Loading. Each section of sail is supported and controlled by its own batten-booms top and bottom, sheet span and luff parrel. Loadings are thus largely divided.

Efficiency. We have seen that a junk sail is not particularly efficient to windward in light weather; under all other conditions, however, it takes a lot of beating. When reaching in a breeze, the flat sail can be adjusted to reduce twist, and then the head allowed to fall away as required in order to feather.

Handling. Due to the full length battens, the sail never flogs, even when head to wind; it swings silently from side to side like a door. The unstayed mast does not transmit shock loads to the rest of the hull. This all makes for a quiet sail with easy gybing.

Sail Drill. There is only one sail, which is permanently bent on the mast. There is thus no headsail changing, no spinnaker drill, no big boy, no wet sails in the saloon.

Reefing. A one-man operation, which can be controlled from shelter.

Locker Space. It may at first seem odd to quote something which doesn't exist as an advantage. But consider the space down below which is made vacant because there are not four headsails and a spinnaker or two to stow away. The fo'cs'le can be returned to the crew, and the cockpit lockers to the bo'sun. And the distaff side of the crew, who always seem to object to water below more than the men (perhaps because she often does the cleaning up) will welcome the fact that all wet canvas stays on deck.

Chafe. The absence of standing rigging means that chafe is largely restricted to the batten-booms rubbing on the mast; the thin lazy-jacks don't seem to cause too much trouble to the sail itself.

Balance. The balanced-lug form, combined with some control over fore and aft position of the CE, means that weather helm can be virtually eliminated.

Short-handed Sailing. General handling is so easy, that the rig is particularly suitable for single-handed sailing, or for family cruising with a weak crew.

DELTA RIG

Colonel Bowden, of Dorset England, has taken some of the best points of the Chinese rig and incorporated them into a delta sail plan, using his experience of flying to develop an aerodynamically efficient rig. There is one balanced sail on a rotating cantilever mast, and advantage is taken of full length battens to shape the sail and keep the whole process of moving under the action of the wind somewhat quieter than we are used to. Unlike the Chinese, however, Bowden uses relatively soft battens, but the sail is supported by a form of wishbone mast, so that development of camber or flow is not inhibited every time the sail is to windward of a single pole.

Reefing might at first also seem to be patterned on the Chinese method, because the yard is lowered so that the sail closes like a fan hinged about the tack. But there is not enough weight in the system for this to be sufficient unto itself, and two lines of reef points can be seen in the photograph. On the other hand, there is only one sheet point on the sail, so that the main boom acts indeed as a main boom and there are no sheet spans; because of the balanced plan of the rig, sheet loads are low. The only other control line is the halyard. Lazy-jacks are not used and, when it is lowered, the sail is automatically gathered on the boom by a pair of collecting horns, one of which can be made out on the port side of the boom, six feet forward of the clew.

The delta sails quietly and well, with light sheet loads and an efficient all-round performance. It doesn't have the Chinese ability to reef easily, nor does it have the same leech control, but it only has two control lines, and a rather better aerodynamic outline shape which gives a docile performance and is easily handled.

THE AERO-JUNK

The affinity between sailing and flying is obvious, so perhaps it is not surprising to find that Jack Manners-Spencer of Aerosystems is, like Tony

Marchaj, Claude Bowden and indeed myself, a sometime pilot. At all events, this former Vulcan flyer, who lives in Beaulieu Hampshire, has developed the original Chinese fully battened lug to what may well be its ultimate form. The photograph and Fig. 19.6 between them reveal the aptitude of my description Aero-Junk. His concept is entirely Chinese in principle, but 20th century technology has been grafted on with happy results, producing an aesthetic looking highly efficient rig.

Plate 19.5 Delta Rig
Col Bowden's *Tentative*, sporting his balanced delta sail; the collecting horn can just be discerned above the head of the helmsman. Note the two rows of reef points, which betray the fact that the battens are not heavy enough to make the sail self-reefing like a Chinese lugsail. *Col Bowden*

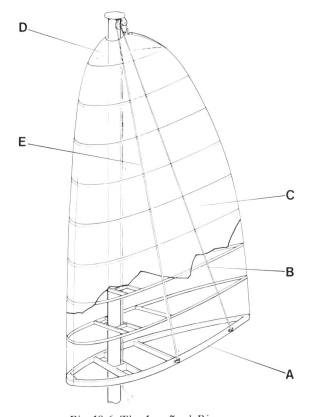

Fig. 19.6 The Aero-Junk Rig
A = Wishbone boom. B = Batten frames. C = Sailcloth skin.
D = Headboards. E = Lazy-jacks.
The principle by which the Gallant aerofoil section pivots on the unstayed mast is
clearly seen. The falls of the halyard and lazy-jack hoist are both inside the
aerofoil, so parasite drag is reduced to a low figure. Drawing by courtesy of Aerosystems.

The unstayed mast and the halyard are both enclosed inside the wing sail,
thus eliminating parasite drag, and there are no parrels. The wing itself is
elliptical in shape, which we decided in Chapter II is the most efficient
outline shape for a sail; it is made up of a series of aerofoil-shaped alloy
frames or battens, which are joined together by Terylene sailcloth panels
running in the grooved T-section frames; see Fig. 19.7. The wing pivots on
the mast, with a proportion of its area forward of the pivot point, so that the
rig is balanced. Like the Chinese junk, there are sheet spans connecting the
lower aerofoil battens at the leech, so that control of twist is available. Again
like the Chinese original, reefing is effected by easing the halyard and letting
the weight of the rig concertina the battens so that they stack on the boom,
where they are maintained by lazy-jacks until they can be tied off.

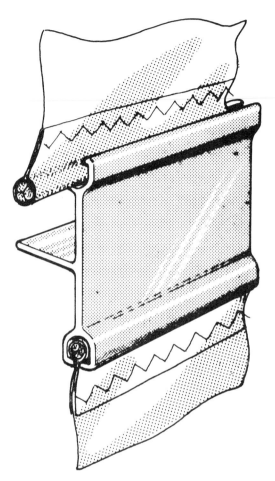

Fig. 19.7 Batten-Frame Section
In Aerosystem's Gallant rig, each section slides in a groove in the upper and lower
arm of the T-section alloy frame. Sections can be removed and put back at will, to
build up the complete aerofoil.

Apart from an entirely silent operation (which it largely shares with the
junk), this sail form also benefits from most of the advantages listed for the
Chinese junk: spread loadings, easy handling, fool-proof reefing, added
locker space, elimination of chafe, a balanced sail plan and silent operation.
Added advantages are clear decks and simplified repairs: if a section of the
aerofoil gets torn, it can be removed from its battens top and bottom by
sliding it from the grooves; it may then be repaired below at leisure, and
reinserted. Depending on design, the lower panels may be interchangeable,
so that a spare may be quickly rigged in any of the bottom three panels,
either side.

Plate 19.6 Aero-Junk

Jack Manners-Spencer's *Cameleon*, showing the principle of aerofoil sails in his Gallant rig (which I prefer to call the Aero-junk). Note the multiple sheets on the lower leech. *Aerosystems*

When I first met Jack Manners-Spencer at Santander in Spain, he had just sailed his boat *Cameleon* from England in $3\frac{1}{2}$ days. She was lying quietly at a mooring, with her aerofoils neatly stowed on top of each other, and had given her crew a trouble-free journey of extraordinary quietness. This is a rig to watch for in the future, for it offers the best of the old and the new technology. Despite its rather high cost, it must join with junk rig in general as a final Best Buy for cruising in this book (from which you will gather that I have been converted to the Chinese connection) – largely because the Gallant

Aero-Junk represents the first significant improvement on the original concept in some 2000 years.

SWING WING

Sunbird Yachts have developed an interesting compromise between their own junk sail and the Aero-junk described above. Like Aerosystems, they have used a wrap-around wing section, but they restrict it to the front two-thirds of the sail, with a fully battened single-sided sail as the aft third; this aft section swings from side to side to give an aerofoil shape regardless of tack; Fig. 19.8. There is a locking mechanism which prevents the leech from swinging too far to leeward, and this would seem to be the weak point in the rig. If it can be made sufficiently robust, efficiency should be good, and I shall watch this with interest in the future.

Fig. 19.8 Swing Wing

This drawing of Sunbird Yachts' aerofoil section with fully battened sailcloth trailing edge is not to scale, but shows the principle. Each batten is restricted from swinging beyond the streamline continuation by a projection forward of the pivot.

Chapter XX

Adding to the Wardrobe

THE SAIL PLAN

Before an intelligent assessment of a boat's sail requirements can be made, a sail plan is desirable. Dinghies and small one-design keelboats present no problem as their wardrobe is usually limited to a number of standard sails, so the owner does not need to spend hours poring over a plan. The larger classes, however, have a wider choice, and a pictorial display is helpful. I do not want to convey the impression that it is not possible to order a sail without a plan, but it will be difficult to make alterations to rig or rating, or to experiment with, say, twin running sails, without one. It will not even be possible to order a mainsail unless certain specific measurements are known. The Sail Maker has to know what is physically possible within the confines of the yacht's spars and rigging. This is in addition to limits imposed by rules and rating, which we shall examine shortly.

If the owner does not already possess a sail plan, it is quite possible that the Sail Maker does, especially if he has made for the boat before. If he has not got one, he may know where to find it; Sail Makers generally get on well with one another, and they sometimes call on each other for rare plans, for they usually pride themselves on not having to bother a customer with such details. A Norwegian owner might write to say that the 6 metre which his father built in 1936 needs new sails. The office immediately goes into action to trace the original plan, either in the firm's records or perhaps from the builder (whose name is found in an old copy of *Lloyd's Register*, and not by worrying the customer). The quotation is sent off with a friendly reference to her last suit, or a request to know whether she still has the roller reefing which the record shows was incorporated in 1947.

It may be, however, that no plan of a boat exists, and that sails are required. In this case the Sail Maker will normally visit the boat to take what measurements he requires, providing the vessel is reasonably accessible and the order warrants the trip. It would be unreasonable to expect him to make a 250-mile journey to measure up for just a small staysail. For the benefit of

377

the owner without a sail plan who is remote from civilization, yet who requires a new sail, I have drawn up a guide to measuring in Appendix F. This is a comprehensive recommendation, to cover a full plan for a yawl or ketch. If just a mainsail is required, it is obviously not necessary to provide all the detail included in the Appendix, for this also covers the foretriangle, mizzen, and general hull shape. Remember, however, that it is important to know the sheer line of the deck for the leech of the genoa, and mast rake is often crucial to the mainsail.

Measuring is not a hard task, but it is one which demands methodical care and good notes. It is not, as might be supposed, essential to climb to the top of the mast, because these distances can be taken by shackling a measuring-tape on to the appropriate halyard and hauling it aloft. The principal points to remember are that you can never take too many measurements for a particular job, and that you should state quite clearly what the distances you find represent. In other words, tell the Sail Maker that you hoisted a steel or a linen tape on the main halyard in a 15 m.p.h. wind (a graduated wire is preferable for all measurements taken aloft where the distance is more than about 35 ft; this is because it will be blown out of the straight line less than a tape-measure); that the shackle and splice at the end of the halyard took up about 5 in; that the boom measurement is from tack eye to clew eye, and not from aft to the mast to the very end of the boom (or vice versa). Above all do not make any allowance for clearance, say between the halyard sheave and the head of the mainsail or between the clew and the outhaul eye for a lashing, without telling the Sail Maker. It is also wise to tell him that you have not deducted anything. He will then make these allowances in the light of his experience, and they are more likely to be right than yours.

I once had a long correspondence with a Belgian who not only made these deductions without telling us, but who also took off some more, to allow for the stretch of the cloth. He sent a sketch of his boat, with measurements marked on the spars as being those found by means of a tape-measure along the lines I have just suggested. We made the sail to stretch to sizes slightly less than the distances he had given, so that there would be 3 or 4 in between the clew and the outhaul eye for a lashing, and rather more between the head and the sheave for a halyard splice and shackle. The result was a sail which was over 3 ft short on a luff of about 35 ft, and 1 ft 6 in short on a foot of some 14 ft. Yet the owner had clearly marked his distances as being between the clew eye and the mast, and between the sheave and the tack. Of course, there was a double error in this case, because he had also tried to teach us our business with respect to making the allowance for cloth stretch and induced flow, again without telling us.

Care should be taken in measuring, not only to avoid the wrong line (topping lift for main halyard), but also to ensure that the halyard is hoisted hard up and made fast securely, so that it does not creep down between two different measurements. It is best to fit a rope downhaul on the halyard alongside the wire or tape, otherwise you may find it difficult to pull down afterwards.

Before I leave measuring, I must just repeat that one of the most important measurements for a mainsail is the distance from the aft face of the mast to the tack-pin; you should also remember to state whether your foot measurement includes this distance or if it has been deducted. Without these details the Sail Maker will not know how much to cut away at the tack so that the sail leads fairly to the pin.

RULES

It may seem obvious to say that all owners should be familiar with the rules governing their class. On the other hand some classes, and I am thinking here mainly of restricted classes and the IOR, have necessarily got such complicated rules that they are difficult to have at one's fingertips. However, the sail locker is something over which the owner has direct control and which he can vary with the years (unlike the hull, once it has been built), so it is important to have an understanding of those rules for your particular class which relate to sails.

Most rules change from time to time, but those dealing with sails are not so fluid that the average man cannot keep up to date with his own particular class. It is a rather different story for the Sail Maker, who has to stay abreast of a whole cabinet full of various rules, some of which he may not need for years on end. Class secretaries would be doing a service to their members if they would remember to circulate Sail Makers, whenever there is an alteration which affects the rig of the boat for which they are responsible. If you are the owner of a rare class of boat, therefore, you should check with your Sail Maker to see that he has all the latest amendments before he makes you a sail.

In this connection, do not forget that the IYRU rules also have something to say with regard to sails. Most of it concerns the Sail Maker and Boat-builder, being about such matters as sail numbers and their positioning, makers' marks, forestay position, etc. However, there is a certain amount about changing sails, sheeting them to spars, and outriggers, which concerns the owner.

The first principle to absorb when interpreting rules is that they mean what they say. This may sound self-evident, but it is sometimes possible to guess at what a rule is designed to achieve, yet it may not put it into the right words. For instance, if a rule says: 'The jib shall not exceed the following measurements when new: luff 20 ft, leech 18 ft 6 in, foot 6 ft 3 in,' then the sail may be made smaller on any or all of the three measurements. It may also stretch over the maximum as soon as it is no longer new, so there is very little control in this rule. On the other hand, a rule which says that the luff length shall be 20 ft, with a tolerance of 3 in, will limit that measurement to somewhere between 19 ft 9 in and 20 ft 3 in. One which gives a *maximum* luff length of 20 ft, with the same tolerance of 3 in, will limit it to between 19 ft 9 in and 20 ft, because the tolerance can only be downwards due to the overriding word *maximum*.

In addition to this, different rules may measure the luff between different points as follows:

    (i) Outside points of head and tack eyes.
    (ii) Bearing surfaces of head and tack eyes.
    (iii) Centres of head and tack eyes.
    (iv) Points where the leech and foot of the sail meet the luff wire.
    (v) Apex points where the leech and foot would strike the luff wire if they were projected.

I recall attending the Prince of Wales' Cup week at Falmouth, where I altered a mainsail for Sam Waters to make it suitable for very heavy weather. This entailed cutting off a parallel piece about 3 or 4 ft deep along the foot, so that it became the equivalent of a heavily reefed sail. In its turn this involved removing the bottom batten pocket altogether. The unfortunate owner was subsequently disqualified when he used the sail, because it did not conform to the rule which said that four battens should be placed 'within 5 in above or below the respective points on the sail which divide the leech into five equal parts'. The fact that he would have been allowed to remove a batten from a full-size mainsail and then roll it down to the same size as his altered sail, made no difference to the literal interpretation of the rules as they then stood. They have since been altered to read that the number of batten pockets shall be 'no more than four, dividing the leech into equal parts, in number one more than the number of batten pockets'.

Equally, just because the rules do not specifically prohibit something, it does not mean to say that it is allowed. A good example of what I mean occurred in a class which now numbers over 20,000 boats. The class rules had a clause which prevented sails being other than according to the plan. With the laudable intention of stopping the rich man having too many gadgets like zippers and specially shaped sails at extra cost, this was interpreted literally so that these devices were ruled out. Unfortunately this also ruled out a simple extra like a Cunningham hole, so an owner was unable to have one sail to cope with a wide wind range, and had to buy one for light to medium conditions and another for heavy weather. Which shows that it is hard to legislate for every contingency.

ORDERING NEW SAILS

Now that we have gone thoroughly into the various factors which affect the size and shape of sails on the average yacht, we can consider the sort of information which the Sail Maker requires from an owner when he orders a new sail.

There is no mystique about ordering sails. Sail Makers are in business to make sails, and they will all give careful attention to the smallest order. The larger firms sometimes have to combat the impression that a sail for a small child's dinghy is beneath their dignity. Nothing could be further from the truth, and they give this as much attention as they do a schooner. Do not be afraid, therefore, to approach any Sail Maker with your request, no matter how small.

You must first, of course, choose your Sail Maker. I am naturally prejudiced, but I would be the last person to try and persuade anyone to leave a Sail Maker he has known for a long time. If there is no reason to leave, stay with him; you know each other's foibles and weaknesses by now and the devil you know is better than the one you don't. If you do not already have a Sail Maker, the choice can often be made by means of discussion with other owners in your club, or else by comparing known prices and quality. Try writing to several different firms; you can sometimes tell quite a lot from the way your letter is answered, besides getting a direct comparison of prices for the particular sails you want. You should remember that, as with a tailor, you usually get what you pay for, and a little extra expense at the start may save you renewal costs too early on. On the other hand, it may well be that a particular firm has a reputation for making the best sails for your class of boat. In this case you must decide whether the reputation is deserved, or whether the top helmsmen in your class would win with whatever sails they used, so perhaps you could try elsewhere at a cheaper price. Sometimes a firm may produce a sail which is an excellent shape, but does not last a long time. It may be that you are one of those who are content with a sail which will win races for half a season, and must then be put aside for another new one of the same calibre. There are plenty of helmsmen in this bracket, and the Dragon is an example of a class where headsails in particular are renewed more than once a season by many of the top owners.

Having selected a Sail Maker, you can place yourself entirely in his hands as I have already implied. He is accustomed to interpreting owners' requirements, and will request all the answers he needs in order to make the sail you want. But if you have read this book as far as this, you are obviously interested enough in what sort of sail you are going to get to be more than a 'Yes-man' and 'No-man' to your Sail Maker. You will probably have your own ideas as to the type of sail you require, and you should put them to him. In this case you should state the sort of sail you want, the conditions for which you require it, and any other factors bearing upon the problem, such as crew weight, spar bend, sheet winches, and so on. Do not try to tell him how to make the sail but if, for instance, you have firm ideas on the amount of fullness you want, try to relate them to an existing suit of similar sails made by the same firm; this will give the Sail Maker a direct yardstick by which to judge your idea of a full sail, which may be different from those of his last customer.

A standard boat with one-design sails will have no need of more than a bare statement that a particular sail is required, coupled with instructions as to whether it should be full or flat. A Dragon mainsail has the same dimensions the world over, so does a 470 or a Finn. On the other hand a 5·5 metre, most offshore racers, a Flying Dutchman genoa or a 14 ft International all have individual requirements. If you cannot supply a copy of the sail plan, the boat's certificate should give a great deal of the information required. Many Sail Makers have special forms for some of the more popular restricted classes, in order to make things easier. The following are some of the basic details without most of which sails cannot be made.

MAINSAIL

1. *Cloth*. State whether you want Dacron, Terylene, Mylar, Melinex or, indeed, cotton. Weight of cloth for racing boats is often governed by class rules so, even if you don't race, it is worth conforming because you will reduce the secondhand value of the boat if you specify a weight outside the rules. See my remarks in Chapter III regarding cloth weights generally and conventional weaves in particular. Now is the time to ask for colour if you want anything other than white for working sails (you may not be able to get it in the heavier weights of Dacron or Terylene, and will have to take what comes where film laminates are concerned).

2. *Length of Luff, Leech and Foot*. Luff and foot will usually be the black band distances; say if they are not. The leech is the one which is sometimes forgotten, but it may be important if the boom has a high cabin top to clear.

3. Distance from the aft face of the mast to the tack-pin. This is variously known as the *knock-back*, the *cut-away*, the *tack back* or the *tack off* distance. It will usually be between $1\frac{1}{4}$ and $1\frac{3}{4}$ in for boats which do not have a roller-reefing gear, and that is the amount which most Sail Makers will allow unless they are warned differently. The distance, of course, has to be subtracted by the Sail Maker from the length of the foot as given on the boat's certificate, so that the clew shall not extend beyond the black band by that amount. A roller gear will usually have a *knock back* of anything from 4 to 9 in, depending on the particular gear.

4. Details of the *mast ramp* (also known as the *mast batten*), if any. This is the ramp on which a luff track is sometimes built up near the lower end, so that it leads fair to the tack when the latter is back 6 in or so (knock back) to accommodate a roller-reefing gear. If the luff fits in a groove, the distance above the tack where the *groove entry* starts should be substituted.

5. *Roller Reef.* If a roller boom is fitted, the Sail Maker must know so that he can tape the lower luff instead of roping it. This will prevent a build-up of rope at the tack as the sail is rolled on to the boom. In addition, he must know the distance from the aft face of the mast to the tack-pin, and the ramp details, if any, as in paragraphs 3 and 4 above. Finally, you should state if you want a row of emergency reef eyelets in the deep reef position as a precaution against gear failure.

6. *Points or Lacing Reefs.* If individual points, or a continuous lacing reef is required, the appropriate type should be specified. The Sail Maker should also be told the spacing needed between each reef, or the distance from the outer black band on the boom to the reef cleats (this is important for jiffy reefing), so that he can fit the reefs at the right height for proper purchase to be put on the reef ear-ring at the leech. If there are no reef cleats on the boom he should be told, so that he knows that he has a free hand over spacing between reefs.

7. *Slides or Grooves.* You would be surprised at the number of owners who specify slides for their mainsail, and completely overlook the fact that they have a grooved boom. State, therefore, how the sail attaches to both the mast *and* the boom. If slides are involved, try and send a sample which fits, as this is the surest way of avoiding errors; send one for luff and foot if they are different. Do not simply say 'one-inch slides', because this could mean four different sizes, as explained in Appendix F.

8. *Rules.* Do not assume that the Sail Maker is conversant with the rules of your class unless he tells you that he is. This is especially important where the rules have recently been changed. Remind him of any sail insignia required, and be prepared to send a full-size tracing if your class is not a well-known one. State the rule on battens if there is any danger of mis-interpretation.

9. *Spar Bend.* If you have a bendy mast or boom, the Sail Maker should be told the maximum bend by means of offsets. The boat should be laid on her side on dry land if possible, while a sail of more or less the desired shape is set, and the mast then bent under the influence of mainsheet and kicking-

strap. Setting the right sail is important, because too flat a sail can restrict the amount of bend, while one which is too full, or no sail at all, will allow the mast to bend too much. A twine should be stretched between the black bands, and the offsets taken every three feet or so.

10. *Racing Number and Name.* A note of the racing number will avoid another letter later on. If you give the name of the boat, the Sail Maker will be able to put it on your sail bags.

11. *Extras.* There are many extras, ranging from slab reefs to spare battens and windows. You will speed delivery if you remember to include them all at the beginning. It is best if a copy of all correspondence is kept for reference.

12. *Mylar.* If the sail is film laminated, ask to be told its maximum upper wind speed.

HEADSAIL

13. *Cloth Weight, Luff, Leech and Foot, Rules and Boat's Name* are all the same as for the mainsail.

14. *Winches.* Say if your sheet winches are particularly powerful.

15. *Type of Luff.* Say whether you want a wire, tape or rope luff and, in the case of polyester, whether it should have a set flow or be adjustable. Is the luff for a grooved stay, to be set flying, or to have hanks or snap hooks? Specify the type of hank if applicable, and give the lowest point on the luff at which the bottom hank can go without fouling turnbuckles or other equipment. State whether the sail is to have a head or tack strop permanently attached.

16. *Forestay Sag.* State the amount of sag in the stay on which the sail will be set.

17. *Extras.* Individual bag colours or stripes are especially important for headsails in these days of constantly changing crews. You are more likely to get the correct headsail hoisted on the stay if you ask for the bag with two red stripes as opposed to, say, the No. 2 jib. Indeed, some designers include this sort of thing as part of their standard specification to the Sail Maker, and add identifying patches on the sails to match the bag, with a further tag such as a black circle to pick out the tack. Ask for some offcuts to be put in as repair material. It is a good idea to specify tan thread for white sails, so that a broken stitch can be quickly spotted. Finally, do not forget that a No.

1 jib may mean the storm jib (i.e. the smallest sail) to some people, the genoa (i.e. the largest sail) to others, and the working foresail to yet others; make sure that you and the Sail Maker are talking about the same sail.

SPINNAKER

18. *Cloth*. Not only weight but also colour enters into it here. I have already discussed cloth weight for spinnakers, and touched on colour. There is no foundation for the belief that one colour attracts wind more readily than another, so the only operational factor which can affect the choice is the question of contrast. It is a good idea to have stripes of contrasting colours in the head, so that the luff can be more readily detected at night to prevent it collapsing. It is also a good idea to avoid those colours which are glaring to look at for too long on a sunny day. Otherwise the question of colour can be, and very often is, handed over to the distaff side of the boat for a decision. I would never dispute such a course.

19. *Sizes*. Spinnakers are often one-design, even for those boats which may vary their fore and aft sails, such as the Merlin Rocket. You may be able to specify reaching, running or heavy weather, but sometimes not even that latitude is allowed. If you are buying a spinnaker for an offshore racer you should either give the maximum luffs and widths (from the boat's certificate), or else the I and J measurements. The Sail Maker will work out the rest from these data, which are all he needs to know.

DELIVERY

Some Sail Makers are poor at keeping delivery promises. You should always try and order well in advance, not only to ensure that you get your sails on time, but also to take advantage of off-season discounts. Allow for two or three weeks' delay in any target date you give, and you should not often be disappointed.

SECOND-HAND SAILS

Before buying a second-hand sail, it is wise to ask yourself why it is for sale. I stated earlier in this chapter that some of the top helmsmen in various classes replace their sails with almost monotonous regularity. You may have thought that this sort of thing is only practised by the very wealthy, but you would be wrong. Imagine the scene at any clubhouse as the dinghies come ashore after an afternoon's exhilarating racing. The local expert has won again, and a beginner profits from the great man's resulting good humour to offer his congratulations.

'I say, well done,' he murmurs, as he casts an appreciative eye over the winner's shining hull. 'You certainly left us standing today. Who made your sails?'

The hero throws out the name of his Sail Maker, and modestly passes the credit for his win to his jib.

'It certainly is a beauty,' says the star-struck beginner. 'I wish I had one half as good.'

'D'you want it?' asks the expert, knowing full well that he has thrashed the stuffing out of it for three months, and that the flow has started to move to the leech.

The upshot is that he sells it for half-price to the tyro, who proceeds to venerate it beyond its deserts, and the expert goes off and gets a new one – with the drive where it should be, further forward.

I am not saying that all experts, or indeed many, do this sort of thing, or that all second-hand sails are blown out. There are many occasions where they can be a useful addition to the locker, so let us examine some of the points to watch when buying.

First and foremost, will it fit your boat exactly as its stands? If it will not, you may end by paying alteration charges which will bring the total cost nearly to that of a new sail. Although the sail may be cheap, you will have to pay labour charges at current rates.

Secondly, you should bend the sail on your boat, to see whether it sets well; take it afloat for a proper trial. If all goes well with this test, examine it carefully along the lines of the points I have listed for a winter overhaul. I will summarize them briefly here:

1. Chafe in way of runners, shrouds and spreaders.
2. Rotten stitching caused by weakening in sunlight.
3. Conditions of bolt rope, with special reference to chafe at the slides and the rope pulling away from the headboard.
4. Wires, with special attention to where eye splices have disturbed the protective covering. Check any spinnaker wires by comparing lengths.
5. Creased leeches.
6. Distortion of the thimbles.
7. Condition of seizings.
8. Do pleats, or a row of empty stitch holes, betray alterations, particularly at the leech, which might suggest a poor shape?

Finally, if you are determined on a sail which will have to be altered, do not take the vendor's word that it is a simple alteration – nor the evidence of this book. Offer to buy it, subject to a Sail Maker of your own choice agreeing to make the alterations for a reasonable sum.

Chapter XXI

The Future

The main factors which contribute to a yacht's performance are the helmsman, the crew, the hull (and its equipment), the sails, and luck. Estimates of the proportion contributed by the sails vary between 25 and 75 per cent but, for the sake of argument, we can say that each of the first four ingredients contributes 25 per cent to the recipe, with luck thrown in as an extra for seasoning. I cannot then be accused of bias. Let me just say in passing that Cornelius Shields is on record as having said that sails are responsible for 75 per cent of a boat's success[38].

Speaking broadly again, the hull with its fittings costs somewhere between 75 and 90 per cent of the total outlay, and the sails are responsible for the rest.

It is heartening for the Sail Maker to note that a general awakening to the importance of sails has taken place. For too long owners were content to make the inevitable economy cuts at the expense of the sail locker. What is the use of spending a year's salary on a boat, only to cut down at the last minute on the very item which is going to make her go? This is surely spoiling the ship for a ha'porth of tar.

Never forget that your sails are your power plant.

We are indebted in part to the spur of international competition for this general awareness. It is fair to say that the British received a rude awakening over successive America's Cup defeats since World War II. Almost everything and everybody was vaguely blamed without deep analysis for *Sceptre*'s failure against *Columbia*, but people really started scratching their heads after *Sovereign* was equally soundly thrashed by *Constellation*. *Lionheart*, of course, never even got through the eliminators.

The whole of the British yacht-racing fraternity was examined both publicly and privately. Nothing escaped criticism. As part of this examination, the Sail Maker had to bear his share. Moreover, the analysis went further into the question, and took a hard look at the raw materials of the business, including the thread with which the sails were made, and the shape of the needles used to do it.

SAILCLOTH

The Sail Makers, of course, did not like to think that the whole responsibility was theirs, and I am not going to be drawn into a fruitless argument about what part should be borne by lack of competition, by the hull, the spars or the crew. There is no doubt, however, that the quality of our sailcloth needed to be improved in common with everything else. It is good to note that energetic and far-reaching steps had results – in the Admiral's Cup at least.

I have already written something about cloth in Chapter III, and it only remains for me to emphasize here what I said there. Sails can only be as good as their cloth will let them, and we can expect that improvement will be best advanced by better weaving and finishing techniques, together with research into new materials.

THE WIND TUNNEL

A primitive apparatus for measuring lateral, forward and downward components of wind-pressure on model sails at predetermined angles of attack and heel, was constructed and used by Mr Linton Hope of Great Britain around 1911 or 1912. At the request of the editor of the *Field*, a series of experiments was carried out to test the relative efficiency of a gunter lug sail, a gaff sail together with its jackyarder, and a high-peaked gaff sail; all had the same area of 500 sq in, the same flow and the same centre of effort. It is interesting to note that they came out in the above order of efficiency, with the gunter lug, which most nearly approached the Bermudian sail in outline shape, ahead of both the others[62].

This early apparatus was mounted in the open, and relied on Nature for its airflow. In 1915 at the Massachusetts Institute of Technology in America, H. A. Everett and C. H. Peabody read a paper on 'Wind Tunnel Experiments with Yacht Sails', and Harold Larner and H. F. Hewins conducted a study into the efficiency of the Bermudian rig. Manfred Currey did a lot of wind tunnel work in Germany before the publication of his remarkable book in 1928[4]. Sir Richard Fairey, of the aviation company which bore his name, conducted experiments at his factory's wind tunnel at Hayes, Middlesex, before the Second World War, but his results have never been published. This roll-call of early pioneers in yacht research would not be complete without the name of Professor Davidson, of *Gimcrack* fame, being mentioned.

All of this experiment is of value, even if it has since been proved that some of it is of limited application, in that it helps to establish the basic problems which are to be solved.

It was not until the late 1950s that a real start was made on the problem in Great Britain. T. Tanner, of Southampton University, had done some earlier personal work on the subject and, when the Red Duster 12-metre syndicate financed a research programme, he was the obvious man for the job. There were at that time three wind tunnels in England especially designed for evaluating sails. The Amateur Yacht Research Society had built an open-air low-speed tunnel at Hythe in Kent, Messrs Ratsey & Lapthorn Ltd had a medium-speed tunnel at their loft at Cowes, and Southampton University had a similar one at Southampton. All these were capable of improving sail design and flow, with Southampton's rather more sophisticated instrumentation in the best position to provide the answers. Tony Marchaj's *Sailing Theory and Practice* and his more formidable *Aero-Hydrodynamics of Sailing* are excellent books on the theoretical side of sails, and are largely the result of years of experience afloat and in the University wind tunnel. I am indebted to him for kindly checking my Chapter II, and commend his books to those who would seek a more intimate knowledge of this subject.

I do not believe that enough has been made of wind tunnels, for it is to science that we must now look if the marginal improvements still possible are to be achieved. At Ratsey's we never seemed to be able to devote the entire energies of one or two executives solely to the wind tunnel for the length of time it would take to mount a really effective investigation. I undertook one or two superficial studies connected with spinnakers and porosity, a trial on adding a shelf to the foot of a 14 ft International mainsail, and a slightly more detailed analysis of the ideal flow in the upper half of a 12-metre mainsail at the time of the *Sovereign* and *Kurrewa V* era, together with some tuft tests, but this is about all that was done in the first five years of the tunnel, which was later regretfully dismantled to make room for more prosaic equipment. Part of the trouble was lack of funds. A Sail Maker's budget is not sufficient to finance a large research programme, and it always seemed a pity to me that post-war America's Cup challenges did not make fuller use of the facilities available. I realize that Southampton University were financed in a research programme, but most of this was paid for by the Red Duster syndicate, which never built a challenger.

WIND TUNNEL REQUIREMENT

The wind tunnel requirement can be divided into two basic elements. First, what outline shape should a suit of sails be (outline design), and secondly what flow should it have (flow design). Because he is nearly always presented with an outline shape by the Naval Architect, the Sail Maker is by nature more interested in flow design. You may think it is time that he took a greater interest in outline design, but this would be like presenting a Boat

Builder with the overall length, beam and draft of the hull and telling him to draw up the lines himself.

Investigations by technical research teams have initially tended to concentrate their efforts principally on outline design. Many sail-testing programmes carried out by aerodynamicists have tried to determine the wind forces acting on a particular boat, and thereby to arrive at the vessel's optimum speed under certain conditions. This requires an exact replica of the hull, rigging and sails, together with a fair representation of both wind and water. At scales below about one tenth, this becomes almost impossible, the stitching and thread of the sails alone can never be reproduced accurately, except in metal; but rigid sails only hold good for the one set of conditions which induce their shape in the full-sized suit of sails. Further difficulties are added by scale effect, and the high tunnel wind-speeds needed if the tests are to be conducted at the same Reynolds number as that prevailing in the full-scale conditions it is hoped to represent. Winds in the order of 100 m.p.h. are demanded, and these once again require metal sails if distortion is to be avoided.

However, the Sail Maker's requirement is not to find out how fast a particular boat will go. It is usually to put the fastest suit of sails on to an existing boat to a given sail plan (outline design) and conditions. In other words, if he wants the boat to go faster, he has to try to make better sails than ones whose characteristics are already known through experience.

His aim is therefore clear: how to improve on a known factor.

Viewed in this light, the problem becomes simpler. If he were to scale down a known suit of sails and take readings in the tunnel, he could then use these as a yardstick against which readings from experimental sails may be measured. He can reasonably trust that errors due to scale effect, stitching, hull and rigging would be the same, or nearly the same, for both models. Provided that the shape and flow of the sails is truly representational, and that both suits are to the same scale and are set on the same rig under the same conditions, their comparative thrusts should also be representational.

ALTERNATIVE SAILS AND RIGS

It has often been said that man is an inquisitive creature, whose restless inventiveness makes him constantly seek improvement. But there is a conservative side to his nature which makes him content with what he has got, even though he has been shown a better way. We have already seen that it has taken 1,500 years for the Western world to get accustomed to the Chinese rig. Around 300 years ago the early Dutch explorers brought back stories from the Far East of native craft which travelled on more than one hull at terrific speeds. Yet the catamaran, trimaran and proa remained essentially Polynesian craft until well into the 20th Century. Similarly, the phenomenon of planing was observed in Britain in the 19th Century, yet nobody seems to have wanted to probe deeper, in order to exploit the advantages of a good power-to-weight ratio, until between the two World Wars. So let us end this book with a look at some ideas which have been started and some which perhaps need further encouragement.

VENTURIS

The venturi® spinnaker was the result of an idea pioneered by M. Lemoigne of France, as a result of his work with vented parachutes, and developed by Ratsey & Lapthorn Inc., of New York. Based on the principle that thrust is deflected downwards by the vents, thus imparting lift to the spinnaker, these sails have been tried in varying sizes since 1961. There is little doubt that they set better than normal spinnakers in very light conditions, but whether they impart extra drive in the process is more doubtful. There are no data as to whether they actually lift the boat by their upwards thrust. I did some wind tunnel experiments with a venturi spinnaker and the results were inconclusive tending, if anything, to show that there was little or no gain in thrust. The principal point in favour of the venturi is that it may prove better on a close reach, because some of the air at the head bleeds off, thus reducing knock-down effect. There is also some increase in stability down wind.

Mainsails have also been made with vents in them, and the fact that they are not now in universal use would indicate that results have not been satisfactory, despite glowing initial reports from those most closely involved.

Vents are a nuisance in a sail, because they catch in spreaders, cleats and any other handy projection, often with disastrous results for all, except the Sail Maker who has to make a new one. I believe, however, that we have not heard the last of them, and suggest that research has so far been misdirected. A vent does not, in itself, promote thrust. Indeed, the opposite is the case, because it allows air to leak from one side of the sail to the other, thus tending to lower the pressure to windward and raise it to leeward. They can certainly be made to encourage the airflow into particular channels, however, and restricted use of them to this end could well pay dividends. I say restricted use, because nearly all venturi sails so far produced – mainsails and spinnakers alike – have had, in my opinion, too many vents. With pressure almost completely equalized on either side, the sail will be robbed of thrust.

The sort of thing I have in mind is one or two suitably placed vents near the leeches of spinnakers to help spread the sail so that maximum area is projected; similar treatment in a mainsail or headsail, to delay separation of the streamlines from the lee side of the sail; a vent near the head of a spinnaker to help lift the sail, and to bleed off some of the wind to lessen knock-down effect.

THE HALF-WINDER

While still sailmaking I was responsible for the half-winder. This is a reaching spinnaker which has part or all of the rear half, or leech area, made of mesh, in order that the sail shall not develop a rearward component of thrust; in addition, the wind is allowed to escape to leeward rather than backwind the lee of the mainsail. Here again, I overdid it. Half the sail developed practically no thrust (as intended) so the leech on that side would not spread. The sail, therefore, collapsed sooner than a conventional spinnaker as the wind went ahead. There is room, however, for development

Plate 21.1 The Half-Winder
A half-winder being evaluated in the Ratsey wind tunnel at Cowes in 1964. The sail did not prove successful (largely because it would not spread properly), but the principle is good, i.e. to use an open mesh at places in a sail where harmful pressure may be equalised before it can promote turbulence or a rear component of thrust. *Ratsey & Lapthorn*

here: again, the top of a reaching spinnaker might have porous mesh incorporated to allow air to bleed off; restricted use of mesh might be beneficial to the leech of a reaching spinnaker; there may be reaching headsails which could profit from allowing some air at the leech to seep from windward to leeward to minimize their heeling effect without loss of thrust.

WING SAILS

The affinity of sails and aircraft wings has been argued for a long time. Whatever views may be held, there is no doubt that a double-sided sail, with a section like an aircraft wing, will make a hull sail very well. One of the major problems to be overcome is that a symmetrical section is inefficient. This means that some system of changing the section on tacking is necessary, so that the windward side is concave rather than convex. This sometimes means an articulated leading edge, or mast, or else a complicated internal system of cranks and levers, which adds to complexity and weight. Another drawback is that the resulting 'sail' is often not transportable, and takes a long time to set up or dismantle.

Considerable progress of this nature has been made by Austin Farrar in the development of sails for C class catamarans. *Lady Helmsman*, sometime winner of what has come to be known as the Little America's Cup, had a wing section mast pivoting at the leading edge, with a conventional fully battened leech. At first it was thought that a fine section to the wing was necessary but, although this resulted in a very close-winded sail, the streamlines broke away quickly as soon as the angle of attacked increased beyond fine limits. Tom Tanner, of the Southampton University Yacht Research Group, suggested that a blunter leading edge would give better results, and this proved to be the case.

It was originally intended to have a loose-footed sail, with a wishbone holding the clew out and down, in order to remove all twist from the head. This it achieved so well that Reg White, the helmsman, complained that it was virtually impossible to control the sail in a fresh breeze. He could not feather the top of the sail while maintaining drive in the lower part. The wishbone was accordingly discarded for a more conventional boom. With its wide mainsheet traveller across both hulls, this was nearly as efficient at removing twist as the wishbone, but allowed controlled development of it if required.

A symmetrical wing, with a leading edge which will incline toward the apparent wind, thus reducing the local angle of attack, is a good theoretical construction. Something can be done along these lines to improve airflow over a normal sail, if a pear-shaped mast rotates sharply toward the wind. It will not be long before wing-shaped masts become more common, even if they are only 6 in or so in chord, and not the rather more unwieldy size used

393

Plate 21.2 The Wing Sail
This catamaran rig was designed for *Lady Helmsman* by Austin Farrer many
years ago. It still looks right.   *J B Moore*

on *Lady Helmsman*. One of the problems to be overcome is the windage caused by the mast which makes the boat unstable at moorings or in the dinghy park.

Experiments have been going on for a long time with wing sails proper, and perhaps what Jack Manners-Spencer calls his Gallant rig, and what I call the Aero-junk (see Chapter XIX), comes closest to the requirement: efficient, balanced, uncomplicated, and no windage at moorings.

FREEDOM RIG

An unstayed mast is likely to be a fairly robust piece of equipment and, if you wrap a sail round it, you will have a form of blunt-nosed aerofoil. It is not calculated to meet the requirements of high speed aviation perhaps, but is a jolly sight more aerodynamically efficient than a conventional sail which is tacked onto the aft face of a conventional mast. What is more, the mast can remain still, yet the aerofoil tends to point towards the wind (because its trailing edge swings from one side to the other like a weather vane, depending which tack the boat is on – like any other sail, in fact).

Garry Hoyt has used this principle to develop his successful Freedom rig, which is well explained by the accompanying photograph. Its most ardent protagonists would never claim that it is as close-winded as a bermudan sloop, but some of them might contend that, because leeway is low, speed made good to windward isn't so bad, particularly in Force 4 and over. Leeway is low because, like the Chinese balanced lug, the unstayed mast tends to flex at the head in the puffs, thus feathering the sail and keeping heeling moment down.

Again like the Chinese rig, there are quite a lot of lines to deal with but, once the sail is up, control is simple, though sheet forces are higher than those of the junk because the Freedom sail is not balanced. Safety aspects include the fact that the wishbone is cocked up at the mast or inner end so that, if the outer end tries to rise, it won't get far before the restriction of the sail itself prevents it developing into a Chinese gybe; secondly, the rig has a high angle of yaw tolerance down wind, so that the boat may swing either side of her course when goose-winged without danger of gybing; finally, since there are no shrouds, stays, diamonds or jumpers, there is no chafe and no compression loading in the mast whence much of the stress is shed by flexing – a quality it shares with all forms of unstayed rig (use of carbon fibres keeps it strong enough).

The rig has been used successfully on a 70 ft boat (the world-girdling three-masted *Kriter Lady II*) but is more usually seen in two-masted form (this is more a factor of boat size rather than rig limitation). As with the Aero-junk, old ideas need to be unlearned, and it may take a little time to find out how to get the most out of the aerodynamics of these modern rigs.

Freedom doesn't look as tidy as Gallant, nor is it so easily reefed, but it has been sailing for longer, so perhaps doesn't deserve to be labelled futuristic. The only reason for not putting the Aero-junk here as well is that it is so closely related to the Chinese rig that it couldn't logically be separated from it. Both developments are worth watching in the years ahead, particularly by cruising families.

FLYING PROA

Captain Cook saw the flying proa during his 18th Century voyages in the Pacific, as did Admiral Anson 25 years before him (and so, almost certainly, did their predecessors in the area nearly a hundred years earlier). While it is tempting to expiate on the type, this is not a book on hulls and, because the proa uses a virtually standard lateen sail (even if it does have its own system of tacking), we must reluctantly pass it by as an example of man's ingenuity, well adapted to the prevailing reaching conditions which give rise to its development.

HORIZONTAL SAILS

The fact that some boats are more stable lying on their sides than upright is well known to many. It would appear logical, therefore, to develop a sail which starts life in the horizontal position. As long ago as 1895 an umbrella sail was tried, and my photograph shows this in action. The idea, of course, is to convert the wind's energy into two components as usual, but in this case one is forward and the second has a vertical or righting moment. The Amateur Yacht Research Society has put forward an ingenious idea for using a modified glider as a kite to tow a boat, either to windward or down wind. This was put to good use in 1982, when a speed record was established in this manner.

WINDMILL

H. M. Barkla, of Scotland, has proposed some interesting lines of thought for the future. At present, he says, effort has been concentrated on driving a hull supported in water, through the water by means of wind power. But what of the opposite state, where a hull supported in the air is driven through the air by means of water power? If a yacht can beat to windward, down current, faster than the current, surely suggests Barkla, an airship hanging a vertical hydrofoil in the water could be made to 'tack' up water,

---

Plate 21.3 Freedom Rig
The sails wrap around their masts and set on wishbones. Like the junk rig, the masts are unstayed and the ride is easy. *Freedom Yachts International*

Plate 21.4 Umbrella Sail
I have always included this 1895 photograph as a sail of the future, and its day must come . . . It is not quite such a simple rig as it may seem, because examination of the print reveals that there is a wire leading from each circular patch, some to the base of the mast and some half way; there are others to the masthead. Though the boat will never capsize (the rig is called a Cyclone Sail on the original print), and tacking should be easy, passage onto the foredeck looks as though it would take a Houdini. *Beken*

down wind faster than the wind. An alternative method of drive would be a water-propeller.

Perhaps this is not possible due to the relative viscosity of the two fluids under consideration (water and air), but there is certainly room for development of the windmill which drives a water-propeller. The late Lord Brabazon of Tara fitted a Bembridge Redwing with just such a system, and he sailed straight into the eye of the wind. He did not make such good speed to windward, however, as conventional Redwings cross-tacking. This was an excellent boat to use for the experiment, because their rules allow 200 sq ft of sail area disposed exactly how the owner likes; there could be no question, therefore, that either system was being favoured. This was some time ago, and there is no doubt that speeds could be improved nowadays, especially if some form of hydrofoil were incorporated into the hull to lessen drag.

CONVENTIONAL SAILS

I cannot leave you with all these rather outlandish ideas as the last impression of this book. For the immediate foreseeable future conventional sails will continue to serve as they have in the past. They will only serve as well as you let them, so take care of them. They are made of a delicate fabric, which does not like mistreatment. They are the soul of the boat, and the motive power. Look after them and they will look after you.

Appendix A

Chart of Equivalent Cloth Weights

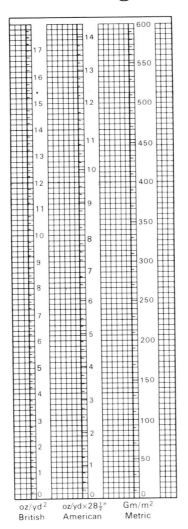

oz/yd² — British
oz/yd×28½″ — American
Gm/m² — Metric

Appendix B

Laundering and Dry Cleaning of Terylene Sails

STORAGE

All sails should be folded or rolled in a manner which avoids sharp creases as far as possible. Sails made from Terylene polyester fibre should be stored under well-ventilated, clean conditions, and dampness which may encourage the growth of mildew should be avoided as far as possible. Whilst mildew growths do not affect the strength of Terylene fabrics, they can cause stains which are unsightly and not readily removed.

WASHING

Small sails can be washed in the bath, and large ones on a clean concrete washdown, using a scrubbing brush and hose where necessary. Terylene sails should be washed in water as hot as the hand can bear and containing soap and washing soda, or any proprietary brand of liquid detergent. At localized areas where soiling is particularly heavy neat liquid detergent can be applied and the treated sail left overnight before washing.

If general soiling is persistent and difficult to remove, the sails may be steeped overnight in cold water containing 1 lb of sodium metasilicate/gallon (100 g/litre). Stainless steel, porcelain or enamel vessels should be used and *not* vessels made of aluminium or galvanized iron. Do not allow the solution to come in contact with galvanized luff wires, hanks or alloy slides. After this treatment the sail should be drained but not rinsed, and then given a warm handwash as described above, with light scrubbing.

REMOVAL OF STAINS

The suggestions below refer to white undyed sailcloth material. Coloured sails which have become abnormally stained should be dealt with by an experienced finisher or dry cleaner, especially when solvents or bleaching agents are involved in the stain-removal technique. Stains should be removed as soon as possible after they appear.

BLOOD

Soak the stained portion in cold water containing half a cupful of ammonia to half a gallon of water. If residual stains are still present after this treatment, damp the stain with a 1 per cent solution of pepsin in water acidified with a few drops of dilute hydrochloric acid, allow to stand without drying out for 30 minutes, and then rinse thoroughly.

MILDEW

Scrub lightly with a dry stiff brush to remove as much of the mould growth as possible and then steep the stained portion for 2 hours in a cold solution of bleach (sodium hypochlorite) at a strength of approximately 1 per cent available chlorine. A proprietary brand of bleach such as Domestos® may be used, 1 part of Domestos being added to 10 parts of water. Wash thoroughly in water and repeat the treatment if necessary. If after the final washing there is any residual smell of chlorine this may be removed by immersing for a few minutes in a 1 per cent solution of sodium thiosulphate (photographers' hypo). Rinse finally with water.

OIL, GREASE, AND WAXES

Small stains of this nature can be removed by dabbing with trichloroethylene or by the use of proprietary stain removers. Heavy staining is best removed by brushing on a mixture of detergent and solvent. This can be prepared by dissolving 1 part of Lissapol NX® in 2 parts of benzene or toluene. Alternatively, a proprietary brand such as Polyclens® may be used. These 'solvent/detergent' mixtures should be brushed well into the fabric, left for about 15 minutes and then washed off with warm water. A well-ventilated place should be selected for carrying out this treatment, and precautions should be exercised if the solvents are inflammable. These treatments will remove oils, greases, petroleum jelly and most lubricating mixtures, but they will not remove stains caused by the fine metallic particles often associated with lubricants. Such stains can be removed by methods described below, after the oil or grease has been eliminated.

METALLIC STAINS

Stains caused by metals, in the form of rust, verdigris or finely divided particles, can be removed by either of the following methods (do not allow the solution to come into contact with galvanized iron or copper):

(*a*) Immerse the stained portion in a 5 per cent solution of oxalic acid dissolved in hot water (1 oz of oxalic acid dissolved in each pint of hot water). The hands and the fabrics should be washed very thoroughly after using oxalic acid solutions, as this chemical is poisonous.

(*b*) Immerse the stained portion in a warm solution containing 2 parts of concentrated hydrochloric acid per 100 parts of water. Wash off thoroughly with water.

PITCH AND TAR

Organic solvents such as perchloroethylene, trichloroethylene, trichloro-ethane (Genklene®), solvent naphtha or white spirit may be dabbed on to the stain to effect removal. Again care should be taken to work in a well-ventilated position, and due precautions should be observed when using inflammable solvents.

VARNISH

Dab the stain first with trichloroethylene and then with a mixture of equal parts of acetone and amyl acetate. Shellac varnish is easily removed with alcohol or methylated spirit. Paint strippers based on alkalis should not be used on Terylene.

ADHESIVE NUMBERS

To remove adhesive numbers, soak in benzene until the glue is softened. After peeling off the numbers, remove the glue from the sail with a rag dipped in benzene.

Appendix C

Thread and Needle Sizes

Cloth weight	Thread weight	Needle size
1–3 oz	Use machine thread	Domestic or no. 19
3–4 ,,	ditto	19 or 18
4–6 ,,	2 lb (light)	18 or 17
6–8 ,,	4 lb (medium)	17
8–11,,	6 lb (,,)	16
11–15,,	8 lb (heavy)	15

When sewing three or four thicknesses of cloth, use a size larger needle and thread than the table.

If repairing head, tack or clew (six or more thicknesses), use two sizes larger needle and one size heavier thread than the table.

If working an eye, use a heavier thread and space out stitches.

If roping, use a size heavier thread, and blunt the point of a size larger needle than the table.

Modern sailcloth is so closely woven that the threads are packed one on the other in a tight weave, so that each pass of the needle carries a high risk of cutting individual yarns, particularly in the lighter cloths where the weave is usually closest. Therefore the fewer stitches in any repair job, the less the chance of weakening the cloth. It is thus a general principle that any hand sewing should be restricted to the fewest stitches possible – which is another way of saying that modern practice is to keep stitches large and widespread, using doubled twine if necessary. This is particularly true of film laminates, which can be weakened by too many stitch holes.

Appendix D
Marshall Half-Tonner

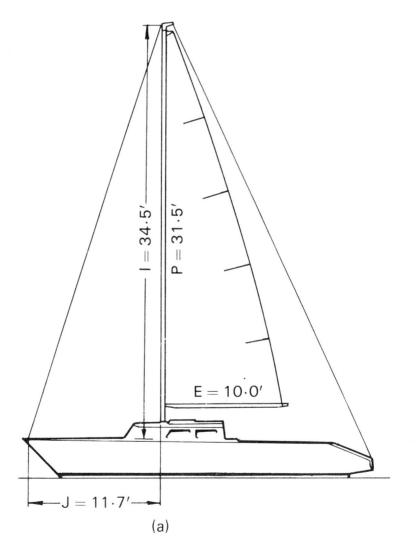

(a)

(b)

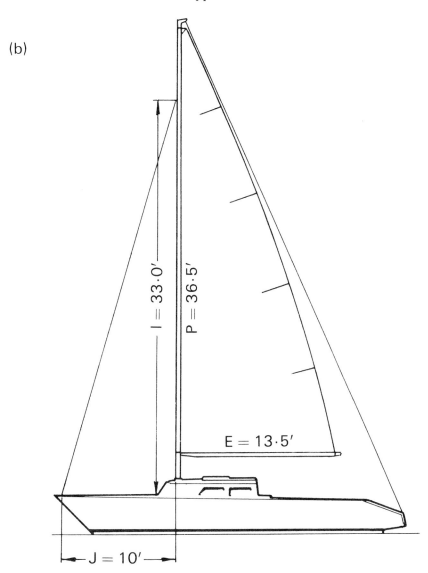

I = 33·0′

P = 36·5′

E = 13·5′

J = 10′

These two rigs, to a common scale, for Roger Marshall's 1983 Half-Tonner, both return the same RSA of 436 sq ft. It will be seen that the fractional rig has over 50 sq ft more actual, or measured, sail area than the masthead sailplan, or nearly 15 per cent extra; the former is better up wind and the latter down wind, if we must generalize.

The effect on rated sail area (and thus on rating) of changing any of the four basic sail measurement limitations (I, J, P and E) in the fractional rig is shown at Appendix E, together with some discussion. See also Figs. 18.1 and 18.2 in Chapter XVIII.

Appendix E

Effect of Sail Area on Rating

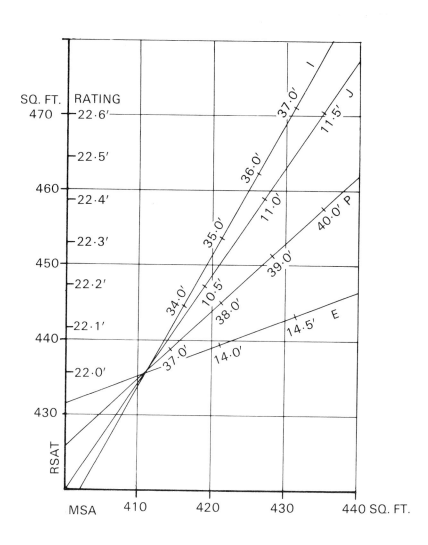

Base boat: I=33·0', J=10·0', P=36·5', E=13·5'; (b) in Appendix D

This graph shows rated sail area (RSA) in the *x* co-ordinate plotted against total actual, or measured, windward-going sail area (MSA) in the *y* co-ordinate for one of Roger Marshall's fractional rigged Half-Tonners. Also in the *x* co-ordinate is plotted the rating achieved for each change in RSAT, provided that all other factors remain the same (any changes in CGF resulting from the change in rig size have been ignored).

The boat was designed to measure under the IOR at 22·0', with an RSAT of 435·7 sq ft; MSA for this rating came out at 411·4 sq ft. Roger has entered on each of the sail parameter curves one or two spot values, in order to show the magnitude of any change compared with its effect on the rating. It will be seen that changes in E affect the rating least (so use this if you want to raise your rating), and changes in I affect it most (but see Fig. 18.1 before you use this to lower your rating, because it can be hard on the pocket). As an example, in moving a rating of 22·0' to 22·2', a bigger J will raise the actual sail area only from 411 to 418 sq ft, whereas increasing E would take it over 440 sq ft.

Appendix F

Measuring a Yacht for New Sails

When a yacht needs new sails and a sailplan does not exist, it will be necessary to measure her if the sails are to fit. It is best if the measurements to be taken are written down beforehand, when there is time to consider what is going to be needed. Working to a list should help to avoid omissions, and the appropriate items should be extracted from the full table at the end of this Appendix. The following comments may be helpful.

General. Always write down the full distance you find, and either make any allowances for sheave clearance afterwards when you come to draw up the sailplan, or else make it clear that no allowance has been made. Measurements from the masthead can be taken shackling the wire or tape to the appropriate halyard and hauling it aloft. Care should be taken, not only to avoid the wrong rope (topping lift for main halyard), but also to ensure that the halyard is hoisted hard up and made fast securely, so that it does not creep down between two different measurements supposedly from the same point. Be accurate, and watch out for sag caused by the wind, as this can make quite a difference over 40 to 50 ft. It is best to fit a rope downhaul alongside a measuring wire or tape, otherwise you may find it difficult to pull down the halyard afterwards. Take too many rather than too few measurements. A steel tape measure is better than a linen one, for the latter may stretch even if it is reinforced; a measuring wire is best of all for it will sag less in a wind, but I realize this sort of equipment is not in common supply.

Jib. The spinnaker halyard may be used if it is more convenient, and if it leads from nearly the same point aloft. You are really measuring the foretriangle here, to establish mast rake and maximum luff distance. Measure to bowsprit end, stem head, forestay on deck and tack fitting, as these will be at least several inches different; don't forget the vertical measurement to the deck, which is the 'I' measurement (you may have to make an estimate of the coachroof here). Many large yachts have a forestay fitting which precludes hanks or snap hooks near the tack, and this is useful to know.

410

Staysail. The same measurements from aloft are needed as for the jib, with the addition of the one to the clew in the sailing position if a boom staysail is used. In the latter case make sure that tack and clew fittings are noted (the jaw width can also be important in some yachts), together with the travel of the clew outhaul slide if one is used. You will see in the table that the maximum and minimum distances from tack eye to clew eye duplicate this measurement, but it is vital to know it, and there is no harm in being doubly sure. There may, of course, be no travel at the clew, in which case there will be only one measurement from eye to eye. If the staysail is fitted to a boom with slides, a sample will ensure a correct fit. You would be surprised at the number of people who tell their Sail Maker that they need 'one inch slides'; this does not tell him whether the slides are internal or external, or whether the track or the slides are one inch (a $\frac{7}{8}$ in internal slide fits a 1 in external track, and a 1 in external slide fits a $\frac{7}{8}$ in internal track). In addition, an external track may not be deep enough to take a particular internal slide which would jam. Thus, if a sample slide is not available, measure the depth of the track as well as the width (a piece of paper pressed over the end of a track section will press the correct imprint into the paper), and also note the amount of room between the underside of the track and the mast if external slides are involved; some heavy slides have thick flanges which will not pass between the track and the mast if there is little room.

Mainsail and Mizzen. Make sure that the luff measurement is taken with the gooseneck in the lowest position, and make a note of the amount of vertical travel. While the wire or tape is aloft, it is quite easy and quick to take the distances vertically to the deck, to the mizzenmast at the deck, and to the counter; none of these is essential, but they will all help to draw up the plan of the boat. The distance from the head to the clew in the sailing position should be taken to the same point you use when measuring the boom from tack eye to clew eye, with the clew in the outermost position if there is an adjustment. Check before taking the leech distance that the boom is the right height to clear the deckhouse or heads in the cockpit. The tack knock back is the distance from the tack of the main or mizzen to the aft face of the mast in question; this is usually $1\frac{1}{4}$ to $1\frac{3}{4}$ in where there is no roller boom, but varies from 4 in to 8 or 9 in for a roller boom, depending on the type of gear fitted. The Sail Maker must know this distance so that he can cut away the tack by the correct amount, in order that the sail shall set properly at the tack and shall not exceed the black band at the clew. If the main halyard is not available for any reason, you can always use the flag halyard, but try and gauge the resulting difference in the distance aloft. Once again it is preferable to supply a sample slide to ensure correct fit; check that luff and foot are not different in this respect. Some boats are fitted with mast ramps, where the track is led away from the mast just above the tack, so that it fairs nicely towards the tack fitting if this is set back for a roller gear. Draw a quick picture of this ramp, showing how high above the tack it starts and finishes, and its vertical distance to the mast at its lowest point. If there is no ramp, the track sometimes finishes well above the tack, so the Sail Maker will need to know not to fit a slide below a certain point. For a grooved mast, substitute the height of the groove entry above the tack for this measurement.

Gaff Sails. If an old sail is available, it should be bent to the spars and hoisted for measuring, as it will correctly give the gaff height and angle even if the sail is a little short on the foot and head. If there is not one, you must hoist the gaff and boom to the best estimate of their sailing positions. In either case two tapes or wires should be used, one attached to the throat and one to the peak. It is important that the distance from peak to tack and clew, and from throat to tack and clew should be taken simultaneously with the gaff and boom at a constant height and angle. Have a good look at the throat eye when the gaff is hoisted, to see whether it is out of line with the rest of the luff and/or head. Don't forget to count the mast hoops. Measure also the top and bottom of the protecting band on the mast in way of the gaff jaws when hoisted, to ensure that the checkwire which will be fitted to the luff will leave the throat correctly positioned at the mast.

Hull. The overall and waterline lengths are usually known without measurement, and a sufficiently accurate guess can be made at the overhangs with the aid of the tape measure on the deck. These details will be necessary for the outline of the hull, as will the freeboard at several convenient points. Freeboard can be established by tying a suitable weight on to the wire or tape, and lowering over the side until the end just touches the water. This establishes the sheer line, which is important for a low cut genoa. Deckhouse details are needed so that the right amount of clearance can be kept between the top of it and the boom. Having settled the outline of the hull itself, don't forget the locations of the various stays and masts where they meet the deck, and the jib fairleads. Note that the measurements from mast to stem, and 'J' are not necessarily the same for a sloop, but establish the position of the forestay on deck in relation to the stem head. Spreaders are not essential, but useful when determining the genoa leech and whether also a particular sail, perhaps an intermediate genoa, will sheet inside the upper shrouds and under the lower spreaders. The mast and boom circumferences have been included in case it may be necessary to make a sail cover for the main or mizzen.

Interpretation. When drawing the plan, start at the waterline and work upwards until the hull is complete. Next settle the position of the masts at deck level, and then establish their rake. There will be a discrepancy at the masthead due to the use of two different halyards (jib and main), and you must allow for the shackle and splice together with the thickness of the mast. Draw all measurements with a soft pencil and the right position should soon be manifest. If one distance is wrong it will be shown up by the fact that all the others are mutually corroborating without it. It is for this purpose that too many measurements are better than too few.

When deciding how big to make the stretched sizes of a mainsail or mizzen to a plan established on these lines, due allowance should be made for clearance at the masthead for the halyard splice and shackle; it is possible that two large wooden blocks with their attendant shackles and eyes may have to be accommodated between the sheave and the headboard. A suitable minimum allowance is 2 per cent of the total distance from sheave to tack, which is 6 in on a 25 ft luff and 1 ft on a 50 ft luff.

Measuring Old Sails. Sometimes old sails are taken as a pattern for size. This is all right for headsails, which spread on the floor to their full size, but a mainsail will not do so without being stretched on the luff and foot. This can only be properly achieved on the spars, and the sail makes a poor pattern on its own, even if it is made of Terylene or Dacron. It is thus preferable to measure the spars along the lines I have just given, because too great a variation will occur if the sail itself has to be measured.

An exception to this rule is the use of an old headsail to establish the size of a new one. The old sail is hoisted on the boat, and the place where the clew of the new headsail is desired can be given by reference to the old one. The instructions to the Sail Maker will then give the sizes of the old sail (luff, leech and foot) and the fact that the clew of the new sail should come, say, 6 in further aft and 3 in lower than the old one. If the luff needs to be longer, this can also be compared with the old sail.

Appendix G

Boat Measurement Table

	Inner jib	Outer jib
JIB		
Halyard in sheave to deck (vertical) ('I').		
Halyard in sheave to bowsprit end.		
Halyard in sheave to stem head.		
Halyard in sheave to forestay on deck.		
Halyard in sheave to tack fitting.		
First hank up from tack (to clear turnbuckle, etc.).		

STAYSAIL
Halyard in sheave to deck (vertical).
Halyard in sheave to stem head.
Halyard in sheave to forestay on deck.
Halyard in sheave to tack fitting.
Halyard in sheave to clew in sailing position.

Boom: tack eye to clew eye.   { Max.
                                   { Min.

Boom: clew lashes or outhaul slide. Slide travel.
Boom: reef cleats from clew in max. position.
Foot: loose, lacing or slides. No. and type of slides.
First hank up from tack (to clear turnbuckle, etc.).

	Mizzen	Main
MIZZEN/MAINSAIL		

Halyard in sheave to tack in lowest position.
Halyard in sheave to deck (vertical).
Halyard in sheave to clew in sailing position.
Halyard in sheave to mizzen mast at deck (main only).
Halyard in sheave to counter.
Tack knock back (distance tack to aft face of mast).
Luff groove, lacing or slides. No. and type of slides.
Foot groove, lacing or slides. No. and type of slides.
Mast ramp details, or distance up groove starts.
Gooseneck travel.
Boom: roller or fixed.
Boom: reef cleats from clew in max. position.

Boom: tack eye to clew eye.   { Max.
                                   { Min.

Boom: clew lashes or outhaul slide. Slide travel.

414

	Mizzen	Main

GAFF SAILS *(Extra to above)*
    Gaff throat eye to peak eye.
    Peak to tack in sailing position.
    Peak to clew in sailing position.
    Throat to tack in sailing position.
    Throat to clew in sailing position.
    Distance throat in sailing position is offset from true.
    Number of mast hoops.
    Gaff laces, groove or slides. No. and type of slides.

    Mast band to tack.   { *Top*
                                  Bottom

HULL
    Pulpit and guard rail height. Continuous YES/NO.
    Length overall (with/without bowsprit).
    Length waterline.
    Bow overhang.
    Stern overhang.
    Freeboard at bow.
    Freeboard at mainmast.
    Freeboard at mizzen mast (or other convenient
        point).
    Freeboard at stern.
    Mast to stemhead.
    Bowsprit length.
    J measurement (mast to outer stay at deck/bow-
        sprit).
    Mast to middle stay at deck.
    Mast to inner stay at deck.
    Distance between masts.
    Mizzen mast to counter.
    Deckhouse height above deck.
    Jib fairleads aft of mast (max. and min. if on track).
    Mast circumference at tack.
    Boom circumference at tack.
    Boom circumference at clew.
    Upper spreaders above the deck, and width.
    Lower spreaders above deck, and width.

Appendix H

List of Mathematical Symbols and IOR Abbreviations

α	Angle of incidence
α_{ef}	Effective incidence angle
A	Area
Ae	Aerofoil chord line
AR	Aspect ratio
β	Apparent course
C_D	Aerodynamic drag coefficient
CE	Centre of effort
C_L	Aerodynamic lift coefficient
CLR	Centre of lateral resistance or plane
D	Aerodynamic drag
ϵ	Drag angle
E	Foot of mainsail
f	Depth of the sail profile (camber)
F_B	Hull buoyancy
F_H	Heeling force (air)
F_R	Driving force (air)
F_S	Side force (water)
F_T	Total aerodynamic force
I	Height of the foretriangle
IC	Height of the foretriangle (corrected)
J	Base of the foretriangle
JC	Base of the foretriangle (corrected)
L	Lift
l	Chord of the sail profile (camber)
LOA	Length over all
LP	Longest perpendicular (headsail)
LWL	Length on the waterline
MSA	Measured sail area
P	Mainsail hoist

q	Dynamic pressure
ρ	Mass density (air)
R	Total hydrodynamic resistance
Re	Reynolds number
RSA	Rated sail area
RSAC	RSA combined abaft masts
RSAF	RSA foretriangle
RSAM	RSA mainsail
RSAT	Total rated sail area
R_1	Total hydrodynamic force
S	Stagnation streamline
S_c	Stagnation streamline (combined aerofoil)
S_h	Stagnation streamline (headsail)
S_m	Stagnation streamline (mainsail)
SA	Sail area
SPIN	Spinnaker rated area
V	Speed (boat or wind)
V_A	Apparent wind speed
V_{mg}	Speed made good to windward
W	Weight of the boat

Appendix I

Beaufort Wind Scale

Beaufort number	Wind speed				Seaman's term	Estimating wind speed	
	knots	mph	metres per second	km per hour		Effects observed at sea	Effects observed on land
0	under 1	under 1	0·0–0·2	under 1	Calm	Sea like mirror	Calm; smoke rises vertically
1	1–3	1–3	0·3–1·5	1–5	Light air	Ripples with appearance of scales; no foam crests	Smoke drift indicates wind direction; vanes do not move
2	4–6	4–7	1·6–3·3	6–11	Light breeze	Small wavelets; crests of glassy appearance, not breaking	Wind felt on face; leaves rustle; vanes begin to move
3	7–10	8–12	3·4–5·4	12–19	Gentle breeze	Large wavelets; crests begin to break; scattered whitecaps	Leaves, small twigs in constant motion; light flags extended
4	11–16	13–18	5·5–7·9	20–29	Moderate breeze	Small waves, becoming longer; numerous whitecaps	Dust, leaves, and loose paper raised up; small branches move
5	17–21	19–24	8·0–10·7	30–38	Fresh breeze	Moderate waves, taking longer form; many white horses; some spray	Small trees in leaf begin to sway
6	22–27	25–31	10·8–13·8	39–50	Strong breeze	Larger waves forming; white horses everywhere; more spray	Larger branches of trees in motion; whistling heard in wires
7	28–33	32–38	13·9–17·1	51–61	Near gale	Sea heaps up; while foam from breaking waves begins to be blown in streaks	Whole trees in motion; resistance felt in walking against wind
8	34–40	39–46	17·2–20·7	62–74	Gale	Moderately high waves of greater length; edges of crests begin to break into spindrift; foam is blown in well-marked streaks	Twigs and small branches broken off trees; progress generally impeded
9	41–47	47–54	20·8–24·4	75–87	Strong gale	High waves; sea begins to roll; dense streaks of foam; spray may reduce visibility	Slight structural damage occurs; slates blown from roofs
10	48–55	55–63	24·5–28·4	88–101	Storm	Very high waves with overhanging crests; sea takes white appearance as foam is blown in very dense streaks; rolling is heavy and visibility reduced	Seldom experienced on land; trees broken or uprooted; considerable structural damage occurs
11	56–63	64–72	28·5–32·6	102–116	Violent storm	Exceptionally high waves; sea covered with white foam patches; visibility still more reduced	Very rarely experienced on land; usually accompanied by widespread damage
12	64–71	73–82	32·7–36·9	117–132	Hurricane	Air filled with foam; sea completely white with driving spray, visibility very seriously affected	
13	72–80	83–92	37·0–41·4	133–148			
14	81–89	93–103	41·5–46·1	149–166			
15	90–99	104–114	46·2–50·9	167–183			
16	100–108	115–124	51·0–56·0	184–200			
17	109–118	125–136	56·1–61·2	201–219			

References

1. *A Preliminary Note on the Results of Rigid Sail Tests in the Unheeled Position*, C A Marchaj and A Q Chapleo. Southampton University Yacht Research Paper No 6. 1961 (p.3)
2. *Aviation Week*. 19th March 1956 (pp.46–7)
3. *Sailing Theory and Practice*, C A Marchaj. Dodd Mead & Co (USA); Adlard Coles Ltd (UK). 1982 (pp.48–9)
4. *Sail Power*, Wallace Ross. Alfred Knopf (USA); Adlard Coles Ltd (UK). 1975 (pp.13–14)
5. *Yacht Racing*, Manfred Curry. Charles Scribners (USA); George Bell (UK). 1928 (p.32)
6. *The Aerodynamics of Yacht Sails*, E Werner and S Ober. 1925
7. *Conference on Yacht Design and Research*, Professor J Sainsbury. Southampton University Yacht Research Paper No 9. 1962 (Ch 3, p.10)
8. Ibid[3] (pp.137–8)
9. Ibid[3] (p.57)
10. *Aero-Hydrodynamics of Sailing*, C A Marchaj. Adlard Coles Ltd (UK); Dodd Mead & Co (USA). 1979 (p.306)
11. Ibid[3] (p.132)
12. *Wind Tunnel Tests of a 1/3rd Scale Model of an X One-Design Yacht's Sails*, C A Marchaj. Southampton University Yacht Research Paper No 11. 1962 (pp.8–9)
13. *Illustrated Experiments in Fluid Mechanics*, David C Hazen. MIT Press, Cambridge Mass & London England. 1972 (p.93)
14. Ibid[10] (pp.230–40)
15. Ibid[3] (p.79)
16. Ibid[10] (p.574)
17. Ibid[3] (pp.107 and 370)
18. *Visual Observations of the Flow Around the Sails of a Model 12-metre Yacht*, C A Marchaj and A Q Chapleo. Southampton University Yacht Research Paper No 4. 1960 (p.5)
19. Ibid[1] (p.6)
20. Ibid[3] (pp.70–4)
21. Ibid[4] (p. 47)
22. Ibid[1] (p.9)
23. Ibid[3] (p.133)
24. Ibid[10] (pp.422 and 581)

25. *Start to Win*, Eric Twiname. Adlard Coles Ltd (UK); W W Norton (USA). 1973 (p.25)
26. Ibid[3] (p.73)
27. *Sails* 1st Ed, J Howard-Williams. Adlard Coles Ltd (UK); John de Graff (USA). 1967 (p.181)
28. *More Sail Trim*, Ed by Anne Madden. Sail Books (USA); Adlard Coles Ltd (UK). 1980 (p.248)
29. *Further Offshore*, John Illingworth. Adlard Coles Ltd (UK); John de Graff (USA). 1969 (pp.66 and 73)
30. *Special Regulations Governing Minimum Equipment*. Offshore Racing Council (Section 10.21.1)
31. Ibid[12] (p.8)
32. *IYRU Sail Measurement Instructions* (Section III–1(2))
33. Ibid[32] (Section III–1(7))
34. Ibid[3] (pp.83–4)
35. *International Offshore Rule*. Offshore Racing Council (Rule 802.6)
36. *Designed to Win*, Roger Marshall. Adlard Coles Ltd (UK); W W Norton (USA). 1979 (p.93)
37. *Yachting*, Lowell North. Ziff-Davis Publishing Corporation. April 1963 (p.74)
38. *Cornelius Shields on Sailing*, Cornelius Shields. Prentice-Hall Inc (USA); Nicholas Kaye (UK). 1964
39. *Yachting World*, Jim Allsopp. IPC Transport Press Ltd. June 1981 (p.67)
40. *Seahorse*, Robbie Doyle. Ocean Publications Ltd. Jan/Feb 1979 (p.69)
41. Ibid[35] (Rule 812)
42. Ibid[30] (Sections 10.21 and 10.22)
43. Ibid[35] (Rule 886)
44. Ibid[35] (Rules 812.1 and 817.3)
45. *Looking at Sails*, Bruce Banks and Dick Kenny. United Nautical Publishers. 1979 (p.130)
46. *Tom Diaper's Diary*, Tom Diaper. Adlard Coles Ltd. 1950
47. *Spinnaker*, R R King. Adlard Coles Ltd (UK); Sail Books (USA). 1981 (p.124)
48. Ibid[47] (p.4)
49. *Tack Now Skipper*, Owen Parker. Adlard Coles Ltd. 1979 (p.7)
50. Ibid[39] Stephen van Dyck. July 1965
51. Ibid[36] (p.28); Ibid[47] (pp.142–6)
52. Ibid[37] Ham de Fontaine. Nov 1951
53. Ibid[35] (Rule 802)
54. Ibid[29] (p.51)
55. Ibid[40] Chris Preston. Jan/Feb 1978 (pp.57–9)
56. Ibid[49] (p.11)
57. *Science and Civilization in China* Vol 4, Dr Joseph Needham. Cambridge University Press. 1971 (p.379 et seq)
58. *Practical Boat Owner*. Oct 1976 (p.50)
59. Ibid[39] Col 'Blondie' Hasler. Jan 1961 (p.15)
60. *Sailing Alone Around the World*, Joshua Slocum. Granada Publishing. 1981 (p.323)
61. *Cruising World*, David Stookey. Cruising World Publications Inc.
62. *Manual of Yachting and Boat Sailing and Naval Architecture* 11th Ed, Dixon Kemp. 1913 (pp.612–9)

Bibliography

The Aerodynamics of Yacht Sails, E Werner and S Ober. 1925
Aero-Hydrodynamics of Sailing, C A Marchaj. 1979
The Best of Sail Trim, Ed by Anne Madden. 1975
Cornelius Shields on Sailing, Cornelius Shields. 1964
Designed to Win, Roger Marshall. 1979
Dinghy Sails, J Howard-Williams. 1978
Expert Dinghy Racing, Paul Elvström. 1963
Manual of Yachting & Boat Sailing & Naval Architecture (11th Ed), Dixon
    Kemp. 1913
Further Offshore, John Illingworth. 1970
Looking at Sails, Bruce Banks and Dick Kenny. 1979
More Sail Trim, Ed by Anne Madden. 1980
Race Your Boat Right, Arthur Knapp Jnr. 1963
Racing Dinghy Handling, Ian Proctor. 1948
Sailing Boats, Uffa Fox. 1959
Sailing Ships, their History and Development, Science Museum. 1932
Sailing Theory and Practice, C A Marchaj. 1964
Sailing to Win, Robert Bavier. 1948
Sailing Yacht Performance, John C Sainsbury. 1962
The Sailor's Word Book, Admiral W H Smyth. 1867
Sail Power, Wallace Ross. 1975
Start to Win, Eric Twiname. 1973
Spinnaker, R R King. 1981
The Story of Sail, G S Laird Clowes, 1936
Tom Diaper's Diary, Tom Diaper. 1950
Voiles et Gréements, Pierre Gutelle. 1968
Wind Tunnel Technique, R C Pankhurst and D W Holder. 1932
Working in Canvas, Percy Blandford. 1965
Yacht Racing; the Aerodynamics of Sails and Racing Tactics, Manfred
    Currey. 1928
Yacht Sails – their Care and Handling, Ernest Ratsey and Ham de Fontaine.
    1957.

PAPERS AND REPORTS

Aeronautical Research Committee 1931–32 (*HMSO Technical Report 1933*)
Amateur Yacht Research Society (*Papers 1955–64*)
Davidson Laboratory, Stevens Institute of Technology (*Technical Memoranda 1935–55*)
National Committee for Fluid Mechanics (*Illustrated Experiments 1972*)
Southampton University Yacht Research Advisory Committee (*Papers 1960–64*)

ARTICLES AND LETTERS

Aviation Week US Magazine 1956
Cruising World US Magazine 1978–82
Practical Boat Owner UK Magazine 1975–82
Sail US Magazine 1975–82
Seahorse UK Magazine 1976–82
Yachting US Magazine 1959–66
Yachting World UK Magazine 1959–82
Yachts and Yachting UK Magazine 1959–82
Yachtsman UK Magazine 1959–66

Index